# PEOPLE OF THE DALLES
## The Indians of Wascopam Mission

STUDIES
IN THE ANTHROPOLOGY OF
NORTH AMERICAN INDIANS

# PEOPLE OF THE DALLES
The Indians of Wascopam Mission

A Historical Ethnography Based on the
Papers of the Methodist Missionaries

Robert Boyd

Published by the University of Nebraska Press
Lincoln and London

In cooperation with the American Indian Studies Research
Institute, Indiana University, Bloomington

First Nebraska paperback printing: 2004

Library of Congress Cataloging-in-Publication Data
Boyd, Robert, 1945–
People of The Dalles: the Indians of Wascopam Mission:
a historical ethnography based on the papers of the Methodist
missionaries/Robert Boyd.  p.  cm.—(Studies in the anthropology
of North American Indians) Includes bibliographical references
and index. ISBN 0-8032-1236-4 (cl: alk. paper)
1. Chinook Indians—Missions.  2. Shahaptin Indians—
Missions.  3. Chinook Indians—Social life and customs.
4. Shahaptin Indians—Social life and customs.
5. Methodist Episcopal Church. Wascopam Mission.
I. Title.  II. Series.  E99.C58B69  1996
973.049741—dc20  95-38916  CIP

ISBN 0-8032-6232-9 (pbk.: alk. paper)

To Ruth

# Contents

# Illustrations

## Maps
*following page 51*

## Plates
*following page 220*

## Figures

## Table

viii

# Preface

I first discovered the writings of Henry Perkins in summer 1977, when I was about to enter the graduate program in anthropology at the University of Washington. I had an interest in Northwest Indian culture change, and knew even then that it would be some aspect of that topic that would be the subject of my graduate research. I had already surveyed some of the literature on Indian missions, but wanted to do more. A search of sources brought me quickly to the bibliography in Robert Loewenberg's *Equality on the Oregon Frontier: Jason Lee and the Methodist Mission, 1834-43* (1976a), where I found a half-page list of Oregon Mission documents held at the University of Puget Sound. I made a day trip to Tacoma to investigate. What I found surprised me. In a small room in the library's basement (the Archives of the Pacific Northwest Conference of the United Methodist Church) was a cardboard box filled with original documents—uncatalogued, unorganized, and obviously barely touched by researchers. Among them was a long handwritten journal, dating from the fall and winter of 1843-44, by one Henry Perkins of the Methodist Mission at The Dalles. I knew virtually nothing about Perkins and had never heard of that document, but a quick perusal revealed that it was full of original observations on Indian culture (particularly aspects of religion), otherwise known largely from information collected by anthropologists nearly three-quarters of a century later, when the culture had changed greatly. It was, quite obviously, an important source on local Indian ethnography, unknown to the anthropological community. There was not enough time to read the entire document or take adequate notes, so—cautiously—I approached a librarian with a question that normally would be unthinkable for a fragile, nearly 140-year-old manuscript: "May I make a Xerox copy?" The answer: "There is a Xerox machine in the basement, five cents a page." Feeling like a criminal, I carefully submitted Henry Perkins's painstakingly hand written original to one of the wonders of twentieth-century technology.

I made a typescript of the entire document and determined to find out as much as I could about Perkins and to learn whether there were more extant unknown gems like the 1843-44 journal. Loewenberg's bibliography also listed the Canse Collection of Henry B. Brewer Papers and H. K. W. Perkins Papers at the Washington State Historical Society (also in Tacoma), so I checked that out as well. There I found, in addition to a large body of correspondence, Perkins's edited autobiography, his two 1843 *Christian Advocate* articles on the history of Wascopam Mission, and the missionary tract version of his report on the remarkable and relatively unknown 1839-40

Wascopam revival, "Wonderful Work of God. . . ." I also discovered that Loewenberg (1976b) himself had written an article on Perkins, which included a few excerpts from the 1843-44 manuscript journal, for the Oregon Historical Society's 1976 commemorative volume, *The Western Shore*. I would later discover that the Oregon Historical Society archives held still another important Perkins manuscript, his description of the 1838-39 revival at Willamette Mission.

I spent the last half of the summer of 1977 collecting materials and taking notes, but for the next four years it was necessary to put the Perkins materials aside, as graduate school took first priority. I was able to return to Perkins briefly in 1981 when, under the direction of historian Keith Murray, I annotated the 1843-44 journal. The following year I submitted the journal and annotations to Priscilla Knuth, then editor of the *Oregon Historical Quarterly*, who expressed considerable interest in the document.

The present volume had its genesis in 1986. Fully aware that the 1843-44 journal was but the tip of the iceberg of the Perkins documents, I submitted a more ambitious proposal to the Oregon Historical Society Press. Encouraged by Bruce Taylor Hamilton, director of the press, we decided that the best way to do justice to Perkins was to create a comprehensive volume that would present all of his major works, placing them in a proper historical and anthropological context, with several interpretive and background chapters that I would write. With the support of the Oregon Historical Society, a manuscript that included the present volume was written in 1987-88.

But the story does not end here. Beset by financial problems, the Oregon Historical Society Press was forced to release several pending publications, including my own, in 1991. The manuscript was then submitted to the University of Nebraska Press, and book 2 of the more comprehensive manuscript is printed here.

# Acknowledgments

Several individuals provided help in this project at various stages in its genesis. Thanks are due to Marilyn Mitchell, director of the Collins Memorial Library at the University of Puget Sound; the Reverend Richard Seiber, archivist for the Pacific Northwest Conference of the United Methodist Church; and the Beinecke Library at Yale University for permitting publication of documents in their possession; to Frank Green and Jeanne Engermann for assistance in 1977 with materials in the Canse Collection at the Washington State Historical Society Library; to David Nicandri, director of the Washington State Historical Society, for permission to publish; to professors Keith Murray, Eugene Hunn, and Pamela Amoss, all members of my Ph.D. committee, who read and commented on what I had written and encouraged me to continue work on Perkins; to Priscilla Knuth of the Oregon Historical Society and Theodore Stern of the University of Oregon, who provided input at an early stage of the project; to Mary Dorsett of the Archives of the Oregon-Idaho Conference of the United Methodist Church at Willamette for help with the collections there, and to Bishop Calvin McConnell of the Portland Area of the United Methodist Church for support for a 1986 visit to the Tacoma Archives; to the Oregon Historical Society, for financial support during 1987 when the bulk of the manuscript was written; to Bruce Hamilton, director of the Oregon Historical Society Press, and the staff of the press for help in preparation of the document; to the Oregon Historical Society Photographs Department, the Stark Museum (Orange, Texas), the Royal Ontario Museum (Toronto), the Detroit Institute of Fine Arts, the Walters Art Gallery (Baltimore), the Smithsonian Institution Archives (Washington, D.C.), and the Oregon Archaeological Society (Portland) for permission to publish visuals from their collections; to the Field Museum of Natural History (Chicago), the American Museum of Natural History (New York), and the Columbia Gorge Interpretive Center (Stevenson, Washington), for photographs of items in their collections; and finally, to Drs. David and Kathrine French, Eugene Hunn, Yvonne Hajda, and Jay Miller, for their valuable comments.

# Introduction

## Historical Ethnography

*People of The Dalles: The Indians of Wascopam Mission* is a historical ethnography, or "reconstruction of a synchronic, ethnographic description of a past stage of culture, especially . . . based on written documents contemporary with that stage" (Sturtevant 1968:454). The book describes the culture of the Chinookan and Sahaptin peoples of The Dalles area, between about 1805 and 1848, based largely upon documents from the Methodist mission at Wascopam, in particular the papers of the Reverend Henry Perkins, who was stationed there from 1838 to 1844. Chapters 1 through 10 constitute the historical ethnography; Appendix 1 is devoted to the reproduction of Perkins's major monographs on Wascopam. The Perkins documents form the core of the database and were the inspiration for this study.

Some prefatory remarks on the nature of historical ethnography are in order. What follows is neither traditional anthropology nor traditional history. An ethnography, to an anthropologist, is a written work describing a particular culture. The classic ethnographic form discusses various parts or subsystems of a culture in a regular sequence. Topics such as subsistence and settlement patterns are covered first, kinship and social structure next, and then politics, religion, and so forth. That format has been followed closely in chapters 2 through 8.

But traditional ethnographies are based upon original data collected in the field by anthropologists through the method of participant observation. This ethnography, in contrast, is based largely upon a body of written documents dating from the 1830s and 1840s. The missionary papers form the primary database; ethnographic field data are decidedly secondary sources—a reversal of the traditional situation in anthropological studies.

From one perspective, a historical ethnography is today (in 1993) probably the only way to produce a rounded ethnographic description of a lifestyle that has been gone for 150 years. The memory ethnography of contemporary and recent Indian informants does not and cannot extend back so far. From another perspective, data amassed from historical records can serve to augment and correct data collected at later times by more traditional anthropological informant interview. Formal ethnographic studies did not begin in The Dalles area until 1905. Anthropologists of that era, moreover, tended to take the statements of their American Indian informants as a literal

1

reading of precontact, aboriginal lifestyles (Steward 1955:296). It is now accepted that the cultures the early informants described had already experienced drastic change. The records from The Dalles examined here come from a period much closer to a precontact state. They record traditions that died out early or had changed by the time the first anthropologists appeared.

Comparison of early historic records with later ethnographic data has the potential of both adding substance to the ethnographic record and providing a better understanding of the processes of cultural change. That method, called "upstreaming" in the ethnohistorical jargon (Axtell 1979:117), is used throughout the book. Typically, the missionary or other historical data is presented first and then critiqued or analyzed in terms of later ethnography or ethnological theory or both. The missionary documents, and in particular the monographs of Henry Perkins reproduced in Appendix 1, serve as a touchstone for reconstruction of most aspects of the culture of the Indians of The Dalles in the early nineteenth century.

The Wascopam documents are also important anthropologically because of the time period in which they were written. It is not often that anthropologists are so privileged (from a scientific viewpoint) as to observe, over an extended period of time, a relatively simple culture in a period of rapid systemic culture change. Perkins and his co-missionaries lived among the Indians at a crucial period, shortly after the devastating mortalities caused by the epidemics of the early 1830s and just before the equally wrenching wars and removals of the 1850s. In that interlude, change was proceeding at a rapid pace and was largely related to the introduction of new things and ideas from the recently arrived Whites. Thanks to the missionary documents, we can see much of that process of introduction and systemic change. For most Native American groups, records covering equivalent periods are not nearly so complete, if they exist at all.

## Perspectives on Culture Change

One way of looking at what was going on in the Columbia Plateau in the early nineteenth century is to view the entire process as a dialectic between traditional cultures that had evolved in situ over several millennia and an invasive culture, with totally different institutions, that insinuated itself into the area and became the prime mover behind the consequent changes in the indigenous culture. The emphasis in that approach is on specific events that occurred when the two cultural entities came in contact and on the accultura-tion processes that developed from these contacts. That dialectic approach has been used before in several studies of Plateau religious change, ranging from Leslie Spier's *The Prophet Dance of the Northwest and Its Derivatives* (1935) up to Christopher Miller's *Prophetic Worlds: Indians and Whites on the Columbia Plateau* (1985). Or, expanding our horizons even more, we can view the Columbia Plateau experience as yet another example of an ongoing, long-term world process, in which smaller traditional cultures come into contact with larger, dominant cultural entities and are destroyed, absorbed, or altered in ways that allow them to persist in the shadow of the prevailing culture. Viewed in that way, it is possible to see similarities in acculturation processes, whether it be between Western European culture and Columbia Plateau Indians or North Chinese civilization and the "barbarian" peoples of highland Kweichow, Yunnan, and Southeast Asia. Eric Wolf's *Europe and the People without History* (1982) is a notable recent example of that kind of scholarship.

## Ethnohistory

This volume is also a species of ethnohistory. *Ethnohistory*—a term used frequently in this book—may refer to either a subject area or a method of research. The subject area of ethnohistory is commonly accepted as pertaining to the history of preliterate peoples—a seeming oxymoron until it is explained that their history is reconstructed from accounts of early literate observers and from the peoples' own oral traditions. The methodology of ethnohistory is eclectic and borrows from both history and anthropology. Because its source material is largely historical, the normal canons of historiography—who wrote the document, when, where, for what purpose, whether it is a primary or secondary account, whether it agrees or disagrees with contemporary accounts, and so on—must be applied. Once the basic historical data have been subjected to the historiographic test and found reliable, they can be interpreted and analyzed as anthropological data, using traditional anthropological method and theory.

There is a special problem in most ethnohistorical studies, especially apparent with missionary records, that must be addressed here. Several observers in the last century described non-Western cultures with what contemporary readers may see as highly charged, ethnocentric (culture-centered), biased, and even bigoted terms. In some cases, the meanings of the words they used have changed, so that what appears to be a slur was not so intended. In other cases, however, the bias was real. Henry Perkins, for instance, though a remarkably tolerant and open-minded man for his time, lost his objectivity when discussing slavery, polygamy, and Indian modes of inheritance. The skill of the ethnohistorian is to look beyond the bias and concentrate on the data contained in the passage. It should be evaluated by the historical canons noted above, and not (necessarily) dismissed because of slanted language. The policy in this volume has been to quote original passages verbatim and to qualify the language when necessary. Bias shown in historical quotations does not reflect the viewpoint of the present author.

Several more purely anthropological methodologies and data sets have been used in this book. The comparative method, in the form of upstreaming, is noted above. The more usual form of anthropological comparison, that is, between neighboring and related cultures within single or adjacent culture areas, is used liberally. Especially in chapters 8-10, which deal with culture contact and change, the concept of diffusion—how traits spread, internal barriers or openness to adoption, the effect of new traits on culture systems—is important. Linguistics (with translations and occasional analyses of Indian terms) has been used throughout. Ethnobiological data and a cultural ecological framework are utilized in chapter 3, studies on social networks in chapter 4, anthropological work on ritual processes in chapter 5, and the theory of culture change (additive, imposed, and syncretistic) in chapters 7 through 10. The final product is a reconstructed ethnography with no single theoretical bias, but with a strong emphasis on processes of culture change, especially in the area of religion. That emphasis is a natural outcome of the nature of the primary documents.

## People of The Dalles: Geographical Scope

Readers will note that this is not a book about a particular "tribe," in any usually accepted sense of the word. The geographic focus of the book is the Wascopam Mission circuit—ranging along the Columbia River from about The Cascades to Celilo Falls. Within that area, although two languages were spoken, there were no linguistic "tribes"; the maximal political unit was the village, and most affairs were conducted on the level of kinship. Ties of blood and marriage connected and crisscrossed the entire region, and people grouped and regrouped into different social entities with the seasons. There were no clear-cut political boundaries, and to speak of a "tribe" in the traditional sense of the word would be both misleading and erroneous. In this part of the Americas such entities have largely arisen and are creations of the contact process.

Thus, although the book deals with Upper Chinookan and Sahaptin speakers, ancestors of peoples who currently belong mostly to the Confederated Tribes of the Warm Springs Reservation or the Yakama Indian Nation, the most meaningful larger unit in the area in prewhite times was what might be called *the region*—an area held together by multiple and crosscutting social ties, or "social networks" (Elmendorf 1971; Hajda 1984; Suttles 1990b). Boundaries of the region are hazy but may be drawn where social connections become sparse—between peoples who have few ties with one another. Looked at this way, the larger part of the Wascopam circuit is indeed a region, or the core of a region. Along this stretch of the Columbia social networks were dense and continuous, incorporating several riverbank winter villages and seasonal settlements and including speakers of both major languages and sometimes other languages as well. Peoples from secondary tributaries converged on the Columbia banks during fishing season, and the mass of interacting humanity during that part of the year probably served more than anything else to identify the largest effective social entity in the area in aboriginal times (Boyd and Hajda 1987).

## Culture Areas

Traditionally, however, anthropologists have used yet another concept, the culture area, in their discussions of supratribal units. Those who read this book closely will note several references to the Northwest Coast culture area and the Plateau culture area. *Culture area* is a term used by anthropologists to characterize a large geographic area, subsuming several ethnolinguistic groups that share a common cultural orientation. The concept goes back to the late nineteenth century, when—in order to compactly display artifacts from the hundreds of distinct American Indian groups and avoid duplication—museum exhibits were organized by culture area. In the Pacific Northwest anthropologists have defined two such areas—the Northwest Coast, including all the peoples from the Alaska panhandle to the California border and inland to the Cascade crest, and the Plateau, incorporating the interior drainages of the Columbia and Fraser rivers. Although there is some quibbling over the boundaries of these areas, the distinctiveness of both is accepted almost without question by a majority of anthropologists.

The significance of the Wascopam area is that (in most culture schemes) it lies squarely on the border between the Coast and the Plateau areas. The line has traditionally been drawn between Chinookan and Sahaptin speakers (Kroeber 1939: map 6), though more recent treatments (e.g., Jorgensen 1980:89, 102–3) include the Wasco-Wishram branch of Upper Chinookans with the Plateau.[1] Regardless of where one draws the line, however, it is clear that The Dalles was a "shatter zone," and there was much mixing of culture traits normally associated with either the Coast or the Plateau. That was particularly true of the Chinookan peoples.

What were the salient characteristics of these two culture areas? Here is not the place for a detailed treatment (see instead the introductions to Suttles 1990b and Walker forthcoming), but a few major traits may be mentioned. The Coast is noted for a heavy reliance on aquatic resources, particularly salmon,

and an associated developed fishing technology; an emphasis on woodworking, including plank houses and dugout canoes; twined basketry, untailored
garments, and anomalous weaving methods; a distinctive art style; an
emphasis on status and rank, slavery, wealth displays and the "potlatch," and
complex ceremonialism (Drucker 1955 and other sources). Important Plateau
culture traits include a diversified subsistence base with an emphasis on wild
root crops, extensive use of earth ovens, seasonally occupied semisubterranean
houses and mat lodges, sweatlodges, buckskin clothing, firstfruits ceremonies,
rite-of-passage feasting, and an emphasis on individually obtained spirit power
through questing (based on Ray 1942). Both the Coast and the Plateau lacked
agriculture and pottery and the developed political and religious structures of
other parts of the Americas (Kroeber 1923); they shared an emphasis on
salmon and the "first salmon ceremony," and kin units were the usual maximal
political structures. The Plateau, after 1730, had the added distinction of
having adopted horse culture in near totality, as well as a cluster of traits
imported from yet another culture area, the Plains.

Viewed as a region, where social networks converge and become denser,
the Wascopam circuit–Dalles region assumes extra significance. In an area
where people from distant areas came together and interacted, there was a
significant mixture and exchange of culture traits. Traditionally, anthropologists have emphasized material items and the trading aspects of The Dalles
marketplace: here goods from the Plateau and the Northwest Coast (as well
as the Great Basin, the Plains, and even California) were exchanged and spread
(or diffused) to distant areas (Teit 1928:121–22; Wood 1980; chap. 3 of this
volume). But the Wascopam circuit was also an area where there was a coming
together, exchange, and spread of ideas as well. Claude Lévi-Strauss (1981)
has emphasized this as it applies to mythology (see his chapter "The Market
Place" in *L'Homme nu*), but, as we will see in the later chapters of this book,
the region was also a crucible for the development and interchange of religious
elements (including both ritual and belief systems). That interchange occurred
during the precontact period, with solely native participants, as well as after
contact, when white fur traders, missionaries, and settlers became part of the
process.

## History of Research

Euroamerican observers have been writing about the cultures of the native
peoples of The Dalles since they first encountered them. Sources on Wascopam area cultures may be grouped into three or four major categories. What
might be called the ethnohistorical database of original observations by
nonspecialists includes the writings of explorers, fur traders, and missionaries,

and from later times, reservation officials and legal caseworkers. There are several monographs and studies by scientifically trained observers (for the most part, anthropologists, including both ethnographers and linguists), dating from the 1850s to the present. And finally, there is a growing body of culture change studies, ethnohistorical in method, that have been written since 1935.

Important original ethnohistorical sources include (1) explorers' accounts: Lewis and Clark's journals (1983, 1988, 1990, 1991) and Charles Wilkes's *Narrative of the United States Exploring Expedition* (1844); (2) fur traders' accounts: Alexander Ross's *Adventures of the First Settlers on the Oregon or Columbia River* (1849) and *The Fur Hunters of the Far West* (1956) and the unpublished Hudson's Bay Company's 1829 "Nez Percés Report" (Black 1829), and "Fort Nez Percés Journal" (McGillivray and Kittson 1831–32); (3) missionary accounts: D. Lee and Frost's *Ten Years in Oregon* (1844), Brewer's *Sketches of Mission Life among the Indians of Oregon* (Mudge 1854), and Perkins's works (present volume); (4) reservation period accounts: Kuykendall's manuscript and published papers on religion and Splawn's *Ka-Mi-Akin, the Last Hero of the Yakimas* (1917), as well as annual reports from reservation officials published in U.S. government *Reports of the Secretaries of Interior and War* in the latter half of the nineteenth century; (5) documents and affidavits collected in association with legal cases in this century: the Seufert Brothers case testimony (1916), Swindell's *Report. . . .* (1942) on fishing rights, and Carter's inventory of fishing sites (1937).

Anthropological investigations (both ethnographic and linguistic) in The Dalles area commenced in 1853, when George Gibbs visited there (see especially Gibbs 1854, 1956); Jeremiah Curtin collected Wasco texts in 1885 (in Sapir 1909); ethnographer and linguist Edward Sapir was at The Dalles in 1905 (1909, 1910, 1990); Edward Curtis (1911a and 1911b) passed through in 1910; Leslie Spier (Spier and Sapir 1930) combined Sapir's notes with his own in 1924–25 into the single most comprehensive monograph on Dalles-area Chinookans; Melville Jacobs (1934) collected Northwest Sahaptin texts in 1929–30; Walter Dyk worked with Dalles-area Chinookan linguistics in 1930–31; George Murdock did ethnographic research among Warm Springs Sahaptins in 1932–35 (1958, 1965, 1980); David and Kathrine French have been collecting ethnographic and linguistic data at Warm Springs since the early 1950s (see especially K. French 1955; D. French 1961, forthcoming); Dell and Virginia Hymes have been studying Upper Chinookan and Sahaptin, also since the early fifties (see especially Hymes 1981); Theodore Stern conducted research among Northeast Sahaptins in the 1960s (1998 *Handbook* chapter); and Eugene Hunn has worked with Columbia Sahaptin informants since 1976 (see especially Hunn 1990; Hunn, Murdock, and D. French forthcoming).

Interpretive works based heavily on ethnohistoric data using the ethnohistorical method include Spier (1935) on the Prophet Dance, DuBois (1938) on the Feather religion, D. French (1961) on Wasco-Wishram culture change, Anastasio (1972) (written in 1955) on southern Plateau social networks, C. Miller (1985) on Plateau religious change, and Stern (1993) on Indian-White relations at Fort Nez Percés.

## The Missionary Papers as Anthropological Documents

I have been able to take an anthropological approach with the Wascopam papers because of their unique content and because of the exceptional characteristics of their principal writer, Henry Perkins. The Wascopam Mission papers are packed with what anthropologists would call primary ethnographic observations. Perkins, the major author of the ethnographic sections of the mission documents, presented much of his Indian information with a sympathy and a depth of understanding that would be the envy of many contemporary anthropologists.

Perkins was not only a missionary; he was an ethnographer as well. To anthropologists that word is usually used in reference to a field-worker in sociocultural anthropology, that is, one who spends an extended period of time living with the members of an alien culture, observing, conducting interviews, and taking notes on various aspects of the people's lifestyles, with the goal of eventually presenting in writing a coherent picture of his subjects' culture (or at least certain aspects of it).

As noted by Robert Loewenberg (1976b:153), Perkins was possessed of a set of qualities that made him admirably suited for that role. He was an educated man, although not overly so, and had read widely on many controversial subjects. He was anything but doctrinaire and had an inquisitive mind that left him open to and often sympathetic with cultural variations that other men simply dismissed (though he did have biases, as noted above). Like most contemporary ethnographers, he learned the language of his subjects, fully aware that it provided an inside view of the workings of the culture. He also lived in the field for an extended, largely unbroken period of time, which allowed him to view the cyclical patterns (seasonal, annual, or in the life cycle) that are not usually noted or fully appreciated by short-time observers. And finally, though he lived among the Indians, he maintained a distance that allowed him to view many customs with an outsider's eye. That role, called participant observation, is an ideal of ethnographic fieldwork. Perkins, like many of our best contemporary field-workers, had a personal history as a marginal man, as an outsider looking in and from that vantage point examining what was inside with an analytical detachment.

## The Missionary Papers

Henry Perkins's monographs on Wascopam comprise the single most important data source for this volume. But Perkins wrote more than what is reprinted here, and he was not the only missionary at Wascopam. I have also used the considerable supplementary information in Perkins's letters, as well as contemporary writings of Daniel Lee, Henry Brewer, and the mission wives. Daniel Lee founded and was co-missionary with Henry Perkins at Wascopam from 1838 until his departure in mid-1843. His *Ten Years in Oregon* (1844, coauthored with Joseph Frost of Clatsop Mission) is (other than Perkins's works) the best single source on Wascopam. Ten Lee manuscripts, mostly letters, but including his five-month 1843 "Dalles Journal" (Archives of the Oregon-Idaho Conference) have also been used in preparation of this volume. Henry Brewer and his wife Laura arrived at Wascopam in mid-1840 and stayed until its closure more than seven years later. The recently republished *Sketches of Mission Life among the Indians of Oregon,* assembled from his papers by Zachariah Mudge (1854), is a second primary source on Wascopam. In addition, thirty Brewer documents (mostly letters), a few with important primary ethnographic observations, have been used here, as have eight letters penned by his wife Laura. Another astute observer of Indian life was Perkins's wife, Elvira. A total of sixteen of her manuscript letters have been consulted.

Twenty-six of Henry Perkins's own letters have been used in preparation of this volume. Not all contain ethnographic data; some are valuable for historical or biographical information. The letters are scattered in various depositories, including the Washington State Historical Society, the University of Puget Sound Library, the Regional Research Library of the Oregon Historical Society, and the Beinecke Library (Yale). All are listed in Appendix 2. Perkins's major works are printed in Appendix 1.

Other major Perkins works not related to Wascopam include chapters 1-6 of his "Autobiography" (Canse Collection) and his eyewitness description of the important 1838-39 Willamette Revival (Daniel Lee Collection, OHS). His eulogy of Narcissa Whitman appears in Drury (1973:2, 392-94). Unfortunately, all of his Sahaptin linguistic documents have been lost (see chap. 10).

The bulk of the Perkins papers, it will be noted, are in the Pacific Northwest. How they got there is a story in itself. In 1930 the Reverend John Canse of Salem, Oregon, published a book, *Pilgrim and Pioneer: Dawn in the Northwest,* on the beginnings of Methodism in the Pacific Northwest. There have been many volumes on that topic, of course, but Canse's was different: it devoted a chapter to Wascopam Mission, put together from the printed accounts of Daniel Lee, Henry Brewer, and from Henry Perkins's *Christian*

*Advocate and Journal* articles. The book was printed in the East, and a copy came into the hands of Grace Albee of Boston, Perkins's granddaughter. In early 1934 Albee wrote to Canse and sent him her own typed (and edited) transcript of her grandfather's autobiography, which was written sometime after his return to New England. Typescripts of some fifty letters (the originals were "falling apart," noted Albee) and a second version of the autobiography, less severely edited than the first, followed in 1952. Canse also collected the manuscript papers of Henry Brewer, and from Methodist mission headquarters in Philadelphia he obtained a large body of original letters from Oregon Mission members that had been sent east in the 1830s and 1840s. During his lifetime (he died in 1954) Canse did not publish any of the Perkins documents, and after his death they were deposited in various archives. The Oregon Mission correspondence (including Perkins's 1843–44 Wascopam journal) was placed in the Archives of the Pacific Northwest Conference of the United Methodist Church, which is housed in the library of the University of Puget Sound in Tacoma. The materials from Grace Albee (including the autobiography and most letters) ended up, with the Brewer Collection, in the library of the Washington State Historical Society, also in Tacoma. A few Canse materials stayed at Willamette, in the Archives of the Oregon-Idaho Conference of the United Methodist Church (for example, Daniel Lee's 1843 "Dalles Journal"), and others (Perkins's account of the Willamette Revival) are now in the Regional Research Library of the Oregon Historical Society in Portland. None of these materials was used by the regional historical community until Robert Loewenberg (1976a) began the research that would culminate in his scholarly volume on the Oregon Mission.

The Perkins documents exist in several forms. Perkins's 1843–44 journal is an original manuscript. All other documents reprinted here, however, have been edited, either by Perkins's granddaughter or by the editor of the *Christian Advocate,* Zachariah Mudge. The locations of the originals (including the autobiography, the *Christian Advocate* articles, and most letters) are not known, if indeed they are still extant. Some of these documents exist in two or three versions. The autobiography was edited and sent by Albee in two typescript editions, the second (1952) more complete and apparently more faithful to the original. The autobiography overlaps with some of the content in Perkins's three *Christian Advocate* articles. Comparing the autobiography with the *Advocate* versions, it is obvious that the two editors (Albee and Mudge) had different ideas as to what should or should not be included and to what extent Perkins's writing should be "improved."

In the absence of Perkins's original manuscripts, the policy followed in this volume has been to recreate the most complete version of the major documents possible. In each case the lengthiest of the extant versions has been used as a base, and passages that had been edited out (or in a few instances substantially rewritten) have been reinserted. The added passages are enclosed in brackets [ ]. The final product, of course, is not original Perkins, but most properly a compilation of the edited versions of his original manuscripts. Not perfect, but the best that can be done under present circumstances.

## Linguistic Usage

Two Indian languages (the Wasco-Wishram dialect of Kiksht or Upper Chinookan and the Columbia River dialect of Columbia Sahaptin: see chap. 2, "Languages") were spoken in the vicinity of Wascopam Mission. Wherever it seemed advisable (for example, for place names), I have included Wasco-Wishram or Columbia Sahaptin terms. My authorities have been anthropologists who have studied and transcribed these languages: David French for Wasco-Wishram and Eugene Hunn for Columbia Sahaptin. Unless otherwise indicated, all such terms come from these two sources. Indian proper names, usually unique and untranslatable, have for the most part not been phonemicized. Instead, the most common missionary spelling is retained.

# 1
# Historical Context

This chapter provides historical perspective on Indian-White dynamics in Columbia Plateau culture history. Direct White influence in the Columbia Plateau began with the Lewis and Clark Expedition in 1805, nearly a third of a century before the arrival of missionaries in the area. The era closed abruptly in November 1847, with the Whitman Massacre and the subsequent abandonment of most Plateau missions. The events in this pivotal forty-two-year period provide a larger historical context for the briefer Wascopam Mission era.

The effective dates for this volume are March 14, 1838, the day Henry Perkins and Daniel Lee left the Methodist settlement at Willamette, through November 18, 1844, the date of the Perkins's departure on the sea voyage that would take them back to New England. The Wascopam missionaries left an extensive record of those six and a half years, a time of exceptional change for the Indians of The Dalles. Their record is exhaustively analyzed in chapters 2 through 10.

This chapter traces three converging timelines: (1) historical events in the Columbia Plateau; (2) the development of the Methodist Oregon Mission, in particular its station at Wascopam, and (3) the life of Henry Perkins, co-missionary at Wascopam and chief author of the documents on which this book is largely based, up to his departure from Oregon. The three timelines converge in the years 1838–44.

## Before the Missions

White men never saw purely aboriginal Columbia Plateau Indians, uninfluenced by any aspects of their own invasive culture. Major changes preceded the Euroamerican arrival by seventy-five years and probably more. The domesticated horse appeared among the Flatheads and Nez Perces by about 1730 and diffused widely through the Plateau (Haines 1938), and a major smallpox epidemic spread through the region sometime between 1775 and 1781 (Boyd 1994b). Horses brought major changes in material culture, subsistence patterns, and intergroup relations (Gunther 1950); the epidemic influenced settlement patterns, social relations, and religious systems. In 1793 Canadian explorer Alexander Mackenzie crossed what is now interior British Columbia, arriving on the Pacific coast at Bella Coola; knowledge of his presence, plus tidbits of information from Indians who crossed the Rockies on horseback to hunt bison, resulted in a vague regional awareness of a different and powerful people to the east (see C. Miller 1985: chap. 3, for a review).

Thus, when the Lewis and Clark Expedition entered the Columbia drainage in October 1805, the native peoples already had prophecies of their coming. Lewis and Clark and their men were the first Whites to come into face-to-face contact with Plateau Indians in their own lands. The explorers passed through The Dalles and the larger region between Celilo and The Cascades twice, in late October 1805 and again in mid-April 1806. Others followed, most notably the Canadian geographer David Thompson, who descended and ascended the entire length of the Columbia in summer 1811. Journals from both of these expeditions remain primary sources on early Plateau Indian culture. Indian traditions of these initial contacts survived for over a century.

## Fur-Trading Companies

A permanent White presence on the Columbia Plateau was not established until the second decade of the century, at fur-trading posts erected by the North West Company. In the southern Plateau, the earliest of these was Fort Nez Percés at the mouth of the Walla Walla, built in 1818 and later renamed after the river itself (Stern 1993). Regular exploitation of Plateau lands for fur began in that year as well, with the annual Snake Country expeditions, which continued into the 1820s until the fur supply in the area was exhausted. The works of Alexander Ross and Alexander Henry and Washington Irving's *Astoria* document that period.

The continuous White-Indian dialogue that began with the building of Fort Nez Percés intensified in 1821 after the Hudson's Bay Company, headquartered at Red River (Winnipeg) took over the trade. In late 1824 the company's director, Sir George Simpson, followed Thompson's route down the Columbia, reconnoitered the territory, and made plans for its exploitation. It was Simpson who dictated transfer of the company's regional headquarters from Fort George (Astoria), at the mouth of the Columbia, to a new site upstream and across from the mouth of the Willamette River, which he christened Fort Vancouver.

The new fort shortly became the mercantile hub and effective political center of the Pacific Northwest, a status it retained for the next two decades, coinciding (during the latter half of that period), with the arrival of missionaries, both Protestant and Catholic. In 1836, at the nadir of the company's domination, American visitor William Slacum described a picketed enclosure containing thirty-four structures, with a 3,000-acre farm, a hospital, and forty-

nine cabins of workers outside. The population of the area was 750 to 800; they
were craftsmen, traders, farmers and officials—Englishmen, Scots, French
Canadians, and Hawaiians.

Each spring a supply ship from London brought a cargo of goods for the
interior and coastal trade: all varieties of material goods and clothing, "hard-
ware and cutlery," sugar and tobacco, guns and ammunition (Slacum 1837).
In late May a brigade of fur-laden bateaux descended the Columbia, arriving
at Vancouver in early June. Here the furs were processed and transferred to the
company ship, which left for England in August. The bateaux returned upriver
in July. The Dalles, eventual site of Wascopam Mission, was therefore passed
by Hudson's Bay Company boats at least twice annually after 1824 (Meinig
1968:78–79). The large collection of company documents from that period
are housed mostly in the Hudson's Bay Archives in Winnipeg; important published works include director Sir George Simpson's 1824–25 journal (Merk
1931) and Chief Factor Dr. John McLoughlin's letters (1941, 1943; Barker
1948).

The Hudson's Bay operation on the Columbia was a great success, and
as such enterprises do, it attracted competition. In 1829 a Boston entrepreneur,
Josiah Marshall, sent two vessels, the *Owyhee* and the *Convoy,* to the Vancouver area in what would be a futile attempt to start his own salmon-fishing
and fur-trading operation. Although that venture is best known for its probable
introduction of the devastating "fever and ague" to the lower Columbia (see
chap. 7), it also had a significant impact on the Indians of The Dalles area. In
early 1829 the Americans hired a Mr. Bache, formerly a Hudson's Bay
employee, to set up a trading station at The Dalles. With Bache upriver and the
*Owyhee* at anchor off Sauvie Island, the *Convoy* made regular trips to Oahu
for supplies. The Americans flooded the market and attempted to undercut the
Hudson's Bay Company monopoly (Morison 1927). Greatly disturbed, Chief
Factor McLoughlin sent James Birnie upstream to establish a rival post.
Within a year the overwhelming resources and manpower of the Hudson's Bay
Company had their effect: the Americans were forced to abandon their
enterprise and leave the river (Barker 1948:60ff). That brief episode
undoubtedly affected the Indians of The Dalles, at the very least introducing
them to a wide range of Euroamerican goods and raising their expectations
accordingly. The sites of the two posts have not been determined. Bache's was
apparently near Big Eddy (DuBois 1938:10); in 1869 tradition placed Birnie's
not far from the eventual location of Wascopam Mission, in the city of The
Dalles, "opposite the Umatilla House, where the China wash house now
stands" (McKay 1869).

## Mission History

Missionary efforts in the Pacific Northwest started late, in 1829, more than a half-century after initial contact. In that year the American Board of Commissioners for Foreign Missions (ABCFM), a joint Presbyterian and Congregational group, sent the Reverend Jonathan Green on board the Boston ship *Volunteer* to reconnoiter the North Pacific coast as a possible site for missionizing. He concluded that there were "great obstacles" to starting a mission but that the best possible site was in the vicinity of the Columbia (1915:99, 103). Six more years elapsed before another ABCFM representative, the Reverend Samuel Parker, visited the Northwest. Parker descended the Columbia; a young assistant, Marcus Whitman, came with him as far as the Rockies. Parker found the Indians of the Columbia ready for Christianity, so in October 1836 Whitman, Henry Spalding, and their wives returned and established the first missions in the Columbia Plateau at Waiilatpu among the Cayuses and at Lapwai in Nez Perce lands.

## The "Macedonian Call"

But Methodists had established a mission in the Oregon country two years earlier than the ABCFM. How that came about is a fascinating story, told in detail elsewhere (see Josephy 1965:94–98; C. Miller 1985:59–62). A thumbnail history goes like this: in 1825, on his Columbia River trip, Sir George Simpson took two Indian boys (Spokan Garry and Kootenay Pelly) back to Red River for schooling. Five years later they returned to their homelands and began teaching rudiments of Christianity to their people. At about the same time, Hudson's Bay post heads and personnel at Vancouver, Colvile, and Nez Percés also began imparting Christian basics to locals, perhaps in response to requests from the Indians themselves (details are given in chap. 9).

The sudden interest in Christianity among Columbia River Indians was apparently region-wide and, with no religious personnel resident, could not be fully satisfied. Hence the famous 1831 "Macedonian Call" from the wilderness, in which four Nez Perce Indians traveled to St. Louis with a party of mountain men to meet William Clark (of Lewis and Clark, then superintendent of Indian affairs for the trans-Mississippi) to request religious instructors for their people. The Nez Perces were directed to Bishop Joseph Rosati, who wrote an account of their visit. Two of the Nez Perces died in St. Louis, and the surviving two succumbed on the way home.

A second account of the visit, supposedly resulting from an 1832 interview with General Clark by Huron Indian William Walker, appeared in the March 1, 1833, issue of the *Christian Advocate and Journal,* the most widely read Methodist periodical of its day. The response to Walker's article led directly to the founding of the Oregon Mission. The president of Wesleyan University, Wilbur Fiske, read the account and penned a letter to the *Christian Advocate and Journal* requesting aid for a mission to the Columbia. The magazine was deluged with contributions and volunteers. Reprinted in several other journals, the Walker article became one of the earliest American "media events" (Billington 1968).

## The Oregon Mission

Jason Lee was Wilbur Fiske's nominee to head the Oregon Mission, and he was formally ordained "Missionary to the Flathead Indians" on June 14, 1833 (Brosnan 1932:32). Between April and September 1834 Jason and his nephew Daniel, along with three lay helpers, traveled overland with the seventy-member party of American explorer and entrepreneur Nathaniel Wyeth. There are several good accounts of the trip (see in particular John Townsend 1839).

At Vancouver, Dr. McLoughlin discouraged the Methodists from starting a mission in the interior; within a month they had selected a site in the Willamette Valley. Here they labored for the next two years without much success, given the depleted population of the valley Indians. The area was malarial, Daniel Lee had to retreat to Hawaii for his health, the teacher Cyrus Shepard was sickly, and a heavy load fell by default on Jason. He therefore wrote a letter east requesting help, and thus began a process that resulted in the arrival of several reinforcements of personnel, which ultimately made possible the founding of the mission at Wascopam.

The enthusiasm that the "Macedonian Call" engendered in eastern congregations spread to Maine Wesleyan Seminary in Kent's Hill, where it infected Elvira Johnson, a student in the school's female department. In early 1836, when the Methodist Missionary Society sent out a new call for volunteers, "Miss Johnson offered her services at once" and was accepted as a member of what became known as the First Reinforcement to the Oregon Mission (Appendix 1, Doc. 1, "Autobiography"). Other members of that party included Dr. Elijah White (see chap. 8 and Appendix 3), a carpenter and blacksmith, and two single women who were betrothed to Jason Lee and Cyrus Shepard of the Mission. A fourth woman, betrothed to Daniel Lee, backed out at the last minute.

## Henry Perkins

Enter Henry Perkins, destined to become founder and co-missionary at Wascopam and author of the documents that form the chief database for this volume. Perkins was a fellow student of Johnson at Kent's Hill. Born in Castine, Maine, in 1814, he had decided, upon the death of the last survivor of his eight-member family in 1831, to enter the seminary. Here, in either 1834 or 1835, he met Johnson, and (in his words) they were "perilous times for susceptible souls. . . . Propinquity has given many a man a partner for life." The two apparently became engaged (Appendix 1, Doc. 1, "Autobiography").

Shortly afterward Johnson—whom Dr. White called "a purer, more truly missionary spirit, and one more zealous in the work to which she had devoted herself, [who] ha[d] not, perhaps, as yet visited [Oregon]" (Allen 1850:23)— volunteered for the Oregon Mission. The First Reinforcement left Boston in midyear, and Henry Perkins stayed behind. That summer, at a camp meeting in Monmouth, Maine, he experienced a "crisis of the spirit," an event that would be repeated three and one-half years later in Oregon (see Appendix 1, Doc. 3). With the next call for volunteers to the Oregon Mission, Perkins applied, and in January 1837 he was accepted.

Despite his "awakening" at the Monmouth camp meeting, a reading of Perkins's autobiography makes it clear that his primary motive in going to Oregon was not commitment to a missionary ideal, but pursuit of the hand of "his own true lady love." He felt deficient in training as a missionary ("I had not been trained at all while at Kent's Hill in homiletics [speech writing]. I had no critical knowledge of the Bible.") (Appendix 1, Doc. 1, "Autobiography"). But Monmouth had introduced him to the felt "religious experience"—which was to him ineffable—"Glory," a kind of "electricity." And his "ever inquiring mind" (Leslie, letter of Aug. 10, 1841, Canse Collection) led him to intensive reading on theology, both on board the ship to Oregon and later. He read everything on that subject he could come by from visitors and from the infrequent mail deliveries to the mission at The Dalles.

Perkins's history and personality had a strong effect on his missionary effort. A consistent underlying experience with and fear of abandonment (by his family, his fiancée, his co-missionary, and ultimately the church fathers) defined many of his "crises" and undoubtedly motivated him to action. When he had the support of those around him—notably in the beginning years at Wascopam—he was capable of great things. He was sympathetic to those defined as outsiders, and (an anomaly among most of his contemporaries) saw the value of and appreciated many aspects of native culture. In his missionizing he was a strong believer in the primacy of the "religious experience" as a requisite for membership in the church; biblical knowledge would follow. His heritage includes an evangelical fervor—probably the single most important force behind the Indian revivals of the 1840s and a major stimulus for the syncretistic Indian religions that arose on the Plateau in years following; a body of linguistic work—including a dictionary and a translation of large parts of the Bible into Sahaptin—presently unlocated and, unfortunately, perhaps permanently lost; and finally, his writings on Wascopam Mission and Indian customs, preserved in Appendix 1 in this volume.

Returning to the chronology, the Second Reinforcement, which also included the Reverend David Leslie and family and Margaret Smith, a teacher, left Boston a few weeks after Henry's appointment. On board, Henry came under "infidel influence," an apparent reference to the Deistic philosophy of Thomas Paine, which got him in trouble with the rigid Smith and members of the Hawaii Mission and even preceded him to Oregon. The reinforcement arrived in Hawaii in the midst of a religious revival, and although Perkins's autobiography notes only the luxurious lifestyle of the missionaries, there is no doubt that he was impressed by and learned from their methods of conversion as well.

On September 4 the party arrived at the Columbia. After some ardent wooing, Henry Perkins finally married Elvira Johnson on his twenty-third birthday, November 21, 1837. The records are silent on events for the next fifteen weeks, until Daniel Lee and Henry Perkins began their journey upstream to establish Wascopam Mission.

## Wascopam Mission

The founding of Wascopam Mission is described in Henry Perkins's own words in chapter 7 of his "Autobiography" (Appendix 1, Doc. 1). A brief history of Wascopam's early years is given in Perkins's "History of the Oregon Mission," Documents 2 and 4. Several collateral sources flesh out what we know about the mission's early years.

Perkins's narrative on the first two weeks at Wascopam stops on April 4. Three days later Jason Lee, on what would be a two-year trip to the East Coast, arrived at Wascopam. He carried three documents: the now-famous "Oregon Memorial," requesting that the United States "take possession" of Oregon south of the Columbia, and letters from Daniel Lee and from Whitman and Spalding, requesting reinforcements for their respective missions. (The first document is reprinted in Brosnan 1933, the second in Loewenberg 1973, and the last in Drury 1973, 1:286-92.) Lee also "preached to more than a hundred Indians in the Chinook Jargon, which was interpreted into the language of Wascopam, and then into Nez Perce [*sic;* probably Sahaptin]" (J. Lee

1916:416). After visiting Waiilatpu and Lapwai, Jason sent a letter back to Wascopam, suggesting that Daniel and Henry "be firm" with their charges, teach them agriculture, and learn the local language(s). Dr. John McLoughlin also passed through Wascopam, on March 24, on his way to a year and a half in Europe. During the nascent years of Wascopam, therefore, the Oregon Mission was under the stewardship of David Leslie, while the head man at Vancouver was James Douglas.

On April 9, as Jason Lee was heading east from Wascopam, Henry Perkins went west to Willamette. On his return he brought his wife and the African American Winslow Anderson. The two men spent the summer building a house. As described by Daniel Lee, there were two ten-foot-by-twenty-foot chambers downstairs, which constituted the living quarters, and two upstairs, which were bedrooms. The Perkinses occupied one; the Lees (Maria arrived in 1841) the other (D. Lee and Frost 1844:250).

The two pictures of the mission compound (plate 1) date from September 1849, after it had been abandoned. From different vantage points, they show four structures surrounding an open plaza of about one acre, connected by a picket fence. The twenty-foot-by-thirty-foot mission house was on the north side, with its front door facing out toward the river. The first floor was split into two rooms, one for each missionary; bedrooms were upstairs (D. Lee and Frost 1844:250), and a twelve-foot-square anteroom was added later. On the east side was the twenty-foot-by-thirty-foot "Spanish wattled house" built in late 1839 by Perkins, Benjamin Wright, and his friends (see Appendix 1, Doc. 3). The 1839–40 revival started in the chapel on the first floor;[1] there was a schoolroom and six small chambers above and a cellar beneath (Farnham 1843:86). In 1841 a barn and "log meeting house for the natives 30 by 40 feet" were built (L. Brewer, letter of Nov. 8, 1841, Canse Collection; H. Brewer, letter of Sept. 23, 1841, Canse Collection).

Peter Burnett, a pioneer of 1843, gave the following description of the mission site:

> The mission houses stand on the southwest side of the river. When you ascend the bank, the sward runs before you in a gentle and regular inclination for about a mile, when it joins a line of hills of moderate altitude, covered with a profusion of pine timber, intermingled with some scattering white oak. Just at the foot of the hill, and on the edge of this timber, stand the mission houses, and between them and the river, are sprinkled numerous Indian huts or lodges. . . . Immediately to the southwest is a fine mill stream, and directly below it a rich bottom prairie skirted with yellow pines and oak. [1880:92]

Nothing remains of the mission compound today, and its exact location is uncertain. In the early decades of the twentieth century tradition placed it "a block east" of Pulpit Rock ("Pulpit Rock" 1925), close to the site of the present Methodist Church (Hillgen 1938:222).

Wascopam was isolated from the other White settlements. Daniel Lee was the one who went to Vancouver or Willamette for supplies, and in mid-1843 he estimated that he had traveled 3,000 miles, including thirty-two trips between Wascopam and Vancouver and twenty-two between Vancouver and Willamette, all by river ("Dalles Journal," entry for May 12, 1843, Archives of the Oregon-Idaho Conference). He also blazed a trail over the Cascades in September 1838 (Appendix 1, Doc. 2; full description in D. Lee and Frost 1844:157-61). It apparently followed an old Indian track and corresponded to the later Barlow Trail, first used by immigrants in 1846. Daniel brought fourteen head of cattle on his return. When he arrived at Wascopam the Perkinses were gone. They had temporarily moved to Willamette where, sometime in November 1838, Elvira gave birth to their first child, Henry Johnson Perkins.

The last half of 1838 was important for religious developments. First, the ABCFM missions of the Columbia Plateau were augmented by two: Tshima-kain near Spokane, under Elkanah Walker and Cushing Eells; and Kamiah among the Nez Perces under Asa Smith. Elkanah Walker's wife Mary had been a classmate of Elvira Perkins at Kent's Hill, and although the two never met in Oregon, they kept up a regular correspondence. The second important religious event was the arrival, on November 24, of the first Catholic missionaries to the Northwest. These were the Belgian fathers Francis Norbert Blanchet and Modeste Demers. The priests initially took up residence at Vancouver, where they replaced the unpopular Anglican Herbert Beaver, and ministered to the large French Canadian contingent. The Catholics turned out to be strong competitors for Indian souls. Demers learned Chinook Jargon in just a month and was shortly sermonizing in it. Blanchet in 1839 devised the Sahale Stick and later the Catholic Ladder, to instruct the Indians (see chap. 10). And both traveled widely in pursuit of converts. Within a month of arrival Blanchet opened a mission at Cowlitz; the first mass at St. Paul in the Willamette Valley was held on January 6, 1839. In April Demers led a mission to Fort Nisqually; during the summer Blanchet visited Forts Colvile, Okanagan, and Nez Percés in the interior (Schoenberg 1962:6-7). The Catholics were aggressive and moved in wherever Protestants were not present.

But enthusiasm was building among the Protestants as well. An emotional camp meeting, reported in full in a manuscript by Henry Perkins, was held at Willamette between December 30 and January 6, 1839. The first of its kind in the Northwest (there were several precedents in the East), it set the tone for the great Wascopam Revival of 1839–40 and the several lesser camp meetings (among both Indians and Whites) that followed (details in chap. 10). By early 1840 Henry Perkins had developed a strong enough command of Sahaptin that he was able to sermonize in it—an accomplishment that certainly increased his effectiveness in the revivals.

Other than the Wascopam circuit revivals, 1840 was notable for the continued expansion of both Catholics and Methodists. In May and June Blanchet conducted a mission to Whidbey Island, while Demers spent three weeks at Chinook. In midyear Jason Lee returned to Oregon after a two-year absence, at the head of the fifty-member Great Reinforcement. Methodists shortly established stations at Nisqually, Clatsop, and Willamette Falls. Wascopam Mission was blessed by the addition of a third couple, Henry and Laura Brewer.

A biography of the Brewers appears in Appendix 3. They were lay people who gradually assumed missionary functions after the departure of Lee and Perkins in 1843 and 1844. Henry Brewer was the mission's farmer; his purpose was to make the mission self-sufficient in food and break the umbilical cord to the west. Before his arrival there had been little agriculture. In 1838 the harvest included only squash and cabbage; in 1839, with Daniel Lee's imported oxen, twenty acres were plowed, but only "25 bushels of the small grains, 75 bushels of potatoes," and sundry other vegetables were harvested (Farnham 1843:86). As Brewer arrived in June, too late for planting, the 1840 harvest was not much better, with only 50 bushels of wheat. But in 1841, with the farm "a mile below us, a flat, prairie lot of 300 acres," 200 bushels of wheat, 50 of oats, 500 of potatoes, plus many pumpkins and "garden vegetables" and a few peas and corn, were harvested (H. Brewer, letters of Aug. 14 and 22, 1840, and Sept. 23, 1841, Canse Collection). The grain, however, still had to be transported downstream to the Hudson's Bay Company mill at Mill Creek five miles above Vancouver.

By June 1841 the Wascopam Mission population had more than doubled. The Great Reinforcement also brought carpenter David Carter and wife, who stayed until late 1841, and Maria Ware, who became Mrs. Daniel Lee. The Perkinses added a second child, Ellen, born on January 12 (which made her the first White child born in what is now eastern Oregon), and Maria Lee gave birth to Wilbur on March 23. (The Perkinses and Lees each had another child while at Wascopam; the Brewers had two.)

But 1841 was a year of troubles in the Oregon Mission. Something happened during Henry Perkins's September 1840 visit to Willamette, his first following the return of Jason Lee, that dampened his spirits. Exactly what is not clear. But we do know that Jason Lee and others were skeptical (and probably envious) concerning the conversion claims of the Wascopam Revival and that most disagreed with Perkins's belief in "immediate salvation" (see Loewenberg 1976a: chap. 4). There was also an ugly battle going on between Jason Lee and Elijah White, which cast a pall over the entire Oregon Mission (Loewenberg 1972) and cannot have failed to affect Perkins. During the first week of 1841, in the Wascopam "Watch Meeting," Perkins announced that he was ready to abandon the mission (M. Lee, "Private Journal," Daniel Lee Collection); shortly afterward he wrote a letter (not extant) to Jason Lee spelling out his intentions. Perkins was not the only disillusioned Methodist at that time: in February Jason Lee received letters of resignation from the two principals at Clatsop. One left; the Reverend Joseph Frost stayed, and Perkins eventually came around after receiving letters from both Jason Lee and David Leslie.

Wascopam, by 1841, was becoming an important stopover spot for travelers. In 1838, as noted above, Jason Lee and John McLoughlin passed through; another notable visitor was Johann Sutter (Sutter n.d.), later famous in California history. In July 1839 Perkins visited Fort Nez Percés and Waiilatpu Mission; in October of the year the twelve-member "Peoria Party" of immigrants stopped at Wascopam: Sidney Smith (1955) and Thomas Farnham (1843) both left descriptions of their stay. In 1840 a few more Americans passed through, and in early October mountain men Robert ("Doc") Newell (1867) and Joe Meek favored the missionaries with their presence (see Victor 1870:282-83).

In 1841 the trickle grew to a flow: the Joseph Drayton party of the United States Exploring Expedition passed through twice in July (Wilkes 1844, 4: Walla chap.); Sir George Simpson (1847:69-70) of the Hudson's Bay Company arrived on August 24, and between August 25 and September 20 Jason and Lucy Lee were present (D. Lee and Frost 1844:250-51). As the Lees left, the first party of overland immigrants passed through (see Joseph Williams 1921); following them on October 9 was the Canadian "Red River party," about 100 strong, on its way to Puget Sound (L. Brewer, letter of Nov. 8, 1841, Canse Collection). Three children from that group were temporarily adopted by the mission family (Mudge 1854:45-46; Brewer 1986:70, 75).

While the Protestant missions were beginning to have problems, the Catholics continued to advance. The year 1841 saw two confrontations on the shifting Methodist-Catholic boundary: in winter and spring at Clackamas village, where Blanchet and the Reverend Alvan Waller argued over jurisdiction and doctrine (see Blanchet 1932:99-103, Blanchet in Landerholm 1956:79-86, 90-94, 103; Waller, diary, Alvan Waller Collection), and again in September at The Cascades, where Blanchet reconverted Indians already claimed by Daniel Lee. In each case the Catholics got the upper hand. The

Methodist discontent of early 1841 resurfaced in 1842, and that fall Nisqually Mission closed. In June 1842 Jesuit missionaries appeared at Vancouver, and a mission was opened at Coeur d'Alene. In March 1843 Father Jean Baptiste Bolduc revisited Whidbey Island and met for the first time with the villagers of southeast Vancouver Island.

But the crushing blow to the Methodists came in August 1843, with the simultaneous departures of Joseph Frost and Daniel Lee. Clatsop Mission was now effectively dead, and Wascopam lost its designated missionary to the Upper Chinookans. Jason Lee would not accept his nephew's resignation, but Daniel went anyway; Henry Perkins bemoaned his departure and for six weeks stopped writing. On the sea voyage home D. Lee and Frost wrote *Ten Years in Oregon* (1844), heretofore the only accessible work on the first five years at Wascopam. The reasons for Daniel's departure were several, including increasing doubts about the sincerity of conversion of the natives, frustration with lack of support from mission headquarters, and his wife's failing health.

Despite that loss, Wascopam continued to be a haven for a string of visitors. A total of 125 immigrants from Missouri passed through in September 1842 (D. Lee, "Ten Years in Oregon," partial draft, Archives of the Oregon-Idaho Conference). Narcissa Whitman arrived on October 29 (just in time to witness an eruption of Mount St. Helens) and stayed until March 1843, while her husband was on his well-known trip to the United States (see Appendix 3). And 1843 was the year for the first of the great overland migrations—more than 1,000 people took their wagons over the Oregon Trail, and most of them passed through Wascopam. Perkins's unpublished account, part of his 1843–44 journal, ranks among the most detailed descriptions of the party (along with those of Jesse Applegate, Sr., and Jesse Applegate, Jr. [Applegate 1914; Schafer 1934], Overton Johnson and William Winter [1846], Peter Burnett [1880], and James Nesmith [1906]).

Three men arrived at the mission September 26, eight on October 1, and sixteen on the October 5. Jason Lee, Narcissa Whitman, and Elijah White all appeared on the seventh, and Jason preached to several rapidly arriving parties before his departure on the sixteenth (J. Lee 1916). Two notable members of the contingent of well-educated New Englanders who led the 1843 immigration arrived on the eighth. These were Asa Lovejoy, yet another classmate from Maine Wesleyan Seminary, well-known today as one of the founders of the city of Portland, and General Morton McCarver, who would later lay out the plots of Linnton and Tacoma. The entry for the twenty-third records the appearance of "Mr. [John] Ricord a lawyer from N. York State," who would eventually become an adviser to the king of Hawaii.

But the majority of the 1,000-member party were, as Perkins noted, "farmers of Missourie . . . for years the friends, & supporters of Methodism in

their respective neighborhoods." The rough-and-ready, frontiersman character
of these immigrants has been noted several times (e.g., Sylvester 1933:267);
but the missionaries' observation that most were Methodists as well has not
been often emphasized. Perkins was elated that several were in the habit of
attending camp meetings; Jason Lee said:

> We rejoice to hear that there are Thirty among the thousand souls in the
> present party, who are said to be professors of religion. If they arrive with
> one spark of spiritual life in them, we trust by the blessing of God, we
> shall succeed in fanning it into a flame. [1916: entry for Oct. 15]

For two months that mass of humanity (according to Perkins) "have been
constantly sweeping by.... Our station has the usual aspect of a hotel or camp"
(letter of Nov. 24, 1843), Canse Collection). "They draw heavily on our little
supplies, but we could not see them pass hungry & starving (H. Brewer, letter
of Nov. 7, 1843, Canse Collection). "Most of our wheat, potatoes, & fat cattle
we have parted with" (H. Perkins, letter of Nov. 24, 1843, Canse Collection).
The people were transported to Wascopam by 140 ox-drawn wagons; some
took jerry-built rafts downstream (four drowned) (H. Brewer, letter of Nov.
7, 1843, Canse Collection); others rode over the Cascades. Eleven children
were "born on the way," one in the Brewers' house (Brewer 1986: entry for
Oct. 14). Perkins's journal gives the experiences of several members of the
party as exemplars.

The immigrants had barely passed before the appearance of yet another
visitor, John C. Fremont, "pathfinder of the West," on the second of his three
exploring expeditions for the United States. Fremont arrived on November 4
and left Kit Carson and most of his forty-member party at the mission "refitting
their equipage," while he canoed downstream to Vancouver for victuals.
Returning on the eighteenth, Fremont left again on the twenty-fourth, taking
with him some horses and cattle bought at the mission, as well as three local
Indians.

Of these three, the "guide to the Tlamath lake ... had been there before and
bore the marks of several wounds he had received from some of the Indians
in the territory" (Jackson and Spence 1970:576). That is undoubtedly the
Indian whose story was told in the entry for August 19 of Perkins's journal
(Appendix 1, Doc. 5); Brewer (in Mudge 1854:165–69) calls him Skakaps;
Fremont's name for him was White Crane. The second, whom Fremont called
Stiletsi, may be the Tenino chief Seletsa (Appendix 3). Both of these men
returned north at Klamath Lake. The third Indian, a nineteen-year-old
Chinook, had "lived for some time in the household of Mr. Perkins" (Jackson
and Spence 1970:577). William (or Billy) Chinook had a very interesting later

history: after some time in the East and in California, he returned to The Dalles and played an important role in the early history of Warm Springs Reservation. He also has a biography in Appendix 3.

The last episode in the history of the Oregon and Wascopam Missions to be considered here began in October 1843, with the dismissal of Jason Lee as head of the Oregon Mission. Several factors contributed to that decision. Most important was that the Methodist Missionary Society was having severe financial problems. But also significant was that Jason Lee was not a good administrator and that complaints had been received about him from several disaffected Oregon Mission members at headquarters in New York. As noted earlier, Jason Lee and Narcissa Whitman were both at Wascopam in October when Marcus Whitman, fresh from his trip to the States, arrived to retrieve his wife. Marcus Whitman relayed the news to Jason Lee that he was being dismissed (Drury 1973, 2:97). Jason was resigned ("Be it so." [Brosnan 1932:213]), but the dismissal apparently affected Henry Perkins strongly. He undoubtedly saw it as yet another abandonment. Book 1 of his 1843 journal, begun after the departure of Daniel Lee, stops abruptly on October 23, the day Jason Lee and the Whitmans left Wascopam. Jason himself took the manuscript east with him. The journal's book 2, started after a six-week delay, is different from book 1—more morose and introspective.

Jason Lee left Oregon in February 1844 and died just over a year later. In June 1844 the Reverend George Gary arrived in Oregon from New York, sent by the Methodist Mission Society to size up the Oregon operation and close down all unproductive efforts. He moved fast, selling the farms at Clatsop and Willamette, shutting down the mission school, and eliminating the debt to the Hudson's Bay Company by selling mission-occupied and -improved property at Willamette Falls to McLoughlin. That last was a controversial decision, as the lots had originally been claimed by McLoughlin but had been given by him to the mission to use (for details see Carey 1932).

Henry Perkins disagreed vehemently with Gary's decision (and indeed the entire policy of retrenchment) and threatened to resign. All that is contained in a scathing manuscript letter to Gary dated July 24. Taking Perkins at his word, Gary detained Alvan Waller, who was about to embark on a ship to the East Coast, and offered him the job of missionary at Wascopam. Waller accepted August 27. Laura Brewer, who was with her husband at Willamette, sent the news in a note that arrived at Wascopam on August 31. Two poignant letters from the Perkinses to the Brewers followed shortly. It appears that Perkins's threat had been a ploy—neither he nor his wife was prepared to leave. But the die was cast; acting superintendent Gary had made his decision, and Alvan Waller had been appointed to fill Perkins's job. During the subsequent visit of Gary to Wascopam, Perkins vacillated, but the superintendent did not waver (see the manuscript [Archives of the Pacific Northwest Conference] and published [1923] versions of Gary's diary).

The Perkinses crossed the Columbia bar in early December, spent some time in Hawaii, and arrived in New England in September 1845. Other than a few letters to Oregon after that time, nothing further is known about Henry and Elvira Perkins. Wascopam Mission continued under the uninspired leadership of Alvan Waller, with the able assistance of the Brewers, until August 1847. But it never regained the influence or focus that it had during the leadership of Daniel Lee and Henry Perkins in its first six years, from 1838 to 1844.

# 2
# Human Geography

On March 14, 1838, Henry Perkins and Daniel Lee embarked on a voyage down the Willamette and up the Columbia that brought them, after a week, to the mouth of Mill Creek (inside the present city of The Dalles), near which Wascopam Mission was to be established.

The banks of the Willamette from the falls to the mouth and the Columbia between the present town of Kalama and The Dalles Dam formed the core of the territory of the "Upper Chinookan" villagers. The stretch of the Columbia between The Cascades and The Dalles made up (approximately) the western three-quarters of what might be called the Wascopam circuit.

The journey to the new mission site took Perkins and Lee through a remarkable landscape, quite unlike that of today. Before dams, dredging, channelization, and other activities of the American immigrants brought the river under control, there was considerable seasonal variation in water level, portions of the shoreline were subject to flooding, and there were several falls and rapids.

The latter features, which impeded river travel and created a need for portages, were also areas of considerable natural beauty and were so noted by most early travelers. The same obstructions that impeded river travel at Willamette Falls, The Cascades, and The Dalles, however, simultaneously produced conditions favorable to the development of salmon fisheries. All three locations were centers of Indian population, with variable numbers of permanent villages, swelled in size at the appropriate season by outsiders who arrived for the fishery. None of those sites exist today in the natural state, having been altered or destroyed by locks or dams. Willamette Locks was built in 1868; The Cascades were destroyed by the construction of Bonneville Dam in 1937, and Five Mile Rapids, Celilo Falls, and other landmarks disappeared under the waters of The Dalles Dam in 1956. To understand what the river was like in Perkins's day, we must resort to historical records.

## Willamette Falls and the "Wappato Valley"

Willamette Falls, besides being the southern terminus of Chinookan territory, was also the southern boundary of the low-lying area called by Lewis and Clark the Wappato Valley, a region that roughly corresponds to the present

27

Portland metropolitan area. The valley's northern boundary was at Kalama, and the eastern boundary was the Sandy River.

One of the best descriptions of Willamette Falls as it existed in Perkins's day comes from the 1843 journal of immigrants Overton Johnson and William Winter:

> At the Falls, the Willammette precipitates down a perpendicular basaltic rock, thirty-three feet, and spreads out as it approaches the precipice, into a broad sheet, at the verge of which it is nearly a half a mile wide. It is divided by two large Islands of rock into three different shoots. The whole descent of the water from the level surface above to that below, is about thirty-five feet. The River for some distance above and below the Falls, runs through a channel cut in the solid rock. On the East side, extending down from the Falls several hundred yards, and back from the water five hundred and fifty feet, there is a perpendicular wall one hundred and fifty feet high; further down the space between the hills and the river increases in width until there is sufficient room for a town of considerable size. [1846:43-44]

Perkins's short description (Appendix 1, Doc. 1, "Autobiography") is one of the earliest extant of that part of the Wappato Valley, downstream from Willamette Falls and the Clackamas River, that corresponds to the central portion of the city of Portland. By combining Perkins's description with similar ones from Alexander Henry (1992:656, written in 1814) and Charles Brackenridge (1931:141, written in 1841), plus an early Coast and Geodetic Survey map (Rockwell 1888), it is possible to reconstruct what the Portland area looked like 150 years ago.

There were two Chinookan Indian settlements near Willamette Falls, one at the site of the present West Linn, the other up from the mouth of the Clackamas at Gladstone. In 1838 the area downstream from the Clackamas to the Willamette mouth was devoid of inhabitants, visited seasonally by Clackamas villagers (who gathered wapato root at Oaks Bottom) or traversed by Whites on their way between Fort Vancouver and the farms at French Prairie in the Willamette Valley. Perkins's "high rocky banks" occur regularly downstream from the falls to where the river widens at Oaks; below that point bluffs recur on the east bank at Mock's Crest. The "low green islands" referred to in the "Autobiography" would have included Ross Island and Swan Island. In the last century the main channel ran to the east of the latter island, which connected to the west bank in times of low water. What is now the northwest Portland industrial area was low and swampy, with numerous lakes (Doanes, Kittredge, Guilds, and Couch), now all drained and filled. Brackenridge, the botanist of the Wilkes Expedition, noted that the banks of that "Shallow basin" were "covered with Willow, Alder, and Dogwood" (1931:141). According to

Henry, there were "large spreading oaks" (1992:656) apparently on Swan Island. Back from the lowland were forests of Douglas fir, broken by "occasional patches of open prairie, which support solitary oaks" (Brackenridge 1931:141). In the early nineteenth century the Willamette was considered to have two downstream branches: one, now called Multnomah Channel, ran along the west side of Sauvie Island, entering the Columbia at St. Helens. That was the "lower mouth" of the Willamette; the entrance to the main branch on the east side of the island was the "upper mouth." Perkins's "delta" is Sauvie Island. Both channels were deep enough to remain open all year long. The "upper mouth in the nineteenth century was itself divided into three branches: shallow sloughs extended to the east and west of the main mouth, separating the islets (Coan and Pearcy), which are now part of Sauvie Island and the mainland, respectively.

## The Cascades

Practically every early traveler on the lower Columbia described The Cascades. From Perkins's time alone there are accounts by Daniel Lee ("Notebook," entry for Apr. 8, 1838, Daniel Lee Collection; D. Lee and Frost 1844:199-200), Charles Wilkes (1844, 4:380, written in 1841), Peter Burnett (1880:136-37, from 1843), Johnson and Winter (1846:37-38, from 1843), George Gary (diary, entry for Aug. 31, 1844, Archives of the Pacific Northwest Conference), and Alvan Waller (diary, entry for Sept. 2, 1844, Alvan Waller Collection). Map 2, dating from 1874, shows the area as it existed throughout the contact era.

Geologically, The Cascades are young: the river channel and most attendant features were formed by the Cascade Landslide, which has been carbon-14 dated (from submerged timbers) to between A.D. 1120 and A.D. 1280 (Minor 1986:7-8). Daniel Lee stated:

> The Indians say these falls are not ancient and that their fathers voyaged without obstruction in their canoes as far as the Dalls. They also assert that the river was dammed up at this place, which caused the waters to rise to a great height far above, and that after cutting a passage through the impeding mass down to its present bed, these rapids first made their appearance. [D. Lee and Frost 1844:200]

Lee (D. Lee and Frost 1844:5-8) suggested a former channel to the north and noted submerged trees and sands as proof of a catastrophe. All his ideas, interestingly, are supportable geologically (except the date, which he set at 300-400 years). A similar, briefer account of geological history appears in Peter Burnett's *Recollections* (1880:136-37), which describes events in 1843.

Lee gives a graphic description of a descent of The Cascades, which should be read in the original for full appreciation. At the head of the falls (about one-fourth mile in length, with a drop estimated at thirty feet by Burnett) the travelers began a half-mile portage on the north side. The canoes were carried by Indians over a narrow path that hugged the bluff. Lee noted the "deafening roar of the Cascades" and an "irregular sheet of snow-white water" (D. Lee and Frost 1844:202). At flood stage, the volume of water in that restricted passage became so great that it was "heaping up . . . mid-channel . . . where it is less broken than towards the shores, and runs with great rapidity" (D. Lee and Frost 1844:203). Three rapids (upper, middle, and lower) followed, the first immediately below the falls, the second a mile lower, and the third another one and one-half miles at the western tip of Bradford Island. In high water the middle rapids were passed by a portage on the north side.

On September 2, 1844, Alvan Waller and George Gary ascended The Cascades on their way to Wascopam. They were more concerned with the landscape than with the river features. The two men entered the Columbia Gorge at Cape Horn, "a high wall of Rock which puts out into the River . . . in deepest water rising in a perpendicular form . . . near three hundred feet." Beyond that were:

> large masses of rock . . . presenting the appearance of ancient and magnificent castles, Domes pyramids etc of enormous height & size, and of even shape and form. . . . One large rock [presumably Beacon Rock] . . . presents the appearance of a huge flattened indian head, nose, mouth, eyes, chin etc clearly visible, on the opposite side the appearance of an African portrait. . . . On the top of this was a small pond, some indians having ascended it by cutting steps in the Rock. [Waller, diary entry for Sept. 2, 1844, Alvan Waller Collection]

The Reverend Gary, making his first trip upriver, was impressed: "The grandest scene by far I ever witnessed, it was indeed fearfully grand; never was I so awed by nature in any form in which I ever beheld her" (diary, entry for Sept. 2, 1844, Archives of the Pacific Northwest Conference).

The two engravings of The Cascades (plate 2) were made from a series of sketches drawn by William Tappan in 1849 (Cross 1850).

## The Dalles

The name The Dalles has been applied to more than one location, creating some confusion. According to Lewis McArthur (1974:721), in contemporary French "dalle meant a stone used to flag gutters." The term was initially applied to that restricted stretch of the Columbia (now under the waters of The

Dalles Dam) also called Five Mile Rapids or the Long Narrows. Here, during low water, the river rushed through a five-mile-long, narrow basalt channel, which McArthur suggests resembled a stone-lined gutter (see map 3).

The Dalles proper was also known as the Great (Grandes) Dalles or (as in Perkins) Lower Dalles to distinguish it from a second feature, the Little (Petites) Dalles or Upper Dalles just over three miles upstream from the eastern end of the main Dalles. Finally, there is the city of The Dalles, some three miles downstream from the lower end of The Dalles itself. The confusion of names has been simplified since 1957 by the obliteration of the two natural features (Great and Little Dalles) by The Dalles Dam. Today only the city remains.

The entire stretch of river from the mouth of Mill Creek to the mouth of the Deschutes was, like The Cascades, quite spectacular and has been described in print by numerous observers. Other notable natural features in the area—moving upstream—included the following (consult map 3). Three Mile Rapids, just east of The Dalles city, was visible during low water, when the low-lying Lone Pine peninsula extended from the south bank of the river. Three Mile Rapids was the site of Tumwater Falls. On the south side of the river, between the mouth of Five Mile Creek and the beginning of The Dalles, was an area of high cliffs that included favored fishing sites of south-bank (Wasco) Chinookans. At the lower end of The Dalles, on the north, was an extension of the river, Big Eddy; on the south there was a series of islands, including Grave Island, the (south-bank?) Chinookan cemetery. Indian (summer?) villages were located on both sides of the downstream end of The Dalles. The north bank of The Dalles itself was Tumwater Fishery, frequented by resident north-bank Chinookans and (in season) visiting Sahaptins. During lowest water, there was only one channel here. But "when the river [was] high . . . besides the main channel, there [were] four or five other small canals through which the water passe[d]. . . . These [were] but a few feet across" (Wilkes 1844, 4:384; a drawing [385] shows those canals). Wishram (*nixlúidix*) and *Tináynu* villages were located on the north and south sides of the upstream end of The Dalles. Just to the east of Wishram was Colowash Bottom, now Horsethief Lake. A mile further was Upper Memaloose Island, followed by the Little Dalles. Three miles above the latter was Celilo (Sahaptin *silaylo*) Falls, commonly known in the nineteenth century by the voyageur term Chutes or Shoots 'falls'. Celilo village (Waiam in the missionary texts) was just above the falls on the south; *sk'in* village was on the north bank.

Descriptions of The Dalles by observers who were in the area in the early 1840s include those in Wilkes (1844, 4:384–85), Simpson (1847:167–68), and Johnson and Winter (1846:35). The series of engravings reproduced in Osborne Cross's "Report . . . of the . . . Mounted Riflemen" (1850) gives an excellent visual impression of the area as it was in 1849; two are reproduced here (plate 2). John Mix Stanley's 1853 "The Dalles" (plate 3) depicts the upstream entry to Five Mile Rapids.

Of all the contemporary narrative descriptions of the area, Daniel Lee's, excerpted below, is best.

> Two miles below the Large Dalles . . . is a dike extending from the south shore three-fourths across, which is bare in low water, turning the current into a deep bay on the north side; but the high water pours over it, and forms a dangerous rapid. Reaching the foot of the Dalls, our attention is arrested by several rocky islands that for ages have borne unmoved the shock of the mighty billows which at an earlier period severed them from their neighbouring rocks. One of these is a depot for the bodies of the dead . . . at the Dalles, the whole volume of the river, half a mile wide, rushes through a deep narrow channel, which the action of the water has formed in the course of ages, through an extended tract of the hardest basalt. . . . A mile brings us to the head of the chasm, which, diminishing in breadth to this point, is here only from thirty to fifty yards broad. . . . More than one thousand Indians, of all ages, pass from May to September on these rocks. . . .
>
> The next object to be noticed is the Small Dalls, two miles further up. Here the river passes through a very deep and narrow cut in the basaltic rock, which rises some twenty or thirty feet above its surface. The water pours through this channel with great velocity, except at high water, when it spreads out over the sands to the eastward. . . . Three miles further we arrive at the Shoots (French, Les Chutes). They are, on the south side, close to the shore, and less than fifty yards over, to a point of rocks widening into an extensive bed, and extending thence across the river to the bank on the north side. This rocky bed, in low water, is mostly dry, but cut here and there with small streams which have opened for themselves a way on its surface. The shoot is nearly perpendicular and from fifteen to twenty feet tall. . . . Here is an excellent salmon fishery, and from two hundred to three hundred Indians spend one-third of the year at these Shoots. [D. Lee and Frost 1844:196-99]

Many early observers, including Lee, speculated on the geologic history of The Dalles area.

## Languages

As stated earlier, the winter villages of the native peoples of the Lower Columbia River were concentrated along the banks of the river itself. The Wascopam Mission papers are one of the best sources—indeed a primary source—on Indian village sites, particularly in the area that was a part of the Wascopam circuit (roughly between The Cascades and the mouth of the Deschutes) during the 1840s, the decade before old patterns were permanently disrupted and most Indians were removed to reservations.

Other than the ties of kinship, the natives of that region identified most strongly with particular winter villages. Aboriginally, there was nothing beyond the village level that could be called a tribal organization. The villages in the Wascopam circuit could be grouped, however, on the basis of primary linguistic affiliation, and that was how Perkins and other Euroamerican observers categorized them.

## Kiksht

There were two languages in the circuit: the first—Chinook in the missionary lexicon, Kiksht according to its speakers—was spoken in villages from The Cascades to Wishram; Walla Walla (missionary term) or Columbia River Sahaptin (linguist's designation) was the major tongue of villages from *Tináynu* at the upper end of The Dalles to the Deschutes. Something should be said both about those languages and about their broader linguistic affiliations.

Kiksht (also called Upper Chinookan) was the easternmost of two (perhaps three) languages of the Chinookan family. The two downstream forms, Chinook proper at the river's mouth and Kathlamet[1] are extinct. The Wasco-Wishram form of Kiksht is still spoken by a few older people on both the Warm Springs and Yakama reservations but no longer survives as the speech of an identifiable community (Hymes 1981).

Spoken Kiksht existed in a number of local dialects, perhaps showing the geographical intergradation that linguists call a dialect continuum (Thompson 1973:982). The dialects probably corresponded to winter-village clusters, which would include at a minimum Clackamas, Cascades, and The Dalles area (Wasco-Wishram, after the major south- and north-bank settlements, respectively). Clackamas Kiksht is represented in the linguistic literature by a large body of material collected in 1929–30 by Melville Jacobs from his informant Victoria Howard and published in the series *Clackamas Chinook Texts* (1958), *The Content and Style of an Oral Literature* (1959), and *The People Are Coming Soon* (1960). For Wasco-Wishram there is Edward Sapir's *Wishram Texts* (1909).

An interesting characteristic of Kiksht and the other Chinookan languages was that, phonetically and gramatically, they were very difficult for non-native speakers to learn to speak fluently. Shortly after her arrival at Wascopam, Elvira Perkins stated, "Our first work is to learn the language, which is far from being harmonious. . . . I could hardly feel reconciled at first to learning to speak a language so full of gutterals, clicks, and hissing sounds" (letter of May 11, 1838, Canse Collection). Henry Perkins said essentially the same in his *Christian Advocate and Journal* report of September 20, 1843 (Appendix 1, Doc. 4). Neither the Perkinses nor anyone else connected with the mission ever learned to speak Kiksht with facility. Perkins himself devoted his efforts to the local form of Columbia River Sahaptin, and Daniel Lee, though assigned Kiksht, apparently never mastered it, as his unfinished lexicon (discussed in chap. 10) suggests.

Perkins also noted in his September 1843 report that "while the Walla-walla and Klikatak are spoken with facility by numbers of the Chinooks, not one of the former tribes, to my knowledge, can speak the Chinook readily." That statement—certainly true, as it is echoed by contemporary native informants—has interesting, and to this writer's knowledge, unexplored social implications. Did it apply as well to non-Chinookan wives (there were many) of Chinookan men? If so, did the husbands and wives communicate via the wife's language, or perhaps via a simplified speech form such as Chinook Jargon? Did the reluctance to learn the Chinookan languages promote the spread of Chinook Jargon? What role did it play in the eventual decline of the Chinookan languages?

## Columbia River Sahaptin

In the 1840s, "Walla Walla" was a collective term applied to the widely dispersed bands of Indians who spoke varieties of the Sahaptin language. Horatio Hale's map (Hale was the "ethnologist and philologist" of the 1841 Wilkes Expedition), reprinted as map 4, is a fairly accurate depiction of their distribution circa 1841.

*Wálawála* ('little river') most properly refers to that band whose territory was centered on the lower reaches of the river of the same name. The Hudson Bay Company's Fort Nez Percés (later Fort Walla Walla) was sited at the mouth of the Walla Walla; at that location—and across the Columbia—Walla

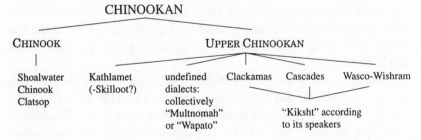

**Figure 1.** Chinookan language family.

Wallas, Cayuses, lower bands of Nez Perces, and Yakamas traditionally rendezvoused during the summer. The Northeast branch of Sahaptins includes Walla Wallas, Wanapams, and Palouses. The most prominent subgroups of Northwest Sahaptins are Yakamas and Klickitats. Columbia River Sahaptins (self-designation *nči wanałáma* or *wanałáma* 'river people'), the group whose territories were closest to Wascopam Mission, include Umatillas (*Imatilámła-ma*), Rock Creeks (*Qmiłáma*), John Days (*Takšpašłáma*), Celilos (*Wayamłá-ma*), Teninos (*Tinaynułáma*), and Tyghs (*Tayx̱łáma*) (Rigsby 1965:48–57). The forms *-łama* (and variations) and *-pam*, incidentally, are locative suffixes meaning roughly "those living at" or "people of" (Schuster 1975:42).

The summer and winter settlements of the Celilos, Teninos, and Tyghs were within the Wascopam circuit and are mentioned in the missionary texts. The Celilo peoples had a winter village *wanwáwi* (Eugene Hunn, personal communication, 1982–93) at the mouth of the Deschutes; *sk'in* was at Celilo Falls, north bank, and *wayám* at historic Celilo village, on the south bank of the falls. *Wanwáwi* was twenty-five miles from Wascopam Mission, Celilo Falls about fourteen miles. *Wanwáwi* (the village at "Chutes River") is mentioned in a letter of August 4, 1839 (H. Perkins, Canse Collection), as one of Perkins's "preaching places," having 200 inhabitants. "Waiam" was visited by Perkins in late May 1840: "spent the whole day visiting from house to house. I judge there were about one hundred in all, every one of which I visited, and talked with many of them, and I think about sixty individuals joined me in prayer" (letter of June 2, 1840, Canse Collection). Perkins also held meetings at *wayám* in early October 1840, when he invited the residents to the upcoming camp meeting, which was held at Kowelapse between the thirteenth

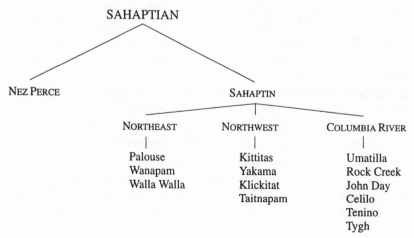

Figure 2. Sahaptian language family.

and the nineteenth (Brewer 1986:64). Alvan Waller held a Sunday meeting at the village on April 26, 1846, which was attended by 100 people.

*Tináynu* village was located at the head of Five Mile Rapids (The Dalles) on the south side, across from the Chinookan village of Wishram (*nixlúidix*). When Perkins visited it in July 1839 there were perhaps 200 people present (letter of August 4, 1839, Canse Collection). That was a summer fishing village; according to the ethnographer of the Tenino, George Murdock, there was a winter village (not mentioned in the missionary literature) "5 miles inland" (1980:134). The Tygh village of "Talhoney" (*tiɬxni*), thirty miles southeast of the mission (at Sherar's Bridge, according to Rigsby 1965:54), is mentioned in a Brewer letter of November 9, 1841 (H. Brewer, Canse Collection). Perkins and Brewer had visited it the preceding summer.

Perkins spent the entire month of July 1839 among the Columbia River Sahaptin peoples between Fort Nez Percés and The Dalles. At the fort itself he preached to 100 Walla Wallas. The several villages "on the small streams which flow into the Columbia from the south" that he passed through were certainly seasonal fishing settlements of Umatilla and John Day peoples, at that time of year scattered liberally along the river's bank in order to take maximum advantage of the summer salmon run (both Lewis and Clark 1988:291–319 and David Thompson 1962:350–53, 371–75 describe that dispersed settlement pattern).

## Columbia Gorge Villages

There is a sizable body of data on aboriginal use areas in the Columbia Gorge, but much of it is misleading. There were several varieties of use areas, ranging from winter villages through seasonally occupied settlements and camps to fishing areas of variable size. In addition, many use areas were abandoned or less used after the disease-caused population decline of the late eighteenth and early nineteenth centuries. The best-known listings of Columbia Gorge use areas (Curtis 1911a:180–81; Spier and Sapir 1930:164–68; Saleeby and Pettigrew 1983) are variably successful in identifying the nature of named use areas, and by combining all in a single list, they give an incorrect impression of a greater population density than was probably the case for either the precontact or early contact periods. The following discussion summarizes the ethnohistoric information from the early nineteenth century (Lewis and Clark through the missionaries), with an emphasis on winter villages, the most stable and meaningful units in a sociocultural sense. Known winter-village and associated sites within the Columbia Gorge area are depicted on map 1.

## The Cascades

The Cascades, located between modern Bonneville and Stevenson, was a first-rate aboriginal fishing area. In the early nineteenth century there were two (perhaps three) winter villages, a number of satellite summer villages, and important fishing stations. Map 2 summarizes that information.

The Cascades people, like other Chinookans, moved with the seasons to areas where native foods, particularly salmon, were most easily taken. At the Upper Cascades, the winter village was *wáiaxix* ("Yehhuh" in Lewis and Clark 1983: map 79), just to the east of Ashes Lake (now flooded), on the north side of the river. In fishing season the *wáiaxix* people moved across the Columbia to the village at Cascade Locks (Lewis and Clark 1991:106, 109); they probably dispersed to other local fishing sites (such as those at the mouths of Herman and Rock Creeks) as well. The Upper Cascades was the site of the major rapids; here also was the most important dip-net fishery on the reefs and rocks just upstream from the modern Bridge of the Gods. The Upper Cascades fishery continued to be used by natives until it was destroyed by Bonneville Dam in 1937. Below the Bridge of the Gods was a rough stretch of river and a portage that terminated at a possible second winter village, *sk'mániak* (at the site of Fort Rains; contemporary Skamania is seven miles downstream), already abandoned when Lewis and Clark visited in 1804-5 (Lewis and Clark 1988:358, 361, 1991:111, 113). There was another stretch of rapids, reefs, and fishing areas near Garrison Eddy at the downstream tip of Bradford Island. Finally, the winter village called "Wahclellah" by Lewis and Clark (probably the ethnographers' *nimišxáya*) was located "on the North side of the river . . . about a mile below the beacon rock" (1991:96).

Lewis and Clark visited The Cascades area twice, in early April and in late October, moving seasons for the natives. Their observations from April 9, below (combined for completeness from the two explorers' accounts) both describe the seasonal movements of the Wahclellah people and give an impression of native houses.

> Wah-clel-lah Village . . . appears to be the winter station of the Wah-clel-lahs and Clahclellars[2] . . . two bands of the Sha-ha-la nation. . . . The greater part of the former have lately removed to the falls of the Multnomah [Willamette Falls] . . . [where] they take their salmon . . . and the latter have established themselves a few miles above on the North side . . . opposite the lower point of brant [Bradford] island . . . rapids, here they also take their salmon. . . .
>
> 14 houses only appear occupied and the inhabitants of those moveing off hourly, they take with them in their Canoes . . . their household effects the bark of their houses, and boards. 9 houses has been latterly abandoned . . . the remains of 10 or 12 others . . . in the rear . . . appears to have been

enhabited last fall . . . they sometimes sink their houses in the earth, and at other times have their floors level with the surface of the earth; they are generally built with boards and covered with Cedar bark. most of them have a devision in their houses . . . several families inhabit one appartment. [1991:96-97, 99]

The Cascades Indians occupied a strategic position on the river and were in continual contact with Whites, who hired native porters to get past the rough area above sk'mániak and traded for salmon, particularly at the upper rapids. Two major Indian-White confrontations took place at The Cascades: the first, in 1813-14 with North West Company traders, was over plunder and passage at the portage; the second, in 1856, was an incident in the larger Yakama War (summaries of both can be found in Beckham 1984).

The ethnohistorical data suggest that by the mid-1830s the settlement pattern, at least for the Middle and Lower Cascades peoples, had experienced a major shift. Depopulation from the "fever and ague" epidemics of 1831 and after certainly had something to do with that (see, e.g., Wyeth 1899:175-76). An 1838 Hudson's Bay Company census indicates that (at that date) 142 surviving Cascades people congregated in a single "winter village Banks of the Columbia opposite Vancouver" (Hudson's Bay Company 1838). They were probably survivors from the former winter settlements at Wahclellah and sk'mániak. In 1841 Father Norbert Blanchet stated, "They leave the sunken encampments and move to winter on the Vancouver islands where the cold is less rigorous and hunting more abundant" (Landerholm 1956:89; cited by Minor 1986:57).

Contact with the Methodist missionaries from Wascopam appears to have been mostly with the people of the wáiaxix villages at the Upper Cascades. In 1840-41, following the Wascopam Revival, the area was the scene of an intense rivalry between the Methodists and newly arrived Catholic priests, Bishops Blanchet and Demers. The spoils, of course, were the souls of the Cascades Indians. Representatives of the two religious groups never met face to face at The Cascades itself but made alternating visits in which each tried to undo the efforts of the other.

When Daniel Lee arrived at The Cascades (presumably the north-bank village at the Upper Cascades) in January 1840, the Catholics had already made some inroads (most likely through contacts with people at the Vancouver encampment, as priests had yet to visit The Cascades itself). In his January 15 letter to Perkins, Lee suggested that the Methodists would have to make a special effort in that area: "I wish you to visit the Cascades. The lambs there want some of the sincere milk of the Word. Remember that the devils there have some agents there to attend to his interests" (D. Lee, letter of Jan. 15, 1840, Canse Collection).

A year and a half later (September 16, 1841), Father Blanchet arrived at one of the summer encampments for a ten-day mission. Excerpts from his report follow:

> The good chief Tamakoun came to clasp my hand; the rest imitated him. . . . I set out to visit the lodges scattered on the shore. In the evening I began to explain the Catholic ladder [see chap. 10], etc. in the presence of forty persons who repaired to me at the sound of the bell. This village was composed of some thirty families . . . only young people, all the elders having been cut down by the fevers. . . . Tamakoun told me that those of the left bank that had embraced the Methodist sect had rejected it a year since. . . . Tamakoun spent entire evenings talking about religion with me. He told me that he had only been two Sundays to hear Minister Perkins, and that, having seen our ladder since 1839, he had constantly refused since then all promises from the Methodist side. . . . I . . . distributed several chronological ladders. . . . The chief already [had] a bell for the summons, received a ladder of which he was charged to give the explanation. Although little versed in prayers, my catchumens knew at least how to do the sign of the cross in their language and to recite the sacraments, recited the words of baptism, and had even learned to sing five canticles in the jargon. . . . I estimate the number of natives of this mission at 150 to 200. . . . I left thirty-four children baptized. The adults yet not being sufficiently instructed to receive this favor. Tamakoun merited it; but his wife not being sufficiently instructed, I awaited an opportunity to baptize them both, and then to marry them. [Blanchet in Landerholm 1956:88–90]

Tamakoun, the leading man named above, is mentioned elsewhere in contemporary documents. Beckham (1984:46) suggests that he may have been the Cascades native who had an interview with the Reverend Samuel Parker at Vancouver in 1835, requesting religious instruction. His name appears on the 1838 Hudson's Bay Company census as Tamagun—married with one wife and three slaves. By the summer of 1841, when visited by the Joseph Drayton party of the Wilkes Expedition, "Tamakun" had at least one son, whose flattened head was sketched by Drayton (plate 4). An infant daughter was baptized by Blanchet at Vancouver in February 1844. Tamakoun's wife Marie was baptized shortly before her death in September of that same year (Beckham 1984:48). In a letter of November 2, 1844, Elvira Perkins referred to "Tumecoon . . . the chief at the Fort" (Canse Collection). He was probably at that time in his winter residence, having been there approximately five weeks (Blanchet in Landerholm 1956:89 dates the 1841 breakup of the summer encampment on September 20).

In July 1847 artist Paul Kane visited The Cascades and made a watercolor painting of Tamakoun (plate 5). For his assistance in capturing two runaway Hawaiian employees of Kane's party, the chief "was rewarded with four blankets and four shirts" (Harper 1971:112). In January 1848 Tamakoun's second wife (also named Marie, aged 30), was baptized; she died on January 19. "Thomas Tamakun Chief of the Cascades, aged about 35 years" followed her in death about nine days later (Beckham 1984:49). Both probably died of measles, which was epidemic at the time.

## Gorge Villages

In their voyage upstream from The Cascades, Perkins, Lee, and company passed "several villages of Indians . . . all on some salmon creek" (Appendix 1, Doc. 1, "Autobiography"). The "Autobiography" does not contain enough information to pinpoint those settlements or determine whether they were in fact (winter) villages or camps established for the taking of spring salmon. Perkins's observation concerning siting at the mouths of "salmon creeks," however, is quite accurate for that stretch of the Columbia Gorge between The Cascades and The Dalles. According to the 1937 survey of fishing sites submerged under Bonneville Pool (Carter 1937), sites at The Cascades and The Dalles were located along bluffs or on rocks at rapids and falls; between those locations, however, they were consistently on tributaries that supported fish runs. Sites named by Indian informants included the mouths of Rock and Herman Creeks; the Wind, Little White Salmon, Big White Salmon, Hood, and Klickitat rivers; and Major Creek. At least four of those—Little White Salmon, Big White Salmon, Hood, and Klickitat River mouths—were both winter villages and warm-season fisheries.

It should be noted, however, that different species of anadromous fish ran at different times in the Gorge tributaries. The greatest Indian presence on any given tributary corresponded with the run season. Most (but not all) streams supported runs of fall chinook and coho salmon, which peaked in September. Spring salmon, however (on present evidence), are known to have run only in the Big White Salmon and the Klickitat rivers (Fulton 1968, 1970). In their late-March ascent of the river, Perkins and Lee probably saw Indians at each of the aforementioned winter-village sites. The only tributaries where they may have seen Indians actually fishing, however (and March is early for spring salmon), were the mouths of the Big White Salmon and Klickitat rivers. It is possible that, at that early date, the Indians were fishing for steelhead (anadromous trout).

Daniel Lee gives a good summary of winter-village sites in the Gorge (D. Lee and Frost 1844:176). Between the villages at the Upper Cascades and the mouth of the Little White Salmon there is no documented early-contact-period village site.[3] The mouth of the Little White Salmon is the probable location of Lee's "Scaltape" (*skałx 'lmax*). Lewis and Clark's map shows three houses at that location, visited October 29, 1805. The inhabitants of the village possessed many furs, including mountain goat, and traded cranberries and root bread (Lewis and Clark 1988:352-353).

Lewis and Clark's maps show a string of houses on the riverbank between the Big White Salmon mouth and the present town of Bingen. The first part of their name for the settlement, "Weocksock Willacum village," is equivalent to the Wascopam missionaries' "Clemiaksuc" (the ethnographers' *łmiyaqsáq*). A number of other names have been applied to that settlement area, perhaps representing subzones within the larger region, occupied or abandoned in accordance with the waxing and waning of the local population during the fishing and winter seasons. The missionaries' "Kowilamowan" (Kiksht *gawilamaixn*; probably the Sahaptin *lawli–pa–amí* [Ray 1936:148]) appears to be next in line downstream, at the site of White Salmon town. *Nánšuit* (Namnit or Namnade are probably Sahaptin [Curtis 1911a:181; Spier and Sapir 1930; Carter1937]), not mentioned by the missionaries, was Underwood, at the White Salmon mouth itself.

Lewis and Clark stopped at the Weocksock Willacum village twice, on October 29, 1805, when there were "14 houses . . . Scattered on the bank" (1988:352), and again on April 14, 1806, when there were "about 20 . . . reather detatched and extent for several miles." On the latter date, Lewis described two types of houses:

> I observed several habitations entirely under grownd; they were sunk about 8 feet deep and covered with strong timber and several feet of earth in a conic form . . . evacuated at present. they are about 16 feet in diameter. nearly circular, and are entered through a hole at the top which appears to answer the double purpose of a chimney and a door . . . you decend . . . by a ladder . . . the present habitations of these peoples were on the surface . . . and do not differ from those of the . . . [Cascades] rapids. [1991:119]

The pit houses were winter dwellings, eminently suited to the chilly winds of the Columbia Gorge. The surface dwellings were plank houses.

Lewis and Clark report that those people spoke Chinookan, though a Plateau influence was obvious: some men wore leggings and moccasins "in the stile of Chopunnish [Nez Perces]," and there were ten to twelve horses, the first encountered on their upstream trip (1991:119). Perkins and Lee also saw their first horses near here on March 20, 1830 (Appendix 1, Doc. 1, "Autobiography"). Lewis and Clark received roots, hazelnuts, and dried berries in trade, and Clark "met Several parties of women and boys in Serch of herbs & roots" in "a handsom bottom"; many "had parcels of the Stems of the Sun flower" (1991:120-21). Eugene Hunn (personal communication, 1982-93) identifies their "Sun flower" as *Balsamorhiza sagittata*. Lewis and Clark's notes strongly suggest that Clemiaksuc was a winter village, augmented by seasonal visitors during the salmon season. The 140 late December 1839 inhabitants met by Lee and company (Appendix 1, Doc. 3, "Wonderful Work of God. . . .") probably represented a core population of Upper Chinookans, who would be joined by others (mostly Klickitat Sahaptins) in the spring.

Lee's visit to Clemiaksuc during the 1839-40 Wascopam Revival is described in Appendix 1, Document 3. Perkins revisited Clemiaksuc in the spring of 1840. He "gave them Christ's sermon on the Mount, as literal as I could translate it. . . . Some catechists were appointed." Nevertheless, it was apparent that Lee's lessons of the preceding winter had not taken hold. Many people violated the Sabbath by performing menial tasks. Sleguahan, a leading man,

> said he wanted another wife—that he spoke to you [D. Lee] about it last winter—and you said you would see about it when you came back—that he had waited a long time . . . and that he wanted another wife very, very much! . . .The way he seems to have understood you was that when you returned, you would provide him with one! [H. Perkins, letter of spring 1840, Canse Collection]

"Nenootletete" (D. Lee and Frost 1844; Kiksht *ninúłdidix*) was the missionary designation for the village on the east bank of the mouth of Hood River. Lewis and Clark passed four houses here on October 29, 1805 (1988:352). The only other mention of the site in the missionary records dates from January 17, 1840, when Daniel Lee met "Witsatsat, one of the leaders from Hood River" at Fort Vancouver (letter of Jan. 15, 1840, Canse Collection). Nenootletete appears in Curtis as Ninuhltidih (1911a:181) and on the Carter (1937) list as Nothdede.

The John Mix Stanley painting "Mountain Landscape with Indians" (plate 6) must have been made in the vicinity of the White Salmon settlements, though it is not possible to be precise as to its exact location.

The next village upstream was the missionaries' "Claticut" (*łádaxat*), located just up the mouth of the Klickitat River. The name is Chinookan and, Anglicized as Klickitat, has been historically applied to the *xwa 'łxway–pam* branch of Northwest Sahaptin speakers who occupied the mountainous south-central portion of Washington state, from Vancouver to north of The Dalles. Ethnographically attested Klickitat winter villages in the area include Claticut itself and *waka'yk-as* and *xwa'txway* up the Klickitat River (Eugene Hunn, personal communication, 1982-93), *lawli-pa-amí* (Kowilamowan?) at White Salmon, and *nakipanik* and *xatxa'ywaša* on the upper White Salmon at the sites of Husum and BZ Corner (Ray 1936:148). The two winter villages near the tributaries' mouths were probably fundamentally Chinookan, with a variable population augmented by Klickitat visitors during the fishing season. The missionary texts also mention a companion village to Claticut, named "Cutcatalk" (see below).

Claticut was visited by Lewis and Clark on April 14, 1806: "This village Consists of about 100 fighting men of Several tribes from the plains to the North Collected here waiting for the Salmon. they do not differ in any respect from those below" [i.e., at Clemiaksuc] (1991:121). That passage says a great deal. The interior people were gathered at that location to take advantage of the spring chinook salmon run. They were identical to the horsemen dressed "in Nez Perce style" met at Clemiaksuc; and they came from the north—Sahaptin territory. Thus we have people of Plateau-type culture—undoubtedly Klickitat—descending upon riverine settlements for a seasonal salmon fishery.

Claticut was an important part of the Wascopam circuit and is mentioned frequently in the missionary documents. Perkins and Lee initially noted it on their way upstream in March 1838. The village was the first important downstream stop made by Daniel Lee, Benjamin Wright, and Tumsowit during the 1839-40 Wascopam Revival. They were there for a full week starting December 17, 1839, and "joined nearly one hundred in society" (Appendix 1, Doc. 3).

After leaving the village, Lee encouraged Henry Perkins to follow in his footsteps. Perkins complied, and on Christmas eve he "rode about eight miles to visit some people down river, opposite Claticut. Found them very stupid" (assumedly meaning they were not interested in what he had to say). Back at Wascopam for Christmas, he left again for Claticut on December 26, where he found the people "in expectation of me." Though Daniel Lee had been dubious about the sincerity of his Claticut converts, Perkins was upbeat. He met twenty to twenty-five in evening prayers and held a class meeting on the morning of the 27th: "Was pleased with their behavior, very eager for instruction. . . . Many spoke freely, feelingly. They need the sincere milk of the Word that they may grow." In the afternoon, he returned to

> Cutcatalk, on the south side of the river, where there are nearly as many men as at Cutcatalk [*sic;* certainly Claticut is intended] but found many of them absent. Assembled them, men women and children, to the

number of thirty-five or forty, and after preaching to them, and giving
them an invitation to visit Wascopam left them and continued home,
where I arrived at twilight. [H. Perkins, letter of Dec. 24, 1839, Canse
Collection]

The location of Cutcatalk is unclear. Claticut was sited on the downstream
bank of the Klickitat River. Cutcatalk may have been on the east bank of the
same river, following the apparent model of Kowilamowan-Clemiaksuc
(separated by Jewett Creek) farther down the Columbia. More likely, on the
model of Clemiaksuc-Nenootletete, it was on the south bank of the Columbia,
below Rowena. Anthropologist Edward Sapir was given the name *geč+geč–ak*
for a site on the Oregon bank of the Columbia, which was possibly Cutcutalk
(David French, personal communication, 1989–93).

In March 1840, on his return from Vancouver, Daniel Lee revisited
Claticut. Shortly afterward he

> went to preach to two villages of the Clickatats resideing inland to the
> northward, and numbering more than two hundred souls. [These could
> be either the two winter villages on the Klickitat or those on the White
> Salmon noted above]. Here he saw such a readiness to hear and to follow
> the teachings of the gospel as had not been surpassed in any other
> place. . . . That numbers of them were converted there was no room for
> him to doubt. Subsequently they attended the campmeeting [April 1840
> at Kowelapse—see chap. 10]. [D. Lee and Frost 1844:190]

Claticut was again visited by Perkins in June 1840 (letter of July 11, 1840,
Canse Collection). The two Wascopam missionaries therefore had visited all
the winter villages of the Klickitats during the 1839–40 season (some a number
of times), had been well received, and had made a number of converts. Those
efforts certainly had an effect on later religious developments among those
peoples.

The area between the mouths of the Klickitat River and Mill Creek is
poorly known, both ethnohistorically and ethnographically. Lewis and Clark
passed a location a few miles upstream from the Klickitat River that they
named "Friendly village"; their maps show a second village of eight houses
between Crates Point and Chenoweth Creek (Lewis and Clark 1983: map 78).
Those may correspond to any of the ethnographers' *škágč, šq'wánana,* and
*capxadidlit.* In the post-1830 records, only one site—Kowelapse (*ġawilapčk*),
downstream from the mission—is mentioned, and that as a meeting place, not
a village. Two factors—the lack of good salmon fishing areas (David French,
personal communication, 1989–93) and postcontact depopulation—may
explain why this stretch of the river was apparently less heavily used during
the missionary period.

## Wascopam Village

Wascopam Mission was established at the site of what is presently the city of The Dalles. The flatlands that bordered the mission site were called by Perkins the "intervale," which (according to Webster) is a New England term for "low flat land between hills or along a river or stream; bottomland." Most of the area was seasonally flooded, yielding "soil like your richest prairies." The Indians had a term for that region as well; according to several sources, it was *wi'nkwat*, meaning "a large indentation in a river or lake bank, useful as a landing place" (Dyk in D. French forthcoming; see also McKay 1869; Sapir 1910:917). The intervale is shown on map 3. Mill Creek, in the middle of the intervale, was called "Hoiss" (perhaps the Jargon haus 'house' [David French, personal communication, 1989-93]), according to Perkins; McKay (1869) supplies the additional information that "the mouth of Mill Creek had the name *Wil–look–it* (*wi'lukt*), meaning looking through an opening or gap." The mission springs were called "*Amotan* (*a-mútan*), meaning the Indian or wild hemp, which grew in abundance at that place."

There are, surprisingly, no accounts of the Indian village located near Wascopam Mission dating from the premissionary period, and only a few specific descriptions in the missionary literature itself. Both Perkins and Lee appear to have been content to devote a few lines to it on first arrival, after which they took it for granted, despite a continuing interaction with its inhabitants. Besides Perkins's "Autobiography" description (Appendix 1, Doc. 1), Lee's "Notebook" (Daniel Lee Collection) contains the following information on the fifteen houses. They were

> built of cedar boards and covered with bark. Each occupies an area of about 15 by 20 feet with roofs a little elevated in the middle. The door is a low narrow opening through the wall covered with a mat. The fire is in the centre and the smoke escapes through an opening at the top. Here the whole household mingles together.

The only other extant description, from 1841, appears in Wilkes's *Narrative*: "There are only a few Indians residing near the mission during the winter, and these are a very miserable set, who live in holes in the ground, not unlike a clay oven, in order to keep warm" (1844, 4:382). Again, as elsewhere in the Gorge, there were two types of dwellings, occupied seasonally.

The Kiksht word *wasq'ó*, meaning "cup" or "horn bowl" (Sapir 1910: 917), is the source of the two names assigned to the village: the Kiksht Ka-clas-ko (according to D. Lee [D. Lee and Frost 1844:176]; apparently the same as Robert Stuart's 1812 "Cathlasko" [1935:54]) and the Sahaptin Wascopam. Cathla (*ga–la–*), the Kiksht prefixes, and *pam*, the Sahaptin suffix, both mean "people of"; hence both names mean "people of the cup" (Yvonne Hajda, personal communication, 1988–93). Brewer states, "A short distance from the square [Mission compound] was a beautiful spring of pure water, which the Indians called 'Wasco', hence the name 'Wasco-pam'" (Mudge 1854:11).

Confusion arises from the fact that the name Wasco has also been applied to a second village, at the site of historic Big Eddy, Oregon, some three miles upstream, and by extension, to all Upper Chinookan villagers who occupied the south (Oregon) bank of the Columbia between approximately Crates Point and Five Mile Rapids. The upstream Wasco has never been known by any other name. That village also received its name from "a cup-shaped rock near the village, into which a spring bubbled up" (Spier and Sapir 1930:168; see also Curtis 1911:181; verified by K. French [personal communication from Yvonne Hajda, 1989]). After 1855 the name Wasco became standard for all south-bank Chinookans who were removed to the Warm Springs Reservation.

Perkins notes "150 inhabitants, who are permanent residents" at Kaclasko; Wilkes has them at the site during winter. Kaclasko was therefore occupied year-round during the 1840s. That "permanency" of occupation may be a postcontact phenomenon dating from the first Euroamerican occupation at Mill Creek in 1829–30 (the Birnie trading post). There is nothing in the earlier literature that suggests permanent settlement in that area. (Lewis and Clark camped on Mill Creek twice, in October 1805 and April 1806, but do not mention a settlement in the area.) In fact, it is unclear at this writing whether the other two villages of the Wasco—Lone Pine (Kiksht name *wacáqʷs*; colloquially Washucks) and Wasco *propre nomo*—were permanent or seasonal. Given the migration pattern of south-bank peoples, they may have been either.

Wasco settlements (seasonal, permanent, or both) and fishing stations were scattered along the river between The Dalles city and Five Mile Rapids (see full list in D. French forthcoming). During the warmer portion of the year, as fish runs came and went and the river level rose and fell, Wasco people moved from site to site. There is evidence that the movement from spring to fall was gradually upstream. Many witnesses in the Seufert Brothers fishing case stated that Washucks was the "earliest" fishing site and that from there the Indians "worked their way upstream as far as Skein" (Seufert Brothers Co. 1916:396). Fish runs began in late March and continued through October, with a peak in autumn. There were no spawning streams in the Wasco area, so all fish were taken along the main stem of the river. Water levels were low in early spring and highest in June. Wasco fishing apparently began at The Dalles intervale when the river was most constricted in spring and then, when the intervale was flooded in late summer, moved upstream to the high bluffs between Five Mile Creek and Wasco village, the core of the south-bank fishery. The progression was from Kaclasko (Mill Creek, spring) to Washucks

(Lone Pine, summer) and finally Wasco (Big Eddy, autumn). Henry Brewer summarized the round as follows:

> the Indians . . . live at the Dalls 4 miles above us in summer during the time for catching Salmon, in the winter near us their habitations are moveable or rather they live under ground in the winter & in the mat houses in summer. [H. Brewer, letter of Aug. 14, 1840, Canse Collection]

## Wishram Village[4]

The preeminent Upper Chinookan village on the north side of the Columbia in The Dalles area was Wishram. It was located at the head of Five Mile Rapids near the eastern terminus of Chinookan territory. During the contact era, it was the single most populous Chinookan settlement.

There have been village sites in that location for several millennia. Wakemup (*wáq'map*) Mound, excavated by archaeologists in the 1950s, was a multilevel site that, in its upper layers, had been built up by centuries of accumulated village refuse. Numerous other sites, pre- and protohistoric, dot the north bank of Five Mile Rapids between Big Eddy and Spedis Valley. They represent a mix of winter and summer villages, campsites, petroglyphs and pictograph sites, and fishing locations, which cumulatively point to a relatively dense population, both seasonal and permanent (Geo-Recon International 1983). Spearfish village, occupied until 1957 when it was flooded by The Dalles Dam, was the lineal descendant of Wishram village (Biddle 1926). The modern community of Wishram (or Fallbridge) is located ten miles upstream, at the site of the aboriginal *sk'in*.

Lewis and Clark stopped at Wishram twice, on October 24, 1805, and on April 16, 1806. Clark's initial description follows:

> proceeded . . . to a village of 20 wood housies in a Deep bend to the Star d Side. . . . The nativs of this village re[ce]ived me verry kindly, one of whome envited me into his house, which I found to be large and comodious, and the first wooden houses in which Indians have lived Since we left those in the vicinity of the Illinois, they are scattered permiscuisly on a elivated Situation near a mound of about 30 feet above the Common leavel, which mound has Some remains of houses and has every appearance of being artificial—those houses are about . . . 20 feet <Square> wide and 30 feet long. . . . Sunk into the earth Six feet, the roofs. . . . Supported by a ridge pole resting on three Strong pieces of Split timber . . . the walls . . . Suported a certain number of Spars . . . the top of which was just above ground . . . the eaves at or near the earth, the gable ends and side walls are secured with Split boards . . . one half of those houses is apropriated for the Storeing away Dried & pounded fish . . . the other part

next the dore is the part occupied by the nativs who have beds raised on either Side, with a fire place in the center . . . each house appeared to be occupied by about three families. [1988:333, 335]

On April 16, 1806, the village had "moved about 300 yards below the Spot it Stood last fall" (1991:128). During the ensuing warm season, most inhabitants would disperse to favored fishing locations scattered along the north bank of Five Mile Rapids—the area known historically as the Tumwater Fishery.

Lewis and Clark named the inhabitants of that area "Echelutes" and distinguished them from the "Eneshurs" upriver. The former term is an Anglicization of *iła'xluit,* which is the self-designation of the villagers; *nixlúidix* is the Kiksht term for Wishram village (Spier and Sapir 1930:164). "Eneshur" refers to upstream Sahaptins, who called *nixlúidix* village *wišxam* (Anglicized as Wishram). Lewis and Clark's October population estimate had 600 people in the twenty-one lodges of Echelute village; in April there were 1,000—a figure that likely includes salmon season visitors, mostly Sahaptins (see Boyd and Hajda 1987).

As the premier Chinookan village, Wishram is mentioned in most travelers' accounts prior to the 1850s. Biddle (1926) surveys a number of those, including visits by David Thompson and Alexander Ross (in 1811), Wilson Price Hunt and Ross Cox (in 1812), Gabriel Franchère (in 1814), David Douglas (in 1825-26), and Nathaniel Wyeth (in 1832). To that list should be added Robert Stuart (visited in 1812), John Work (in 1824), Aemilius Simpson (in 1828), and John Townsend (1839:35). Based on some of those sources, Washington Irving (1836) also describes the village. It is obvious that Wishram was a landmark and notable place.

Visitors to Wishram in Perkins's time included mountain man Thomas Farnham (in 1839), Hudson's Bay Governor Sir George Simpson (in 1841), and Joseph Drayton's party of the (American) Wilkes Expedition (in 1841). The Wilkes *Narrative* states:

> Wishram . . . is situated on the left bank of the river, and its proper name is Niculuita. . . . There are now [July] in this village about forty good lodges, built of split boards, with a roof of cedar bark. . . . The Indians that live here . . . number four hundred regular inhabitants. . . . They appeared to have more comforts about them than any we had yet seen. [1844, 4:414-15]

July was a time for several anadromous fish runs. The Americans also describe Tumwater Fishery, swollen by visitors from the interior. The following passage is both ethnocentric and judgmental but nevertheless conveys the color and flavor of the summer fishery.

The Dalles is appropriately called the Billingsgate of Oregon. The diversity of dress among the men was greater even than in the crowds of natives I have described as seen in the Polynesian islands; but they lack the decency and care of their persons which the islanders exhibit. Their women also go nearly naked, for they wear little else than what may be termed a breech-cloth, of buckskin, which is black and filthy with dirt; and some have a part of a blanket. The children go entirely naked, the boys wearing nothing but a small string around the body. It is only necessary to say that some forty or fifty live in a temporary hut, twenty by twelve, constructed of poles, mats and cedar bark to give an idea of the degree of their civilization. [Wilkes 1844, 3:383; Clark (Lewis and Clark 1991:128-29) also describes clothing]

Lewis and Clark state that during the fishing season *nixlúidix* was "the Great Mart of all this Country"; pounded salmon, horses, bison robes, beads, and tools were the commodities exchanged (1991:129). Alexander Ross subtracts salmon from that list and adds tobacco; most commodities, according to him, "change hands through gambling. . . . The long narrows is the great emporium or mart of the Columbia, and the general theatre of gambling and roguery." He claims that during midsummer there might be upwards of 3,000 Indians in the camp "at the head of the great narrows" (1849:117). That would include, assumedly, the swollen summer settlement at Wishram as well as the adjacent flat camping area at Spedis Valley (see map 3).

A second, later account of the summer fishery at The Dalles comes from Father Pierre DeSmet, in July 1846.

Indians flock . . . [to] the great Dalles [Five Miles Rapids] . . . from different quarters of the interior, to attend, at this season of the year, to the salmon fisheries. This is their glorious time for rejoicing, gambling and feasting; the long lent is passed; they have assembled in the midst of abundance. [1905:556]

## Population

Throughout the lower Columbia drainage, at the beginning of the nineteenth century, there was more than enough salmon to serve as a staple food for riverbank population, besides providing winter subsistence for neighboring interior peoples as well. In that stretch of the river occupied by Kiksht-speaking villages, the prevailing pattern was for interior peoples to flock to the riverbanks in the summer for the fishery. A glance at Lewis and Clark's autumn and spring population estimates for the mid-Columbia shows the

Table 1. Lewis and Clark's Population Estimates

|  | Late October 1805 | Mid-April 1806 | Percent Difference |
|---|---|---|---|
| The Cascades | 1,300 | 2,800 | 215 |
| The Cascades to The Dalles | 1,800 | 2,200 | 122 |
| The Dalles | 600 | 1,000 | 167 |
| Subtotal (Kiksht area) | 3,700 | 6,000 | 162 |
| Columbia Sahaptin[5] | 3,500 | 4,500 | 129 |
| Total | 7,200 | 10,400 | 144 |

SOURCE: Lewis and Clark (1990:474–89).

magnitude of that movement. On their downstream voyage in late October 1805, when the explorers made their first estimate, most mid-Columbia peoples had retreated to winter villages; on their return trip in mid-April large numbers were massing on the Columbia's banks for the spring salmon run. Almost one-third more people were on the main Columbia in April 1806 than had been there the previous autumn. The great majority of those may be assumed to have been Sahaptin peoples (particularly the Northwest branch of that language), or, to use Perkins's term, "Walla Wallas." For a more detailed treatment of seasonal population movement on the Lower Columbia see Boyd and Hajda (1987). More than thirty years after Lewis and Clark, Henry Perkins provided a second estimate of the number of Indians in that area. In "Wonderful Work of God . . ." (Appendix 1, Doc. 3) he gave 1,000 as the total for the Wascopam circuit. That would include, at a bare minimum, those Indians (Chinookans and Sahaptins) who resided in winter villages along the Columbia between Fort Vancouver and (approximately) the mouth of the John Day. On the above table, that corresponds to all the peoples in column one, exclusive of the easternmost "Pishquitpahs," who lived above the John Day, a total of 5,600. The difference in numbers is due almost entirely to disease mortality in the intervening years (see Boyd 1985, 1990).

Similar numbers appear in other contemporary documents. In March 1843 Perkins said there were around 1,500 total Chinookan speakers, "including the Indians . . . at the Falls of the Willamette" (Appendix 1, Doc. 4); in 1841 Wilkes stated that 1,500 was the number who "visit the Dalles during the fishing season" (1844, 4:382) (compare to Ross's 3,000 thirty years earlier [1849:117]).

Jason Lee's statement on the Wascopam circuit population appears most complete and accurate:

> At the commencement of our Mission March 1838, there were 1,000 thousand Indians, who reside chiefly near the Station. The labours of the Missionaries extend to 1,000 more, the proportion of adults, to children, is nearly as 3 to 5. Baptism has been administered to 840 adults, and 560 children. Embracing others who have not be en baptised, the whole number that have been received under the special care of the Mission is about 1,600. [J. Lee, letter of Aug. 10, 1842, Archives of the Pacific Northwest Conference]

After 1844, under Alvan Waller, more Indians were contacted, chiefly to the north among the Yakamas: "Our circuit extends to a . . . diameter of . . . one hundred miles. . . . The number of souls properly within our present circuit cannot be less than two to three thousand" (Waller, letter of Aug. 15, 1845, Archives of the Pacific Northwest Conference).

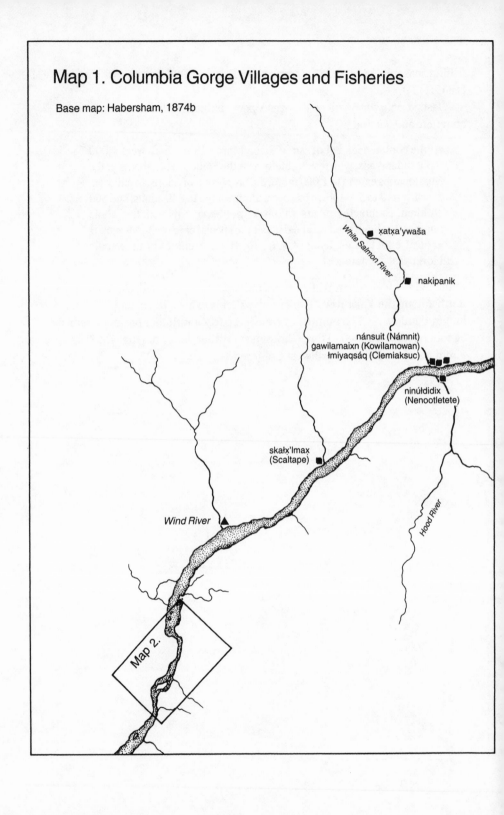

# Map 1. Columbia Gorge Villages and Fisheries

Base map: Habersham, 1874b

White Salmon River

xatxa'ywaša

nakipanik

nánsuit (Námnit)
gawilamaixn (Kowilamowan)
łmiyaqsáq (Clemiaksuc)

ninúłdidix
(Nenootletete)

skałx'lmax
(Scaltape)

Wind River

Hood River

Map 2.

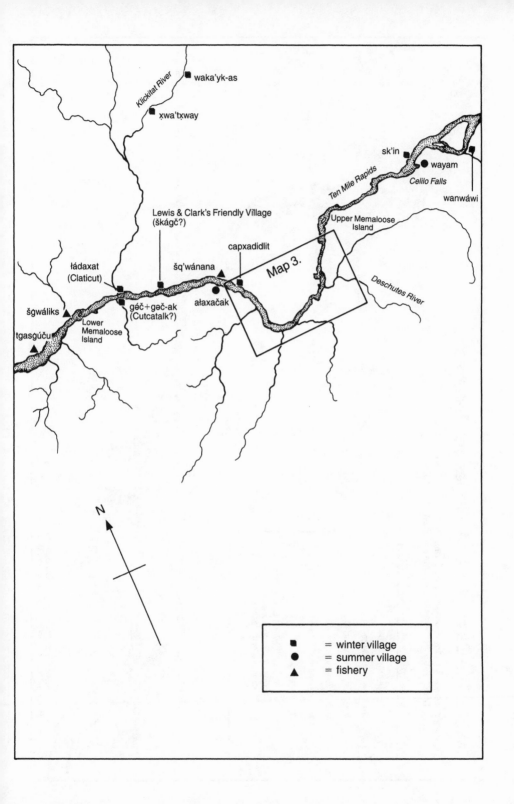

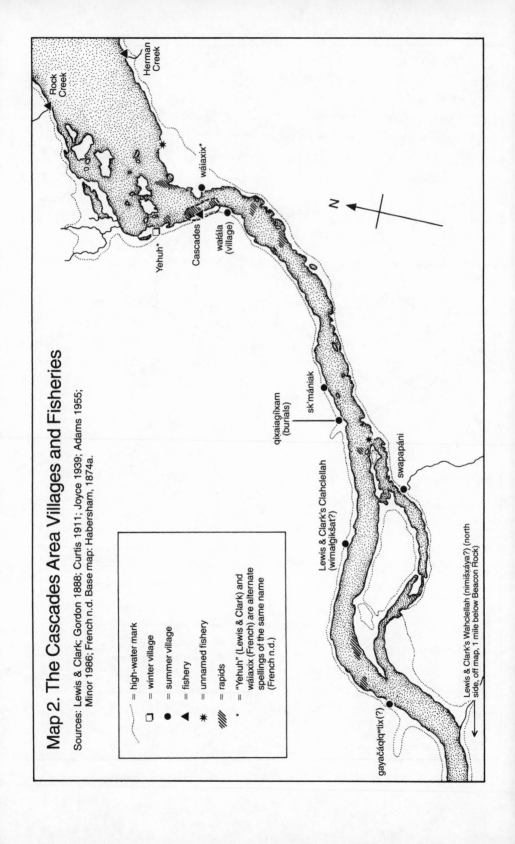

# Map 2. The Cascades Area Villages and Fisheries

Sources: Lewis & Clark; Gordon 1888; Curtis 1911; Joyce 1939; Adams 1955; Minor 1986; French n.d. Base map: Habersham, 1874a.

⌒ = high-water mark

☐ = winter village

● = summer village

▲ = fishery

✳ = unnamed fishery

▨ = rapids

* = "Yehuh" (Lewis & Clark) and wáiaxix (French) are alternate spellings of the same name (French n.d.)

Rock Creek

Herman Creek

wáiaxix*

Yehuh*

Cascades

watála (village)

N

qixaiagíłxam (burials)

sk'mániak

swapapáni

Lewis & Clark's Clahclellah (wímałgikšat?)

Lewis & Clark's Wahclellah (nimíšxáya?) (north side, off map, 1 mile below Beacon Rock)

gayačáqłqʷtix(?)

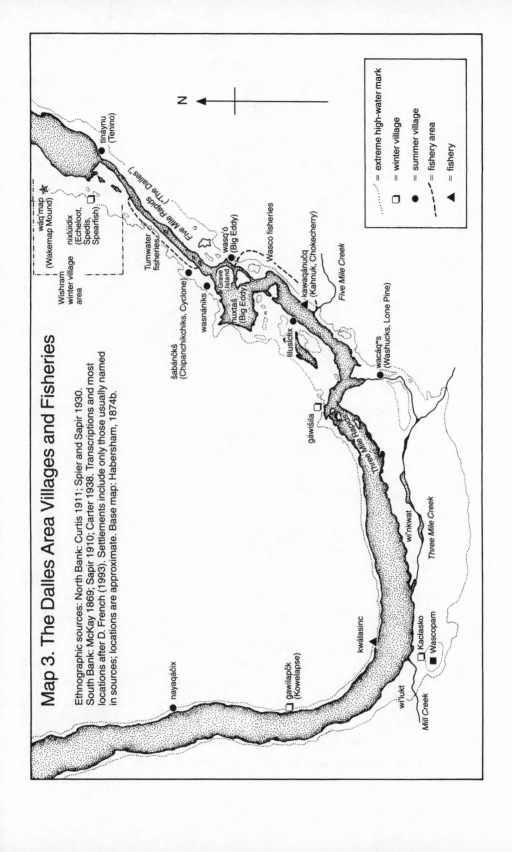

# Map 3. The Dalles Area Villages and Fisheries

Ethnographic sources: North Bank: Curtis 1911; Spier and Sapir 1930.
South Bank: McKay 1869; Sapir 1910; Carter 1938. Transcriptions and most
locations after D. French (1993). Settlements include only those usually named
in sources; locations are approximate. Base map: Habersham, 1874b.

N

wáčʼmap
(Wakemap Mound)

Wishram
winter village
area

nixlúidix
(Echeloot,
Spedis,
Spearfish)

tináynu
(Tenino)

Tumwater
fisheries

*Five Mile Rapids ("The Dalles")*

šabánčkš
(Chipanchikchiks, Cyclone)

wasnániks

wasqʼó
(Big Eddy)

Grave
Island

ĥuxtáš
(Big Eddy)

Wasco fisheries

iłiusłdix

kawaqánučq
(Kahnuk, Chokecherry)

*Five Mile Creek*

wacáqʷs
(Washucks, Lone Pine)

gáwiẃśila

*Three Mile Rapids*

wiʼnkwat

*Three Mile Creek*

nayaqáčix

gawilapčk
(Kowelapse)

kwálasinc

Kaclasko
◼ Wascopam

wiʼlukt

*Mill Creek*

= extreme high-water mark
□ = winter village
● = summer village
= fishery area
= fishery
▲ = fishery

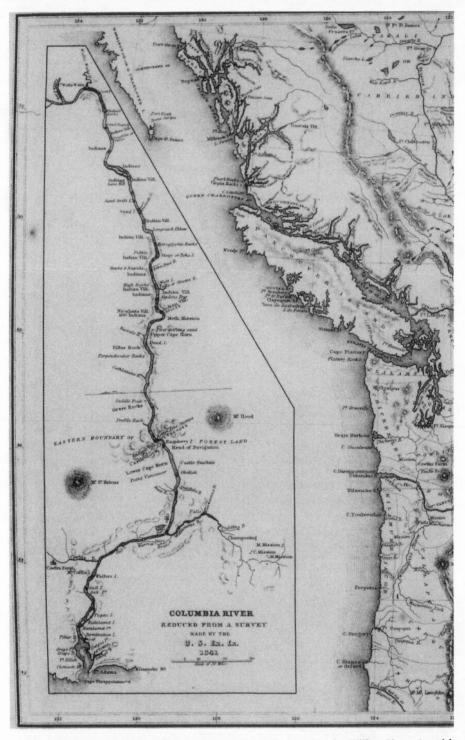

**Map 4.** "Map of the Oregon Territory," by Horatio Hale; from Charles Wilkes, *Narrative of the United States Exploring Expedition* (vol. 5, 1849). Courtesy Oregon Historical Society, Portland.

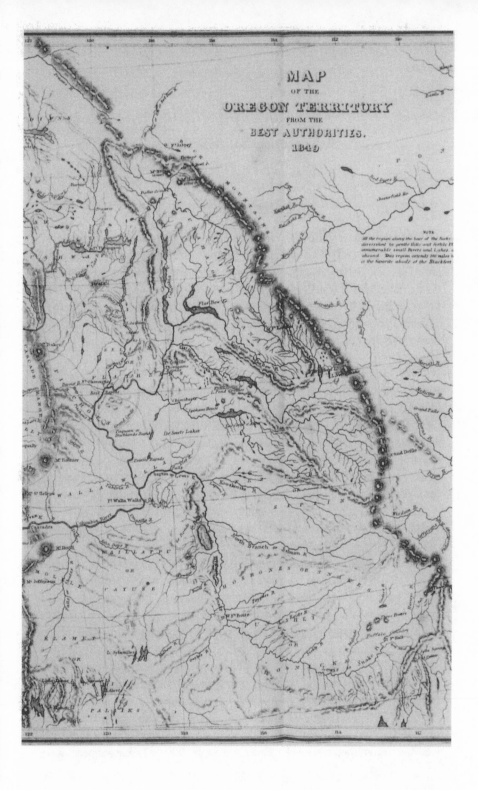

# MAP
### OF THE
# OREGON TERRITORY
#### FROM THE
### BEST AUTHORITIES.
## 1849

# 3

## Subsistence and Economics

### Subsistence

The Indians of the middle Columbia were a nonagricultural people: they grew no crops (except tobacco) and had no domestic animals except the dog (and after 1730, the horse). Salmon was a staple food, and it pervaded their culture. As we have seen, it was the salmon run that drew large numbers of people to the river banks in the warm season, and the abundance of the run helped support a population that, by the standards of hunting-gathering peoples, was dense and large.

*Salmon*

Five species of salmon occur in the Columbia; three species were taken in abundance by the Indians between The Cascades and Celilo (Spier and Sapir 1930:170). Spring chinook run from March to May, summer chinook in June and July, and fall chinook in August and September. September is the optimal spawning month. Coho salmon run in fall and spawn shortly afterward. Sockeye run in June and spawn in upstream lakes. Chum and pink salmon are of negligible importance in the Upper Chinookan-Columbia Sahaptin area. All those species belong to the genus *Onchorhyncus* (the first three are *O. tschawytscha, O. kisutch,* and *O. nerka,* respectively). In addition, nineteenth-century Whites as well as natives commonly classified steelhead, or ocean-run trout *(Salmo gairdneri),* with salmon, because of its similar anadromous habits (Hunn 1980). Perkins and his contemporaries called that fish "salmon trout." Of the four important anadromous fishes, chinook, coho, and steelhead spawned in middle Columbia tributaries; sockeye, of lesser importance, merely passed through the main river on their way to spawning lakes in the upper river drainage (Fulton 1968, 1970; Netboy 1980).[1] Besides salmon and steelhead, lesser "run" species included lamprey eels, taken in June at falls, and various species of suckers, taken in spring at spawning streams in The Dalles area (Hunn 1990:155, 158–59).

Salmon fishing methods in the Gorge were relatively limited (Handley in Seufert 1916). Seines were rare that far upstream. Basket traps and weirs were used on salmon run creeks (Spier and Sapir 1930:177). Large spears were often used in falls. But dip nets—of two varieties—were most common. One of these, the regular dip (or sweep) net is smaller and moveable. This net moves with the current and catches fish traveling upstream. The stationary set or bag net is larger and catches fish moving with the current, generally in eddies (Curtis 1911a:95; Schoning et al. 1951:13–17). The best dip-net sites are narrows, rocky cliffs, and islands, where the fish runs are close to shore. Scaffolding or platforms were often extended out over the river to get closer to the fish (Sapir 1909:185; Kuckup in Seufert 1916; Stuart 1935:52). Scaffolding and a dip net are depicted in the Kane picture from The Cascades (plate 7).

Shortly after their arrival at Wascopam, old Canacissa, "one of the principal men of the village," showed Perkins and Lee his "rock from which he caught salmon." Fishing stations throughout that area were family owned. The station itself was narrowly defined—perhaps a single rock or a short stretch of cliff. At major fisheries, there were clusters of such sites— sometimes in very great density (Celilo Falls, in 1954, had about 480 such sites; Spearfish village in 1941 had 120) (Swindell 1942:175; Corps of Engineers 1955:4).[2] "Ownership" was loosely defined. The primary owner (elder family head) had first access to the site, but once he was done fishing, another more distant relative might take over, and so on down (Jensen, Wannassay in Seufert 1916; Schoning et al. 1951:10). Given extensive kinship ties, by both blood and marriage, a single individual might have rights in fishing stations over a wide area. One Indian might move sequentially from one site to another (Kuckup in Seufert 1916) in which he had rights, through the season, with the fish runs. That flexibility made it more likely that most Indians caught enough fish to get their families through the winter. It also contributed to the fluctuating and ethnically mixed population at the major summer fisheries.

Fish were normally processed at or near where they were taken. That might mean flensing and drying on racks or in the rear of mat lodges.

> We always had small fir poles that we used to gather up in the mountains. . . . We put up a scaffold and made a flat roof to dry our salmon under the shade. . . . The women folks always cut different kinds of reeds and tules out of swamps, and dried them, and wove them together and made mats . . . that went over the salmon, and the salmon dried underneath. [Shea-Wa in Seufert 1916]
>
> After they catch a salmon, they take them to their dry-house, cut them up, hang them up. . . . I can remember perhaps about fifty years ago [circa 1866] that Indians had long dry-houses as long as this building is here now. And they had it fixed so as they could cut their salmon and hang them up there at different places. . . . This dry house is generally built right

where the villages was . . . at Wah-sucks and . . . Wasco and . . . Tenino.
[Dick in Seufert 1916]

Dr. Shea-Wa was from *sk'in* village at Celilo Falls; Charley Dick was a
Wasco-Wishram. The Stuart painting depicts a salmon camp and dry-racks
at Celilo; the Drayton etching shows a dry-house in The Dalles area (plates 8
and 9).

Perkins mentions salmon drying, boiled salmon, and "women busy in
dressing and curing salmon" in his journal entries for August 13-14, 1843
(Appendix 1, Doc. 5). The women may well have been preparing the "dry
salmon" that he mentions as a Wascopam trade item in March 1838. That dried
and pulverized product, today called "sugar salmon," is described in many
early accounts (e.g., Farnham 1843:89; Wilkes 1844, 4:383-84; D. Lee and
Frost 1844:181; Spencer in Seufert 1916; Lewis and Clark 1988:323, 325).
Curtis gives the most complete account:

> In the preparation of itkilak [*it–k'i'lak*; *č'lay* in Sahaptin] (pounded
> salmon) the salmon was beheaded and gutted, and with a sharp knife the
> two halves were separated from the backbone and the skin. The clear
> strips thus obtained were laid on a platform in the hot sun for a day. The
> next morning the flesh was soft, and the women squeezed it through their
> hands into shreds, placing the mass in large dishes or in a pit lined with
> grass or matting, and mixing with it the large quantities of roe taken from
> the fish. It was then thoroughly worked over with the hands and spread
> on a piece of matting. After a thorough drying for two days, or more if the
> sun was not hot, it was pounded fine in a maple mortar with a stone pestle
> and then rammed tightly in baskets of split cattails lined with fish skins.
> Such a package weighed from 100 to 150 pounds, and was the product
> of about 100 salmon. Fish prepared in this way kept for months. [1911a:
> 94]

The figures given by Curtis for the size of the pounded salmon baskets are no
exaggeration: Clark estimates the weight at 90-100 pounds; twelve baskets
formed a stack; and at Wishram he "counted 107 Stacks of dried pounded fish
. . . which must have contained 10,000 w. of neet fish" (Lewis and Clark
1988:335).

The Dalles area was ideally suited to an aboriginal salmon processing
industry: not only was it able to produce a great enough surplus of salmon both
to lay away for winter and to trade, but the hot, dry weather of August and
September was ideal for drying fish. In addition, fall-run chinook ("white
salmon") were leaner and had a lower oil content than did those of spring and
summer, making them easier to dry. Most salmon were probably split and air
dried and consumed locally (David French, personal communication,

1989-93). Pounded salmon, however, was a specialty of The Dalles and was likely to be traded to downstream peoples who inhabited damper areas not amenable to its production.

Perkins's journal states that the Indians "secrete all their salmon . . . in the ground . . . near their winter quarters" (Appendix 1, Doc. 5, entry for Aug. 19, 1843). That was probably split and dried salmon. According to Clark,

> the mode of bur[y]ing those fish is in holes of various Sizes, lined with Straw on which they lay fish Skins in which they inclose the fish which is laid verry close, and then Covered with earth of about 12 or 15 inches thick. [Lewis and Clark 1988:331]

Daniel Lee and Henry Warre (D. Lee and Frost 1844:177; Warre 1976:64) say the pits were dug in sand. Perkins says the holes were filled before the Indians departed for the huckleberry harvest; according to Lee interior peoples might steal the fish while the owners were gone (D. Lee and Frost 1844:177).

## Plant Foods

The mission records contain some information on other native foods that were gathered in season. Perkins's description of the huckleberry month (Appendix 1, Doc. 5, entry for Aug. 19, 1843) is the single best early record of huckleberry gathering in that area extant. The species in question was the mountain huckleberry, *Vaccinium membranaceum* Dougl. ex Hook. (*a–undiax* in Wasco-Wishram; *wíwnu* in CR Sahaptin). The "berry month" centered on September; in Perkins's journal the Indians began to leave August 19 (Appendix 1, Doc. 5, entry for Aug. 19, 1843); Brewer's journal has them returning on October 10 (in 1840) (1986:65). In modern times, the early-to-mid-August start of the huckleberry harvest is the occasion for one of the four seasonal firstfruits celebrations held by Sahaptins and Chinookans at Yakama and Warm Springs (Schuster 1975:86; Hunn and French 1981:88–89).

South of the Columbia, huckleberry fields were southwest of Mount Hood, on the upper Sandy, and around Olallie Butte (D. Lee and Frost 1844:158; Abbot 1857:30, 99–101; Murdock 1980:135–36); to the north, the chief fields were, and continue to be, in the "Indian Heaven" area southwest of Mount Adams (Ray 1936:149; Filloon 1952; Norton, Boyd, and Hunn 1983).[3] All the fields were named, and they were connected by well-worn trails.

Women collected the berries in large baskets; one or two basketfuls (two to four liters) was a day's work (Norton, Boyd, and Hunn 1983:132). The berries were usually dried on mats next to a smoldering log until they looked like raisins (Filloon 1952:5). Perkins's "four or five pecks of nice dried berries" equals 32 to 40 dry quarts of 35 to 44 liters. The berry-salmon mixture he mentions is a delicacy that is rarely seen today (Eugene Hunn, personal communication, 1982-93).

A second on-the-spot missionary observation of the berry harvest was made by Henry Brewer, at the Mount Adams fields, on September 15, 1845.

> "Indian Berry Ground" Here are a large company of Indians, busily engaged in picking whortleberries: these they dry by the fire, and preserve them for future use. They spend a month or more here, every season. The absence of our Indian converts so long a time during the berry season, being surrounded as they are by every possible bad example, and separated from the watchful care of their teachers, in many cases proves very injurious to their piety. [Mudge 1854:52-53]

Acorns (Sahaptin *wawawči*; Kiksht *a–gúlul*) were probably another specialty of the Wascopam natives, given the profusion of oaks *(Quercus garryana* Dougl. ex Hook.) in the area. "The finest grove of oaks that I have seen in the country," said Perkins on his arrival (Appendix 1, Doc. 1); Brewer noted, "At no great distance they resemble an apple tree orchard" (H. Brewer, letter of Aug. 14, 1840, Canse Collection). Along with pounded salmon, acorns were one of the commodities Perkins saw at The Cascades being taken downstream by Wascopam natives to trade (Appendix 1, Doc. 1); to the east, the acorns that Lewis and Clark saw at the John Day had been procured from "the nativs who live near the falls below" (1988:317).

The following two quotations from the missionary records give a complete description of acorn processing.

> Acorns, which are abundant some years, are used as an article of food. These are gathered and baked with heated stones—a method of preparing food common to both the Indians and Pacific Islanders. Heated stones are put into an excavation in the ground three feet across, and covered with leaves or grass so as to prevent the articles to be cooked from burning. Then these are laid on and carefully covered in the same manner. Last of all, earth is spread over the whole to keep in the heat, and the process of baking is done up in real native style. After the acorns are thus prepared, deep pits are dug near the water, in which they are buried in mud, where they remain through the winter; when they are taken up and eaten, much improved, it is supposed, by the soaking process. [D. Lee and Frost 1844:181]
>
> Saw some females on the bank of a small stream, taking Acorns from holes where they had been buried, below low water mark, and remained in water all winter. Having been roasted before they were deposited in the earth, they had now reached the vinus fermentation, and had lost entirely their bitter and acrid taste; and are doubtless a pleasant food for the

Indians, though not very nutritious. Thus prepared, and eaten with dried
or pounded salmon, these acorns, no doubt, in the absence of all other
vegetable food, tend to promote health. [J. Lee, letter of Mar. 27, 1843,
passage dated Feb. 13, 1843, Archives of the Pacific Northwest Confer-
ence]

Buried in the mud under water, the bitter tannic acid was leached out of the
acorns. In late winter and early spring, the lean season of the Indian year, there
were indeed no fresh vegetables, as Jason Lee states.

Two other fall crops mentioned by Perkins are hazelnuts and chokecher-
ries. Hazelnuts *(Corylus cornuta* Marsh; *a–q$^w$lál* in Wasco-Wishram; *kkuuš*
in CR Sahaptin) were collected by women and eaten fresh or stored. Choke-
cherries *(Prunus virginiana; i–k'áxanin* in Wasco-Wishram; *tmiš* in CR
Sahaptin) were eaten fresh or dried–either whole or mashed with the seeds
(Hilty et al. 1972:15).

The last class of important foods for the Wascopam area natives consisted
of various root crops. The season for root gathering was spring through early
summer. On March 25, 1838, shortly after his arrival, Perkins noted that there
were only 47 people at Kaclasko, the remainder of the 100–150 residents he
had estimated earlier being "away" (Appendix 1, Doc. 1). Daniel Lee's
"Notebook" entry for April 1 notes that "at this season, the women are abroad
obtaining a supply of roots among the surrounding hills" (entry for Apr. 1,
1838, Daniel Lee Collection). April, it might be noted, marked the end of the
lean season. Spring chinook followed in late April or early May, when stores
of dried salmon were running low. Similar entries appear in missionary
documents from later years. Following the April 1840 Camp Meeting, Daniel
Lee

started down the river, preaching to the Indians wherever he found them,
they having broken up their winter residences, and pitched along here and
there on the river in stations convenient for obtaining a good supply of
roots. [D. Lee and Frost 1844:193]

On May 3, 1841, Brewer stated, "Nearly all are gone after roots and to the
Dalles" (1986:68).

The products in question at that time would be, in particular, two species
of *Lomatium, L. canbyi* Coult. and Rose *(wa–q'wáɬ* in Wasco-Wishram; *lukš*
in CR Sahaptin) and biscuit root, *L. cous (wa–čxwán; xawš),* and the bitterroot,
*Lewisia rediviva (i–biáxi; pyaxt)* (Hunn and French 1981). All three grow in
arid, rocky areas and are either eaten fresh or dried. *Lukš* may be ground into
a meal that can be made into a mush or pudding or formed into finger cakes;
*xawš* may be ground into pellets and used as a soup thickening; dried, peeled
bitterroot is boiled like potatoes (Hilty et al. 1972:8–12). Descriptions of

biscuit root and bitterroot by botanist Carl Augustus Geyer (1846) (a contemporary of Perkins who left Oregon on the same boat) are also available. The three roots are the focus of one of the contemporary southern Plateau peoples' "first fruits feasts," the root feast of early spring (Hunn and French 1981).

*"Starvation"*

The arrival of the first root crops signaled the beginning of the end of the "lean season" for the Wascopam natives. Perkins refers to that period in his discussion of the April 1840 Camp Meeting:

> The number of natives in attendance was not large. . . . Many at the time were literally starving, or just gaining a meagre subsistence from their daily employment of root-digging, which at this early season afforded the bare means of sustaining life. [Appendix 1, Doc. 2]

References to starvation are common enough in the ethnohistorical literature to merit some attention, for they seem to contradict the commonly held stereotype of salmon-zone Indians as living in a world of food abundance. The problem here is not so much gross quantity or variety of wild foods as it is seasonal availability (see Suttles 1960b for an extended discussion). Large quantities of food there certainly were, particularly salmon, and there was a considerable variety of alternate supplemental foodstuffs. Unfortunately, that largesse was only available for the taking in certain localities during the warm season of the year. From November through March there were virtually no fresh foods available—almost everything eaten had been preserved and stored. Depending upon natural vagaries—a bad run of fall salmon or an unusually cold or long winter—there might be food shortages at winter's end. Food shortages might have caused hunger, some dietary deficiencies, and perhaps malnutrition, but actual deaths are seldom recorded in the literature from the area (for one example see Sapir 1909:227-29). The word *starvation* should be taken with a grain of salt. Although Indians died infrequently, it is clear that by the beginning of spring, throughout the Columbia drainage, they were hungering for fat, oily spring salmon and nutty *Lomatium* roots and would spare no time or effort to procure them as soon as they became available.

Daniel Lee and Joseph Frost mention the lean season at The Dalles and Clatsop, respectively (1844:177, 313), and it is discussed in other contemporary accounts (Parker 1838:215; Wilkes 1844, 4:386; Simpson 1847:94). The clearest exposition of the seasonal food problem at The Dalles, however, comes from Lewis and Clark.

> I have seen none except dryed fish of the last season in the possession of the people above [Five Mile rapids], they subsist on roots principally with

some dryed and pounded fish. . . . The inhabitants of the rapids at this time take a few of the white salmon trout [steelhead] and considerable quantities of a small mullet on which they principally subsist. [1991:131, entry for April 17, 1806][4]

There was great joy with the natives last night in consequence of the arrival of the Salmon. . . . They informed us that those fish would arrive in great quantities in the Course of about 5 days. . . . One of these fish was cought . . . dressed and being divided into small pieces was given to each Child in the village. this Custom is founded in a Supersticious opinion that it will hasten the arrival of the Salmon. [1991:300, entry for April 19, 1806]

The second of the preceding two quotations is a description of the first salmon ceremony (see chap. 6; Appendix 1, Doc. 5, entry for Aug. 15, 1843).

## The Hunt

According to the early ethnographers of the Upper Chinookans, Spier and Sapir, "hunting took a secondary place" in food-getting activities (1930:180). It is therefore not surprising that hunting of deer—the usual prey—is only mentioned a few times in the missionary literature. Spier and Sapir state that deer were usually taken in winter, and the missionaries verify them. Perkins, in late March 1838, notes that hunters from "several" Gorge villages "had been out for some time" and had "eight or ten canoes, heavily laden" (Appendix 1, Doc. 1); Jason Lee, also in late March (of 1843) in the Gorge, describes the killing of a doe who was roped and drowned in the river (letter of Mar. 27, 1843, Archives of the Pacific Northwest Conference); Alvan Waller, on February 19, 1847, mentions driving deer in deep snow:

Several reports of the success of the indians (some twenty miles below us) in killing deer this month. The snow being deep in the mountains the deer are driven down Crust forming on the snow renders it almost impossible for them to get about. The indians on snow shoes go out with their dogs and with clubs kill great numbers. In some instances a man kills twenty or thirty in a day. I judge from reports that they must have killed no less than five hundred. [Waller, letter dated Feb. 3, 1847, Archives of the Pacific Northwest Conference][5]

The winter of 1847 was especially severe, so a large haul of venison would have been welcomed. According to Spier and Sapir (1930:180–82) deer were taken with bow and arrow, clubs, or in pitfalls.

Curtis (1911a:94) states that the people of Wishram village normally obtained their venison in trade from the Klickitats. It is therefore probably

significant that all three of the preceding ethnohistorical accounts occurred in
the Columbia Gorge, probably in the area of Clemiaksuc-Claticut villages,
seasonally co-occupied by Chinookans and Klickitats. A few Chinookans,
nevertheless, may have specialized in the hunt. Individuals joined multiethnic
"task forces" of Plateau peoples who traveled to the Great Plains to hunt bison
(Anastasio 1972:163–65). A Chinookan was depicted by Alfred Jacob Miller
at the Green River rendezvous (Wyoming) in the summer of 1837 (plate 10).

On venison processing, Perkins states, "They . . . cut it up in large pieces,
build a large fire, build a scaffolding of poles over and lay on the meat until
smoked and dried" (Appendix 1, Doc. 1). Daniel Lee gives a description of
meat processing (in this case, horse—on the difficult cross-Cascades trip) that
matches both Perkins's and Spier and Sapir's closely:

> Four crotches were set in the ground, and four poles were laid into them;
> and across these several other ones, both ways, a few inches apart,
> forming a kind of Indian gridiron. On this was soon spread a bountiful
> supply of horseflesh, and built under it a fire of dry bark, which soon
> dried, smoked, and roasted it "closh," good. [D. Lee and Frost 1844:160]

*Seasonal Movement*

At this point in the narrative, it should be obvious that the Kiksht- and
Columbia River Sahaptin-speaking peoples were seasonally migratory. Their
year was split into two well-defined segments. From approximately November
through March, the cold season, when they stayed in their winter villages, they
might merit the term *sedentary.* But from March through October, small family
groups moved from place to place, gathering seasonally available wild foods.
The missionaries tolerated but disliked all this moving around, as it interfered
with their conversion program. According to Henry Brewer:

> they do not like to stay but a little while in one place they are here and
> there they visit the Clamets, Klickitats, snake Indians, Walla Wallas etc.
> In the spring they go off to get roots, in the summer they are at the salmon
> grounds, in the fall they go another direction after berries in the winter
> they are here. [H. Brewer, letter of Jan. 1, 1842, Canse Collection]

Something remains to be said about the logistics of that travel. The
missionaries never discuss the problem in detail, but there are numerous
references in context. River travel, of course, was via Indian canoe; on land,
people traveled on foot or on horseback (a postcontact addition) over
well-worn trails. While traveling, the Indians camped in various kinds of
temporary dwellings.

According to Perkins, goods for the new mission were transported from Fort Vancouver in 1838 via "small Indian canoes." That is all the records have to say on the subject, and there is no mention of any other type of vessel prior to the rafts for downstream travel constructed on the spot by the immigrants of 1843.

On the lower Columbia there were a number of canoe types, of variable sizes. The best description of types is in Lewis and Clark (1990:262-72). The smallest canoes in use in Chinookan territory were variations of the "shovel-nose" class used in quieter stretches of the river, marshes, and tributaries; those found in The Dalles area ranged from twelve to twenty feet (Spier and Sapir 1930:186).

The usual river canoe, however, and the type certainly used on the Columbia up to The Dalles, was the typical Chinook (sometimes "Nootka") canoe with a raised prow. According to Clark that variety ranged from twenty to forty feet long (Lewis and Clark 1990:270). The Perkins vessel, which held three people plus "all our luggage" must have been a small Chinook canoe, probably between twenty and thirty feet long.

The third form of canoe used in Chinookan territory was the seagoing or "Kilamox" variety, upwards of fifty feet long. Lewis and Clark did not see it above tidewater. Both Paul Kane and Clark sketched the three major types of Columbia River canoes; the Kane sketch reprinted here (plate 11) has not been previously published.

Peter Burnett, one of the immigrants of 1843, describes how canoes were manufactured near Vancouver:

> Chinook canoes . . . are substantially of the same model as the clipper-ship, and . . . are made out of a solid piece of white-cedar timber. . . . It is easily split with wedges. The Indians . . . cut and burn down the tree . . . and split it into quarters. Then they hollow out the inside of the canoe, mostly by burning. For this purpose they kindle small fires along the whole length . . . which they keep steadily burning; and, by careful and constant watching, they cause the fires to burn when and how they please. The outside they shape with their tomahawks; and, before these were introduced, they used sharp flint-stones for axes. These canoes are usually about thirty feet long, three feet wide, and two feet deep, and are sharp at both ends, with a gradual taper from near the center. No craft could have a more handsome model, or run more swiftly. They are light, strong, elastic and durable. [1880:131]

It should be emphasized that all the canoes pictured by Kane were dugouts, and in aboriginal times they were made only with stone tools.

Traveling lodges (a common ethnohistorical designation) might be either mat lodges (such as those described in Wilkes at Wishram, chap. 2 above) or mat tipis. Both were in use locally, as this description by Daniel Lee (from the April 1840 Kowelapse Camp Meeting) indicates:

> The wigwams were made of willow-poles set in the ground in a circular or oblong form, inclining toward the centre at an angle of fifty degrees, and enclosed with mats of grass, having a large opening at the top, and a door at each end, with a fire in the middle, and sometimes two fires, when the tenement was long, and then it was occupied by a large number, perhaps thirty. [D. Lee and Frost 1844:190]

The mat longhouse noted by Wilkes was twelve by twenty feet and held "forty or fifty" people. A second missionary description of the mat lodge, this time in Yakama territory, comes from Alvan Waller's 1845 diary.

> Their Houses are either of a circular, conical form, or oblong circular at each end poles set up and fastened at the top form the frame, and skins sewed together or Mats or both the covering, an aperture at the top at evening the smoke from the fire in the center beneath to escape. The door, formed of a skin or Mat, stretched on stick is either in the side or at one end. [Waller, diary, entry for May 1, 1845, Alvan Waller Collection]

Those two accounts are consistent with the ethnographic data on Plateau structures (Spier and Sapir 1930:202-3; Ray 1939:137-39; Rice 1984). A contemporary description of a tipi may be found in Burnett (1880:132).

For the western half of the Gorge there is a dearth of descriptions of temporary structures but a wealth of pictures. Speaking of The Cascades(?), Brewer states

> The lower country Indians ... winter lodges, being partly underground, are covered with boards. These they take down in the spring, bury the boards in the excavation in which they have lived, and construct a summer, traveling lodge of a kind of rush, or coarse grass. [Mudge 1854:27]

Paul Kane's 1847 pictures include two versions of Vancouver-area Chinookan mat lodges (one unpublished), the interior of a Chinookan plank house, and an exterior view of a Vancouver Klickitat plank lodge (Harper 1971:240-41). In John Mix Stanley's 1853 "Mountain Landscape with Indians" (plate 6), the downstream mat lodges all appear to be small, single-family dwellings, whereas their upstream counterparts are multifamily units.

On matting, Schuster reports the following, for the Yakamas:

Ordinary cattail rush[es] or a bullrush called tule . . . were sewn together
with Indian hemp, ranging in length from 6 to 20 feet. The longest mats
were hung inside a lodge to be used for lining and insulation. Small mats
were made for use as plates and platters. [1975:130]

## Economics

### Cayuse-Nez Perce Visits and "Trade"

There is strong evidence, both ethnographic and ethnohistorical, for considerable warm-season movement and visiting by lower Columbia peoples. The
Wascopam papers, however, reveal an unexpected variation on that pattern
of seasonal movement and visiting. Each winter, apparently during the entire
life of the Methodist mission (1838 to 1847), a group of Cayuses and Nez
Perces annually set up camp near Wascopam (H. Perkins, letter of Jan. 1, 1841,
Alvan Waller Collection; D. Lee and Frost 1844:163; Waller, letter of Feb. 3,
1847, Archives of the Pacific Northwest Conference; Mudge 1854:30-31; H.
Brewer 1986:71, letters of Jan. 1, 1842, Jan. 1, 1844, Feb. 25, 1846, Canse
Collection). Their purpose, according to Daniel Lee (D. Lee and Frost
1844:163), was to "exchange horses and buffalo robes for salmon; and to pass
the cold season, which lasts about two months, where wood can be easily
obtained, which is not the case between this and the Blue Mountains." Some
years later, from an upstream perspective, Henry Spalding reported: "Great
Nos of Nez Perces were returning from the Dalls or Long Narrows, where they
go every winter to exchange Buffalo Robes, cords, Parfleshes, Appishmores,[6]
meat, horses etc for pounded Salmon" (1846).

The Nez Perce and Cayuse visitors appear to have arrived shortly before
Christmas each year; they were generally gone by mid-February. The numbers
involved were not small. Perkins, typically, considered their presence to be
an opportunity: "Great numbers of Indians here from the Upper Country—some 50 lodges on both sides of the river—say 500 souls. Surely the
fields are white ready to harvest" (letter of Jan. 1, 1841, Alvan Waller
Collection).

The ethnographic record does not mention cold-season settlements of Nez
Perce speakers outside their focal territory; neither does it preclude it. Nez
Perces, like their downstream counterparts, were seasonally migratory: during
the warmer months they ranged over a wide territory, often at considerable

distances from their traditional lands on the lower Snake and Clearwater rivers; in winter they retreated to sheltered villages within the focal zone (Schwede 1970; Marshall 1977). After acquiring horses, however, some bands traveled to the Plains to hunt bison and frequently wintered there (Haines 1960; Anastasio 1972:130-36). In the early decades of the nineteenth century, some Plateau peoples began to cluster around permanent posts established by fur companies during the winter off-season (Chance 1973).

What exactly were those outsiders doing at The Dalles at that season of the year? Daniel Lee's assertion that they came to trade horses and bison robes for salmon and to be near a reliable source of firewood sounds logical but raises questions and is certainly incomplete. First, for the lower Columbia region (downstream from The Dalles), the trade of wealth or luxury items for food or subsistence goods, if true, is unusual. Traditionally, wealth items and subsistence goods circulated in separate spheres; there was little overlap between the two (Hajda 1984:248-52, 1987).

It might be profitable to examine the trade items more closely. Pounded salmon (described above) was a Dalles specialty and in demand among outsiders. (One suspects that the demand was gustatory, as the upstream and downstream peoples who are documented as trade recipients—Nez Perce and lower Kiksht-speaking villagers—had plenty of salmon, processed in other ways, of their own.) Other local specialties (e.g., wapato, from the Wappato Valley, and sea mammal products from the Tillamook area) may have been downstream equivalents of pounded salmon (Hajda 1984:232-35).

Upstream peoples, according to Lee (D. Lee and Frost 1844:163) and Spalding (1846), traded mostly nonfood items (horses, bison robes, parfleches) for salmon. Downstream peoples exchanged the following:

> Wahclellah [Beacon Rock Cascades] village[:] the Grand Cheif and two others of the Chee–luck–kit–le–quaw Nation [Clemiaksuc-Claticut villages] arived from below. they had with them 11 men and 7 womin and had been trading in the Columbia Vally for Wappato, beeds and dried Anchovies [*sic:* eulachon, another local specialty] etc in exchange for which they had given pounded fish Shappalell [a root cake], beargrass, acorns boiled berries etc. etc. [Lewis and Clark 1991:99-100, entry for April 9, 1806]

The only nonfood items in that list are "beeds," which may have been aboriginal, introduced by Euroamericans, or both. Horses were not present in the Northwest before 1730 (Haines 1938); bison robes, available in quantities large enough for trade, were probably a by-product of horse acquisition and hunting trips to the Plains (as above). The important nonfood goods, in other words, were the result of indirect contact with Whites or largely introduced by Whites. A trend to overlap in the two spheres of exchange appears to be mostly postcontact (Hajda 1984:250).

What did Lee's "exchange" consist of—that is, what were the mechanisms of trade? That is a problem rarely discussed in the ethnohistorical literature. All we know for sure is that the items in question changed hands—exactly how that was accomplished is not spelled out. There are many possibilities. The first that comes to mind is barter or direct exchange: horses and skins for dried salmon. Most exchanges of that sort probably took place between recognized trading partners (*yalupt* in CR Sahaptin) from the different ethnic groups (Marshall 1977:105–6; David French, personal communication, 1989–93). Perhaps there was a medium of exchange between the spheres: "ahshahs" (dentalia) are a possibility. Some goods changed hands through gambling (cf. Ross 1849:118), though gambling is usually mentioned as a warm-season activity and is unlikely to have involved subsistence goods (Desmond 1952). The following description of *yalupt* comes from Stwire Waters, born near Lake Vancouver in the early nineteenth century and later resident at Yakama. Dentalia and gambling are discussed later.

> I come to see you. I bring blankets, furs, beads, clothing and many things with me. These, I give to you. I do not say anything. I leave them without words, You are glad to see me. You take me in and feed me. We are Yah-lipt. I am your Yah-lipt; and you are my Yah-lipt. Maybe I have come from another tribe, come with pack horses loaded for my Yah-lipt. I stay several days. Then I say: 'Now I go back home.' You say 'All right!' Then you order your boys, the young Indians, to round up your horses. You select maybe ten, maybe twenty of best horses and give them to me. We have had a good time, and I go home feeling fine.
>
> Yah-lipt is not loaning things, is not the way the white people do business. White man goes to another white friend says: 'How long? When you pay back?' The white man says 'Thirty days, sixty days, I pay you back.' That is not Yah-lipt. Indian never says any thing about paying back. Let it alone. Never speaks that he wants paid back. That is good, the Indian way. The Old Indian way of friends! [McWhorter n.d., "Chief Waters' Definition of yah-lipt or Yah-y-lipt: 'great friendly,'" file 1516]

There are other interpretations of the Lee passage. The first is that salmon may not have been traded at all. That supposition is based on ethnographic and more recent ethnohistorical data. First, although there are no explicit accounts of ethnic Nez Perce or Cayuse fishing at The Dalles in the early nineteenth century (contra Walker 1967), there is no reason to assume that certain individuals and families did not do so. They would have obtained rights to use fishing stations through intermarriage with resident Upper Chinookan or Sahaptin owners, a practice that persists to the present and explains why enrolled Nez Perces, Umatillas, and others from distant areas claim fishing privileges in parts of the lower Columbia well outside their traditional territories. Present at The Dalles summer fishery at scattered fishing stations, those people would have prepared their own dried salmon, cached it in pits, moved on to other subsistence areas in the fall, and returned to consume it in midwinter, when they camped near Wascopam. There Nez Perces would gather and consume their own salmon; no trade would be involved.

Second, goods may have changed hands through a nontrade mechanism: gifting, a normal practice among affinal kin (in-laws) in much of the aboriginal Northwest (e.g., Suttles 1960a). As noted above, intermarriage was pervasive in the region, and it was through intermarriage that outsiders gained rights in certain resource areas. Intermarried Chinookans and Sahaptins, Cayuses and Nez Perces, in addition to sharing fishing sites, probably circulated food gifts. Marriages were validated by the exchange of gifts (see chap. 5), and gift giving between affines probably persisted afterward as well (Spier and Sapir 1930: 217-21; Murdock 1980:140-43). Gift giving accompanied all life-cycle rituals (K. French 1955) and was usual at other ceremonials. In those milieus donor and recipient need not be related.

Finally, after Anastasio (1972:171) (for the Plateau as a whole): "Goods would also be exchanged between groups to initiate or confirm friendly relations." The latter form may have something to do with the occasional perplexing ethnohistorical references to a "tribute" of goods demanded of resident Dalles peoples by their winter Cayuse and Nez Perce visitors, and to presents requested by Cascades and Dalles villagers of travelers through their stretch of the Columbia. White observers may have seen or experienced only the first round of what was expected to be an ongoing reciprocal relationship.

The missionary accounts suggest tribute, not reciprocity. Brewer's January 1, 1842 letter states:

> Mr Spalding's & Dr Whitman's Indians are here at present, they came in hostile warlike manner. Our Indians to appease their wrath gave them horses, guns, blankets, etc & now they have but little left to keep alive until Salmon comes again. [H. Brewer, Canse Collection]

The usual arrival ritual of the interior peoples certainly suggests an image of conquering overlords. Again, after Brewer (from 1844):

> Our congregations on the Sabbath are now large, the Cayuse and Nez Perce are here. These two above named tribes made quite a grotesque appearance a few days ago when they arrived. It was quite an *Indian* affair. If we had not known their customs and ways we might have been afraid, for it had the appearance of war. At a distance we saw a large body

of them coming, we heard their drums & the report of their guns, upon a near approach they began to yell & sing and make all manner of noises, & their horses prancing & running in every direction, (Indians never observe any order in their marches) & they were the most fantastically dressed of any I have ever seen (the chiefs had considerable red about them) their horses were also dressed to suit their liking, no two alike, one horse I noticed with a Buffalo's scalp horns and all on his head, another with Black feet scalps flying in the air etc. etc. In this manner they came into our yard when a part alighted & commenced drumming, yelling & dancing, after going over this performance they left us and went around the village, at the same time their wives were erecting their lodges. [H. Brewer, letter of Jan. 1, 1844, Canse Collection, edited version in Mudge 1854:30-31]

To a reader of European heritage the above might conjure up images of barbarian hordes descending upon defenseless central European villagers. Actually, the staged entrance of a party of guests into a grand ball would be a more apt comparison. The Nez Perce behavior was apparently standard procedure when arriving at large gatherings. (For a similar account, see the descriptions of the arrival of the Nez Perce delegation at the Walla Walla treaty grounds on May 24, 1855 [Kip 1897:10; H. Stevens 1900:34-35].)

There may have been much more than the presence of salmon, firewood, and trade opportunities that drew Nez Perces and Cayuses to The Dalles. Large multiethnic gatherings held on the Plateau during the warmer months were always festive occasions, with considerable socializing and visiting of relatives, playing of the bone game and horse racing (Desmond 1952). The latter two activities were less likely during midwinter, the Northwest sacred season. At The Dalles, as elsewhere on the Plateau and Northwest Coast, the period around Christmas and New Year's Day appears to have approximated the traditional time for Winter Spirit Dances (Ray 1939:102-13). Indeed, multiethnic winter spirit displays, coupled with intermarriage, which allowed the transmission of personally owned spirit powers among ethnic groups, certainly helps to explain the wide distribution of religious traits discussed in chapter 6.

A remaining problem with the Nez Perce and Cayuse winter presence at The Dalles concerns its time depth. As noted earlier, there is a possible parallel with the historic concentrations of various interior peoples around Hudson's Bay Company forts, where there were employment opportunities and hangers-on were assured of provisions from the company's stores (Chance 1973). But Wascopam was a mission, with very limited resources, which was hard pressed to supply itself for a bad winter, to say nothing of supporting 500 visitors. None of the other reasons for the Nez Perce and Cayuse presence given above has anything to do with the mission per se. The interior winter camp probably predates 1838. By how much, however, is a question of a different order.

All of the reasons listed above for the winter presence are aboriginal, modified in different degrees by White influences, direct or indirect. The Dalles has been a major fishery for many millennia, and the sharing of fishing stations through rights gained by intermarriage is certainly a very old custom. The Dalles has certainly been a trading center for a long time as well. The nature of goods exchanged, however, has undoubtedly changed due to White contact. Glass beads as trade items date to the last decades of the eighteenth century; bison robes in quantity and horses date to the middle and early parts of the century. It is also probable that the quantity of goods increased during that period as an outcome of enrichment from the fur trade (trade enrichment and substitution is well known from the British Columbia coast—see Codere 1950). A second postcontact change, depopulation from successive epidemics of introduced diseases, particularly smallpox, probably diminished population densities at The Dalles and made room, given the unchanged resource base, for outsiders (Boyd 1985). The newly enriched Nez Perces and Cayuses would be more than willing to establish economic bonds with the salmon-rich inhabitants of The Dalles. The tempo and proportion of interethnic marriages that allowed access to fishing sites probably increased after the first smallpox epidemic of the 1770s. Increased intermarriage would augment the multiethnic nature of winter ceremonies. Given those trends, the most likely hypothesis for the Nez Perce and Cayuse winter camp is that it existed, in much attenuated form, prior to 1730 but developed to its recorded size as a result of White influence, mostly indirect, in less than a century.

## Three Aspects of Exchange

Three aspects of exchange, barter, dentalia ("ahshahs"), and gambling, noted above, are mentioned in Perkins's writings and may be discussed here. Barter was assumedly a common means of exchange at trade marts such as The Dalles, but the mechanisms of Indian-Indian barter are nowhere discussed in the ethnohistorical literature. The gap is not surprising, as Whites were not party to purely Indian transactions and had no reason to describe them. What we do have is a considerable body of descriptions of Indian-White barter.

Hajda (1984:222–28), whose discussion of trade is the most complete, cites many relevant examples from the ethnohistorical literature. It is obvious from those citations that Chinookan peoples, up and down the river, were accomplished bargainers who knew how to play the market. That trading acumen was shared with coastal peoples and was too well developed to be a postcontact phenomenon. Whites, when they began trading with coastal natives in the late eighteenth century, were not dealing with amateurs. Perkins expresses a quite typical frustration when he mentions the impossibility of rendering the natives "any satisfactory equivalent for their labor." It fluctuated with need and the natives' perception of how much they could get out of the Whites: "Since the multiplication of Whites in the country . . . the pay of an Indian is more than doubled" (Appendix 1, Doc. 2).

Lewis and Clark described the situation:

> they are great higlers in trade and if they conceive you anxious to purchase will be a whole day bargaining for a handful of roots; this I should have thought proceeded from their want of knowledge of the comparitive value of articles of merchandize and the fear of being cheated, did I not find that they invariably refuse the price first offered them and afterwards very frequently accept a similar quantity of the same articles. [1990:164-65, quoted in Hajda 1984:224]

A mere three years after the discovery of the Columbia, Captain Charles Bishop was chagrined to find that "after bartering and shewing them a great variety of articles for the whole day we did not purchase a Single Fur" (in Bishop 1967:56, quoted in Hajda 1984:223). Other statements of that sort, revealing a surprised admiration for Chinookan trading skills, appear regularly in Astorian and Hudsons' Bay Company documents.

An eloquent account of the frustrations inherent in dealing with Chinookan traders is Hudson's Bay trader John Work's journal (1824), which describes his experiences trading salmon on the Columbia. Work set out with "a small outfit of tobacco, axes, hooks, rings, files, knives, beads, & a little ammunition." The first day (May 18) at Chinook, the natives "demanded such an exhorbitant price" that there was no trade. Upstream Indians insisted upon high prices plus "Rum, ammunition & shirts & different other articles which we have not got." The traders paid "very high" prices for sturgeon. As they moved upriver, however, and the salmon run improved, asking prices dropped: at The Cascades "12 salmon is bought for a small axe . . . 1 for a brass ring." The traders found that they were ill prepared to supply what the natives wanted—tobacco and buttons were hot items. After trading, Work thought there were no more than two dozen buttons left on his men's clothes. Supply and demand fluctuated wildly.

In his 1843-44 journal, Perkins mentions "ahshahs" (Indian money) (Appendix 1, Doc. 5, entry for Dec. 10, 1843). In Columbia Sahaptin, áx̌šax̌š is the word for dentalia (tooth or tusk shell in colloquial English), a medium of exchange among the Northwest Coast Indians. The shells came from a limited area on the western coast of Vancouver Island, in Nuu–chah–nulth (Nootka) territory and were exchanged from one group to the next as far south as California and as far east as the Plains. The singular methods of gathering those rare shells is described in Drucker (1951:112). Alexander Ross discusses dentalia use on the lower Columbia in the second decade of the nineteenth century:

> The circulating medium in use among these people is a small white shell called higua [more usual rendition: 'hiaqua' in Chinook Jargon] . . . and may be found in all lengths, between three inches down to one-fourth of an inch, and increase or decrease in value according to the number required to make a fathom [six feet], by which measure they are invariably sold. Thirty to a fathom are held equal in value to three fathoms of forty, or four to fifty, and so on. So highly are the higua prized, that I have seen six of 1 1/2 inches long refused for a new gun. But of late, since the whites came among them, the beaver skin called enna, has been added to the currency; so that, by these two articles, which form the medium of trade, all property is valued, and all exchange fixed and determined. [1849:95-96, cited in Ray 1938:100]

There is no doubt that dentalia circulated in precontact times; they have been found in northern Plains archaeological sites over 1,500 years old (Wood 1980:103). Slaves may have served a similar function, as in Perkins's exchange with Bear-Cap: "'Slaves' said he 'are our money, as dollars are yours'" (Appendix 1, Doc. 5, entry for Aug. 19, 1843). New candidates for exchange media appeared with White trade: besides Ross's beaver pelts, there were blue and white trade beads (Hajda 1984:231-32) and (in British Columbia) Hudson's Bay blankets (see also Griswold 1970:32-42). All three intermediaries helped to anchor prices and injected a degree of stability into the wildly fluctuating, rapidly changing market that was the Pacific Northwest of the early nineteenth century.

Dentalia, as wealth items, were frequently exchanged as gifts at Chinookan life-cycle rites. Their role in a marriage ceremony is described in chapter 5.

Chinookans also used dentalia as a form of conspicuous consumption: they wore the shells on their persons. According to Daniel Lee:

> It is not unfrequently the case that you may meet with an Indian with a bunch of these, say ten or fifteen, tied together and hung in each ear, and one sticking through a hole in the ligament which divides the nostrils. [D. Lee and Frost 1844:101]

Edward Curtis, in the first decade of the twentieth century, took photographs of Wishram people wearing dentalia jewelry. The nose ornament, worn by both men and women, appears in four photos; a kind of frontlet, consisting of alternating rows of dentalia and beads worn over each shoulder appears in three, as does a head covering, made of dentalia alone, which cascades down the neck (Curtis 1911a: following 90, 92, 120, 130, 132, plates 278-79, 281). The head covering has a border of strings of shell beads that dangle over the brow; that appendage, minus the head covering itself, appears to be the same as the "heavy bandeau" worn by the Chinookan girl sketched by Paul Kane in 1847 near Fort Vancouver (plate 12).

Perkins's passage on gambling, present in the 1952 manuscript, is lacking in the published version of "Wonderful Work of God. . . ." (Appendix 1, Doc. 3). Its omission probably relates to Perkins's lack of success in dealing with the practice. In fact, there is no real evidence that he ever made a concerted effort to stop gambling. It was simply too pervasive a part of Indian culture.

Ross asserts that at The Dalles summer trade mart, valuables "generally change hands through gambling" (1849:118). Without coordinate evidence, it is impossible to be more specific, but it appears that gambling was so common a means of redistributing goods that it challenged the expected mechanism of barter. In the present century, as during the last, traditional forms of gambling still occur at pan-tribal gatherings.

Perkins's discussion says very little about the specifics of middle Columbia River gambling. Numerous forms were known, and many are still practiced today (see Desmond's 1952 *Gambling among the Yakima*). The "hand game" (also known as "bone" or "stick game") was for men; an equivalent for women used beaver teeth dice. Wilkes gives a contemporary description of the bone game, shinny, and two other team games involving targets (1844, 4:367). There are others: the following description of the hand game is from Spier and Sapir.

> Any number of individuals could play. Seated on the ground, each of the parties had a plank laid before them on which to beat with eighteen inch long sticks while they sang. Four finger-long gambling bones made of deer shin-bones were used. Two (called "men") had a piece of buckskin tied around a groove at the middle; the other two ("women") were unmarked.
>
> The leader from each side sat in the middle of his row. He rolled all four bones in his hands, then passed one "man" and one "woman" to one man on each side of him, always an assorted pair. These hid them one in each hand, swinging their hands to and fro in front of their bodies. The object of their opponents was to guess in which hand the "men" were hidden. The leader of the opponents . . . announced his guess by hand movements. . . . If he correctly guessed the way in which one of the hiders held them, his side took that pair of bones. Then he guessed again for the other pair. If he missed on the second guess, his pair returned to their former owners. [1930:267-68]

# 4

# Social Structures

Any discussion of Northwest Indian economics leads inevitably to a consideration of social structure, as the two were inseparable. The missionary papers say little about the intricacies of Upper Chinookan and Sahaptin kinship, as most of it was beyond the missionaries' ken or interest and a full understanding would have required fluency in the native language. Although Euroamerican and Indian family organization was broadly similar, many native kin categories and relations differed from those to which Westerners are accustomed. One wonders how Henry Perkins's Sahaptin lexicon (no longer extant) dealt with the latter problem.

What the missionary accounts do discuss, however, are interactions among significant groups and categories of people—interactions that were in many cases based upon kinship categories and structures and that are important in gaining a complete understanding of aboriginal social structures. I have chosen to group those relationships into two broad categories: horizontal, or interactions among peers (for example, kin relations), and vertical, or relations among people of differing statuses (for example, chiefs, shamans, slaves).

## Horizontal Relations

### Kinship Networks

In "Wonderful Work of God. . . .," Perkins states, "An Indian tribe is like a great family, every member connected with one another; and as all the members of a family feel a mutual interest, so with all the members of any one tribe" (Appendix 1, Doc. 3). What he was referring to was the rapidity with which, by means of kinship ties, word of the Wascopam Revival had spread from one village to another. Those social ties operated in lieu of any developed political institutions; in fact, the networks established by kinship between villages were, in that part of the Northwest, the closest equivalent to a tribal structure in existence. Kin ties were extensive between winter villages, among village clusters, and even beyond the boundaries of ethnolinguistic groups. They formed the warp and woof of native society. As an expression of the role of kinship in Northwest society, Perkins's statement is a gem: a contemporary anthropologist could not say it any better.

Since 1960 many anthropologists have been interested in the role of kinship networks among the Coast Salish, Sahaptin, and Chinookan peoples of western Washington and the Columbia Basin. Their reconstruction goes as follows. Throughout that area marriage ties with individuals from distant groups were preferred, especially among the higher-ranking individuals of a given community. Marriages were cemented by gift exchanges between families and carried with them life-long economic ties. Establishing marital links with high-status, wealthy families from other areas not only increased one's own family prestige but provided access to important resource areas as well. In the Wascopam area, an especially important example of shared access was (and remains) family-owned fishing stations. That access served as a form of insurance in times of need. If food supplies in any given area failed or were insufficient, a family could, and often did, move to join relatives in a more prosperous area. The social system, on an economic level, was "adaptive" (Suttles 1960a; see also Elmendorf 1971; Schuster 1975:51–52; Hajda 1984).

The great mobility of middle Columbia River peoples—an inescapable effect of their subsistence round—ensured that family ties would be reinforced regularly. Sisters, for example, dispersed in marriage among several villages, might meet in April at the salmon fishery, in May in the camas meadows, or in September in the huckleberry fields. Such convocations, though fundamentally economic in nature, were inherently social and always festive, accompanied by visiting, gambling, and athletic contests. Life-rite ceremonies (birth, puberty, marriage, death—see chap. 5), often accompanied by feasting and gift exchange, brought relatives together. And there was, and still is, considerable visiting at other times of the year among relatives scattered by marriage.

Such a system is eminently suited to the rapid diffusion of new ideas and techniques over a wide area. High-status individuals with exceptionally broad kin networks were in the best position to serve as the agents of such change. Tumsowit and Yacooetar, the two Indians who were most responsible for spreading the "Work of God" beyond Wascopam in 1839–40, occupied such focal positions in the social network. As a shaman and high-ranking man (if not a chief), each had multiple wives, and hence many relatives in neighboring villages. Perkins's and Lee's establishment of good relations with those two was fortunate, and their employment of them as aides was a fortuitous, if not wise, use of the Indian system.

It has been suggested that, in both the prehistoric and early historic periods, many region-wide ceremonial elements spread over broad areas in ways such as those noted above (Elmendorf 1971:372–75). The early historical record on Plateau nativistic religions suggests that Indian prophets took advantage of the system to transmit their messages. With Tumsowit and Yacooetar traveling among local villages and serving as the missionaries' exhorters, we see what was basically a native system in operation, though serving Euroamerican ends.

## Division of Labor

Within that kinship network, a basic horizontal relationship was that between husband and wife. The missionaries were very interested in the marriage rite itself and assembled considerable data, which will be presented in the section of life rites (chap. 5). Another missionary concern was with the male-female (husband-wife) division of labor. On the Plateau, as among hunter-gatherers in general, the economic aspects of the marital tie were very important. A marriage bonded two individuals with complementary economic roles into a single functioning productive and consuming unit. And on the Plateau those roles were quite distinct and different from those to which the missionaries were accustomed. Perkins notes (Appendix 1, Doc. 1) that women did basket work and gathered roots and berries. Complementary male tasks were woodwork and hunting. Wilkes notes other aspects observed in the summer of 1841: "The men are engaged in fishing and do nothing else. On the women falls all the work of skinning, cleaning, and drying fish for their winter stores" (1844, 4:383). Perkins apparently held very strong views on women's roles, as he did on slavery, views that he shared with other Columbia Plateau missionaries. Elvira Perkins, Laura Brewer, Narcissa Whitman, Mary Walker, and others were all educated, strong individuals. All came from New York and New England, a region also characterized by strong abolitionist sentiment. In his discussion of women's roles and slavery on the Plateau, Perkins loses his usual objectivity.

It is an exaggeration to say, as Perkins did, that native women "labored like Virginia slaves" (Appendix 1, Doc. 1). Though the female workload certainly involved a degree of heavy labor, chances are that much of it was temporally restricted. Intensive root digging, berrying, and fish processing were concentrated into a few months, and—particularly in the case of root gathering—likely restricted to a manageable number of hours in each workday. There was not so much to do in the winter. Despite the visibility of male subsistence activities (fishing and hunting), women's contribution to the food-getting effort on the Plateau was substantial—one authority, in fact, has estimated that upwards of "70% of food energy [came] from plant foods harvested by women" (Hunn 1981:132).

That last quotation underlines the value of the woman as an economic partner in the Plateau marital union. Even though it may seem distasteful from a Western perspective, it is useful to keep that economic contribution in mind when discussing Plateau marriage variations such as polygyny (many wives) and marriage with prepubescent girls.

## Reciprocity and Visiting

Visiting and gift exchange, as stated above, were usual and expected ways of reinforcing social ties—both of kinship and friendship—in Plateau society. The missionaries unwittingly inserted themselves into that system and had a most difficult time adjusting to it. Indian-style visiting and reciprocity conflicted directly with American customs of privacy, private property, and self-sufficiency. Throughout the missionary papers there are many incidents of direct conflict in those matters. Close study of the incidents helps clarify the dimensions of those practices in both societies.

At the simplest level, the missionaries found themselves besieged by Indian visitors, who came unannounced at all hours, "begging" (the missionaries' word). Perkins, shortly after arriving at Wascopam, notes, "Parties of Indians from all parts of the surrounding country were every day coming and going. . . . It would have been a strange thing for a native to pay us a visit without begging for something" (Appendix 1, Doc. 2). After a period of adjustment the visits seem to have become less frequent.

The Brewers (Henry and Laura), shortly after their arrival in summer 1840, had similar experiences. Kindly people, but not as outgoing as the Perkinses, they seem to have been frequent targets of native importuning. Laura reported that

Indians thronged the house. They came early and often, and were seldom in a hurry to depart. They expected to be treated with something to eat, at any time. In the absence of presents of food they became morose and prejudiced. [Mudge 1854:13]

Laura, of course, was not being "friendly." To protect her privacy, she locked her doors, but that did not work: "The visitors would rattle them violently, rap at the windows, and perhaps shout for admittance" (Mudge 1854:13).

Five years later, that behavior persisted:

It usually begins in the morning about breakfast time, and some days it is come and go, come and go until night, unless I turn porter and fasten the door upon every one that goes out, and attend upon the call of every one that wishes to come in. They have a great many little wants, one wants a little salt, another a needle & thread, another a little meal for the sick, another medicine for the eyes, another has a 'Po.lak.ale tumtum' or dark heart or stomach, and wishes medicine suited to that case, another wants to get a shirt cut out, or perhaps, (as one did today) brings a blanket to have me cut him a coat, for such a favor as this, all that they seem to think is due on either side is to give them a needle & thread to make it, and then they are content, however, for the last garment mentioned I required them to bring me a Mat. [L. Brewer, letter of Apr. 29, 1845, Canse Collection; see also Waller, diary, entry for May 24, 1845, Alvan Waller Collection]

The missionaries, of course, had more possessions and were thus more often the subjects of requests. Laura was perfectly within her rights in expecting a return, though asking for it immediately may have been in poor form.

More serious misunderstandings sometimes arose from native expectations of reciprocity. Two instances from the missionary literature were: (1) An Indian gave the missionaries a horse, and then sometime later "stole" a heifer, which he believed was his due (see complete discussion in chap. 8); and (2) A native house burned down while its owner was attending a sermon; the Indian demanded that Rev. Waller replace it. Reciprocity in material goods as a means of sustaining or reinstating a balance among social groups reappears in the missionary texts like a leitmotif and appears to have been pervasive in Indian society.

Among more formalized interactions between social groups, in those cases usually involving nonrelated persons, the Wascopam records mention gambling (discussed in chap. 3), the smoking ceremony, and a competitive game, probably shinny.

Perkins and Lee, upon arrival at Wascopam, went "through the ceremony of smoking with all the principal men of the village." The Reverend Samuel Parker gives a more detailed description of a smoking ceremony, probably among Upper Chinookans, in 1835.

> They use but little tobacco, and with it they mix freely a plant which renders the fume less offensive. It is a social luxury, for the enjoyment of which they form a circle, and only one pipe is used. The principal chief begins by drawing three whiffs, then passes the pipe to the next person in dignity, and in like manner it passes around until it comes to the first chief again. He then draws four whiffs, the last of which he blows through his nose in two columns, in circling ascent, like a double-flued chimney. While thus employed, some topic of business is discussed, or some exploit in the chase, or some story of the battle field, is related, and the whole is conducted with gravity. [1838:246]

The smoking ceremony was a specifically Plains Indian tradition that had probably spread to the Northwest in relatively recent times. The practice was modified to suit local conditions. Plateau peoples, who had no agriculture, did not usually have tobacco, and used kinnikinnick *(Arctostaphylos uva-ursi)* instead. Throughout most of western Oregon, the local species *(Nicotania attenuata)* was the only cultivated plant (Kroeber 1941:13-20); seeds were broadcast in plots that had been prepared by burning to produce ash (D. Douglas 1953:59); the harvested leaves were mixed with kinnikinnick. As a scarce local commodity with high cultural value, tobacco became an important trade item. Stone pipes are known archaeologically from the Plateau for at least the last 2,000 years. There were two forms: the elbow pipe, usually associated with Upper Chinookans, and the tubular pipe of the Columbia Sahaptins (Ray 1942:188).

In the above examples, smoking was a social lubricant, to be used among friends and visitors. Smoke was also occasionally swallowed in order to produce an altered state of consciousness and facilitate contact with one's guardian spirit. That is reported by Alvan Waller in a letter dated February 3, 1847 (Archives of the Pacific Northwest Conference), and Jason Lee (letter of Mar. 27, 1843, Archives of the Pacific Northwest Conference) describes such an incident observed in The Cascades area:

> Found one man suffering with a severe burn on his back and shoulder; occasioned by his swallowing Tobacco smoke till he *died* (as the Indians expressed it); and fell into the fire. . . . I have seen one or two go through the operation of smoking themselves *dead,* but the practice is not common.

On March 24, 1838, Perkins's journal notes "a beautiful green about a quarter mile from . . . the village . . . where all the men resort occasionally for a game of ball" (Appendix 1, Doc. 5). That is the only mention in the local ethnohistorical literature of what was probably the local form of shinny. McWhorter (n.d.) cites Wasco Jim, born in 1828 at Winkwat, who called it *wal–kul–kul* (Kiksht *wa–k'al–kal;* David French, personal communication, 1989–93); Curtis (1911b:159) mentions the Yakama form *watloktlokkit* (probably *wax̃ikx̃ikit* "clubbing it repeatedly" [Eugene Hunn, personal communication, 1982–93]), and Desmond devotes a page (excerpts below) to the game as it was played on the Yakama Reservation in the mid-1940s.

> Each team consisted of from ten to twelve players. Each player provided himself with a shinny stick about four feet long . . . curved toward the end somewhat like a golf club. . . . The ball was usually a rounded oak burl about four inches in diameter, hardened by fire. The playing field was from 200 to 250 feet long with a pair of stakes at each end for goals. The stakes were usually set about twenty feet apart, and a hole about a foot in diameter was dug between the stakes for goals. . . .

> The two teams formed lines near the goal posts. The leader of each team stood near the hole in the center of the field in which the ball was

placed. At a signal from the supervisor, each leader tried to hit the ball . . . to his team . . . all players broke ranks and tried to hit the ball . . . between their goal posts or into their goal hole. . . . Each goal counted one point, and each game was played for five to ten points. A single game lasted two hours or more. [1952:14]

Two other games that might be played by teams on a field were noted by Wasco Jim and by Joseph Drayton of the Wilkes Expedition. The first involved shooting an arrow through a rolling hoop. The second had two teams throwing spears at goal poles fifty feet apart (Wilkes 1844, 4:367).

## Conflict

Conflict resolution, in a society that was kin based and lacking distinct political and legal institutions, operated differently than in the cultures of the invading Euroamericans. Two forms, blood revenge and the less focused variety—similar to scapegoating—that manifested itself in what the records often call "doctor killing," are mentioned in the missionary records.

In the 1843–44 journal, Perkins describes an incident in which Klamaths hired two Wascopam men to avenge the murder of one of their own by an "enemy" group ("Shasta," according to Brewer in Mudge 1854:51). The idea was to obtain "blood for blood" and thus (perhaps) bring the matter to a close. Unfortunately, it backfired. One of the mercenaries was killed by the "enemies," and the Wascopam villagers decided the Klamaths were to blame. One of their people was required in restitution for the slain Wascopam. Perkins, correctly assuming that the incident might develop into an ongoing feud ("war" is his term), intervened, and a Klamath woman, betrothed to the deceased, was presented to the man's brother (following the custom of the levirate—see chap. 5), and the Wascopam-Klamath dispute was brought to a close. It is important to note that that matter remained at the level of a feud and did not develop to a general "war of every man against every man" (Thomas Hobbes in Service 1979:52). The aboriginal lower Columbia pattern of intergroup conflict was, in fact, closer to the back-and-forth feuding of the Hatfields and the McCoys than to more complicated warfare with pitched battles, numerous casualties, and the taking of lands. The goal was restitution of balance, not conquest. In that sense the Chinookan villagers differed from their neighbors to the east, the Cayuses and the Nez Perces, who had a more complex form of intergroup conflict similar to that of the Plains (see Anastasio 1972:142–46).

Parker was also intrigued with lower Columbia blood revenge. He described it in more detail:

> Their custom of punishing the crime of murder . . . coincides with the custom of the Jews. The nearest relatives of the murdered person are the "avengers of blood.". . . They kill the murderer if they can find him; and in their own tribe or nation they do not extend the punishment to any other person, so that "the fathers are not put to death for the children.". . . If one is killed by a person belonging to another nation, if they cannot obtain and put the murderer to death, they will take the life of some of the relatives of the murderer; or, if they fail of this, some one of the nation must atone for the crime. And if this cannot be done immediately, the debt of blood will still be demanded, though years may pass away before it is cancelled. [1838:194-95]

Parker's description is identical in its particulars to ethnographer Kalervo Oberg's discussion (1934) of feuding among another Northwest Coast people, the Tlingits of the Alaska panhandle.

There are other examples of such feuds in the missionary literature. On the lower Chinooks, see D. Lee and Frost (1844:97); on the details behind the "Cockstock incident" at Oregon City see chapter 8. Allen records the following account from The Dalles:

> Two Indians were said to have been chopped entirely to pieces. . . . The squaw and daughters of one of the deceased set up a mournful wailing. . . . The disturbance had been caused by family feuds. It seemed that formerly a member of the family had been killed and as was the custom, his friends had slain his slayer, and *his* friends in return one of the *other* family, till with the last two the males of both families had become nearly extinct. [1850:277]

For more detail on that incident, see the biographical sketch of Papeus (Appendix 3). Feuds of that sort had the potential of going on ad infinitum, with a cumulative effect upon the participating units.

In his 1843-44 journal (Appendix 1, Doc. 5, entry for Dec. 23, 1843) Perkins discussed the practice of "doctor killing," which was very common among the Indians in the vicinity of The Dalles. "Doctor killing" is a complex issue, which seems to be a product of numerous factors—social, ideological, and historical—operating simultaneously in particular societies. Clusters of "doctor-killing" episodes are known from two other Northwest Indian groups in the mid-nineteenth century: the Takelmas (upper Rogue River) and the Nisquallys (south Puget Sound) (Boyd 1984).

Daniel Lee's parallel account of the phenomenon at The Dalles is more complete than that of his co-missionary:

the most influential persons among the people are the medicine men or conjurers, who can, it is believed, set the evil spirit of disease at defiance, cast it out where it has dared to enter, and make it seize with an unwielding, deadly grasp the objects of their displeasure. The people believe that they hold intercourse with the spirits, that they can see the disease which is some extraneous thing, as a small shell, or a pipe or a piece of tobacco, or some material substance which they (the doctors) describe. It is firmly believed that they can send a bad "tamanawas" [Chinook Jargon: spirit power] into a person and make him die, unless it be cast by some other medicine man. If a threat is made, or it is intimated by one of them that a certain person will not live long, no sooner does he hear of it than he is alarmed and feels himself a dead man. For their services they are paid in advance, and often their demands are high and their practice is lucrative. When their patients die, they restore the fees. This is necessary for their own security, for otherwise they might be charged with having caused his death, which would render them the mark of revenge. If one of the order is his rival or enemy and he wishes this obstacle to his own advancement removed the affirmation that he caused the death of some person will probably be followed with his death by the relatives of the deceased. Several deaths from this cause took place at the dalls the first year after the station [Wascopam] was occupied, and this is a common occurrence among the many surrounding tribes. [D. Lee and Frost 1844:179]

The Indians did not possess the germ theory of disease; death from disease was attributed to supernatural means including object intrusion, spirit possession, and soul loss; shamans (the proper anthropological term for that kind of curer) had the ability, using those means, to both "cure" and "cause" disease. They might, therefore, be blamed for disease deaths, particularly those that came about under unusual circumstances. That is the ideological basis behind the phenomenon.

On another level, it might be noted that "doctor killing" is really another variety of blood revenge, except that in that case the object of revenge is more likely a member of the in-group, not an outsider. "Doctor killings" and sorcerer or witchcraft accusations are all very similar. Spier and Sapir (1930:247) point out that such accusations were especially likely when there was an underlying social tension between the parties involved, as well as when a disease was particularly severe or unusual. People who were associated with unusual happenings—who "rocked the boat" socially, who looked and acted differently—were likely to be the objects of sorcery accusations. Among the Paiutes, southern neighbors of the Chinookans and Sahaptins, fear of sorcery accusations "constituted the strongest motivation for behaving socially"

(Whiting 1950:79) among a family-level society, lacking institutionalized means of social control. For Columbia River Sahaptins, Murdock suspects that "in-group sorcery primarily served a judicial purpose" (1965:170).

Sorcery accusations have been called measures of a society's internal "strain gauges" (Marwick 1964:285). It is also significant that they tend to increase in periods of social dislocation and change (M. Douglas 1970:xx-xxi). Lee (above; see also H. Brewer, letter of Aug. 22, 1840, Canse Collection) notes the concentration of "doctor killings" in the "first year of occupation" at Wascopam; in the three regions of the Northwest where "doctor killing" was prevalent, there is a trend toward more killings in periods of epidemic disease (Boyd 1984).

The review of "doctor killings" in the vicinity of The Dalles (Upper Chinookans, Columbia River Sahaptins, Cayuses) uncovered twenty documented instances between 1837 and 1855. The two quoted below occurred close to or during the time of Perkins's 1843–44 journal. The first is reported by Rev. Gustavus Hines, with the date June 2, 1843:

> Mr. Ogden[1] ... found the Rev. H.K.W. Perkins dispensing to ... some three hundred Indians ... the work of reconciliation through a crucified Redeemer. There was sitting in the outskirts of the congregation an Indian woman who had been for many years, a doctress in the tribe, and who had just expended all her skill upon a patient, the only son of a man whose wigwam was not far distant, and for the recovery of whose son she had become responsible, by consenting to become his physician. All her efforts to remove the disease were unavailing, the father was doomed to see his son expire. Believing that the doctress had the power of preserving life or inflicting death according to her will, and that instead of curing she had killed his boy, he resolved upon the most summary revenge. Leaving his dead son in the lodge, he broke into the congregation with a large butcher-knife in his hand, and rushing upon the now terrified doctress, seized her by the hair, and with one blow across her throat, laid her dead at his feet.[1850:190]

An incident among the Cayuses was described by Marcus Whitman on March 11, 1844:

> A most barbarous murder occurred on the night of the 11th inst a short distance from our door. The murdered was a sorcerer and became a prey to that superstition, being murdered by his intimate friends. A death having taken place in the family of a brother of the murderer, at a distance from this place, a messenger was sent to bring the news and orders for the younger brothers to kill the Sorcerer; which was promptly obeyed the same night. It was perpetrated in a public gambling scene and no-one attempted to avert the blows, but all fled and left them to complete the

work of death, which was done with a sword in the most shocking manner. [M. Whitman in Hulbert 1941:89–90]

One of the latest and most interesting clusters of "doctor-killing" incidents occurred in early 1853 at The Dalles. General Benjamin Alvord, then in charge of Fort Dalles, was approached by

> several of the chiefs of the ... Waskows, Wishrams, and Des chutes ... to invoke my aid to suppress a most extraordinary custom which prevailed among them of killing their doctors ... or medicine men, if they did not cure their patients. During the previous winter three doctors in that neighborhood had been killed for that reason, and it was done by the relatives of the deceased. [1884:364]

William Chinook (see biographical sketch, Appendix 3) was interpreter for the delegation of chiefs. Alvord's proposed solution to the problem, reminiscent of what Elijah White had attempted a decade earlier (see chap. 8) was to impose the rule of law on that people. In his words:

> If a murder was committed, the punishment should be administered, not by the kindred of the murdered man, but in the name of the law. ... To permit the punishment of the accused to be administered without investigation by a brother or son or father of the person killed only leads to indiscriminate slaughter. ... If they wished to check this unfortunate custom of killing doctors, they must first make known this new law, and afterwards arrest the next offender, and after careful trial and assured evidence and conviction of his guilt, he should be sentenced to be hung. [1884:365]

It was, needless to say, very presumptuous (though not at all atypical) of Alvord to expect that a simple explanation, through an interpreter, of a completely foreign and very complex system involving a law code, trial by jury, and punishment by hanging, developed through many centuries of English jurisprudence, would be fully understood and rapidly and completely assimilated by middle Columbia Indians. Three months later, when a smallpox epidemic hit Wishram, claiming 257 lives (Bolon 1854), a "celebrated medicine-man" who "did not cure the small-pox" was brought to justice. The villagers put him on a horse with a rope around his neck and hanged him. No law code, no weighing of evidence, no jury. Alvord was shocked. "That is as much as they learned by all the preaching of the priest[2] and myself" (Alvord 1884:366). Indeed.

## Vertical Relations

### Shamans and Chiefs

Shamans and chiefs were the two most important vertical statuses among mid-Columbia peoples. Both, if successful, held considerable prestige and had access to more wealth than their fellows. At Wascopam in 1839–40 Perkins and Lee befriended the shaman Tumsowit and the chief Yacooetar (see biographical sketches, Appendix 3) and took advantage of their influence to spread the "Work of God."

Shamans and chiefs differed not only in their duties, but also in the ways their positions were obtained: the shaman's powers were acquired through the establishment of relationships with spirit powers obtained in a vision quest; the chief's influence arose mostly from his focal position in the kin network. The difference, in sociological terms, is between achieved and ascribed statuses. There was some overlap, of course (shamans tended to run in families—often high-ranking); and individual capabilities could make or break a particular chief.

Both shamans and chiefs were wealthier than their neighbors; but while the former achieved his wealth in the form of payment for services rendered, the latter gained his by dint of his focal point in the kin system: he had access to and could manipulate the myriad social channels through which wealth flowed.

The only detailed nineteenth-century account of how a shaman obtained his powers again comes from Benjamin Alvord:

> The young candidate, about ten years of age, is sent out to sleep by himself on the ground or in a lodge, there to await communications from their good spirit, or "Tamanoise." This spirit appears in the shape of a bear, eagle, coyote, buffalo, or some wild bird or animal. If the child, when he returns in the morning, has heard nothing, he is sent back again, and they will continue to send him day after day, and night after night, to sleep alone in this way; and he is often made to fast the whole time, until he is worried into believing or asserting that he has had some wonderful visitor, in his sleep, in the shape of the spirit of some animal. He will tell to some medicine dignitary what he has heard and seen, who will instruct him that when he is in want of anything he must call on that spirit to assist him in all his undertakings. This seals his character as being destined to the profession, but until grown up he does not act as a doctor. Long fasting and stoicism under it, are regarded as an essential part of the process. With the Waskows, if the boy when sent out to sleep by himself should

on his return, ask for food, he is looked upon as utterly unfit for any such high trust. On reaching manhood the novitiate is initiated into his sacred profession in a medicine dance, which is associated with their idolatrous worship. The idols are the "Tamanoise" or the genii of certain animals. Their movements and expressions are imitated in the dance. During the ceremony of initiation some of the chief doctors chant suitable songs or incantations, and make certain passes not unlike those made by mesmerists to put the candidate to sleep. When awakened from this sleep, he is pronounced fit for practice in his lofty and potent profession. [1884:365]

Everyone had spirit helpers (see chap. 6); the difference with shamans was that their guardian spirits gave curing powers and tended to be stronger than other spirits; shamans could also have several spirit helpers simultaneously (Ray 1942:240).

Chiefs, throughout the Pacific Northwest, tended to be the most senior members of high-ranking kin groups. Chiefs normally were present at the village, rarely at the tribal, level. The consensus among Northwest anthropologists and the more astute nineteenth-century White observers is that that office did not represent any concentration of political authority.

These were not the strong chiefs that most Euroamerican immigrants had grown accustomed to from other parts of the Americas and expected to find in Oregon as well. In his 1843–44 journal Perkins comments, "The chiefs here have but little authority, & the people do pretty much as they please" (Appendix 1, Doc. 5, entry for Sept. 30, 1843). That quotation may be added to a body of similar ethnohistorical statements, including those by Samuel Parker: "They do not exercise authority by command, but influence by persuasion" (1838:235); Charles Wilkes: "There are but few chiefs to whom the appeal for redress [for theft] can be made and they exercise but little control over such a lawless crew" (1844, 4:386); Asa Smith, on the Nez Perces: "The power of the chiefs amounts to very little & the people do which is right in their own eyes" (cited in Drury 1958:139); and Hudson's Bay governor Sir George Simpson, on the renowned Chinook chief Concomly:

> Concomelly is the principal man of the Chinook tribe from the circumstance of his being the most wealthy having a number of Slaves and a large stock of Hyaques Beads and other property but he has little controul over them, indeed every Flat Head Indian who is possessed of a slave considers himself a Chief. [Simpson in Merk 1931:97]

The lack of power obviously impressed the White observers; otherwise they would not have mentioned it so frequently.

So what did chiefs on the middle and lower Columbia do? The anthropological record is by no means clear on that question. Similarities between chiefs among the Wishram Chinookan and Tenino Sahaptins of The Dalles include, most prominently, the following points: the position was hereditary (in the male line), it was a named office (*icta'mx* in Kiksht; *miyúux* in Columbia Sahaptin), there was one or more chiefs per (winter) village or community (tribal chiefs are "clearly postcontact"), the chief possessed wealth and multiple wives, and the chief had a role of *primus inter pares* in disputes. There are vague references to a "council" among the Wishrams and "sub-chiefs" among the Teninos. The Wishrams are also supposed to have had a war-chief (typical of the Plateau) and spokesmen for their chiefs (both a Northwest Coast and a Plateau pattern) (Spier and Sapir 1930:211–13; Murdock 1980:143–44).

The missionary records add some information on this matter. First, it should be noted that references to chiefs are common—there was apparently no ambiguity about their identity, though the content of their roles is not always clear. In the Upper Chinookan area there were two chiefs of note: Tamakoun at The Cascades (see chap. 2, above) and Yacooetar ("Equator") at Wascopam (see biographical sketch, Appendix 3). Both were men of wealth and influence: Tamakoun had slaves, Yacooetar at least two wives. Given their status and their roles in handling intergroup affairs, they were logical candidates to serve as representatives of their communities in interactions with the Whites; both appear to have manipulated that role to increase their own wealth and influence.

Yacooetar was termed a "war chief"; as there is no reference to any other chief at Wascopam at that time, he assumedly occupied both roles. There is some ethnohistorical information on an earlier Upper Chinookan chief, Tilki, who held the office at Wishram in the 1830s. In Perkins's day, Tilki was dead, and there is only one citation in the mission papers to "Tilki's son" (H. Perkins, letter of June 2, 1840, Canse Collection). There is nothing to suggest that the son had inherited his father's position nor that he had any influence over the Wishram villagers.

Tilki himself is first mentioned in the "Fort Nez Percés [Walla Walla] Journal," entry for January 25, 1832, as "Watilka (Chief of the Dalles)." Ten months later American explorer and entrepreneur Nathaniel Wyeth met him:

Just below the Dalles . . . there are here many Indians Tilky & Casineau[3] are here the chiefs and very clever ones. . . . We encamped for the first time on the river among timber among which I saw a kind of oak and ash. Indians Plenty one chief at whose lodge we stopped a short time gave me some molasses obtained from fort below to eat He had a large stock of dried fish for the winter 4 tons [sic] I should think roots &c he was dressed in the English stile Blue frock coat pants. & vest comported himself with much dignity enquired my name particularly and repeated it over many times to impress it on his memory his sister was the squaw of an American of the name of Bache who established a post on the river below the great dalles three years ago last fall and who was drowned in them with 11 others the following spring the remains of the fort I saw also the grave of the woman who died this fall and was buried in great state with sundry articles such as capeau vest pantaloons shirts &c. A pole with a knob at the top is erected over her remains at the foot of the Dalles is an island called the Isle of the Dead. [Wyeth 1899:183, 175]

Samuel Parker encountered Tilki three times during his 1835-36 journey.

October 12, 1835:

Tilki, the first chief of La Dalles Indians, engaged to furnish me with a canoe and . . . three . . . men to carry me to Fort Vancouver. [Parker 1838:132]

February 14, 1836:

[Vancouver Sunday service:] I met with . . . Indians from La Dalles. . . . They came in single file, the first chief leading the way. When I prayed with them, they all kneeled down except two or three, and these were reprimanded by the chief for impropriety of conduct, which was soberly received and implicitly obeyed. . . . The first chief, at the close of service wished to speak; and on permission being given, he spoke a short time to his people, and then told me . . . a white man gave them a flag, and told them to set it up on a pole, on Sundays, and meet and pray, sing their songs, and dance around the pole bearing the flag; and that they had done so a long time. He wished to know if it was right. [Parker 1838:254-55]

June 8, 1836:

In the narrow, broken channel of the La Dalles . . . we had to make three portages. Our canoe was so large that twenty Indians were not too many to carry it safely. Their mode of carrying, is to invert it upon their heads and shoulders, and then it is with difficulty and danger that they pass the steep and rocky ravines. When we came to the last portage, the Indians were not willing to take hold again unless we would pay them in powder and balls; and although their demands were reasonable, yet our stores were not adequate to meet them, and they would not perform the labor without the required article. I engaged Sopelay, and another influential chief, to induce their men to perform the labor of making this last portage, and promised that I would send them the demand from Fort Vancouver, and for their security I would give them a talking paper. They stated to their people my proposal, and were about to succeed, when Tilki, the first chief, who had become familiar with an American trader,[4] laughed at their credulity. Sopelay, however, stated to the people, that he had seen me at the fort, and that he heard me teach the Indians good things, and did not believe I would deceive them. He prevailed, and the men took hold of the work. [Parker 1838:306-7]

Tilki is named as "first chief" in both the first and third Parker passages, but Sopelay's speech in passage three casts some doubt on the identity of the unnamed "first chief" in passage two. It was most likely Tilki but may have been Sopelay. This encounter at Vancouver is discussed later, in the context of religion (chap. 9).

Dr. John Townsend, who came to Oregon in 1835 with Jason and Daniel Lee, is the last to mention Tilki.

June 30, 1836:

Encamped in the evening at the village of the Indian chief Tilki. I had often heard of this man, but I now saw him for the first time. His person is rather below the middle size, but his features are good, with a Roman cast, and his eye is deep black, and unusually fine. He appears to be remarkably intelligent, and half a century before the generality of his people in civilization. [1839:243]

September 6, 1836:

The Indians told us with sorrowful faces of the recent death of their principal chief, Tilki. Well, thought I, the white man has lost a friend, and long will it be before we see his like again! The poor fellow was unwell when I last saw him, with a complaint of his breast, which I suspected to be pulmonary. I gave him a few simple medicines, and told him I should soon see him again. About two weeks since he ruptured a blood vessel, and died in a short time. [1839:252]

That short biography contains many clues about the role of chiefs in contact-period Upper Chinookan society. First, note the consistent references to "first chief . . . principal chief," implying ranking and the presence of subchiefs such as Sopelay. Second, Tilki is called both "clever" and "intelligent," suggesting that he held his role on the basis of more than heredity. Tilki had some control over his subordinates (for example, the reprimand), but it was by no means absolute (Sopelay and the others disagreed with him). Tilki was an acknowledged intermediary: a "friend" of the Whites, who had "become familiar with an American trader," and who transmitted information between Parker and his people. He established ties with the influential newcovers: his sister had married the American trader Bache, and he had acquired molasses and clothing from the Whites. Tilki was wealthy, with "4 tons" of dried salmon. He seems to have had a focal role in ceremonial affairs (according to Drucker 1983:87, a prime function of Kwakwaka'wakw chiefs). And finally, there is his relationship to canoes and portages.

That latter point may have been more important than has been heretofore acknowledged in the ethnographic literature. On the downstream trip, Tilki furnished the canoe for Parker and arranged for oarsmen; on the return another "influential chief" provided those services, and Tilki scoffed at them. The 1916 Seufert case testimony contains some interesting information on canoes, portages, and chiefs. Dalles area Indians moved regularly from one bank of the Columbia to another, but not everyone owned canoes. There were three important portages: canoes, owned by chiefs, were kept at each, to be freely (?) used by whoever needed them. It may well be that portages or canoes, or both, were property of chiefs, and that their control helped determine chiefly influence. Elsewhere on the Northwest Coast, canoe ownership was a mark of wealth; chiefs, who were custodians of their kin group's wealth, would own more and larger canoes; some important economic activities requiring cooperating groups directed by a leader were conducted in canoes (for example, whaling and reef-net fishing [Drucker 1951:48–56; Suttles 1990a]).

Finally, some comparative and historical notes: Plateau chiefs, while sharing many of the traits listed above, seem to have had a greater degree of influence over wider groups (Anastasio 1972:177–82). That is apparent in the biographical sketches of Tawatoy ("Tuetasomittlecum") and Piupiumaks-maks, Cayuse and Walla Walla chiefs (see Appendix 3). Historically, the office of chief benefited and was strengthened by White contact. Downriver chiefs such as Concomly and Cassino took advantage of their role as intermediaries to develop power bases of their own. They tried to monopolize or manipulate trade so that wealth flowed into their hands, they married their children to Whites, and the newcomers reinforced the chiefs' positions by continuing to deal with them as representatives of their people in matters of increasing cultural importance. On the southern Plateau chiefs sought to increase their wealth through the accumulation of horses and cattle, and in 1843 their powers were increased and their positions formalized by the imposition of Indian Agent Elijah White's law code (chap. 8). The broad pattern throughout the Northwest was the same as elsewhere in native North

America: the office of chief became stronger as a result of the interaction between Western and aboriginal societies.

In his August 17, 1843, journal entry (Appendix 1, Doc. 5) Perkins notes two native functionaries: "heralds or 'sap-a-wanp-tlam-a'" and "news-bearers or 'tai-mu-tlam-a'."[5] Perkins says that the "sapawanptlama" was "a man, such as I use every sabbath to proclaim my words to the people, & which we sometimes term a 'crier'." Spokesmen, who served chiefs, are known ethnographically for most Plateau Indians (Ray 1942:229; Schuster 1975:54). According to Spier and Sapir, Wishram

> chiefs were provided with spokesmen who repeated to the gathering in a loud voice what their principals said. . . . The spokesman might be any man; it is not clear that there was any specialization of function here . . . a shaman also had his spokesman who repeated aloud what the spirit communicated to the shaman. [1930:213]

The use of such a spokesman would certainly underline the importance of the chief.

Perkins says that the "sapawanptlama" was "a man, such as I use every sabbath to proclaim my words to the people, & which we sometimes term a 'crier'." The missionaries' utilization of a preexisting native functionary was not only convenient but astute as well, for a herald "lends dignity and public worth to a statement" (Theodore Stern, personal communication, 1982). At the beginning of his ministry, when Perkins spoke only Chinook Jargon, the crier apparently served as translator as well. There was a need for translations into both Kiksht and Sahaptin. After Perkins began to preach in Sahaptin, the needs changed, and it is not clear whether one crier repeated his words, or translated into Kiksht, or whether there were two criers present performing both functions. Perkins's "taimutlama" or newsbearer is not reported anywhere as a separate position, though Desmond assigns both functions to Yakama "criers" (1952:7).

## Slaves

At the bottom of the social scale in Upper Chinookan society were the slaves—a true class apart from the body of native-born freemen. While there was continuity among the free class—a chief might include among his relatives the poorest and least honorable members of his society— slaves, who were obtained from outside groups, had no local relatives and were thus outside of the social network. They were property, pure and simple. Slavery, along with the treatment of women, was a concern of Perkins. "Whatever I might be in the United States of America, in Oregon I am 'an immediate abolitionist.' I have seen so much of this sickening business, that my soul revolts at the idea of its contin[uance] for a time however short." His August 19, 1843, discussion of the practice (Appendix 1, Doc. 5), however, includes not only an emotional tirade on the treatment of slaves, but a number of ethnographic nuggets as well.

Slavery was a complex practice. Slave raiding and trading appear to have increased during the contact period, and are discussed in chapter 7; slave burial is covered in chapter 5. Here the concern is with the role of slaves in the socioeconomic system. First, it should be pointed out that slavery was typical of the Northwest Coast culture area but unusual on the Columbia Plateau. At The Dalles, on the border of the two areas, slaves appear to have been held by Upper Chinookans, while Sahaptins provided the supply by raiding distant peoples and trading their captives at The Dalles for other kinds of wealth.[6] Among Upper Chinookans, it was only high-ranking and consequently wealthy people (particularly chiefs) who could afford to purchase slaves. Slaves were simultaneously symbols of wealth and producers of more wealth through their labor. In a prestige-conscious, acquisitive society like that of the Chinookans, they were very desirable to have.

Perkins's confrontation with the slave owners was a confrontation with some of the most powerful people in native society—the "principal men of the village" who owned them, and the leaders of the "Kaius & WallaWalla" trading party (on the model of later expeditions, men such as Tawatoy of the Cayuses and Piupiumaksmaks of the Walla Wallas) who supplied them. An attack on slavery was an attack on one of the most important means such men had to maintain and increase their wealth and prestige. "Slaves are our money, as dollars are yours," said Bear-Cap, threatening Perkins with his whip. The prices obtained for slaves quoted by Perkins underline their importance. In the Klamath country, slaves were purchased for "a horse for each" (then worth "about ten dollars"), a commodity that the leaders of the trading party had in large numbers. At The Dalles, slaves could be sold for "more than double this price ... 100 per cent profit," which in one case amounted to "5 large blankets, worth four dollars apiece, & about eight dollars in Indian money [dentalia] beside." The blankets and dentalia were themselves nonutilitarian but could be used as prestige-enhancing mechanisms—the former given away at feasts, for instance, the latter used in a marriage-gift exchange or even displayed conspicuously in the form of jewelry for the chief's wife. The resident villagers who purchased the slaves might use them in ways similar to the Sahaptins' material wealth—in prestige-enhancing exchanges and as conspicuous wealth—but they were also likely valued as capital goods—which, as additions to a family's labor force, increased its productive capacity and freed up some members for other pursuits.

This latter function seems logical from the nature of the slave-trading system at The Dalles but is in fact not well supported by direct local ethnohistorical evidence. Elsewhere on the Northwest Coast, the evidence is somewhat better: slaves provided "undifferentiated labor," especially in helping females in food processing; they were involved in

> "all menial offices," bringing water, cutting wood, making canoes, assisting in building and repairing houses, supplying masters with fish, manufacturing cloth, cooking, collecting berries, waiting on family and guests, and paddling canoes. [Donald 1983:111-14]

Most of those activities (exclusive of those related to woodworking) were, in fact, women's work among Upper Chinookans, and that may explain both Perkins's equation of women and slaves and the silence of most (male) observers, who were not concerned with nor privy to women's activities. It is now established that, in the mid-Columbia, women were important economic producers.

The following passages from the missionary records address the issue of slave labor and treatment.

> They are put to the same service which women perform. . . . They are generally treated with kindness; live in the same dwelling with their masters . . . [Parker 1838:197]

> The service to which the slaves are subjected is the most menial. They dress the food taken in the chase or in fishing, draw water, and provide wood for the fire. [Brewer in Mudge 1854:25]

> They do the principal part of the work and drudgery. . . . Slaves generally are as well, or better clad than their masters, and as to food fare equally well. [Waller 1843]

Note the range of opinions on the treatment of slaves. Perkins, from his strongly abolitionist stand, paints the bleakest picture, but on close examination, he seems more concerned with clothing, cleanliness, and denial of burial privileges than with day-to-day treatment. Brewer echos Perkins, but his words are not so strong. Both of their accounts were prepared with a particular audience in mind, which was strongly abolitionist. Waller's statement, made about the same time as those of his cohorts, may be a corrective to their antislavery zeal. Parker's contribution, written without reference to the slavery issue in the states, is probably the most objective. His equation of slave and female labor and location of living quarters is consistent with the ethnographic information from elsewhere on the coast and with the factual details that underlie Perkins's emotional account.

## Head Flattening

Among all the peoples of the lower Columbia drainage, head flattening was usual among the nonslave segment of the population. In the transition area of The Dalles, the practice was common among Chinookans but limited to certain women among Sahaptian speakers. From the Euroamerican perspective, head flattening was bizarre and merited comment from nearly every early observer. Perkins is unusual in that he mentioned it only once, in reference to Yacooetar, who stood "unique among his tribe for one singularity—his parents did not flatten his head." Brewer's description of the practice appears in Mudge (1854:28); Narcissa Whitman's, from The Cascades, follows:

> I saw an infant here whose head was in the pressing machine. . . . The child lay upon a board between which and its head was a squirrel skin. On its forehead laid a small square cushion, over which was a bandage drawn tight around pressing up its head against the board. In this position it is kept three or four months or longer, untill the head becomes a fashionable shape. [Drury 1973, 1:99 (diary entry for Sept. 11, 1836)]

Brewer describes the cradleboard: "wider at the head than foot; upon the edge of this board a narrow piece of skin is fastened, with loop-holes at short distances." Cords passed through those holes, and held the immobile child tightly. Brewer states that flattening continued for upwards of a year. The ethnographic (Spier and Sapir 1930:256) and ethnohistoric sources agree that the procedure was difficult, and some infants died. The results are visible in the pictures of Tamakoun's son and Kane's Clackamas Indian (plates 4, 13).

# 5

## Ritual Behavior:
## Life-Cycle Ceremonies

The Wascopam Mission records contain probably the best extant information on early Upper Chinookan and Columbia Sahaptin ritual behavior—particularly in the areas of life-cycle ceremonies (in anthropological jargon, "rites of passage") and winter ceremonies. Both persist today, in altered form, among reservation communities. Life-cycle ceremonies have been studied intensively by anthropologists (see two Ph.D. dissertations: Kathrine French's 1955 "Culture Segments and Variation in Contemporary Social Ceremonialism on the Warm Springs Reservation, Oregon" and Helen Schuster's 1975 "Yakima Indian Traditionalism: A Study in Continuity and Change"). Winter ceremonies (covered in chapter 6), on the other hand, are to this day poorly known to outsiders. The mission records show that winter ceremonies in The Dalles area were surprisingly complex, with many activities similar to those of better-known Indian cultures of Washington and British Columbia.

Information on ritual behavior is recorded in Perkins's 1843-44 journal (Appendix 1, Doc. 5), in D. Lee and Frost's *Ten Years in Oregon* (1844: 163-64), and in Brewer's *Sketches of Mission Life* (Mudge 1854:23-24), as well as in many of Brewer's manuscript letters. Alvan Waller did not approve of "heathen practices" and has little to say about them. The missionary descriptions, previously little known and difficult to locate, constitute primary ethnographic data and are assembled here for the first time.

### The Beginnings of Life

As is true in most hunting-gathering cultures, pregnancy and the first few years of life were particularly difficult for the Indians of The Dalles. The missionary records contain several references to two aspects of that problem, infanticide and the high infant-mortality rate, which they found particularly abhorrent.

Infanticide is not uncommon among non-Western cultures around the world. It should be emphasized that the practice tends to occur in societies with a normally high infant-mortality rate and is most frequently explained as a response to difficult economic conditions, for example, the inability of the mother to feed and care for a second child without threatening the one she already has, or situational economic privation (for hunter-gatherers, a bad winter or failure of usual food resources). There is also evidence that more infants are killed in situations of rapid change, deculturation, and anomie (see Dickeman 1975).

Two excerpts from the Methodist missionary literature cite such reasons, one by Jason Lee at Willamette Mission, dated October 29, 1834, and another by Frost at Clatsop, dated February 1842:.

> An old squaw attempted to kill her grandchild by strangling it, & when prevented by one of the settlers . . . she was very angry and inquired who would take care of it, now its mother & father are dead, & added "It is good to kill it." [J. Lee 1835]

> Mrs. Frost had a conversation one day with an Indian woman who called at our home with her little son, whom we used to clothe. This woman told Mrs. F. that she had destroyed her infants previous to this. . . . When asked the reason why . . . she said that as they had become very poor, and had no slaves, the drudgery all fell upon the woman; and if they had many children they were prevented from doing their work; so that when their husbands came home weary and hungry, and found no fire and no roots to eat, they were angry, called them lazy, and abused them. Therefore, in order that they might relieve themselves of much trouble and care and escape abuse from their husbands . . . they destroyed their infants. [Frost in D. Lee and Frost 1844:314]

Perkins discusses another instance of infanticide in his September 1843 *Christian Advocate and Journal* report (Appendix 1, Doc. 4). In that case, the proximate reason for the act was a malformation of the child's stomach, which was attributed to the breaking of a pregnancy taboo by the father. In Chinookan society parents were subject to a lengthy list of taboos (see Boas 1894:241-43; David French and Kathrine French [personal communications, 1989-93] have recorded "prenatal tabus for fathers" from Wasco informants). The Wascopam infanticide was performed quickly and efficiently by a shaman, who was paid for his effort. Henry Brewer, who retells Perkins's story, supplies the additional information that the father was "Homaz a brave and distinguished Wascopam" (Mudge 1854:31-32).

Each of the above incidents was reported in such a way as to shock its intended audience, with an unspoken motive of gaining support for the missionary effort. They still shock today. Yet placed in the context of a difficult, changing Indian culture, the reasons are justifiable and the measures rational.

Incidents like the above were uncommon; the high infant mortality rate resulted mostly from natural causes. As Perkins relates in his 1843-44 journal

(Appendix 1, Doc. 5, entry for Dec. 24, 1843), "So great a proportion of the heathen die while in a state of infancy." The following quotation from Henry Spalding, Presbyterian missionary at Lapwai, gives some of the reasons for the high infant mortality among the neighboring, seminomadic, Nez Perces:

> Many births are premature from the hardships the women are exposed to from being almost constantly on the horse or under the burdensome packs. . . . A great proportion of the children die within the first four days from violence done them by hard traveling, heat of the sun beating upon their bare heads, and exposedness to cold, or from want of nourishment. [1840:231]

## Feast of the Naming[1]

To this writer's knowledge, Perkins's descriptions of the naming and ear-boring rites among Dalles-area Indians are the only ones from the nineteenth century. Both rites are described ethnographically in several sources from the reservation period.

Perkins's account of the naming ceremony (Appendix 1, Doc. 5, entry for Dec. 10, 1843), in fact, is considerably more complete and coherent than either of the standard ethnographic records (Curtis 1911a:179; Spier and Sapir 1930:258–59). It also adds details that make many of the constituent activities intelligible in terms of traditional Northwest Coast practices.

Perkins dates the naming rite at "generally . . . during the first year"; Spier and Sapir place it at six months to two years, Curtis at one to three years. Perkins suggests that wealthier parents might hold the ceremony earlier, as they would not have to spend much time amassing the requisite gifts. The timing of the naming rite was also certainly influenced by the high rate of infant mortality. As Spier and Sapir note, "A child named when still very small might die"; it was simply good sense to "wait and be certain before giving it a name" (1930:258).

A naming ceremony bestowed "personhood": a genealogical and social identity upon a child who had heretofore occupied a rather ambiguous and generalized status. Spier and Sapir call it "the greatest event in a Wishram's life." All sources agree that the name given the child was inherited from a late relative and that the name had "lain fallow" for a certain period of time.[2]

Dividing Spier and Sapir's and Perkins's accounts of the naming ceremony into segments, as Kathrine French has done for recent Warm Springs ceremonials, reveals a remarkable degree of consistency between the 1840s rites and those practiced at the turn of the century. From each period the rites have (1) parents inviting relatives ("both sides," according to Perkins; "and

friends," according to Spier and Sapir); (2) a feast; (3) an elderly man who
announces the name (Spier and Sapir note that there might be two speakers,
the second repeating the statements of the first; Perkins has the speaker being
hired and paid with dentalia); (4) "publication" of the name to the audience and
spirits of the native cosmology (Perkins notes that the speaker gave a history
of the name; Spier and Sapir state that the name giving symbolized rebirth of
its former owner); (5) audience response that verified the name ("axi" to each
statement in Spier and Sapir; repetition of the name in Perkins); (6) presents
to the audience (according to Perkins, in order of "dignity"); (7) the cutting up
and distribution of an elk skin by the speaker; and (8) requests from the
audience for valuables, which the parents were bound to give (Perkins lists
shirts, knives, and guns; Spier and Sapir horses and blankets). Perkins notes
distributions of dentalia and rush mats not mentioned by Spier and Sapir.

The two accounts augment and do not contradict each other—a correspon-
dence that suggests close attention and objectivity on the part of each observer.
Note, for instance, the similarity between the pronouncements of the speakers.
In Perkins:

> Hear ye earth, water, & fire; ye heavens, sun moon and stars; ye clouds,
> & trees, & rocks, & all creatures in air, earth, & sea (naming over the
> things of the animate & inanimate creation in regular order), and all ye
> people, old men & old women, young men & maidens, & ye children this
> name.

And in Spier and Sapir:

> We want the mountains, the rivers, the creeks, the bluffs, the timber to
> know that this man or woman is now named so and so. . . . We want to let
> the fishes, the birds, the winds, snow and rain, the sun moon and stars
> know that so and so has become as though alive again.[3]

A most interesting aspect of the Feast of the Naming, and one that ties it closely
to Northwest Coast practices, is the attention paid to feasting and gift giving.
A "grand feast" and gift giving were characteristically associated with all rites
of passage (and certain other occasions as well) in aboriginal coastal cultures.
In its developed form, among the wealthier coastal peoples, of course, that gift
giving was the potlatch. Among poorer and less complex peoples of the
interior it was expressed differently. The Upper Chinookans, as peripheral
members of the coastal province, emphasized the gift-giving aspect in their
ritual behavior more strongly than did their neighbors to the east.

Perkins implies that it took some time to collect the wealth and resources
that were necessary for a successful naming. That was very true of north coast
potlatches. He notes that the speaker was paid for his services with dentalia,

which was also distributed to the audience. That suggests that the audience was being paid as well—probably on the coastal model, for their attendance and recognition of the new name. Perkins's statement that presents were given "to each according to their dignity" is pregnant with meaning for Northwest Coast ethnologists. A hallmark of the North Coast potlatch was that guests were seated and gifts distributed according to a strict order of ranking. That was another form of social recognition, but for the audience, not the person for whom the celebration was being held.[4] The ripping apart of an elk hide and distribution of the pieces has its equivalent on the North Coast in the (postcontact) shredding of Hudson's Bay Company blankets as a part of the potlatch ceremony. All that is not to say that the Wascopam people were potlatching. Their ceremonies merely included many elements that, elsewhere, were consolidated and developed into a more complex ceremonial. The most comprehensive discussion of the basic elements of North Coast potlatching is still Homer Barnett's "The Nature of the Potlatch" (1938); for a summary of the various theories on the potlatch see Suttles and Jonaitis (1990).

Today, among the amalgamated Upper Chinook–Sahaptin peoples of Warm Springs and Yakama, the basic segments of the naming ceremony persist, though they have changed in relative importance. At Warm Springs in the 1950s, feasting, gift giving, and requesting gifts still occurred, but the only important segment was "Pronouncing the Name." That segment, moreover, might be factored out and combined with other ceremonies (K. French 1955:115–16). Also important in recent times on both reservations is the ceremony called in English the "baby trade." The crux of that ceremony is the exchange of goods between the families of the father and mother. The similarity in form of baby trades to wedding trades (described below), plus the silence of the ethnohistoric sources on ceremonial exchanges in the early years of life raises the possibility that they are an innovation, or elaborations of small family affairs originally restricted to Sahaptins (Kathrine French, personal communication, 1989–93).

### Feast of the Boring

In the case of the ear-piercing rite, the Feast of the Boring (Appendix 1, Doc. 5, entry for Dec. 10, 1843),[5] the ethnographic sources are fuller than Perkins's account. Spier and Sapir discuss the ceremony among the Wishram (1930:261); Boas treats the Kathlamet version (1894:242); and Curtis has two sentences on the rite among the Yakamas (1911b:9).

Spier and Sapir's account of the rite is the most complete. The three main sources agree that the rite was practiced for both boys and girls; they differ as to time (Spier and Sapir say when "a few years old"; Perkins says "generally during the first year"; Boas reports that the Kathlamet performed it twice, at one month and at one year). Spier and Sapir indicate that the father's father was host; among the Kathlamet it was the father. The practitioner was an elder male or female adept, according to Spier and Sapir; an old woman "juggler," according to Perkins; and a man with the requisite spirit power among the Kathlamet. Spier and Sapir have the baby on an elk skin; Perkins reports it bound to a cradleboard. Perkins is the only one who mentions perforation of the nasal septum; Spier and Sapir note that both the ear lobes and the auricle were bored; the number of holes gave prestige, with five (the ritual number) preferred; the Kathlamet drilled two holes in the first ceremony and five in the second. Perkins is the only one who mentions the tool, a bone needle (Spier and Sapir say the instrument was unknown); Spier and Sapir report a sinew loop inserted in the new hole and note singing and dancing by the audience; among the Kathlamet, according to Boas, there was dancing only. Payment went to the practitioner, according to Spier and Sapir, but to the practitioner and the audience among the Kathlamet, according to Boas. Gifts are mentioned in both of the more recent accounts.

Curtis has several photos of Wishram men and women with pierced nasal septa, always with a small dentalium through the hole. Dentalia nose ornaments conferred status: Curtis says "anybody without it 'looked like a slave'" (1911a:93). Earrings, like nose ornaments, might be made of dentalia shells. Both the Cayuses and the Nez Perces also perforated the nasal septum (Theodore Stern, personal communication, 1982).

Even in Perkins's time, that rite was "fast being laid aside." In the early twentieth century it was not practiced at all for boys (Spier and Sapir 1930:261), and by midcentury it survived among girls as single-hole piercing with "no ceremony and no significance attached to the event" (K. French 1955:44; see also Schuster 1975:104).

## Marriage

Perkins does not give a description of Upper Chinookan marriage ceremonies. But there are two excellent detailed manuscript accounts, by Henry Brewer and Alvan Waller, of a single wedding, performed at Kowelapse on December 18, 1846. Brewer's account, up to the final stages of the ceremony, is reprinted below. The last few lines are from Waller. An abridged version of Brewer appears in a letter of January 1, 1847 (Western Americana Collection) and in Mudge (1854:28–30).

### An Indian Marriage
It is customary among the Indian tribes at the time of the marriage ceremony to exchange property as a formal binding contract. The

bridegroom & his friends on their part usually present horses, the more wealthy as high as fifteen or twenty horses; whereas those in more moderate circumstances will give ten, five or as low as two. The Bride & her friends on their part in return present, clothing, food (salmon usually), tin ware, beads, shells trinkets etc. When a young man is about to be married they give us to understand that he does not purchase his wife in the light of a bargain, but only exchange property to ratify the engagement. We had frequently witnessed some parts of their marriage ceremonies but never witnessed a ceremony through until the following.

Joseph the young man who had lived in Mr. P[erkin]s' family, gave us a friendly invitation to his marriage. Accordingly we went accompanied by mr W[aller]. to a village three miles below. The ceremony was commenced by the bridegroom & his friends taking five horses, (in this instance) to the door of the father of the bride & tying them. This was the signal that the bridegroom & his friends were ready to commence the ceremony. And now the bride & her mother commenced looking over their beads, shells etc. And after some time had elapsed, a fathom of large beads was handed to an old man 'the crier' who tied one end to a stick & held it up in the air & the other end he held in his hand & then as he went to the house of the Bridegroom he mumbled or uttered a certain something indistinctly, though we understood him to mean, Look here! this is given in exchange for one of the horses (it was not expected I presume an equivalent or full value of the horses in return, though beads & shells are considered as their money & upon which they place a high estimate.[)] in like manner for the next horse they gave a fathom of Clameth shells. the crier proceeding as before & uttering the same sounds, & so on for a third horse a fathom of Iroquois [*sic:* hiaqua] shells, in this way all of the horses were soon disposed of.

In the next place a number of young women (Wassenes) [*sic:* probably Sahaptin *wapsíni* = "unmarried woman"] perhaps fifteen in number arranged themselves in order three in a row with each a tin plate or some article of tin ware, each row connecting themselves together with a string of beads, in this manner they marched to the bridegroom's house, chanting as they went, & entered and deposited what they brought, & in return they received some small article handkerchifs, a piece of buck skin etc which they appropriated to their own use. The next in order is the combing, the young man having previously prepared himself with elk & beef tallow & also combs. his mother & an assistant proceeded to the brides house & commenced greasing & combing her head unmercifully, a short time however answered when the combs were left in her hair & the tallow presented to her mother & they return, she having the privilige of distributing the tallow among her female friends. The next business is the feast, his friends followed him to the bride's house where he took his seat on a mat at her right hand, & his friends surround him in a circle

all seating themselves on mats on the ground as this is the common way
of sitting for all indian tribes. The bride now went to a vessel where she
had previously prepared a large quantity of dried pounded salmon &
cammas roots mixed together with salmon oil to suit the taste, & served
this up on small mats made for the occasion to the friends of the bridegroom only. After eating what they chose they took the mats & what
remained thereon & returned home. . . . Mr. W. & myself not being fond
of such food, they gave us some Indian bread, made from Cous a kind of
root pounded & dried in the sun. this we were pleased to call our wedding
cake. [H. Brewer, letter of Jan. 1, 1847, Western Americana Collection]
During the repast (water for drink suplying the place of wine) the young
man pulled off his shirt and gave it to one of his friends sitting near. In
some cases the bride groom is striped entirely naked probably would have
been in this case if we had not been present. This I suppose may signify
that he now forsakes Father, Mother and friends and cleaves to his wife.
Some part of his clothing is sometimes returned. Supper over conversation was entered upon. The ceremony for the day considered ended. . . .
On the way home we met the step-father of the young man and learned
that he had been out to cut dry wood which the friends of the bride-groom
were on the next day to carry to the house of the friends of the bride and
have the second part of the wedding, eat and drink etc. I did not go to see
what was done. After marriage the bride in most cases remains at home
with her friends one year where her husband also resides, and according
to custom is not expected to have any particular business but to comfort
and see to his wife. Is not this a little Jewish? [Waller, letter of Feb. 3,
1847, Archives of the Pacific Northwest Conference]

There are a few significant differences between the Brewer and Waller
accounts. Brewer's is generally more complete, until the final stages, but
Waller includes two elements that Brewer omits. First, previous to the greasing
and combing of the bride's hair, Waller noted that her attendants "break a
string of beads and cast them on her head." Second is the removal of the
groom's clothing.

Brewer and Waller did not witness events following the feast. What
happened after that time is most fully reported in Spier and Sapir:

The youth now remained with his bride's family. After a few weeks
they took baskets, food, horses, etc. and with the girl's relations went to
the groom's former home. The bride's mother spread a blanket for the girl
to stand on. They then poured baskets of beads, pouches, etc., over the girl
as she stood before the house. The groom's family appropriated these.
She sat down and her mother-in-law removed her finery. In its stead she
draped blankets, shawls, and lengths of cloth over the bride, which the
latter's female relatives then removed.

Then food was placed for the visitors to eat. The groom's family gave presents to the bride's to carry away with them. The bride's people went out to where they had left their packs and made a pile of things for the groom's relatives. The bride's relatives then returned home, leaving the couple in residence with the groom's family.

After an appointed interval, only a week if they wished to hurry the affair, the couple and the groom's relatives again visited the bride's. Again there was the exchange of presents and feasting. Finally, after a brief time the couple were taken in the same fashion to the groom's home, which was to be their permanent residence. [1930:219]

The two standard ethnographic accounts of Upper Chinookan marriages, both collected from informants in the early twentieth century, are Spier and Sapir's "Wishram Ethnography" (1930:218-19) and Curtis's "The Chinookan Tribes" (1911a:90). An "Indian Marriage Ceremony" from Yakama, probably dating from the 1870s, is described in Kuykendall's "Indian Traditions, Legends, Superstitions" (1973). Contemporary Warm Springs and Yakama wedding ceremonies are detailed in K. French's and Schuster's dissertations (K. French 1955:73-89; Schuster 1975:452-60).

The modern wedding trade (papšx$^w$ít in Yakama Sahaptin) is an extremely important life-cycle ceremony and (in its more elaborate manifestations) is quite similar to the Kowelapse marriage reported by Brewer and Waller. Without going into great detail, a summary of the major ceremonial segments observed by Kathrine French at Warm Springs in the fifties and by Helen Schuster at Yakama in the seventies is instructive. In both cases there was initial property exchange (sometimes with a "messenger"; combing and greasing of the bride's hair (sometimes with trinkets poured over her); "dressing the bride" with clothes then taken by the groom's family; an exchange of goods between families as groups (sometimes with the bride's relations connected by strings of beads); and final feasting (by either side).

On the whole, the major elements of the aboriginal ceremony have been preserved. But that does not mean that recent ceremonies preserve the exact form of the Brewer-Waller account. In fact, there is considerable variation from one marriage to another. As K. French has pointed out, "ceremonial segments" exist as discrete units and can be omitted, moved around, and combined in different ways. In particular weddings, both the format (order of presentation of segments) and elaborateness (number of segments) may be quite different. What is true today was likely true in the past as well: the Kowelapse wedding involved well-to-do families; most early-nineteenth-century weddings were probably much simpler.

That individual variation makes it difficult to propose hypotheses about change, other than what seems logical and obvious. Certainly there has been a change in type of goods exchanged (horses and dentalia are rare), and some simplification in ritual has occurred (paid intermediaries and greasing the bride's hair are rare). But on the whole the continuity is impressive.

Back and forth, back and forth. What that ritual (particularly in its aboriginal form) emphasizes most strongly is gift exchange between two families that would, in later years, remain bonded both socially and economically. The marriage ritual was not, as both Brewer and Spier and Sapir point out, bride purchase but an "exchange [of] property to ratify the engagement" (H. Brewer, letter of Jan. 1, 1847, Western Americana Collection). Economic gain was not a motive, for (as Perkins states) there was "a pretty equal exchange of property between the parties contracting." Bonding, social and economic, was more to the point. According to Spier and Sapir, "Formal visiting did not end with marriage. The effort of the two families was directed toward maintaining friendly relations by visiting, feasting, and exchanging gifts" (1930:270). The social ties of the in-laws (affines) would persist and be constantly reinforced by economic exchanges.

Economics, in fact, underlies most of the marital-union variations mentioned by Perkins (Appendix 1, Doc. 5, entry for Aug. 19, 1843) and Spier and Sapir (1930:217-20). Perkins's discussions of polygyny, sororal polygyny, and child betrothals indicate that he understood the economic basis of those customs, even though he found it difficult to reconcile them with Christian morality.

"O this polygamy!" Perkins mentions the custom (specifically polygyny, or one husband with many wives) several times, usually in a disapproving tone. The first passage, however, dating from a letter of spring 1839, shows bemusement with the practice.

> After meeting [at Clemiaksuc] Sleguahan got up and said he wanted another wife,—that he spoke to you [Daniel Lee] about it last winter,—and you said you would see about it when you came back—that he had waited a long time,—that you had passed in the night,—that he did not see you, and that he wanted another wife very, very much! etc. I was utterly astonished at the man, and at you too, if ever you put him off as he says you did, with a promise to attend to it when you came back. The way he seems to have understood you was that when you returned, you would provide him with one!

That was most likely a misunderstanding, because Perkins's next statement on the subject (fall 1839; see Appendix 1, Doc. 2) emphasizes that they had "taught that Christianity allowed but one wife to each man." It is clear, however, that neither Perkins nor Lee took any steps to enforce monogamy. The custom was bound up too tightly with the aboriginal social system. Which wives would be dismissed, and how would they and their children be supported, to say nothing of possible antagonism of the husband? "For a time we had to let things be, only stipulating that if a man had one wife, he should take no other during her lifetime." Polygyny persisted into the reservation period.

Polygyny was a preferred and prestigious mode of marriage throughout the aboriginal Pacific Northwest. Usually, of course, due to the restrictions of the sex ratio, only a few wealthy and high-ranking males were able to have more than one wife. The outlay required to espouse a high-ranking wife or multiple wives may have eliminated most men from the running, but for those who could afford it, it brought multiple benefits. In comparison to social prestige and economic factors, sexual advantages paled. Plural wives were a visible sign of wealth, and wives were producers, whose contributions in the economic division of labor were significant indeed (see chap. 4). More important, however, was the fact that, in the marital union, a man bonded with not just one other person, but with a whole family. Multiple wives brought more ties with more families and increased one's social and political network. More family ties brought more economic benefits, in the forms of ongoing affinal gifting and preferred access to economic resources.

Examples of polygynous husbands in The Dalles area include Skookum, the warrior and aspiring successor to Tilki at Wishram in 1836, who had five wives (Townsend 1839:249); Yacooetar, chief at Wascopam, who had two and "put one away" (Mudge 1854:38), and Kis–kis, the warrior killed at Klamath, who had two families, at Wascopam and at Wishram, and had just married a new wife. Matches made with families from other villages or ethnolinguistic groups, such as those of Kis–kis, were especially auspicious, for they extended the husband's network of influence considerably. The "great chief" Concomly, of the lower Chinook, made a fine art of that marital diplomacy, having wives from neighboring and upriver Chinookan villages and peoples (Chehalis) as well.

Perkins notes (Appendix 1, Doc. 5, entry for Aug. 19, 1843) that a man might marry sisters, or even take a child bride. Both customs are verified by Spier and Sapir (1930:218). Keeping the alliance and economic functions of marriage in mind, both practices make eminent sense. The anthropological term for the first is *sororal polygyny*. A frequent rationale for that arrangement is that "sisters tend to get along better than unrelated co-wives." Perkins states that jealousy was often a problem in polygynous households (Appendix 1, Doc. 5, entry for Aug. 19, 1843).[6] Spier and Sapir state that boys and girls as young as two might be married to one another and that a man might marry a baby girl. In all child marriages the in-law relationship, with its alliance and economic benefits, began immediately, but the couples did not reside together nor begin sexual relations until both were mature. Perkins's statement *"There are no old maids."* also underlines the nonsexual functions of marriage. Most women past childbearing age had networks of relatives and might be productive workers. Widows apparently did not remain in that status for very long. Upper Chinookans practiced both the levirate, whereby a widow married one of her deceased husband's male relatives, and the sororate, whereby a widower espoused a female relative of his deceased wife. Both of those customs had the effect of keeping the bonds between two families intact.

## Death Customs

### Funerals

There is very little information in the missionary texts on funerals per se. Like most contemporary observers, the Wascopam missionaries were more impressed with the material manifestations of death—cemeteries, graves, and grave goods—and had little to say about the ceremonials that preceded and followed interment. Brewer again is the only source on funerals. The following is from *Sketches of Mission Life.* . . . (Mudge 1854:23; a manuscript version has not been located):

> . . . a most dismal howling, in lamentation for the dead, which often lasts seven days,—the length of time being determined, somewhat, by their regard for the deceased. Women are the chief mourners, and are often hired for this purpose. . . . As soon as the breath leaves the body, the corpse is bound up, by those accustomed to the business, in a blanket, or skin, and the neighbors and friends make presents to the relatives of the deceased, of beads, shells, and sometimes of more valuable articles, depositing them on the corpse. . . . The Dalls Indians carried their deceased to an island in the Columbia River. . . . After the ceremony of placing the corpse in its resting place is over, the immediate friends of the deceased retire to a secluded spot . . . and for a number of days give themselves up to a purifying process, washing and rubbing themselves as if to remove some infection. This done, they are then ready to return to contact with society.

Curtis has the most complete ethnographic description of a funeral (1911a:96–99); there are additional details in Spier and Sapir (1930:270–71). On the first night, the survivors collected in the house of the deceased. At one end was the body, attended by two hired overseers *(iyahihhlihlih [iyak'i'lixlix],* perhaps the same as the Sahaptin *tlchacha kutkutlama [łčača kutkutláma]* named by Perkins); the survivors congregated at the other end, where those who had the same guardian spirit as the deceased sang his spirit song (Yvonne

Hajda, personal communication, 1988-93). The overseers (according to Kuykendall 1889:93, individuals "who have the tlchachie [ghost] spirit") had the power to hear the ghost, who might make specific requests. They washed the body, wrapped it in a skin, and lashed it to a plank. On the second day, the ghost became restless, and the overseers sang their own special spirit songs to placate it. While the body lay in state in the middle of the house, "the relatives danced round it in a circle . . . single file." Probably at that time small gifts from the mourners ("sea-fish bone beads, sea-shell beads, round glass beads, and strings of Chinese cash") were tied to the corpse (Spier and Sapir 1930:270). The undertakers then transported the corpse via canoe to the closest "Memaloose island," where they deposited it on the *simas* (bed platform in Umatilla Sahaptin, according to Theodore Stern, from a personal communication, 1982) at one end of the family charnel house, and then left, shutting the door behind them. Mourning continued for five days (more or less, depending on status). It consisted of "Crying aloud from shortly before sunrise until the middle of the morning, ceasing then for about an hour, and wailing again until mid-afternoon, when [the mourners] washed their faces and ate" (Curtis 1911a:99). All the mourners cut their hair short. According to Spier and Sapir, the five days of wailing were succeeded by five days of sweating, to cleanse and purify the bodies of the survivors of pollution (1930:270).

On December 17, 1839, in the midst of the "Great Revival," Daniel Lee, Benjamin Wright, and Tumsowit began their mission to Claticut. That was the day after the death of a (probably influential) man, and "half the village was in mourning." In the days that followed, Perkins said, "mourning for the dead was taken up in mourning for themselves, as sinners" (Appendix 1, Doc. 3). If Perkins is correct, Lee and company took advantage of the ritualized transition period that was mourning and, consciously or serendipitously, manipulated it to serve their own ends. But the evidence can be interpreted variously. It is by no means clear whether the "cries of mercy," "pouring out of souls," and "repenting" that the missionaries perceived did in fact represent a "birth of the spirit," or simply the culturally patterned fashion of expressing grief over a death. Perhaps it was both. Regardless, when the Claticut Mission was completed, Lee and his coworkers had "joined nearly one hundred in society."

## Burial

Again, there is impressive continuity between aboriginal and recent burial practices. In the mid 1950s, undertakers, funeral songs, ritualized mourning, grave goods, and sweat-bathing persisted. Burial was in a coffin, however, and interment rites were from the contemporary *Wáašat* religion (K. French 1955:61-65). The elements that have disappeared from the present ceremony (burial in charnel houses on islands, loud public wailing) appear to be those that were most at odds with Christian practices.

Perkins (Appendix 1, Doc. 5, entry for Dec. 23, 1843) gives a particularly coherent and complete account of burial practices, the best in the literature, both ethnohistorical and ethnographic. He prefaces his discussion with the remarkable admission, for a missionary, that he considers the native "way of interring . . . on the whole . . . very good." The reasons he gives are practical: wood was scarce and coffins were hard to come by. Others at the mission were not so tolerant. The discussion of burial islands in *Sketches of Mission Life . . .* (which presumably related the opinion of Henry Brewer, but may in fact be that of his editor, Zachariah Mudge) includes the following statement:

> The aspect of this place is truly dismal, and speaks mournfully of the necessity of the correcting influence of the gospel, by which the dead might be laid beneath the ground, in hope of a glorious resurrection. [1854:23]

To round out the argument, from George Gary:

> The Indians think our way of burying the dead is very unfeeling; we do not clothe the bodies sufficiently; we do not furnish them with sufficient supplies for the various emergencies of their future state etc. etc. [1923:169]

Perkins states that there were three burial islands in the vicinity of Wascopam. Those included Lower Memaloose Island (Lewis and Clark's Sepulchre Island), just downstream from the mouth of the Klickitat, which apparently served the Chilluckitequaw villages (Scaltape, Nenootletete, Clemiaksuc, and Claticut); Grave Island, three miles upstream from Wascopam, the probable cemetery of the south-bank (Wasco) Upper Chinookans; and Upper Memaloose Island, three miles up from Wishram, which likely housed the dead of the north-bank Upper Chinookans (Wishram). *Memaloose* means "dead" in Chinook Jargon. Grave Island and Upper Memaloose were submerged under the waters of The Dalles Dam in 1957; the last of the remains from Upper Memaloose were removed prior to inundation (Sprague 1967: 141).

The standard ethnographic source (Spier and Sapir 1930:270-71) is, relatively speaking, not very good, and is derivative on burial customs. The best sources other than Perkins are also historical and include Farnham (1843), Applegate (1914), Gary (1923), and Kuykendall (1973, 1889). Lewis and Clark, usually a good source, describe vault burials at The Cascades in some detail but have only a few notes from a visit to Lower Memaloose and say nothing about the other two burial islands. Farnham and Gary, like Perkins, describe Grave Island; Applegate and Kuykendall discuss Upper Memaloose. Farnham's account is dated October 15, 1839:

> Mr. [Daniel] Lee pointed to . . . the "Island of the tombs." . . . We climbed up a precipice of black shining rocks 200 feet; and winding among drifts of sand the distance of 100 yards, came to the tombs. They consisted of boxes 10 or 12 feet square on the ground, 8 or 10 high, made of cedar boards fastened to a rough frame, in an upright position at the sides, and horizontally over the top. On them and about them were the cooking utensils and other personal property of the deceased. Within were the dead bodies, wrapped in many thicknesses of deer and elk skins, tightly lashed with leather thongs and laid in a pile with their heads to the east.[7] Underneath the decayed bodies were many bones from which the flesh and wrappings had fallen; in some instances a number of wagon loads. Three or four of the tombs had gone to ruins; and the skulls and other bones lay strewn on the ground. The skulls were all flattened. I picked up one with the intention of bringing it to the States. But as Mr. L. assured me that the high veneration of the living for the dead would make the attempt very dangerous, I reluctantly returned it. [Farnham 1843:88–89]

The only significant difference between Perkins's and Farnham's accounts is that the latter has "cooking utensils and other personal property" atop and around the vaults. Four years later, Perkins mentions that "formerly . . . valuables" including "guns, bow & arrows kettles, axes . . . were all wrapped together with the body but this is now very much laid aside." George Gary, in 1844, adds the information that "these are family sepulchers . . . kept in some sort of repair from generation to generation" (1923:169). Curtis maintains that before "about the year 1840" Wishram's "house of the dead was on the bluff behind the village," but that "because the bodies were being stripped of valuables" (presumably by Whites, though that is not stated) it was moved to Upper Memaloose Island (1911a:99). That may explain why there are no descriptions of Upper Memaloose predating 1843. The move may be related to the termination of placement of valuables around burial houses on Grave Island, noted by Perkins, above.

George Kuykendall was a physician at the Yakama Reservation between 1872 and 1882 and wrote the chapter on Indian religion and mythology for Elwood Evans's *History of the Pacific Northwest* (Kuykendall 1889). His account of mortuary customs not only includes a description of Upper Memaloose, but the best supplementary data on the specialist who handled corpses and secondary burial.

> Islands in the Columbia were favorite burial places, being more out of the reach of coyotes and other wild animals. . . . The Indians deposited their

dead in houses built of bark or cedar boards. The corpse was lashed to a post or board in an inclined position until the fluids had drained away and finally it was placed horizontally. . . . The bones were well wrapped up, and carefully placed on platforms elevated about two feet. The remains of families were placed side by side, with heads to the west. . . . The "dead-houses" were covered over and shut in with care. . . . Some of the Chinooks used to put dead infants in quiet, still pools of water. (Kuykendall 1889:92, 94; reordered for clarity)

Applegate also noted bodies floating in a pool and added data on grave images, which are otherwise mentioned only by Spier and Sapir. The date for the following quotation is November 1843.

The islands known as "Mimaluse" connected with the main land on the north shore when the river is low. We passed a pond or small lake on which were floating many rafts made of logs on which were dozens of dead bodies rolled in blankets or Klisques ["mats" in Chinook Jargon] mats. . . . I came to a pen built of logs and in this were bodies rolled up like those on the rafts. . . . Near the pen stood . . . a little old black man. . . . Others who passed that way across the island said they saw dead bodies everywhere on rocks, on rafts, in old broken canoes, and these little wooden devils were legion. Someone said they were put there to protect the dead, a sort of scarecrow. . . . Mimaluse island was the Golgotha of the Waskopum tribe. [Applegate 1914:52-53]

Kuykendall comments on corpse handlers:

The work of handling the corpses or bones was done by one man, who had received the tamanowash spirit or power, from the ghosts. He was called "thchach–au koot–koot–tla," turner of the bones of the dead. This old man, for he was usually past middle life, was well paid for these services. While working about the graves or corpses, he pretended to hold communications with the dead, and was heard talking, apparently asking or answering questions. [1889:93]

The term "thchach–au koot–koot–tla" is, of course, akin to Perkins's "tlchacha kutkutlama." It translates in Sahaptin as follows: *łčača* = ghost; *kutkut* = work; *la* = agent; and *ma* = plural (Eugene Hunn, personal communication, 1982-93). Perkins says that specialist's "express business is to bury the dead"; he also apparently was the one who cleaned and rewrapped the bones in secondary burial. The Kiksht term is *iyak'i'łixłíx* (*iyahihhlihlih* in Spier and Sapir 1930; *klak–i–kli–kli* according to Kuykendall 1973:27). People who had a special guardian spirit power qualifying them to prepare and dispose of the bodies of the dead are known from other Northwest Coast cultures. For the Skagits, June Collins reports that the guardian spirit for the native undertaker was *s.kayú*? (akin to Perkins's "skep," Appendix 1, Doc. 5, entry for Aug. 26, 1843) 'the skeleton spirit' (1974:233).

Kuykendall's description of secondary burial, assembled from his manuscript and published accounts, corroborates Perkins:

> The Indians about the Cascades and down to Vancouver used to go in the fall when the fishing season was over in canoes up to the islands where their "dead houses" were to re clothe the dead. [1973:27]
>
> On arriving, in the morning, at the place of sepulture, the Indians sat off at a little distance, and gave directions as to the reclothing of their dead friends. . . . The custom was to scrape off all the decayed animal matter from the bones of the dead, and then to wrap them in blankets, or robes made of the skin of wild animals, putting in such articles as moccasins, knives, beads, pipes, and red pigments for painting the face, etc. . . . The old klaky-kle-kles, or persons who work among the bones of the dead, say they can hear very distinctly the voices of those recently buried. After some time, the sounds are less distinct; and the voices sound as if the spirits were talking "through their noses." Later on, when the body has nearly crumbled to dust, the tones get down to faint whispers; and when the last vestige of the bones and body are gone, the voices cease entirely. [1889:93-94]
>
> Sometimes they redressed the dead each year sometimes only every two three or four years. . . . The putting on of new blankets and garments was appreciated by the departed spirit—it really added to his comfort and respectability in the spirit land. . . . [Eventually] the bones were gathered together into ossuaries. [1973:3-4]

Spier and Sapir state that "bodies were not reburied" (1930:271). That is clearly wrong, as Perkins, Kuykendall, and Curtis (1911a:99) all verify the practice. Lucullus McWhorter's manuscript "Second Sight of Wal-a-musk-kee" (n.d.: file 1514), dating from 1918, describes the duties of a Yakama corpse handler.

The predominant form of burial among Sahaptin-speaking peoples in historic times was interment in talus (rock-slide) slopes (Ray 1942:217-18). The location of Perkins's talus burial—eight miles above Wascopam—would be in the neighborhood of Brown's Island at the Short Narrows. There are no known surviving burial sites in the region, only now-submerged petroglyphs on the island itself.

Several talus burials are described in two archaeological studies, one from The Dalles (Caldwell 1956) and one from Miller's Island, upstream from Celilo (Strong, Schenck, and Steward 1930:16-25). Burial number 17 from

Miller is described below:

> ... directly behind and about 500 m. distant from village [132 housepits].
> For perhaps 250 m along the cliff, beyond the talus slope, were fragments
> of human bones and artifacts uncovered from the sand by the wind. ...
> Several graves were marked by ... irregular piles of basalt fragments. ...
> Burial 17. ... The north and east sides at least were bounded by split
> boards badly decayed. The floor also seems to have been covered with
> boards over which tule matting was apparently spread. Another layer of
> boards ... had apparently been placed over the corpse. Bodies: number
> indeterminate ... one adult skull. ... One, possibly two, children. ...
> Artifacts ... [included] 138 copper beads ... 140 shell beads. [Strong,
> Schenck, and Steward 1930:23]

Some graves from The Dalles were still, in 1930, "marked by wooden staves."

Grave goods were usual on the Northwest Coast. Perkins mentions grave
goods in two contexts. First, inside the corpse's wrappings were two classes
of goods: the deceased's own "best" clothing, in which he was dressed, and
"all kinds of trinkets" (including "beads, shells, copper & brass coins, knives,
spoons"). Those "trinkets" apparently correspond to the "gifts" tied to the
corpse by mourners at the funeral. Second, "wrapped together" or (more
likely) "laid with the corpse" was "property" (including "guns, bow & arrows,
kettles, axes"). On the model of lower Columbia grave goods, this class
included the most personal, gender-specific possessions of the deceased, those
that would accompany the body to the afterlife. Those were also the items that
were routinely "killed"—usually by punching a hole through them. "Killing"
had the dual functions of symbolically making the goods "dead," like the
owner, and rendering them useless to the living, thus discouraging grave
robbers.

That duality of grave goods appears to have been usual throughout the
Chinookan area. On the lower Columbia, bodies were generally deposited in
raised canoes, but the grave goods were broadly equivalent. At the mouth of
the Cowlitz, in March 1847, Paul Kane examined a canoe burial:

> I found it lavishly decorated with numerous articles, of supposed utility
> and ornament, for the convenience of the defunct in the journey to the
> world of the spirits. These articles consisted of blankets, tin cups, pots,
> pans, kettles, plates, baskets, horn bowls, and spoons, with shreds of cloth
> of various colours. ... All the articles appended to it were rendered
> useless for this world by either tearing, breaking, or boring holes in
> them. ... On examining the interior I found a great number of ioquas and
> other shells, together with beads and rings: even the mouth of the
> deceased was filled with these articles. [1859:139]

That particular canoe also had "a bow and arrow, paddle, spear," and a digging stick inside it.

On the lower Columbia, as the above quotation indicates, "killed" property might be affixed (nailed) to the canoe, hung from it, laid atop it, or suspended from poles around it. Grave poles, with or without affixed grave goods, appear in several paintings and sketches of Chinookan canoe burials and Kalapuya graves from the lower Columbia. From Grave Island, Perkins notes "a small pole" with a "strip of scarlet cloth" (Appendix 1, Doc. 5). Grave poles are known archaeologically from The Dalles, but none of those upriver examples have grave goods attached. Given the wide distribution of grave poles, Perkins's theory that they were "introduced by the traders" is probably incorrect.

Richer individuals might have much more elaborate grave goods. Perkins notes that horses might be interred with their owners; that practice is verified by Lewis and Clark, who observed it upstream, at a communal vault on Blalock Island (in Sahaptin territory) in October 1805:

> We also Saw the Skeletons of Several Horses at the vault & great number of bones about it, which Convinced me that those animals were Sacrefised as well as the above articles to the Deceased. [1988:312]

A late description of a horse burial is included in Kuykendall's (1887) "Death of the Wisham Chief's Daughter." Horses would, of course, be more likely to be found in Sahaptin burial sites, because they were more common and more culturally important among that people than they were among Chinookans.

Slaves, on the other hand, were infrequent among the Sahaptins, although general among the Chinookans. Interment of slaves with their masters is reported for the lower Chinook (D. Lee and Frost 1844:233) and Upper Chinookans (Curtis 1911a:99). Perkins, in fact, rescued a slave boy from a grave in August(?) 1844. The incident is reported in a letter of Mrs. Perkins (Sept. 1, 1844, Canse Collection), in George Gary's diary (Archives of the Pacific Northwest Conference), by Brewer (Mudge 1854), and, most dramatically, in Allen's *Ten Years in Oregon* (1850). George Gary gives the most detached and probably reliable account of the incident:

> A man lost his son; this man had a slave of perhaps ten years of age; this son formerly thought much of this slave and now his father determined this boy must be buried with the body of his deceased son . . . to wait on him. . . . They bury their dead in boxes above ground. . . . The box is large and holds many bodies. . . . The living boy's feet were tied together at the ankles; his hands also at the wrists . . . the boy was put onto many old corpses . . . face downward and then the dead body put onto him. In this condition he spent one night. . . . The dead body put onto him was but

larger than his own . . . during his dreadful night, he squirmed about so that he rolled the dead body off him, or he probably would have died before morning. . . . Br. Perkins by purchasing the slave with . . . three blankets and a shirt . . . saved the little fellow from the sepulchre of death; here he is at Br. Perkins', ankles and wrists very sore from the efforts he made to break loose from the bonds of death. [1923:166–67, 169 (entries for Sept. 8 and 12, reordered for clarity)]

Additional details are as follows, assembled from the four sources. The slave owner was a wealthy Klickitat, Siminese. His son had died (probably) from the whooping cough, which was prevalent on the Columbia in the summer of 1844 (see chap. 7). The Perkinses were informed of the burial by the influential Wasco Yacooetar ("Equator") and paid a professional undertaker to retrieve the slave. The boy was taken into the Perkins household and named (apparently by Mrs. Perkins) Ransom.

When a slave died of natural causes, he was denied all funeral and burial privileges. That was consistent with the status of nonperson—the property of someone else, without any social standing or relatives in the local community. Slaves were left to die untended, a fact that was recorded by many observers besides Perkins. According to Alvan Waller on August 19, 1842: "When they die [they] are cast out among the bushes without burial, and are generally devoured by wild beasts. . . . Slaves are not considered tillicum, that is, people, but dogs" (Waller 1843). Brewer (in Mudge 1854:25, 44) records two instances of exposure and abandonment. His melodramatic manuscript account of the second, which occurred on September 8, 1844, shortly after the Ransom incident, follows:

Picture to yourself a poor Clameth or Shasty slave a girl of perhaps 16 years of age, away from her home & friends in a land of strangers, among those who care but little for her, and after living here months, perhaps years she is taken sick and then her master mistress and all leave her alone to die, without food without clothing—the stones were her bed, no one near to hear her cries—nothing, save the swift running Columbia as it rolled and whirred at her feet unless perchance a raven in her flight or a wolf may be drawn near by her moans and cries—she died, the stones were her grave, naught covered her body save the veil of darkness, which was drawn over once in twenty four hours. This dear brother was the sight that made my heart bleed and I pray God I may never see another of the like. . . .

[September 9:] I proposed to bury the body . . . but it was more than our olfactories could endure. [H. Brewer, letter of Sept. 24, 1844, Canse Collection]

Property, beyond the personal possessions that were "killed" and placed near the corpse, was distributed among the male blood relatives of the deceased. In the case reported by Perkins (Appendix 1, Doc. 5, entry for Dec. 24, 1843), a man died and his property went to his brothers, leaving his wife and children without; Lee and Frost (1844:165) mention the case of a man who attempted to get his deceased sister's property from her widower. That system, of course, makes sense in a society with a bias to the male line, as was the case throughout the southern Northwest Coast. But it was very hard for immigrant Whites to understand (see also chap. 8).

# 6

## Ritual Behavior:
## Spirit Beliefs and Ceremonies

### Cosmogony and Spirits

At the time of the missionaries' arrival at Wascopam, Perkins says (Appendix 1, Doc. 2), the Indians had "no knowledge whatever of the idea of a universal Father of the human race who made and loved them." In terms of the purely aboriginal belief system that statement is true: Northwest native religions had no concept of a high, omnipotent god responsible for creation, but believed instead in a multiplicity of nature spirits. In terms of postcontact belief systems, however, Perkins's statement is not completely accurate. By the early nineteenth century an amorphous concept of "The Great Chief Above" (*sáxali tayí* in Chinook Jargon) had already worked its way into the belief system (see chap. 9).

A very important actor in aboriginal mythology, associated with several specific acts of creation, was Coyote (Perkins's "common prairie wolf," or "Talipaz").[1] Coyote was the most prominent of a cast of hundreds of anthropomorphized animal characters and nature spirits whose activities during the ill-defined Myth Age were described in the native mythology. Coyote should not be thought of as a god in the Old World, theistic sense; neither was he a true creator, though he, more than any other spirit, tended to be associated with the creation of various phenomena in the mythology and the "creation of order out of disorder" (Yvonne Hajda, personal communication, 1988-93). According to anthropological folklorist Melville Jacobs, "Indians' economic activities, handicrafts, and customs were announced by Myth-Age actors . . . and in only a few instances were causally determined by them" (1960:x). Coyote's experiences during the Myth Age were often the subject of a connected cycle of myths not unlike that of Reynard the Fox or Bre'r Rabbit in European and African American folklore.

Jacobs states (for Clackamas Chinookan mythology, essentially the same as that of The Dalles Chinookans) that each Myth Age actor had a specific personality, prototypical of character types that were well known to all Indians. Coyote most often represented "an audacious and sadistic adolescent"; he might also "stand for a well-to-do village leader who concerns himself with the peoples' welfare" (1960:x). Kuykendall's summary of Coyote's character as expressed in Sahaptin–Upper Chinookan mythology, though marred by a few ethnocentrisms, is particularly eloquent nevertheless:

> He traveled over the earth, met and subjugated the monsters, demons and tyrant gods that were destroying the people. He always was the friend of the Indian and an enemy of their foes. While he is represented in their myths as performing wonderful and supernatural things . . . such as transforming the face of nature, changing living beings into stone, transforming himself into a feather, a little mewling baby, or anything that might forward his purposes . . . he often found himself outwitted and circumvented even by some small and insignificant animal, and is spoken of as doing the most ridiculous and absurd things, and getting into predicaments of the most painful or ludicrous nature. . . . He is represented as being very acute and cunning, and as resorting to all sorts of stratagems, fair or unfair, to accomplish his objects. He was sick, hungry and poor at times. . . . He is represented as being interested in games and amusements, and as favoring and ordaining dances, promulgating laws, introducing industrial pursuits, teaching the Indians how to cook food and do various other things for their welfare and happiness. He was angry or amused, and enjoyed a joke or trick, and frequently suffered because of his ignorance or folly. In short, Coyote was a being with the qualities of a real coyote and a live Indian. The Indian's god was, in short, like himself,—full of treachery and deceit, ignorant yet cunning, wise in some respects, yet full of folly and childishness. [1889:64]

Other myth actors were more monodimensional than Coyote: Grizzlies were evil; Blue Jay was crazy; Bear Woman was a "kindly mother," and so on (Jacobs 1960:x).

Chinookan storytelling was, as described by Jacobs and his successor in the study of Chinookan literature, Dell Hymes, an art form. The printed page does not adequately convey the depth of meaning of a literature that was originally transmitted only by word of mouth. Chinookan myths were presented with a terseness and compactness of language, that allowed the listeners to fill in a considerable amount of meaning, both cultural (shared meanings, such as Coyote's personality) and individual (for example, psychological motivations). The "recitalist" (Jacobs's term), if skilled, embellished his stories with vocal modulations, "gestures and mimicry" (Jacobs 1960:x). The tales themselves possessed an internal poetic structure and cadence, preserved in the original language, that has been lost through transcription and translation. Dell Hymes has attempted, with considerable success, to reconstruct the literary form of many Chinookan tales in English (see, e.g., Hymes 1981).

Coyote tales from The Dalles area are very common in the folkloristic literature. From Perkins's time, both Paul Kane and George Gibbs relate Sahaptin Coyote tales (Harper 1971:113-14; Gibbs 1956:140ff.). Several stories collected from the reservation period of the 1870s are reprinted in Kuykendall (1889:64-82, see also 1973). Turn-of-the-century collections made by ethnographers appear in Curtis (1911a:106-54) and Sapir (1909:3-148, 264-73). A large body of Yakama tales collected by Lucullus McWhorter in the first and second decades of the twentieth century was published in 1992 (Hines 1992); a more recent Yakama collection is Virginia Beavert's excellent *The Way It Was: "Anaku Iwacha"* (1974). Jacobs's "Northwest Sahaptin Texts" (1934:54-101) and "Clackamas Chinook Texts" (1958:1-99) contain Coyote tales collected in the 1920s and 1930s. And finally, Jarold Ramsey's 1977 *Coyote Was Going There* includes Coyote stories from various Northwest languages.

In his 1843 journal Perkins discusses (Appendix 1, Doc. 5, entry for Aug. 26) nature spirits in general and their relationships to the beings of the Myth Age and to living men. His gloss "guardian . . . spirit" is a perfectly adequate definition of the (Northwest) Sahaptin word tah (*taax̲*). Curtis defines the Yakama tah as "the guardian spirit, and . . . the supernatural power which it bestows" (1911b:10), and Schuster calls it "a supernatural power" (1975:114). Perkins says tahmas (*taax̲-ma*) is the plural of tah; Curtis gives tahinsh (*taax̲-inš*) as "one who possesses a guardian spirit." The words for *guardian spirit* are different in neighboring languages: in contemporary Columbia Sahaptin the word is *šúhat*; in Upper Chinookan it is *i-yuɫmax̲* (Spier and Sapir 1930:237); in Nez Perce it is *wéyekin* (Walker 1968:18). Tah is related to the Chinook Jargon word tamanawas (the spelling varies), which, as used by White Jargon speakers, has a much broader (and vaguer) definition, inclusive of both guardian spirits and the powers they confer (Gibbs 1956:125-26). Kuykendall says, on tamanawas:

> I have a great many times asked intelligent Indians to explain to me what Tamanowash is and I never have had any illustration except by way of illustrative cases. The old Indian idea is that in everything there is a kind of vital essence or force independent of the material being itself. This force or influence may be communicated to a man, may reside in him or be subject to his bidding or the man may be ruled or dominated by this influence or spirit. . . . Tamanowash is a kind of general term of the invisible force. . . . "Tah" is the special manifestation of Tamanowash in some particular form or shape. [Kuykendall 1973]

Perkins separates the spirit world into two classes: "skep-ma" or "evil geniuses . . . demons," and "tahma," the "spirit[s] of an opposite character . . .

succourers." Despite the fact that other early observers made a similar distinction (Gibbs, in 1865: "According to the Chinooks, every man has a good and a bad tamahnous" [1956:126]; Eells [for Puget Salish]: the "angelic spirits" or tamahnous and "demons" who cause illness [1985:366-67]), it is not likely that Northwest Indians dichotomized the spirit world into two broad categories that could be labeled good and evil. Those characteristics smack of Christianity and were probably superimposed by the observers (Pamela Amoss, personal communication, 1982). The linguistic evidence does suggest strongly that guardian spirits (*taax̱-ma, šúhat, i-yułmax̱, wéyekin,* etc.) were conceptualized by the natives as a special class of spirits. But it is harder to make a case for native recognition of all disease-causing spirits as a class unto themselves. Perkins's "skep-ma" appears to be a term applied to a specific kind of spirit, not all spirits that were capable of causing illness, or that an outsider might consider demons.

The guardian-spirit belief is widespread in native America and universal on the Northwest Coast and Plateau. Ruth Benedict's classic "The Concept of the Guardian Spirit in North America" (1923) draws heavily on Columbia Plateau ethnography for its empirical basis. The "common element" in the guardian-spirit concept, according to Benedict, is that:

> some animal, or voice, or thing appears to the suppliant and talks with him, describing the power bestowed upon him and giving him songs, mementoes, taboos, and perhaps ceremonial procedures, and thereafter remains his life-long protector. [1923:20]

Beyond that, particulars differ. Among the Indians of what are now Oregon and Washington, guardian spirits normally conferred a particular "power" (skill or talent), obtained near puberty in a "spirit quest" and not displayed until the winter ceremonies, when the power was expressed through song and pantomime. The spirit quest itself was performed by both boys and girls under the supervision of an elder and involved spending a specified period of time alone in an isolated place, often in the mountains, during which one underwent privations and performed tasks and encountered a spirit (of a sort known to him from the culture's epistemology), usually in a dream or vision (Ray 1942:235-40).

## Spirit Quest

There are several ethnographic descriptions of mid-Columbia spirit quests: for Upper Chinookans, Spier and Sapir (1930:239-40) and Curtis (1911a: 101); for Sahaptins, Curtis (1911b:10) and Murdock (1980:145); and for Nez Perces, Walker (1968:18-21). Perkins's account (Appendix 1, Doc. 5, entry

for Aug. 26, 1843) is one of the best in the ethnohistorical literature. Marcus
Whitman's description of the quest among the Walla Wallas (Northeast
Sahaptin) and the Cayuses, dated April 7, 1843, not quite five months earlier
than Perkins's, follows:

> their legend is that the present race of beasts birds reptiles & fish were
> once a race of men who inhabited the globe before the present race. That
> they were doomed to their present state from that of men, but that still
> their language is retained & these beasts birds reptiles & fish have the
> power to convey this language to the people into whom they transfix
> themselves as they think them able to do. For the very important purpose
> of obtaining this transfixture boys were required to leave the lodge &
> repair to the Mountains alone & there to stay for several days without
> food in order to be addressed in this maner by some of the supernatural
> agencies & received the transfixing of some one or more beast bird reptile
> or fish into his body. Some return without any assurance of the kind.
> Others believe themselves to be addressed & are very free to tell what was
> said to them & what beast or bird addressed them while others profess
> great secrecy & claim great reverence on account of their Majick
> possession.[2] At these times they profess to be told what is to be their
> future character & in what way to secure honour, wealth, & long life, how
> they will be invulnerable and if wounded by what means they may
> recover themselves. [M. Whitman in Hulbert and Hulbert 1938:298-99]

Perkins's account is similar enough to Whitman's—even to the repetition of
the phrase "birds, beasts or reptiles"—to suggest that it was influenced by that
of his older colleague. Two distinctive features of each account—Perkins's
"talismans" of the guardian spirit and Whitman's learning to speak the
"language" of the animal guardian—are documented elsewhere (Spier and
Sapir 1930:239; Walker 1968:22).

It is interesting to examine some of the Indian "conversion experiences"
during the 1839-40 Revival with what is known about the aboriginal spirit
quest. Tumsowit, the shaman and first convert, spent a fortnight "alone among
rocks & hills"; Tumeocool spent most of one day praying alone behind a hill
before his conversion. At Claticut, in December 1839, the "sound of prayer
was heard in every direction—in the houses, the woods, and prairies"; at
Wishram, the "rocks & prairie for half a mile around rang with prayer . . . 50
[were] engaged in such wrestling." And at Clemiaksuc, a woman "fell to the
ground, and lay two hours as one dead" before "retreating to the woods,"
where she was "overcome by the power of God" (Appendix 1, Doc. 3). In the
aboriginal scheme of things, it was quite possible to acquire a guardian spirit
(or many spirits) at any time in one's life—by chance encounter (as Perkins
notes in Appendix 1, Doc. 5), in dreams—or by undergoing privations that

might induce a suggestive psychological state. Here the evangelical belief in spiritual rebirth and the native practice converged and overlapped. Though the missionaries perceived those behaviors as Christian conversion experiences, to the Indians they were probably a new form of power quest.

The case of the Clemiaksuc woman is instructive and by no means unusual. She may have passed out or gone into a trance state, but—as the natives put it—"She is dead." Middle Columbia natives viewed a loss of consciousness, entry into a trance state, or recovery from a debilitating illness as potential avenues for making contact with the supernatural. All those conditions, in anthropological terminology, are *liminal* states, "neither here nor there; they are betwixt and between the positions assigned and arrayed by law, custom, convention, and ceremonial" (V. Turner 1969:95). In a liminal state one might contact the supernatural: the adolescent's vision quest introduces him to his guardian spirit; the shaman's trance state allows him to contact his spirit powers and rid his patient of disease-causing spirits; the Indian prophet's coma transports him to the supernatural world, where he receives a message to bring back to the real world, and so on.

Many times in the ethnohistorical literature from the Upper Chinookan area, various forms of altered states are described by native observers as varieties of "death." The Clemiaksuc woman, fainted or in a trance, was "dead." Daniel Lee describes a Chinookan from The Dalles who

> was blind of an eye, which had been destroyed by a violent inflammation, that nearly caused his death. But in his extremity he fancied some kind visitor from the invisible world, who assured him he should recover; upon which he soon revived, greatly to the surprise of his friends around him, who viewed his restoration as mysterious, since they looked upon him as one dead, and on this account he received the name of Uk-woui-a-neete, that is, "heart," or "life." [D. Lee and Frost 1844:155]

In late January 1843 Jason Lee observed Cascades natives swallowing tobacco smoke, which intoxicated them: "smoking themselves *dead* . . . (as the Indians expressed it)" (letter of March 27, 1843, Archives of the Pacific Northwest Conference). And then there is the gruesome example given by Joseph Frost at Clatsop of the Indian who passed out from overeating, was "pronounced to be dead" by the Indians, and, still groaning, was buried alive (D. Lee and Frost 1844:284-85). In the above examples, not only the terms but (in most cases) the behavior of the Indians indicates that all those states were seen and treated as varieties of a single experience. The underlying shared characteristic was passage out of normal consciousness, often to a state of unconsciousness. When one died *(really* died—ceased to live) and was interred, he or she entered the spirit world. Apparently, in the Indian conception, when one passed out of normal consciousness, he or she also entered the spirit world, and hence "died." That belief persisted into the early twentieth century, as verified in Lucullus McWhorter's manuscript "Vision of an Aged Warm Springs Woman": "To the Indian, an unconscious or coma state is being 'dead.' 'My wife died twice in one night but came back to life again.' wrote a Warm Springs man in telling me of an epidemic in his household" (n.d.: file 1514).

## Curing

Aboriginal beliefs and practices concerning disease causation and curing were closely tied to the system of beliefs surrounding nature spirits. As noted above, certain spirits were considered to cause disease. And shamans (curers, or medicine men) routinely utilized their own powerful guardian spirits as aides during curing sessions.

Perkins nowhere describes Indian curing in detail, though he mentions curers often (most prominently in the derogatory reference to the "wretched system of superstition . . . the constant shameless juggling of a large class of medicine men," Appendix 1, Doc. 4). Despite Perkins's omission, descriptions of aboriginal curing are very common in both the ethnohistorical and ethnographic literature for the mid-Columbia. Important accounts include (1) The Dalles Chinookans: Lee and Frost (1844:179–80), Brewer (in Mudge 1854:21), Waller (diary, 1845, Alvan Waller Collection), Rousseau (1965: 246), Curtis (1911a:104–6), Spier and Sapir (1930:246); (2) Columbia Sahaptins: Murdock (1965:257–58), and (3) Northwest Sahaptins: Kuyken-dall's 1881 "Indian Doctoring" (1973). The most complete accounts are those of Lee and Frost, Waller, and Kuykendall.

Mid-Columbia peoples perceived most illnesses as being caused by supernatural means. According to Verne Ray's Plateau culture-element distribution lists, important causes include intrusion of a foreign object into the body, spirit possession, personal spirit loss, and soul loss. Object intrusion seems always to be the work of a "malignant shaman"; spirit possession may be due to the activities of a malignant shaman or a lost spirit; and spirit loss may occur because one's personal spirit is "lost, wandering" or because it is "stolen by a malignant shaman" (Ray 1942:242–48). Soul loss seems to have been, in the early contact period, not typical of the region, but limited to its western fringe (Spier and Sapir 1930:244; Ray 1942:247). "Natural" illnesses, mostly bodily ailments, were recognized and treated with medicines, usually by a specialist with knowledge of herbal remedies (Splawn 1917:408).

Curing methods corresponded to the prevalent theories of disease causation. Following is one of the more complete ethnohistoric accounts of a curing session involving removal of a disease-causing object, from a manuscript diary of the Reverend Alvan Waller, successor to Perkins:

Their mode of operation is to place the patient on the back in a naked state a company of men of half a dozen or more are placed near with some sticks or poles laid horizontal before them on the earth they with small clubs in their hands strike on their sticks before them in a regular manner, or in unison, at the same time setting up a chant, as the operator directs—he at first placing himself at the feet or side of the patient, girted tight about the breast, with a dish of water near him, into which he frequently puts his fingers, then putting them into his mouth sets up an indescribable spitting, blowing, & whistling or whizzing noise altogether. Soon applies his hands or fists to the bowels, or parts supposed to be affected, pressing, gouging, wringing & twisting, frequently applying the mouth, & sucking constantly keeping up a hideous noise nearly allied to the infernal regions, puffing, blowing, spitting, jabbing, grunting & heaving . . . as if in the most intense agony—features distorted & eyes ready to leave their sockets. This is kept up for hours. At length the operator with a hideous shout, brings out as he and the people suppose the skookum or cause of the disease, & with a great force introduces his hands into the dish of water! Sometimes if the case is a severe one, one or two persons jump upon the shoulders of the operator to hold him down. . . . A little time elapses, he arises in the greatness of his strength & with an awful puff or blast with his mouth throws out his arms at full length & casts the skookum to the winds. Should the person continue sick this process is continued day after day. [Waller, diary entry for July 19, 1845, Alvan Waller Collection]

Despite his colorful language, Waller probably does not exaggerate in his description. The term *juggler,* applied by Perkins and many of his contemporaries to native curers, has an implicit connotation of sleight-of-hand and trickery. "Skokum" (usually skookum), by the way, is Chinook Jargon for "ghost or evil spirit" (Gibbs 1863:23). It also means "strong" (Yvonne Hajda, personal communication, 1988-93).

It is interesting that all the accounts of curing from The Dalles listed above describe curing by object removal or exorcism; spirit or soul loss is nowhere mentioned. Common elements in mid-Columbia curing procedures include: (1) presence of an audience, who beat on wooden planks and sing, (2) assistants to the shaman, (3) a smoke by the shaman prior to diagnosis, (4) singing by the shaman and (sometimes) possession by his spirit helpers, (5) sprinkling of water and passing of hands over the patient's body, (6) removal of an object, sometimes visible, by kneading or sucking on the body, and (7) "cooling" of the disease object by immersion in water, followed by tossing the spirit into the air (Ray 1942:242-43).

## Pat–ash

Perkins's discussion of "pat–ash . . . the likeness . . . in wood, or other material
. . . of the supernatural visitor" (Appendix 1, Doc. 5, entry for Aug. 26, 1843)
is very interesting, as it documents a practice that died out early in the contact
period throughout most of the lower Columbia. Pat–ash apparently subsumes
a number of objects: actual images, power sticks, power boards, medicine
bundles, and talismans. The root *pata–,* in Sahaptin, means "to stand up, or set
upright" (Eugene Hunn, personal communication, 1982-93).

Images representing guardian spirits are mentioned sporadically in the
ethnohistorical literature on Upper Chinookans in three contexts: in the rear
of a lodge near the chief's bed, in winter ceremonies, and at grave sites. In 1814
at the Cascades, Alexander Henry saw images

> at the foot or in front of the chief's bed planted in the ground at equal
> distances. Four figures of human heads, adorned with a kind of a crown,
> about two feet high, and rudely carved and painted. . . . the outer side of
> these figures, at both ends are placed in the ground, two large flat stones
> erect and painted. [1992:649]

There are two accounts of pat-ash in the winter ceremonies. From The
Dalles, Brewer noted, in a letter of March 11, 1847 (Western Americana
Collection) "little images" carried by dancers that were presented to spectators
in a "waving manner or a dancing motion." A Kathlamet tale, "The Nisal,"
describes "a small figure of a supernatural being made of cedar wood" that
"danced . . . to and fro" whenever its owner sang his spirit song (Boas
1901:201-6). From the neighboring lower Chinooks, Boas describes a
"manikin (a figure made of cedar bark)" that guided a shaman to the land of
the dead to recover lost souls (1894:206). Images representing guardian spirits
were common components of shamanistic paraphernalia throughout
aboriginal western Washington and British Columbia.

Ethnohistorical mentions of images at grave sites include the "little black
men" noted by Applegate at Upper Memaloose Island in 1843 (chap. 5). Lewis
and Clark recorded grave images at The Cascades on October 31, 1805:

> I observed Several wooden Images, cut in the figure[s] of men and Set
> up on the <South> Sides of the vaults all round. . . . I cannot Say certainly
> that those nativs worship those wooden idols as I have every reason to
> believe they do not; as they are Set up in the most conspicuous parts of
> their houses, and treated more like ornaments than objects of aderation.
> [1988:361]

Kuykendall's discussion of The Cascades images states:

Some of the images had arms and in some instances eye sockets were cut out and round shining stones or the half of large beads were set in as eyes. Lips and oral cavity were cut and small shells or pieces of shells were set in to represent teeth. The face and eyebrows were usually painted. . . . When a death occurred in the family of one of these men who owned two or three of the images one was stood up in the dead house by the side of the deceased. . . . the same as any other personal property and were not intended to represent any person. [Kuykendall 1973]

A few of those grave figures survived into this century, when they were collected by the locals and placed in museums. The wood figures shown in plate 14 all come from two cemeteries: Grave Island (nos. 1-3) and Upper Memaloose Island (no. 4). Numbers 3 and 4 might be called either images or grave figures.

In Pandosy's Yakama dictionary there are at least two words, probably related to Perkins's pat-ash, that refer to objects other than images per se that might also be infused with spirit power. The first of those is *pa-tish,* which Pandosy glosses as "large branch" (1862:39). Throughout much of the region north of the lower Columbia, shamans and common people carved representations of their guardian spirits on poles that were used in winter dances. Spier states, "It is strange that neither Dr. Sapir nor I learned of [that] type of carving among the Wishram" (Spier and Sapir 1930:271), but in fact "shaman's wands" are known archaeologically from The Dalles (plate 15). Spier and Sapir do refer to a Chinookan performance, "the dance with the thumping sticks," that involved "forearm"-length "billets" of wood, not mentioned as carved, that became infused with spirit power, moved, and pulled those holding them with them (1930:243-44).

Kuykendall, who never saw the performance but had "heard it described by a great many eye witnesses," gives the most detailed description of it. The following is his manuscript version. The incident occurred

at the Cascades. . . . An old doctor who became quite famous for his exploits in making sticks dance used to keep five "Tamanowash sticks" for his seances. They are from one inch and a half to two and a half inches in diameter and from two to three feet or more long. All gathered into the lodge. . . . After the old doctor had sung four times then any person present was invited to take hold of one of the sticks as the old man sung and kept time with his hands the person was jumped about by the stick which began hopping up and down.

As the old tamanowash man warmed up and sung louder and faster, the stick danced more vehemently and the party holding it was instructed to keep it from moving and hold it still. The more strenuously he tried to resist the dancing the more violently it hopped up and down and around the lodge. Finally the stick raised up and jerked up violently the uplifted arms of the one who was trying to hold it. At last being overcome he fell over in a cataleptic state holding on to the stick with a death grip.

The old tamanowash man then stopped his singing and went to the one who had fallen over and stroked him or made some passes over his head when the rigidity relaxed and the man or woman wakened up as from sleep and was soon all right again.

Indians familiar with the performance have described the sensations they felt on taking hold of the Tamanowash sticks to be almost exactly the same as that experienced when holding the electrodes of a magnetic battery. They say their muscles are thrown into a state of powerful contraction so that they cannot let go their hold by any effort of the will.

The Indians declare that the rods turn around at the doctors command or at the motion of his hand. . . . The doctors who use the tamonowash sticks in seances for amusement or show use them also in treating the sick. While the assistants of the doctor are seated in rows . . . pounding or beating on the board or pole before them the Doctor places the "tamanowash stick" in the hands of the patient and if a cure is to be effected the sick person will as the drumming and singing goes on be raised up in his bed and may be made to stand on his feet. [Kuykendall 1973]

The performance occurred elsewhere in the lower Columbia drainage and western Washington. The Tualatin Kalapuyas had a spirit power, "(shaman's) carved (three foot long) dancing stick power" (named *ask^w i 'tit,* similar to the Upper Chinookan term for the performance, *wa 'kc 'kwīti 't* (Spier and Sapir 1930:243–44; Jacobs 1945:181). Gibbs, in 1865, gives a resume of the performance among the lower Chinook, stating that

The sticks are bars of cedarwood, carved and painted, and are sometimes smeared with grease and feathers. . . . Mr James Strong of Cathlamet witnessed the performance of To-tilikum, the chief at Woody Island. . . . Ho-hoke or the Raven, a Cowlitz Indian, and a very old man living on the Puyallup, are the only others who have been named to me as possessing it. . . . The Klickitats state that they have not the power themselves but have seen others exercise it among the Chinooks. [1956:137–38]

Similar to power sticks were power boards, well known from western Washington but present among Chinookan peoples as well. John Townsend describes figures "rudely carved and painted upon a board" to which "the Indians ascribe supernatural powers" in houses at Chinook village (1939:253); Paul Kane made a painting of the interior of a Chinookan house in which a power board can be clearly seen (Harper 1971: plate 37). At The Cascades in

1814, Alexander Henry mentioned a "broad plank erect on which are rudely carved some figures" (1992: 649); at a village between Claticut and Wascopam, in 1805, Lewis and Clark "observed in the lodge of the Chief . . . two wide Split boards with images on them Cut and painted in emitation of a man" (1988:351); and at Wishram, Curtis mentions "an upright cedar plank carved into figures of birds and animals . . . at the rear of . . . the house of a medicineman" (1911a:92). In the Wishram tale "The Maiden Sacrificed to Winter," recorded by Curtis (1911a:150), carved cedar boards were placed next to a dancing platform on which a girl danced and sang her guardian-spirit song to overcome an illness.

Pandosy's Yakama dictionary also translates *pa-ta-she* as "plume" (1862:52). One of Brewer's winter-ceremony dancers (see below) carried an "image in one hand & a stick with large black feathers attached to it in the other." Feathers were an important part of the postcontact native religion of the middle Columbia termed by Sahaptins either Waptashi 'feather' or Waskliki 'spin' (DuBois 1938:5). During initiation to the Feather religion, novices held eagle feathers in each hand and involuntarily spun in circles. In regular services, feathers were held in the right hand and waved in time to singing. They were considered to be "cleansing devices" (DuBois 1938:30, 38–39, 44).

Finally, there is a word resembling pat-ash in Nez Perce, *ipétes*, which refers to "a sacred package of a particular tutelary [guardian] spirit" (Walker 1968:19). In this case, the spirit is resident in something that seems to be akin to the medicine bundle of the Plains Indians. According to Walker:

> The *ipétes* . . . had a power all its own, and great care had to be taken with it . . . an individual would know what his *ipétes* should be like soon after undergoing the spirit-dance validation of his tutelary spirit. . . . The ipetes was considered a very personal piece of property like the associated [spirit] song. . . . It was used whenever the individual had recourse to his tutelary spirit. . . . A small "eye" of the *ipétes* customarily was worn on a string around the neck in the form of a feather, a shell, or some other suitable symbolic object. The costume worn at the spirit dance or when entering a risky undertaking requiring power bore a close resemblance to the *ipétes*. [1968:22]

The small objects contained in the bundle appear close to Perkins's second, more specific meaning of pat-ash: "visible representations of the *'tah-ma'*" such as bear claws and a wolf's tail "sometimes worn on the person . . . a sort of charm" (Appendix 1, Doc. 5). Coale (1958:138) describes the Nez Perce "*ipätis*" as charms given to a quester by a spirit, such as "a claw, feather, fur, stone, or any like object." Perkins notes that "all such charms, amulets,

talismans etc. . . . are always buried with the body" (Appendix 1, Doc. 5, entry
for Aug. 26, 1843). Bone, stone, and antler effigies and amulets are commonly
occurring archaeological finds in The Dalles region. A few have holes in the
tops, indicating that they were suspended, perhaps on a cord around the neck.
Two cremation pits, at the Leachman site and at Miller's Island (both in
Sahaptin territory) have yielded particularly impressive assemblages of finely
wrought bone and antler figurines (Steward 1927). Those pieces depict quite
clearly two of the hallmark traits of the lower Columbia art style: the skeletal
rib cage and the owl-like eyes. Other motifs include a smiling mouth with
central (protuberant?) tongue and often elaborate headdresses (Strong
1961:133).

Pat-ash, following Perkins and the above, refers to a large class of objects
that shared the characteristic of being infused with spirit power. They included
spirit images, power sticks, power boards, and medicine bundles. Feathers,
claws, and other animal body parts might represent a spirit, as well as
(probably) small carved images and amulets. The latter might be worn on the
person, kept in a medicine bundle, and buried with the body.

## Aut-ni

Perkins had considerable difficulty making precise translations from biblical
English into colloquial Sahaptin. The English and Sahaptin lexicons simply
did not have words that were equivalent, and Perkins spent much time
wrestling with shades of meaning and connotations in both languages. His
philological wanderings led him to doubt the accuracy of the biblical writ,
itself a translation of the original Hebrew or Greek. In the 1843-44 journal he
went so far as to ask Secretary Pitman for his advice on particularly vexing
translation problems.

The most interesting of Perkins's ethnosemantic musings involves the
word aut-ni and several of its derivatives. The following discussion is based
upon several communications from Eugene Hunn, himself an ethnosemanticist
and student of Columbia River Sahaptin. Perkins translates aut-ni as "sacred,
hallowed, or sanctified" (Appendix 1, Doc. 5, entry for Aug. 15, 1843). The
word is composed of the verb stem aw or awt, which, broadly, subsumes such
English concepts as "to be sacred, holy, polluted . . . to purify or [interestingly]
to vomit." The form ni is a nominalizing suffix. i-au'ni (Appendix 1, Doc. 5,
entry for Jan. 13, 1844) includes the root aw plus i, a transitivizing prefix, and
ni, the qualitative adjectivizer; hence, "making holy." i-au-las is more
elusive: it includes aw and i, as above, plus either la 'one who', yielding the
meaning "one who makes [something] sacred," or nas, which would make the
word (roughly) "I was made holy." shap-a-autsha, according to Perkins, is
a verb, based upon the root awt, meaning "to prohibit" (Appendix 1, Doc. 5,

entry for Aug. 15, 1843). Analyzed, *šapa* is a causative prefix; *ša* is a continuitive aspect suffix. As Perkins realized, and Hunn emphasizes, such interpretations are exceedingly difficult, and the above translations should be "considered as best guesses" (Eugene Hunn, personal communication, 1982-93).

However loose, the above analyses do uncover some very interesting points. Hunn notes that awt is also the root of the Columbia Sahaptin word for the native tobacco *(Nicotania attenuata), awt-pamá. pamá* means "for, belonging to"; hence *awt-pamá* = "for holiness, pollution." An example of Cascades natives smoking to intoxication—that is, entering an altered state of consciousness or "becoming dead" was given earlier. According to Hunn, "an infusion of native tobacco was drunk as a purgative after the death of a close relative with whom one has just shared food" (Eugene Hunn, personal communication, 1982-93).

That leads us to the translation of the root *awt* as "to vomit." Among the Nez Perces, vomiting was a recognized means of cleansing and achieving a "satisfactory state of spirituality" (Walker 1968:19). The Reverend Asa Smith reported on November 11, 1839, that Nez Perces induced vomiting as part of a prehunt ritual:

> A few days ago I witnessed a practice among the Indians which they perform at this season preparatory to hunting deer. They run small sticks down their throats into their stomachs to cause themselves to vomit. The sticks are small timber osiers. Four are usually taken at a time & passed down more than a foot in length & held there till he commences vomiting. Soon four more are taken in the same way & this is repeated 8 or 10 times during the same morning. The rest of the day is spent in washing the surface of the body in water heated by hot stones dug for the purpose at the margin of the water. . . . They have an idea if they do not vomit themselves and wash they will not be skillful in killing game. [A. Smith in Drury 1958:122-23]

Among Nez Perces "cleansing and purging" such as the above was also a part of "formal preparation preceding the [spirit] quest" and was normally resorted to "during periods of crisis or in preparation for some undertaking, the outcome of which was uncertain, such as hunting, gambling, or warfare" (Walker 1968:19).

## First Salmon Ceremony

Perkins, however, does not use the word aut-ni or its derivatives in reference to either smoking or purging. Instead, it appears in his discussion of the first salmon ceremony (Appendix 1, Doc. 5, entry for Aug. 15, 1843) and is used specifically in reference to the blood of the salmon, which the Indians "considered to be 'aut–ni'—or . . . sacred." According to Perkins, the blood from a beheaded salmon—the first of the year—was collected in a "basin," kept for five days, and then poured back into the river.

Such a treatment of the fish's blood is nowhere reported in the ethnographic literature. Although the first salmon rite was almost a cultural universal in the Pacific Northwest, other peoples returned the fish's bones, not its blood, to the water. Spier and Sapir's account of the first salmon ceremony at Wishram, collected in the early twentieth century, does not mention special treatment of either blood or bones. Yet there is no reason to doubt Perkins's account—the treatment of blood is fully consistent with its status in the winter ceremonies; and the other elements of the salmon rite are consistent with what is known from other parts of the culture region. What he may be describing is an element of the precontact ceremony that dropped out at a very early date.

Perkins's reference to a "basin, or small dish" is both perplexing and provocative. Without a more complete textual description we cannot be sure, but it could be either a wooden vessel or the archaeologically familiar shallow basalt "mortar." Two examples of the latter are pictured in plate 16 (originally published in E. Strong 1961:134–35). The function of those artifacts has never been determined, but on the lower Fraser, similar vessels, containing water, were used by shamans in various rituals: to cleanse (purify?) their hands, for divination, and in female puberty rites (Duff 1956:56–59). According to Wilson Duff, "most of the [Fraser] bowls of animal and human form are assumed to have been used for ritual purposes, holding sacred oil, powder, or water" (1975:40–41). If Perkins's reference to a "basin" is indeed that type of stone vessel, its ritual use by a shaman on the lower Columbia is consistent with the use of similar artifacts on the Fraser.

The Wishram first salmon ceremony, as described by Spier and Sapir (1930:248–49), was conducted by a shaman, with all village members present. The people feasted when the shaman had completed the ritual dismemberment. There is no mention of the ritual treatment of blood, nor of a five-day sacred period. The ethnographers mention several fish, not one, and they are baked in a pit, not boiled. The ritual was followed by "prayers . . . accompanied by drum and bell," which "suggest that the reference is to the days of the šmúxala cult," which postdates the reservation period (Spier and Sapir 1930:248–49). The first salmon ceremony has been practiced continually since aboriginal times by Columbia Sahaptin peoples (particularly at Celilo), but the recent ceremony is, in most of its particulars, a Wáašat rite (see, for example, McKeown 1959). Perkins's account is the only detailed description that predates the late-nineteenth-century period of greatest elaboration of postcontact nativistic religions. Kuykendall's brief description of the middle Columbia first salmon ceremony, which probably dates from the 1870s, appears to contain transitional elements: the fish's head is torn off without benefit of a knife, and the leader, who has salmon "tah," makes an address "sometimes if not always to his patron saint instead of the Great Chief" (1973).

The standard references on the first salmon ceremony are Erna Gunther's "Analysis of the First Salmon Ceremony" (1926) and her "Further Analysis of the First Salmon Ceremony" (1928). In many areas of the Northwest, as part of a general resurgence of Indian religions, the ceremony is being revived today (Amoss 1987).

## Winter Ceremonies

The Wascopam Mission papers preserve what is undoubtedly the most complete description of the Winter Ceremonies—the major religious events—of The Dalles area Indians. The description is particularly important because—as with the first salmon ceremony—those rituals disappeared rapidly after the mid-1800's, and by the time the ethnographer Sapir questioned informants in 1905, they were fragmented memories. Perkins describes some elements in his journal entry for August 26, 1843 (Appendix 1, Doc. 5), and Daniel Lee devotes two pages to them in *Ten Years in Oregon* (D. Lee and Frost 1844:163–64). But by far the most complete account comes from the manuscript papers of Henry Brewer. Brewer and Alvan Waller together attended a single performance in December 1846. An abridged, edited version of Brewer's account, "The Indian National Dance," appears in Mudge (1854:24–25), but the manuscript version, which follows, is more complete.

> I have thought I would devote a few lines, giving you some information of the dance I attended last winter. I have known ever since I have been here that in the month of Dec. the Indians have a great dance but I never would consent to go until last Dec. I accompanied Br Waller, taking along with us some of our most friendly Indians. The scene I saw enacted there that night, beggars all description. It is impossible to give you a correct idea. you need to see it to realize it fully—As we entered the house a tall middle-aged indian was on the stage who had nearly passed through his performance & soon after sat down. The house was crowded to overflowing. The fire of an Indian house is always in the centre & the smoke escapes through an opening in the roof. The stage or place on which the actors performed was back of the fire. It was composed of thin boards raised probably 8 inches from the ground & covered over with an Elk skin. The next actor that came on the stage was a juggler—I believe they are considered the best actors. He commenced with a low singing noise

dancing at the same time taking the lead in the different songs nearly all the congregation assisting. On one side of the house on a high stage were two swinging poles one long and the other a short one. The longer one was ordinarily used by keeping time in striking it against the end of the house, during the height of the performance both were used. Every few moments the actor would swing his right arm & stop to recover strength at the same time some few would make a response however he would stop but a moment & continue on with the old tune or a new one, every time he would increase in exertion. At this stage of the performance the sweat ran in streams down his naked body for he had nothing on but a blanket belted around his loins with a pistol at his side. During the height of the performance a part of his audience rose as by magic & commenced beating with their feet. all voices were at the highest pitch & the two poles were beating most furiously. About this time two young men stepped up upon the stage behind the actor the younger had nothing on but a pr of pants who immediately threw himself with his back upon the back of the actor with his arms over the shoulders of the actor who at the same time caught hold of them. the other young man held his feet up & in this manner he danced some time—this was about the closing up of his performance—One or two others performed without any thing remark-able when we heard a noise above us & then who should make his appearance before us but a man naked or only his shirt held before him with his arms & breast gashed in different places & the blood streaming down. I began to think he came from "Tother world" It seems he came down through the roof before us—He went through his performance nearly like the one I have described only he had quite a bundle of flax & beads & which were distributed to the female singers I had forgotten to mention that during some part of different performances little images were presented before us in a waving manner or a dancing motion & then would be taken in. When this last actor was about through who should come in but a man painted black with a little image in one hand & a stick with large black feathers attached to it in the other hand. He took his station by the fire with a low grumbling singing, swinging motion, apparently unconscious of all that was going on around. About this time a small puppy dog was thrown near my feet, when a young man com-menced beating the breath out his body & before he was half dead threw him into the fire & then pulled him out & took a knife & cut him open while the poor little dog was still half alive & then took the warm blood & commenced giving it to this niger dancer who drank three handfuls of it down freely & then he was ready to mount the stage & dance with energy & life. By this time I became so disgusted that I wished myself out of that place, but the crowd prevented it. It was all I could do to stay there. After he passed through his dance, Br Waller gave them a talk, warning them of the folly of such a course & enviting them to give it up after which we left for home as it was nearly midnight. . . . They usually have their dances continue 4 or 5 days & nights together, the women dancing some part of the time. But I have worried your patience— [H. Brewer, letter of March 11, 1847, Western Americana Collection]

Two notable characteristics of the above passage are (1) its similarity, in broad outline, to the Winter Spirit Dancing as practiced throughout most of aboriginal western Oregon and Washington, and (2) the presence of distinct performance elements, well known among the highly complex winter ceremonies of coastal British Columbia, which suggest historical ties to the north and imply a more elaborate ceremonial development than has hitherto been reported from the lower Columbia.

Ethnologist Verne Ray has written most extensively on the winter ceremonies of the Columbia River drainage (see "The Winter Spirit Dance" in 1939:102-22, 1942:248-53). According to Ray:

> The Winter Guardian Spirit Dance is the major religious ceremony of the Plateau, dwarfing all other rituals by comparison. It forms an elaborate complex which is readily identifiable . . . so characteristic is the combination of elements. And yet those elements, in their individual distributions, are highly variable. [1939:102]

The usual elements of the Winter Spirit Dance, as it occurred among the Sahaptins and Chinookans, include the following (based on Ray 1939:102-22, 1942:248-53):

1. The dances were held during the two coldest months (December and January, "60 days"); performances took place in a large house with a prominent center pole; individual dances lasted five days.

2. New guardian spirits were "made obvious" to the audience. Novices, who had kept their guardian spirits secret since their quest, began to experience spirit illness. At the Winter Ceremonies, a shaman diagnosed the illness and then gave the novice his song. The novice then danced and the audience followed suit.

3. The ceremony was open to all others who had guardian spirits, and they might now perform their own spirit songs and dances. Symbolic clothing ornaments identified the spirit.

4. Shamans were the usual sponsors of the ceremonies, attended by a spokesman and assistants. The shaman not only guided the novices but performed various tricks, including handling of hot rocks and the swallowing of fire or boiling water.

5. Gifts were contributed by the shaman and all attendees, placed on an elevated horizontal board, and distributed to everyone in the final days of the ceremony.

The ceremony witnessed by Brewer and Waller had some of those elements, but not others. Element groups number 1 (timing and location) and number 4 (role of the shaman [here called juggler]) are quite clear. The singing of guardian spirit songs (element group 3) may be represented by the sequence of actors with varying performances, and the initiation of a novice may be the back carrying of a young man by a juggler. There is no mention of gift giving or receiving (it is, in fact, not mentioned in any of the Wascopam accounts).

Two other descriptions from the mission literature, from Thomas Farnham and Daniel Lee, present skeletal outlines, which retain the specifics of the 1846 ceremony at Wascopam but lack the special performances.[3]

> In order to keep up their influence among the people, the conjurers of a tribe, male and female, have cabalistic dances. After the darkness of night sets in, they gather together in a wigwam, build a large fire in the centre, spread the floor with elk skins, set up on end a wide cedar board, and suspend near it a stick of wood in a horizontal position. An individual seizes the end of the stick, swings the other end against the cedar board, and thus beats noisy time to a still more noisy chant. The dance is commenced sometimes by a man alone, and often by a man and woman. And various and strange are the bodily contortions of the performers. They jump up and down, and swing their arms with more and more violence as the noise of the singing and thumping accompaniment increases, and yelp, and froth at the mouth, till the musician winds up with the word "ugh"—a long gutteral grunt; or until some one of the dancers falls apparently dead. When the latter is the case, one of the number walks around the prostrate individual, and calls his or her name loudly at each ear, at the nose, fingers and toes. After this ceremony, the supposed dead shudders greatly, and comes to life. And thus they continue to sing, and thump, and dance, and die, and come to life through the night. [Farnham 1843:88]

> The nights among the Dalls Indians were spent in singing and dancing, and their carousals could be heard a mile. One, and then another of the medicine men would open his house for a dance, where it was generally kept up five nights in succession; men, women, and children, engaged in the chant, while a man, or a woman, or both, danced on a large elk-skin spread down on one side of the fire, that blazed in the centre of the group, keeping time to the loud-measured knocking of a long pole suspended horizontally, and struck endwise against a wide cedar board, the dancer

jumping, and invoking his "tam–an–a–was" or familiar spirit; until, exhausted, he falls as one dead, by the overpowering influence of his "familiar." To arouse him from this deep slumber requires the skill of a medicine man, or "Mesmeriser," who going around him peeps, and mutters, and hoots, at his toes, fingers, and ears, and wakes his tam-an-a-was; when he shudders, groans, opens his eyes, and lives again! [D. Lee and Frost 1844:163]

Common elements here are night-time dances held in a house with central fire, sponsorship by a shaman, elk skins on the floor, the distinctive swinging pole-and-board drum, chanting by the audience, and dancing by an individual who falls "dead" and is revived by a shaman. All those elements, save the latter, appear in the Brewer-Waller performance. The "death" and revival is clearly a specific example of the initiation of a novice as described by Ray, and it may be the equivalent of the back dancing in Brewer-Waller.

So much for the basic outline of the ceremonies. The three missionary records—Brewer, Perkins, and Lee—all mention special elements, many of which are widespread in the Northwest, some as far afield as British Columbia. All three mention gashing the body with a knife; two list dog eating; Lee includes fire eating; Brewer has back dancing; and Perkins has "wandering naked in the snow," which, as we will see, probably forms a single element with Brewer's man who enters through the roof and his black-painted man.

## Back Dancing

Back dancing is mentioned only a few times in the ethnohistorical-ethnographic literature, and only for Wishrams and Nez Perces. It appears to have been, in its usual form, a means of transferring power from a more experienced individual (usually a shaman) to a novice and thus can be considered part of the initiation-of-a-novice stage of the spirit dance (Walker 1968:24). The exact nature of power transferral appears to have varied: Walker cites the above, generalized form; Spier and Sapir (1930) note it as part of a shaman's initiation; Gibbs's example (1956) involves a cure; and the Wishram text "A Singing and Dancing Festival" (Sapir 1909) has elk-people using it to transfer hunting power to various animal spirits. Neither of the two ethnographic accounts (Spier and Sapir 1930:241; Walker 1968:24), based upon informants' memories, is very complete; the two ethnohistoric accounts (Brewer [Mudge 1854:24–25] and Gibbs), based on personal observations, are more comprehensive. Gibbs's account, following, is very similar to Brewer's and may in fact reflect a performance by the same shaman. Tumsowit (see biographical sketch, Appendix 3) was the principal Wascopam shaman in the late 1830s. He was also Perkins and Lee's first convert during the Great

Revival but, as Jason Lee noted, had "backslidden" by 1843. Tumsowit's cure probably dates from 1853.

> A remarkable instance was related to me by Dr. [George] Suckley and by Lieut. Archibald Gracie (5th Inf.), both of whom were present at the time. An Indian named Tomasowit, a great medicine man at The Dalles, was the operator. The patient was a young girl who had a spinal affection [*sic*]. The Wascoes had a dance which lasted five days, and the whole band were assembled in a lodge, at one end of which there was a board platform somewhat raised. Tomasowit stood upon this, dancing, swinging and shouting, and tearing off, as his excitement increased, one article after another of his clothing, until he stood perfectly naked. At length he exclaimed, "I feel a wind coming which will make me strong enough to put her to sleep." And becoming apparently exhausted or weak from his exercise, he grasped the pole, which supported the roof, at the same time stooping so as to bring his back into a horizontal position. His knees shook under him and his voice subsided into a low, monotonous song. The girl was then brought in and laid upon him, with her back to his, her head lying over his shoulder and kept in her position by a couple of squaws who held her legs. She had on only a shift. Meantime the people present kept on singing and pounding upon boards, and the man continuing dancing and singing. In a short time, perhaps ten or fifteen minutes, the girl went to sleep. She was then laid on the floor, and the Doctor kneeling by her commenced a low, wailing cry. The Indians stated that no one but he could awaken her. As the slumber passed off, she commenced crying, then singing louder and clearer and finally got up and danced with all her strength. [Gibbs 1956:135–36]

Brewer's description leaves out the final stages. The person on the back eventually goes "to sleep" (Gibbs 1956:136), becomes "unconscious and stiff as a board" (Spier and Sapir 1930:241), or goes "into a trance" (Walker 1968:24). When the back dancing was over, the novice, now "strong . . . danced once more" (Spier and Sapir 1930:241).

## Skep Spirit

"Skep (pronounced scape)" is what Perkins calls "the spirit of some dead person, which . . . wanders about invisibly, and is capable of entering into the bodies of the living" (Appendix 1, Doc.5, entry for Aug. 26, 1843), where it causes illness and death and many of the "frantic-insane" behaviors observed during the winter ceremonies. The word almost invariably refers to a particular kind of spirit, which has several recurring characteristics and a complex of associated behaviors. Both Dell Hymes (1980:410) and Wayne Suttles (1987) have noted that cognates of the word exist in several Salishan, as well as

Sahaptian and other Penutian languages.[4] Although the originating tongue is unknown, Suttles says that "the initial s– suggests a Salish source" (1987). In (Umatilla) Columbia Sahaptin, the term is glossed *sxáyp* (Theodore Stern, personal communication, 1982); the (Wasco-Wishram) Upper Chinookan form is *i–šgíp* (David French, personal communication, 1989–93).

Skep behaviors seem to fall into two clusters: one is characteristic of peoples of the Columbia drainage, including speakers of Salishan, Sahaptin, and (probably) Chinookan languages; the other is shared by Salishan-speaking peoples of Puget Sound and the Gulf of Georgia.

In the Columbia drainage the skep spirit is a "spirit-ghost" (Ray 1942: 238–39)—the disembodied guardian spirit of a deceased person— that makes itself known to a living person as an invisible voice, often in a dream. It is sometimes depicted as a skeleton. Skep is a dangerous spirit, which may cause a wasting illness or death, on the one hand, or produce moodiness, uncontrollable behavior, or insanity on the other. The skepi is prone to gash himself with a sharp instrument, usually on the legs or arms. There is an unquestionable association with blood: drinking of one's own blood, dog's blood, or bird's blood is reported. On the eastern Plateau there is an association with property: the skepi both desires it and dispenses it in a give away or feast. Three examples of the Columbian skepi follow.

> [Yakama:] a few doctors profess to have a very strange and mysterious "tah" known by the name of skaiep. . . . It is the prince or ruler of all the tamanowash spirits. . . . It comes to the tawaties [shamans] as a voice and is never seen. . . . This is the spirit or tah that causes insanity and all forms of madness. If a man is spoken to by skaiep and commanded to do any thing he is bound to obey or he may die immediately or he may become insane and wild . . . skaiep has commanded the doctors to do the most painful and distressing things. One was to swallow alive a great quantity of water beetles, another instance . . . to sing tamanowash songs daily and nightly for five years. . . . If this skaiep . . . leaves or is driven out by some other tamanowash man then the medicine man so deserted will immediately die—usually they say he becomes a raving lunatic and persists in jumping into the fire until he is roasted to death. [Kuykendall 1973]

> In Umatilla [Columbia Sahaptin] I have *sxáyp* "a power, often Skeleton, that may confer curing power." *I–sxáyp–i* ("one who has *sxáyp* power") has acquired the spirit of a deceased person. The spirit is dangerous to acquire: having sought out the spirit, [the quester] sought to "domesticate" it to himself, but for some three months or more . . . was in danger of being driven to slash his upper arms and thus killing himself. A vigil had to be mounted over him (or her) to prevent this from happening. Once

acquired, the spirit gave powers of clairvoyance but continued to be dangerous to others. [Theodore Stern, personal communication, 1982]

[Nez Perce] *Isḥép* comes in a dream. The person to whom this comes sings a song in a strange language, dances violently and continuously, and must give away all possessions. Usually it causes death, but if the afflicted lives through the winter and summer until fall, *isḥép* will thereafter belong to him and will do no harm. This may come upon a person at any time and in any place, but generally it begins in the medicine ceremony.... While dancing they cut themselves across arms and legs with flint-points..... The Nez Perce who used [the *Isḥép* song] was a man who in his vision had seen a skeleton, and therefore he had the ability to cure convulsions, since this malady is believed to be caused by the bones being twisted out of joint. [Curtis 1911a:72n, 183n]

There are some unique traits in those accounts: clairvoyance in the Umatillas, and the convulsion cure among the Nez Perces. Both Curtis and Walker, who describe the Nez Perce *isḥép*, note that its owner became "very desirous of property," which he amassed and, over several years, gave away in order to demonstrate his prowess (Walker 1968:25-26). That behavior, akin to potlatching on the Coast, seems to be uniquely associated with skep behaviors only in the eastern Plateau.

Skep behaviors among the Coast Salish people are somewhat different. Not one of the accounts gives a good description of the spirit itself, though it is occasionally called red and is sometimes said to convey strength and war power. Self slashing and blood coming from the mouth are prominent behaviors. Firewalking or handling and dog eating are occasionally mentioned. There is, significantly, no mention of the spirit as a spirit-ghost. Neither is the skep stated to be particularly dangerous to its owner nor cause him to lose control or become insane. Two detailed examples of the Coastal skep from the ethnographic literature are found in Haeberlin and Gunther (1930:72) and in Collins (1974:155-56) (both Puget Salish).

Verne Ray, in "Lower Chinook Ethnographic Notes," claims that a secret society, including gashing, was introduced among the Chinooks of the Columbia mouth from the north "at a very late date" (1938:89). The Chinookan name for the society has not survived. Ray's evidence suggests that it was a form of the Nuu–chah–ulth (Nootkan) Wolf Dance (1938:91).

In fact, Ray's evidence can be interpreted two ways. Some elements—teaching by a mentor, an initiation fee, the black-bear guardian spirit, and the bleeding mouth—suggest a derivation from the north. Others, however, seem to have equal or stronger ties to skepi performances among peoples to the east. Those include gashing, fire walking, and a terminal period when the initiate "wandered alone along the beach and through the woods" (1938:91). The evidence is by no means strong enough to draw a definite conclusion, but it seems likely that there were two ceremonial layers among the lower Chinook: an older substratum with ties to the east, and a much later overlay from the north. It seems unlikely, on the basis of the ceremonial elements recorded in the Wascopam Mission papers, that the bulk of those behaviors were recent diffusions from the north, as Ray suggests.

## Gashing

There is a small body of ethnohistorical-ethnographic data from the Chinookan area that describes ceremonial gashing. (Besides Perkins and Brewer, above, they include McWhorter n.d., manuscript description of a Wasco female puberty dance; Townsend 1839:249; D. Lee and Frost 1844:64; Dunn 1845:91-92; Kuykendall 1889:83; Boas 1894:208; Spier and Sapir 1930:242; Jacobs 1958:505-6). The accounts are very consistent: the performer, in a state of excitement, cuts the loose flesh of his torso and arms with a knife, drawing blood, which he sometimes drinks, and producing scars, which are subsequently displayed as proof of his strength and invulnerability to pain. Three examples follow:

> [Clatsop, ca. 1835:] In times of pretended inspiration . . . they seize a fleshy part of the body, about the stomach and ribs, in one hand, and plunge a dagger right through the fold, without drawing blood. This act is taken as a proof of their invulnerability. . . . I have seen some of them thus gashed all over in front of the body. While I was in charge of Fort George, one of these crafty old priests prepared to perform this operation in my presence. He grasped a handful of his flabby flesh, and drew his dagger. But I instantly checked him. [Dunn 1845:91-92]

> [Wishram, Sept. 6, 1836:] We observe on the breasts and bellies of many of the Indians here, a number of large red marks, mostly of an oval form, sometimes twenty or thirty grouped together. These are wounds made by their own hands to display to their people the unwavering and stoical resolution with which they can endure pain. A large fold of the skin is taken up with the fingers, and sliced off with a knife; the surrounding fibre then retreats, and a large and ghastly looking wound remains. Many that I saw today are yet scarcely cicatrized. There is a chief here who obtained the dignity which he now enjoys, solely by his numerous and hardy feats of this kind. He was originally a common man. . . . The whole front of his person is covered with the red marks of which I have spoken . . . he will probably be chosen chief. . . . He is named by the Indians *"Skookum"* (the strong). [Townsend 1978:249]

[Wishram(?), 1860s:] While the drumming and dancing went on, the shamans grew excited and gyrated about frantically. Finally the more bold bared their arms, and with a butcher knife cut deep gashes across the fleshy part of the arm. Sometimes several were cut about half an inch or more apart. Blood flowed profusely; and the demoniac conjuror sucked it out and drank it, or even ripped out the strips of flesh with his teeth and devoured them like a ravenous beast. These extravagant performances were thought by the common people to indicate great bravery and manhood; and the performer showed the scars afterwards with evident pride. [Kuykendall 1889:83]

Dunn's is the only account that comes from the lower Chinook. It differs from the others in the lack of blood. Other than that, the only obvious difference among the various descriptions is in the role of the performer. Most accounts do not specify; Dunn, Kuykendall and Daniel Lee make him a shaman, while Townsend (above) quite clearly makes him a lay person.

## Dog Eating

Another ceremonial element mentioned by both Perkins and Brewer is dog eating. Dog eating was the central ritual in the Nutlam society, best known (and named) from the Kwakwaka'wakw. Either as a separate society or as a ritual element it has been reported from virtually every coastal culture between the Tlingits and southernmost Coast Salish (Drucker 1940:229). It is briefly mentioned in a myth collected by Edward Curtis at White Salmon (1911a:152–53), but otherwise the Wascopam Mission records contain the only documentation of its occurrence among Upper Chinookan-speaking peoples. Besides Perkins and Brewer, Alvan Waller noted the ritual:

Today an Indian died two miles distant. . . . I learned the probable cause of his death, viz: last winter the Indians had a great dance during which they took a live dog, put him upon the fire till dead & his hair most singed off, he also partly roasted. One of the Indians let his blood out, which the Indian just deceased with two or three others, catched in their hands and drank, after which this Indian ate most or all of the dog, singed as he was, entrails & all, since which he has not been well, but has slowly wasted away till his death. . . . A year ago last winter at the Falls of the Wallamette an indian thus ate a dog after which his long hair was cut off, singed & cut off by him. If he lived through this operation he was to be denominated a great doctor among his people, also a chief or ruler. He was sick sometime & came very near dying but finally recovered & lives to enjoy the acknowledged honors. [Waller, diary, entry for May 23, 1845, Alvan Waller Collection]

Amoss (1984) describes the ambiguous status of the dog in Northwest Coast thought—not like other animals, as they were domesticated, but not human either—dogs were somewhere in between. Wolves, the wild relatives of dogs, ate dogs; humans, in the Cannibal Dance when wild, "ate" other humans; humans, possessed by wolf-spirits in the Nutlam dance, ate dogs. Drucker, noting the relative simplicity of the dog eating dance among the northern peoples, plus the widespread distribution of its basic elements, hypothesized that it is of considerable antiquity and "comes the closest to representing the ancestral ritual on which the more complex dancing societies were patterned" (1940:229). There is indeed something archetypal in the ceremonial act of dog eating. And, interestingly, like the other widespread ceremonial act discussed here—gashing—blood is present and prominent. Blood, of course, was what Perkins was referring to when he began his discussion of the Sahaptin concept of "*aut-ní*" or "sacred" (see Appendix 1, Doc. 5, entry for Aug. 15, 1843).

# 7

# Culture Change at Wascopam

Culture change among the Indians of the Pacific Northwest proceeded at a very rapid pace: in less than a century, from initial contact with Spanish ships in 1774 to the establishment of reservations in the 1850s, native populations dropped to less than a quarter of their original numbers, they were removed from their original homes, with few exceptions their fishing and gathering economies were disrupted, their material cultures were displaced and altered by White influence, their kin structures and social networks were loosened or unraveled, and their religious systems were wiped out, forced underground, or folded into new, semi-Christian configurations.

The Wascopam Mission papers document a period of intense culture change at The Dalles. Culture change resulting from indirect White influence on the mid-Columbia goes back to the latter half of the eighteenth century; direct contact with Whites dates from the arrival of Lewis and Clark in 1805. With the exception of the temporary Bache and Birnie trading posts in 1829–30, sustained, unbroken contact with Whites in The Dalles area did not begin until the arrival of Perkins and Lee in March 1838. From that date on the pace of Indian culture change quickened rapidly, and there was a rapid shift from indirect, selective processes to more aggressive, coercive, and super-imposed change. The open give-and-take influence of the Hudson's Bay Company traders was replaced by the more intense, yet still benign, methods of the missionaries, and then, beginning in Perkins's last two years, the draconian, superimposed methods of the White settlers, exemplified by Elijah White's law code. In the middle 1840s the latter kind of pressure increased, leading to conflict and open warfare by late 1847 and forced removal to reservations by 1858. The Perkins years were important and pivotal: before 1838 the local Upper Chinookans and Sahaptins still had control of their destiny; by late 1844 they were well on their way to losing it.

There is a considerable amount of information in the Wascopam papers on change in four broad areas of native life: disease and depopulation, material culture, social control, and religion. Each of those topics will be dealt with in sequence. The first two are covered in this chapter, the last two in chapters 8, 9, and 10.

## Disease and Depopulation

Perhaps the most fundamental of all changes began well before White contact, and in ways not yet fully understood it affected all segments of aboriginal culture, loosening and preparing the Indians for the eventual onslaught of new ways. That was the introduction of new infectious diseases and the high mortalities those diseases brought with them. Nearly all the highly infectious diseases we are familiar with today were not native to the Americas, and once they were introduced they spread rapidly, with devastating effects.

The process of disease introduction in the Pacific Northwest is summarized in Boyd (1985, 1990). The first European disease to affect The Dalles area was a major smallpox epidemic, sometime between 1775 and 1781 (Boyd 1994b). The epidemic spread throughout the region, and although mortality figures are not known, all accounts agree they were high, certainly exceeding the 30 percent average for virgin-soil smallpox epidemics. A second smallpox epidemic passed through the southern coast a generation later, in 1801-02. White traders introduced venereal diseases and tuberculosis to the lower Columbia in the early decades of the nineteenth century, and in 1824-25 an unidentified "mortality" spread through the Columbia basin. It is safe to assume that by 1829 there were less than half as many Indians in the Pacific Northwest as there had been a mere fifty-five years earlier, when direct contact began.

In 1830 another epidemic, the "fever and ague" appeared at Fort Vancouver and in the Wappato Valley, and in 1831 it spread to the Willamette Valley and The Dalles. Its demographic effect on the Kalapuyas of the Willamette Valley has been discussed elsewhere (Boyd 1985: chap. 3). For the Chinookan peoples, a comparison of Lewis and Clark's 1805 population estimate of 9,800 (Boyd and Hajda 1987:313) and Perkins's 1843 estimate of 1,500 gives an idea of the magnitude of loss. That 85 percent decline, concentrated in the first years of the epidemic, was strongest among the downstream peoples, especially in the Wappato Valley. Horatio Hale, ethnographer of the Wilkes Expedition, said:

> The region below the Cascades ... suffered most from this scourge. The population, which before was estimated at upwards of ten thousand, does not now exceed five hundred. Between the Cascades and the Dalles, the sickness was less destructive. There still remain five or six villages, with a population of seven or eight hundred. [1846:215]

As noted earlier (chap. 2), Jason Lee's estimate of the Wascopam circuit population, 1,600, was a decline of 71 percent from Lewis and Clark's estimate of 5,600, which was for approximately the same area. The farthest upstream extent of the illness was the mouth of the John Day, according to Simon McGillivray (1831–32); at Fort Nez Percés only a few isolated cases were recorded. Mortalities were also fewer at the mouth of the Columbia (Boyd 1985:121). The geographic extent of fever and ague provides one clue as to its identity. A second clue comes from its temporal occurrence: the first fever and ague cases appeared regularly each summer, peaked in early fall, and stopped with the onset of winter. Epidemiologically, those patterns fit the characteristics of malaria in temperate zones. Malaria is carried by a mosquito vector, in the Northwest *Anopheles malculipennis,* which is uncommon along the coast and in the dry interior and which breeds in summer and early fall. That pattern plus other clues (the historic occurrence of malaria in Oregon, medicines used by Whites, symptomatology) indicate that fever and ague was malaria, although other diseases were certainly present in the 1830s as well and, superimposed on malaria, contributed to the high Indian mortality.

Both Whites and Indians were affected by fever and ague, but Whites, who knew how to care for those afflicted with the disease, and who had proper medicines, rarely died. Practically everyone at Willamette Mission, White and Indian, suffered from fever. Perkins's *Christian Advocate and Journal* account (Appendix 1, Doc. 4) of the effects of the disease on a trip to Willamette—itself a summary of a September 12, 1840, letter to Daniel Lee (Canse Collection)—is one of the two most complete nonepidemiological descriptions in the historical record (see also Bolduc 1979:118). Perkins's "sickly season" was, of course, the warm months of late summer and early fall, when fever and ague was most prevalent in the interior valleys of Western Oregon. Intense febrile episodes—such as those experienced by the Indian who died, alternating with "chills of the ague"— the problem of twenty-month-old Henry Johnson Perkins—were typical symptoms of malaria. Temperature extremes—such as the "intense" heat noted by Perkins—tend to bring on spells of fever or chills; measures that further disrupt the body's temperature-regulating system, such as immersing oneself in cold water (a common Indian response), bring on death.

Perkins's administration of calomel (mercurous chloride, a cathartic) probably did not help his Indian's condition. For others (according to the letter), Perkins used quinine, the most effective medicine for malaria (as well as a strong antipyretic), which was apparently provided by Dr. William Bailey. The reference to "miasma" (swamp gas or low fog), is pertinent, as it was commonly assumed in the nineteenth century to be the cause of the type of fever that would later be named malaria (from *mala aria* 'bad air' in Italian). The role of Anopheline mosquitoes in the transmission of malaria was not discovered until 1897.

Other diseases that appeared in the 1830s—including tuberculosis, meningitis, and influenza—contributed to Indian mortality. James Birnie's letter of February 27, 1840, from Clatsop (appended to chap. 5 of "Wonderful Work of God....," Appendix 1, Doc. 3), supplies additional information on population decline among the lower Chinooks. Birnie mentions chronic venereal disease (a common problem around most trading posts, but negligible near The Dalles at that time), which often leads to sterility and miscarriage, causing a decline in the birth rate. Abortion and infanticide, practiced aboriginally to a limited degree, appear to increase in frequency in situations of cultural disruption and anomie (see chap. 5). Birnie's account, though short, is very similar in its particulars to two later papers on the causes of population decline among the Nuu-chah-nulth of Vancouver Island (Sproat 1868: chap. 27) and Puget Sound Salish (Eells 1887).

With the beginnings of the great migrations over the Oregon Trail in 1843, new diseases arrived. In 1844, outbreaks of whooping cough and dysentery are recorded in the Wascopam papers. The first mention of whooping cough is in a January 1 letter by Henry Brewer (Canse Collection); Henry Perkins notes it in his January 21 journal entry (Appendix 1, Doc. 5), and Elvira in a letter of February 8 (David Leslie Collection). The disease is mentioned in Daniel Lee's "Dalles Journal" between January 23 and February 15 (Archives of the Oregon-Idaho Conference). According to the Perkinses, whooping cough was contracted by Cayuses in the Rocky Mountains during summer 1843 (at a rendezvous?), "& from them it has spread through the Wallawalla tribe & is now spreading through this & will probably sweep through Willamette" (E. Perkins, letter of Feb. 8, 1844, David Leslie Collection).

Brewer's description of that miniepidemic, from letters of January 1 and February 13, follows:

> [January 1, 1844:] The whooping cough is quite prevalent among the children in this vi[cinity], ours & Br Perkins children are now afficted [sic] with it, we dread the disease because of its length some[times] it is six week before it arrives at its highest pitch & then six weeks more in going off. [Canse Collection]

> [February 13, 1844:] We have two sweet babes . . . they are now both recovering from the whooping cough. Br Perkins children are also afflicted with the same disease. Mrs. Masters, wife of one of the emigrants has been in my family 4 months her infant son was taken ill with the cough . . . died one week ago . . . the first white child that has died at this station. . . . A number of Indian children are also afflicted in the same way, some have died—Last evening when I was out of doors I heard cries and lamentations from the village again, it is truly distressing to the

ear, this morning Br. Perkins interpreter [Luxillu?] called upon me for
a coffin & said his little Susanna died last evening. [Canse Collection]

The dysentery epidemic is not mentioned in any of Henry Perkins's
writings, but it appears prominently in documents of his contemporaries and
should be mentioned here. The disease, sometimes called the bloody flux, was
first recorded at Fort Vancouver in August. Some "four hundred Indians . . .
in the vicinity of the Fort" died, as well as thirty at Cowlitz and "numbers" at
The Cascades (Boyd 1985:179). The disease was epidemic at Wascopam in
October, after the Perkinses' departure. The Brewers were distressed, as their
daughter Susan was especially sick, and they did not know how to treat her (L.
Brewer, letter of Oct. 16, H. Brewer, letter of Oct. 27, 1844, Canse Collection).
A year later, in a letter to Elvira Perkins, Laura Brewer summarized the
outbreak:

> Soon after . . . you left, the dysentery, which you recollect was raging in
> the village below us [Nenootletete?], made its appearance here. While
> Mr Brewer was gone, several were brought here from the village below
> to obtain medicine. Three or four were in our yard at one time. All I
> believe died. In all about thirty. One was Ticicash, Carnicissa's son. . . .
> There is no doubt that he would have lived, if Tumsowit had let him alone.
> He worked on him till the evening he died, when at his urgent request, he
> was brought here, but it was too late. [L. Brewer, letter of Aug. 15, 1845,
> Canse Collection]

Both the whooping cough and the dysentery outbreaks hit the youngest
segment of the population especially hard. Those circumstances were destined
to be repeated in November 1847, when the well-known measles epidemic
preceded the Whitman Massacre, the abandonment of Wascopam Mission,
and the start of the Cayuse War (Boyd 1994a).

## Material Culture

### Influence of the Hudson's Bay Company

In the first installment of his *Christian Advocate and Journal* report, "History
of the Oregon Mission," Perkins noted that "fighting and bloodshed had been
mostly put an end to through the influence and exertions of humane gentlemen
of the Hudson Bay Company" (Appendix 1, Doc. 2). Though that statement
has its qualifiers, as we will see, it was in large part true. The Hudson's Bay
Company played a major role in establishing a degree of tranquility in the
Northwest of the 1830s. It would not be an exaggeration, in fact, to speak of
a "pax H.B.C." imposed, in particular, by the firm hand of Chief Factor John

McLoughlin. The Hudson's Bay Company was primarily an economic organization, which operated in a political vacuum. The company did not exert political control over the Indians of the area, but to allow for the continual unimpeded movement of people and goods, it was sometimes necessary to take noneconomic actions.

The usual tactic was to provide a show of force and selective punishment of prominent wrongdoers. A precedent for that policy was the punitive North West Company force sent to The Cascades in January 1814, which cleared up a long-festering problem of difficult passage on that stretch of the river (summary in Beckham 1984:27–43). At least two incidents involving Indians and Whites between 1828 and 1829 were dealt with by McLoughlin with quick surgical action. The first was the Clallam Expedition of 1828. The Clallams had killed five men and taken a woman captive. The Chief Factor responded by sending a party of sixty men: a "large village" at New Dungeness was "destroyed" by cannon, and perhaps twenty-five Indians were killed (Ermatinger, letter of June 17, 1828, 1980:96–114). In 1829 the ship *William and Ann* ran aground at Clatsop Point, all lives were lost, and the hulk was looted by the Clatsops. The initial assumption (later disproved) that the crew had been murdered by the Indians prompted McLoughlin to send a punitive expedition of fifty-nine to the coast (letter of Aug. 5, 1829, in Barker 1948:19–22). To quote the Chief Factor, "Three of their chiefs were killed and lost their heads, their village was burnt down and their canoes and everything else that could be found destroyed" (letter of Mar. 19, 1830). George Simpson concluded, "The example which has been made of the Clatsops has done much good throughout the Columbia, as the Natives have not for a length of time been so quiet & orderly" (1830). A third punitive expedition, to southern Oregon to punish the attackers of Jedediah Smith's 1828 party, was deemed not necessary, and the stolen goods were obtained by other means (McLoughlin in Clarke 1905:216–17). As late as August 1840, following the killing of two people at Pillar Rock, McLoughlin sent identical letters to Jason Lee, Father Blanchet, and the Willamette settlers informing them of his intent to punish the killers. Two Indians at the site were shot to death, and a third was hanged "in the presence of all his countrymen" (McLoughlin 1840).

Under the Hudson's Bay Company regime there was a free flow of goods and a corresponding selective change and enrichment of native material culture. The process of adoption of some of those new items, and the changes they brought in their wake, is a fascinating subject, mentioned often in the Perkins documents.

## Livestock

The adoption of livestock by the Indians of the southern Plateau is an example.

Horses preceded Whites to the Plateau in the middle of the eighteenth century and brought many culture changes with them. The process of their adoption has been discussed in several works (e.g., for the Plains, see Ewers 1955; Haines 1960; for the Pacific Northwest, Anastasio 1972:127–30; Boxberger 1984).

Cattle were rare and valuable in early Oregon, and both Whites and Indians went to great lengths to obtain them. Until 1836, when Whitman and Spalding brought 15 cattle over the Rockies (Drury 1973, 1:183), all livestock in the Northwest were owned by the Hudson's Bay Company, which lent them to settlers for their milk but forbade slaughter and claimed all calves. In 1837, mountain man Ewing Young determined to break that monopoly and made his well-known drive to California to obtain stock. In October, Young's Willamette Cattle Company returned with 630 head for the valley settlers.

The new Wascopam Mission required oxen for plowing as well as milk cows; hence Daniel Lee's September 1838 cross-Cascades trek to acquire them. The Wascopam herd grew rapidly. Two years later, Brewer stated: "We have 30 head of cattle, among them are 9 cows . . . four give milk. . . . We have ten very good hogs, one yoke steer . . . four horses" (letter of Aug. 14, 1840, Canse Collection). "We are not obliged to cut grass for our cattle or raise grain for our swine the latter keep fat on acorns all winter & the former on the large rich fields of grass" (letter of Aug. 22, 1840, Canse Collection). In late September 1841 Brewer planned to slaughter "4 or 5 hogs & 2 or 3 beef" for winter provisions (letter of Sept. 23, 1841, Canse Collection).[1]

Euroamericans desired cattle for their milk-producing and draft characteristics as well as for their meat. None of those qualities, however, explains the Indian desire for herds. A taste for dairy foods is definitely culturally acquired and must be introduced early in life in order to overcome the body's natural intolerance to lactose. Draft animals are of greatest use in plowing the earth, which of course is a necessity only in agricultural societies. Indians did not drink milk, nor did they plant crops. So why did Indians want cattle? Two factors seem important. First, Plateau peoples undoubtedly noted the similarity of cattle to bison (the Sahaptin term for cattle, *músmicin*, is the same as the name for bison) (Eugene Hunn, personal communication, 1989). Since the middle of the eighteenth century task forces of Plateau peoples had traveled over the Rockies to take bison, which were valued for their meat and hides. Why travel to the Plains when you could raise ersatz bison at home? It took a while to build up the herds to the point where meat and hides could be taken on a sustained basis, but some entrepreneurial Indians were willing to wait. A second factor was prestige. Certain scarce commodities, held in large quantities, had social value. Such commodities might also be used as working capital to obtain other goods. Strictly utilitarian value was beside the point.

That kind of acquisitiveness was very much characteristic of Northwest Coast and (to a lesser extent) Plateau cultures and provided a motivation for the entry of cattle into late-contact-era Indian cultures.

As early as 1837 Plateau Indians were expressing a desire for cattle. In April of that year William Gray (who had arrived in Oregon with Whitman and Spalding) began his overland return to the States, accompanied by Ellice (see chap. 8) and three other Nez Perces, who hoped to trade horses for that valuable new commodity. The Nez Perces turned back at the Green River rendezvous, however, and Gray went on with the horses. When he returned to the Northwest in August 1838, he had no cattle and the Nez Perces were angry (Drury 1973, 1:236-37, 308, 323).

By 1840 the success of the Wascopam and Waiilatpu herds was becoming obvious to the locals, and Indians who traveled to Willamette and Vancouver could not have failed to be impressed by the large herds owned by the Whites. It may have been about that time that, in the words of A. J. Splawn:

> Chief Kamiakin, about 1840, brought the first cattle to the Yakima valley from Ft. Vancouver, having exchanged horses for them with the Hudsons Bay Company. Not long afterwards Chief Owhi of the Kittitas procured cattle at Ft. Nisqually driving them over the Nah-cheez Pass. Talth-scosum, chief of the Ko-wa-chins at Rock Island, traded horses for cattle with the Hudson's Bay people at Ft. Nisqually and drove them to his range. Other Indians soon followed their example. [Splawn 1917:286-87]

Among the "others" were the Nez Perces. In mid-1841 one of the members of the Wilkes Expedition recorded that Plateau Indians at Willamette were in search of cattle: "Heard that a party of the Nez Perce Tribe of Indians were on their way to the Settlement with fur, horses, etc. to exchange with the settlers for cattle" (Emmons 1841). Six months later, at Lapwai, Henry Spalding noted, "6 persons have cattle, several are expecting to take horses to the Willamette next spring to exchange for cows" (1842).

In April 1845, when Alvan Waller made his circuit of the Yakama country, he found small herds in the hands of many local headmen: "Skillim" [Skloom] had "twenty head of horned cattle and over a hundred head of horses"; "Kamiacan" and "his brother . . . Shawiwi [Showaway] . . . have several head of cattle & horses" (letter of Apr. 26, 1845, Canse Collection). In a later letter Waller stated, "I know of three brothers who have between them I think not less than one hundred head of horned cattle" (letter of Aug. 15, 1845, Archives of the Pacific Northwest Conference).

Kamiakin (k̓amáyaqan, according to Hunn, personal communication, 1982-93) had, by 1855, acquired considerable influence among the Northwest

Sahaptin peoples and was recognized in the Yakama Treaty as head chief of
the newly constituted Yakama Nation. His influence had been gained by
traditional means: extensive social networks (his father was Palouse, his
mother Yakama; he married a Yakama and a Klickitat; he had other ties
through his brothers) and accumulation of considerable movable capital (herds
of horses and cattle), which he obtained through long-distance trade.
k̓amáyaqan was also the first Yakama to grow crops—a fact recorded both by
Waller and by k̓amáyaqan's biographer Splawn. It is notable that the adoption
of cattle and crops was apparently made without direct White influence and
on his own initiative—marks of a genuine innovator.

With that model established, a desire for cattle spread among related
peoples. Hence, by mid-1844, we have the remarkable trip of a task force of
mid-Columbia peoples to the Sacramento Valley to obtain herds of cattle
(Heizer 1942). The innovator in that case was almost certainly Piupiumaksmaks of the Walla Walla: with a residence near Waiilatpu Mission, a son who
had been at Willamette Mission when the California herds arrived, and a
friendship with k̓amáyaqan, he was in a favorable position to understand the
potential value of cattle. The other principals of the party were likewise local
luminaries: Tawatoy of the Cayuses, Kip-kip Pahlekin, a Nez Perce, and
perhaps even Spokan Garry (Josephy 1965:240). Leaders and incipient leaders
like k̓amáyaqan, they were just the kind of people one would expect to take
such a long, risky trip in order to obtain prestigious goods. There is no evidence
that that trip did in fact produce cattle (Brewer in Mudge 1854:62 stated they
were left behind), but by the midfifties Piupiumaksmaks at least owned large
herds of both cattle and horses (Stevens 1900, 1:403).

## Crops

Agriculture did not catch on so easily among the Indians. It should be recalled
that Pacific Northwest Indians were a fishing and gathering people, with no
tradition of agriculture other than the broadcasting of seeds of tobacco, a
nonfood item, in a bed of ashes. Perkins notes that there was considerable
interest among the Indians when he and Lee planted their first garden of
parsnip and cabbage seeds in March 1838: twenty Indians observed intently,
and Canacissa and Tumsowit helped turn the soil. During the second year,
however, Indians stripped an acre of corn and dug up many potato plants. They
were, of course, merely "gathering" those foods. In year three, with twenty
acres under cultivation, according to Daniel Lee:

> One field of several acres we held in shares with some of the Indians, who
> helped to fence and plough it. The ground being new, the returns were
> small; and even these were partly stolen. These discouragements, with

the abundance of salmon, and roots and berries easily obtained, prevented them from ever again, while the writer dwelt among them, degrading themselves by an attempt to till the soil! [D. Lee and Frost 1844:175]

Although the attempt at agriculture failed, the Indians had developed a taste for one crop, potatoes, and Perkins records another example of theft in his 1844 journal (Appendix 1, Doc. 5, entry for Sept. 30). More than fifty bushels were taken, and three or four men from another village dug up more in the middle of the night and spirited them away on their horses.

Among all the domesticated plants brought by Euroamericans to the Pacific Northwest, the potato was singular. In many ways it resembled wild root crops that the natives already harvested. Its taste was similar to both spring beauty *(Claytonia lanceolata)* (N. Turner 1978:172–74) and to wapato *(Sagittaria latifolia)* (Suttles 1951:141), a starchy tuber gathered in lakes in the Wappato Valley (Portland Basin) and traded upriver and downriver from that location. At The Dalles, wapato was a rare commodity, greatly prized. Potatoes not only tasted like wapato but were prolific and probably kept better as well. It is hardly surprising that the Indians scoured the fields.

A second similarity of potatoes to native root crops was in their harvesting and care. On the Plateau, lomatiums, camas, and other root crops were dug up by women with digging sticks and transported in burden baskets. On the Coast, among some peoples, wild camas, which grew most profusely on wet prairies, was tended by semiagricultural methods: plots were burned over and weeded; soil was turned over by digging, and stems with seed pods were buried; there was occasional transplanting (N. Turner 1983:211). Only planting from seeds separates those techniques from true cultivation. And, at certain locations on the coast, that is precisely how Indian agriculture began—with potato plots, replanted annually.[2] On the Coast, where the camas-gathering tradition was strong, potato cultivation spread rapidly. It was virtually universal among most Coast Salish peoples by the middle of the nineteenth century (Suttles 1951).

Despite the failed attempt at Wascopam, cultivation did take hold on the lower Columbia and at Waiilatpu, and at approximately the same time that Perkins and Lee were making their attempt. The earliest account comes from the Reverend Herbert Beaver, at Fort Vancouver, in 1837:

Nearly two hundred of the Klickatack Tribe of Indians have congregated, for agricultural purposes, on a large plain about fourteen miles distant from the Fort, during the last summer, when I have paid them several visits . . . their first attempt at cultivation being made, this year, with potatoes, Indian corn, and peas, furnished them by Chief Factor McLoughlin. Having no place in which to store it, they have brought hither several bushels of the last named product to be reserved for seed till next year. Their little gardens are well fenced, and altogether do them great credit. Indeed I was surprised at the regularity and cleanliness of their potato rows; and I cannot help thinking, that much good might be done among them by encouraging their praiseworthy efforts, in continuing a supply of various seeds, and in providing them with a few agricultural implements, particularly a plough and harrow, which they already possess horses to draw. [Jessett, ed., 1959:58-59]

The "large plain" was probably Lacamas Prairie, a fertile "wet" prairie above Camas, Washington. In March 1838 Margaret Smith (Perkins's shipmate) visited the area and saw Indians planting (Bailey 1986:121). The endeavor was apparently a success—in 1853, just before removal, Klickitats were still maintaining potato plots in Vancouver-area plains (McClellan 1853: entry for July 31).

At Waiilatpu, following the example of Marcus Whitman, some Cayuses also began planting. Whitman grew a large variety of crops in the fertile soil of the Walla Walla valley in an attempt to achieve agricultural self-sufficiency, and he encouraged the Cayuses to grow in hopes that it would keep them in the vicinity of the mission. In March 1837, before they decamped to the camas grounds, several "labored very hard to prepare ground to plant" with fifteen hoes supplied by the missionary (Hulbert and Hulbert 1936:279-80). In 1838 Whitman lent the Indians two wooden plows and reported:

It is really amusing to see them break their horses to work generally one man or woman leading in front & one on each side with sticks, & one holding the plough. . . . Several of them have already planted from half to an acre of potatoes & have considerable fields of corn, and peas. [Hulbert and Hulbert 1936:312-15]

Whitman requested a large quantity of plows and hoes from the East.

At the same time, at Lapwai, the Spaldings began to introduce the Nez Perces to agriculture:

About 80 families have been engaged here several weeks, in breaking land with hoes and planting. Most of them finished last week, and have left for a season to obtain roots fish and [sic] which is their principal food. They will be obliged to continue to wander more or less until they can sustain their families by raising cattle and cultivating their land. I think they would immediately adopt a settled mode of life, if it were consistant for them. The little they raised last year was (with very few exceptions) reserved for seed this season. [E. Spalding 1838]

Spalding's sensitive observation recognized that it would take some time for the Nez Perces to integrate this new practice into their traditional system.

Vancouver, the source of Yakama cattle, may also have been the source for the limited cultivation that Alvan Waller reported in Yakama lands in late April 1845 (letter of Apr. 26, 1845, Canse Collection). Waller visited several bands scattered throughout the Yakima valley. The headmen of two groups, Moninneck and his brother and k̓amáyaqan and his brother Showaway, both grew potatoes, corn, and peas. k̓amáyaqan even showed Waller a corn crib, which in late April had only a few sacks left from the previous summer. As far as Wascopam was concerned, in a letter of August 15, 1845, Waller reported, "They have done more the past year in cultivating the soil than ever before" (Archives of the Pacific Northwest Conference). Fifteen had planted crops.

Reasons for the successful agricultural attempts at Vancouver, Waiilatpu, and Lapwai versus the lag at The Dalles were several, including the better soil of the three former locations, access to more reliable supplies of agricultural tools and seed, and better models and more active encouragement on the part of the personnel at the former three stations.

## Clothing

One class of material culture that appears to have had virtually no barriers to adoption by the Indians was clothing. In fact, the process of adoption of Western-style clothing among Dalles-area Indians seems to say something about the functions of apparel in human societies at large. Purely aboriginal clothing, worn by the larger part of the population at the beginning of the century, was utilitarian and not much more. Yet certain high-ranking individuals, with more access to wealth, apparently added items to their wardrobe that served less as protection from the elements than as statements of their means (examples below). As the access to Western clothes improved, more and more people began to wear them, producing the hodgepodge of clothing types observed by Whites at The Dalles in the 1840s.

On his arrival at Wascopam, Daniel Lee described the clothing of the villagers as follows: "Some of them were draped in Buffalo robes, some in deer skins, and others wore a Shirt and trousers, or a Shirt only, and Some were quite naked" ("Notebook," entry for Mar. 24, 1838, Daniel Lee Collection). The occasional nakedness of Indians usually went unremarked by the Whites. Perkins, however, was embarrassed by Hanecunewitt's lack of clothing (Appendix 1, Doc. 1), and George Simpson, at "Les Dalles" in August 1841, was bemused: "At the landing-place we found about thirty women and children, all the men being absent, fishing. These good folks, generally speaking, were nearly as naked as when they were born" (1847:168).

The missionaries, of course, made an effort to clothe the masses, within their means. Especially at Willamette Mission, several contemporary letters refer to the efforts of Dorcas Societies in the eastern churches—groups of women who made clothes for distribution to the poor. The problem was not of great moment, however, and eventually solved itself. At Willamette Mission, Margaret Smith conducted classes in sewing for Kalapuya women (Bailey 1986:105). At Wascopam, Elvira Perkins and Laura Brewer were less concerned with such "domestic arts."

Two types of apparel worn in precontact and early-contact times that were worn as statements of wealth were dentalia shells (see chap. 3) and bison robes. Both were nonlocal items, in short supply, acquired through long-distance trade. Bison hides were obtained from the east, particularly from Nez Perces, who acquired them on regular bison-hunting trips to the Great Plains. Dalles-area peoples occasionally joined such hunting expeditions, as well as making occasional appearances at Rocky Mountain rendezvous, along with mountain men and several other tribes. Bison robes on the Plateau appear to have been the functional equivalents of several types of woven blankets on the Northwest Coast (such as the Chilkat blanket of the north and the mountain-goat–dog-hair blankets of the central coast).

Plains-type clothing apparently diffused into the Columbia Plateau very late, following the adoption of the horse. The traditional Plateau pattern, according to Erna Gunther (1950:176–77), was bark clothing and simple buckskin garments with some decorative painting and puncturing. Once the cross-mountain bison hunts began in the middle of the eighteenth century, however, a complex of Plains traits, including, among others, beaded clothing, feathered headdresses, and porcupine-quill embroidery, flowed across the Rockies and were quickly adopted by the Plateau peoples.

Shortly afterward, when Euroamericans appeared on the lower Columbia, their clothing too became a desired trade item. On October 28, 1805, downstream from The Dalles, Lewis and Clark met "an Indian with round hat Jacket & wore his hair cued" [he Said he got them from Indians below the great rapid who brought them from the whites] (1988:347). Tilki, "chief of the Dalles" in the early 1830s, wore "English stile Blue frock coat pants. & vest" (Wyeth 1899:175; see chap. 4 above). Perkins's own descriptions of the apparel of Wamcutta and Tawatoy (Appendix 1, Doc. 1) show that individual wardrobes could become quite elaborate indeed. Wamcutta was dressed "in the French style" with a bison robe over all. Tawatoy had "a neat underdress of white blanket, trimmed with blue . . . a pale red robe, fringed and colored with various figures . . . covered nearly half with various beads," moccasins, and a cap. Wamcutta was a prominent local, Tawatoy a Cayuse chief.

There are several pictorial representations of middle-Columbia Indians from the 1840s and 1850s wearing items of White clothing. An 1841 drawing by Henry Eld, probably in the Umatilla area, shows a native in a French sailor's cap and greatcoat standing in front of a tipi. Many of Gustavus Sohon's Walla

Walla treaty sketches depict Indian notables with French caps (Nicandri 1986); it is tempting to speculate that Tawatoy's cap (above) and the "valuable" cap that was the object of the gambling dispute settled by Perkins in November 1839 (Appendix 1, Doc. 3) were of that type. One truly remarkable 1856 drawing by Eugene de Girardin shows the Cayuse "Cut Mouth John" wearing a French military jacket, complete with brass buttons and epaulets, a tall hat with a fur tail atop, and a dagger through his belt.

Increased trade opportunities arising from the presence of American immigrants brought a flood of new types of clothing to The Dalles during the forties. In July 1841 Wilkes states, "The diversity of dress among the men was greater even than in the crowds of natives I have described as seen in the Polynesian islands" (though the women were still "nearly naked") (1844, 3:383). Five years later a somewhat bemused Father Pierre deSmet noted "a complete metamorphosis" in dress from what he had seen in 1844. One Indian, for instance, was clothed as follows:

> A roundabout much too small for him, a pair of tights with straps, with an intervening space showing the absence of linen, form his body dress, while an old-fashioned lady's night-cap with large frills, and if he be rich enough, a sailor's glazed cap carefully balanced above it, constitute his head-dress; a pair, and sometimes half a pair of brogans, complete the ludicrous appearance of this Indian dandy. Some appear parading thro' the camp in the full dress of a wagoner, others in a mixture composed of the sailor's, the wagoner's, and the lawyer's, arranged according to fancy; but the favorite article of ornamental dress appears to be the night-cap with its large frills. [1905:556–57]

Women's outfits at that time consisted of more sensible and functional calico dresses. The men's clothing, however, was more a form of conspicuous consumption. Availability determined the larger part of what one wore—and the Indians were being presented with the entire array of the immigrants' castoffs. Suddenly, the market was flooded. White clothing, formerly limited to the wealthy, was now available to a great many. Everybody wanted new clothes, and it did not make much difference how they looked on one's person. The rapid rate of change temporarily left the Indians' usual taste in apparel behind.

## Tools

A second example of relatively simple additive and replacive acculturation concerns tools. On April 4, 1838, Perkins mentions the Wascopam natives' desire for "tools . . . such as saw and draw shave . . . axes" (Appendix 1, Doc. 1). In fact, the desire of the Indians was probably not so much for particular tools as it was for tools made of a particular material—hard iron or steel. The Northwest Coast woodworking tool kit consisted of adzes: axe-like stone blades inserted in a straight, hand-held antler haft; chisels: finer blades, hafted in wood, driven with a heavy stone maul; and elk-antler wedges, used for splitting red cedar planks. The blades, of nephrite, basalt, or other hard stones, were made by a laborious process of pecking and grinding (Stewart 1973: chap. 3).

Despite those limited tool types, Dalles-area Chinookans made "dugout canoes, paddles, bailers, wooden bowls, mortars, troughs, ladles, spoons, bows, and cradleboards," in addition to (dependent upon local availability of wood) plank structures (Spier and Sapir 1930:188). The Dalles is just beyond the eastern border of distribution of western Red Cedar *(Thuja plicata)*, the tractable, all-purpose Northwest Coast wood. Spier and Sapir (1930:188) note that the local woodworking tradition paled in comparison to that of the Northwest Coast proper but was superior to that of the Columbia Plateau.

Iron was in demand as a trade item on the Northwest Coast from the very beginning of Euroamerican contact; in July 1774, when the first Spanish ship stopped off the Queen Charlotte Islands, the local Haida Indians took all the iron knives the crew owned and wanted more of a larger size (Rickard 1939:25). Many early voyagers reported iron implements in the hands of natives; since iron has been found at the precontact Ozette site, and as there was no indigenous smelting tradition, it is now assumed that coastal Indians salvaged iron from wrecks of Japanese junks (Quimby 1985). The material was therefore well known, rare, and in demand because of its superior cutting ability. Indians would go to great lengths to get iron: the Nuu-chah-nulth chiefs Maquinna and Callicum, in exchange for "copper and iron articles . . . took off their sea-otter garments . . . and remained in the unattired garb of nature on the deck" (John Meares, 1788, quoted in Rickard 1939:30-31). Lewis and Clark (1990:249-51, 1991:28-29) mention iron knives on the lower Columbia; they are occasional archaeological finds in Oregon (see, e.g., Cressman 1948; Phebus 1978:121).

## Guns and Slave Raiding

Another category of material culture in which the Euroamerican product was obviously superior and Indian demand was correspondingly great was weaponry. Guns were unquestionably more effective than the aboriginal equivalents, bows and arrows and clubs, both in the hunt and in slave raiding or "warfare."

The addition of guns to the aboriginal cultural inventory not only increased the efficiency of hunting and raiding but had secondary effects in the social sphere. The diffusion of guns appears to have been correlated with an increase in slave raiding. Peoples with guns were at a competitive advantage and used them to increase their supply of slaves and, indirectly, their wealth. Peoples who did not have guns were the source populations for slaves and in some cases appear to have suffered significant population and territorial loss. Those processes appear likely but have not been proven. As of 1993, there is no detailed study of the diffusion of guns among Pacific Northwest Indians in the early nineteenth century.

Available evidence indicates that the process of diffusion was slow. Supply apparently was the determining factor. Guns could be traded to Indians by individual traders, but to be useful they required a continual supply of ammunition, which the Indians could not manufacture themselves. Hence, even though some lower Columbia Indians are recorded as owning firearms in 1796 (Bishop 1967) and in 1805-6 (Lewis and Clark 1988, 1990, 1991), guns probably did not have any significant cultural impact before 1811, the year of the establishment of the first permanent land-based fur-trading post at Astoria.

Between 1813 and 1824 the North West Company was the supplier of firearms to the Indians; after that date it was the Hudson's Bay Company. It is not clear exactly how great the Hudson's Bay Company trade in firearms was: officially the company discouraged it, but observers such as the American William Slacum claimed otherwise. At least, it is clear that, through the years, the supply of guns among Indians increased.

An indication of that fact is found in the price of firearms, recorded in Hudson's Bay Company records. In 1824, the year Fort Vancouver was established, prices (in beaver skins) for major trade commodities were:

> Axes, common—1; Blankets, 3 pt.—6; Blankets, 4 pt, green—10; Beads, per lb.—1; Buttons, per doz.—1; Flints, gun, per doz.—1; Guns, common N.W.—20; Rifles, English twist—40; Gun powder, per lb.—3; Knives—1; Kettles, per lb.—2; Rings, brass, per doz.—1/3; Thimbles, per doz.—1/2; Vermillion, per lb.—4 [Simpson in Strong 1959:239-40]

In 1829, as a result of the abortive American attempt to wrest the Columbia River trade from the company, prices plummeted. A revealing letter dated Aug. 5, 1829, from McLoughlin states:

> Guns were kept by us at a high price from policy to prevent the numerous population getting armed and as they are not animal hunters Guns are of little or no use to them in procuring food . . . an opposition . . . in the River . . . have reduced the price of Guns, from eighteen beaver to three, of Blankets from five to one Beaver, and every other article in the same proportion. [McLoughlin 1941:76]

Guns that had cost thirty beavers in 1824 were going for one-tenth of that price five years later. In the interior, the portals for entry of trade items in 1829 were the Bache and Birnie trading posts near Wishram and on Mill Creek. Although there is no proof that the supply of firearms did in fact increase, or that Indians bought more, the probability is very high.

The strongest case for diffusion of guns facilitating increases in slave raiding has been made for the "Ucletas" (the Lekwiltok, a southern Kwakwaka'wakw group supplied by American coastal traders), who carried out extensive and destructive raids among the gunless Gulf of Georgia and Puget Sound Salish in the 1830s (Taylor and Duff 1956). In Western Oregon, the possession of guns allowed river-mouth Chinooks to raid their upstream relatives (Bishop 1967:118-90) and Tillamooks to take slaves from their southern neighbors (D. Lee and Frost 1844:133). In the 1830s armed Klickitat horsemen entered the Willamette and Umpqua valleys, where they raided scattered bands of Kalapuyas (see, e.g., Applegate 1851).

The source of most Dalles-area slaves was south-central Oregon and northeast California. The peoples of that area—Klamaths, Shastas, Takelmas (Rogues) and Achumawis (Pit Rivers)—were off the main lines of commerce, and in the 1820s and 1830s seem to have had neither horses nor guns. Hudson's Bay Company trader Peter Skene Ogden's account of the first encounter with the Klamaths, dated November 29, 1826, is instructive:

> [lower end of Klamath Marsh:] For many years past they informed us the Nez Percey Indians have made different attempts to reach our Villiage but could not succeed and even this last summer we discovered a war party of Cayouse & Nez Percey, who were in search of us but did not succeed, but now they will have in future your road and altho we have no fire arms we fear them not. [1961:33]

There are several accounts in the Wascopam papers of Columbia River expeditions to obtain slaves from the Klamath country. Both Perkins (journal entry of Aug. 19, 1843, Appendix 1, Doc. 5) and Brewer (in Mudge 1854:50-51) describe a summer 1842 incident in which two Wascopam slave traders were employed by Klamaths to kill a Shasta in a distant village as an act of blood revenge. The Wascos were the only ones with guns. In August 1843 Perkins mentions a "task-grouping" of Wascos, Cayuses, and Nez Perces, who brought in fourteen slaves, "captives of the Chasti tribe" (Appendix 1, Doc. 5, entry for Aug. 19, 1843). Although those slaves had certainly been taken in a raid, the Columbia River peoples had supposedly purchased them. Who did the raiding was not stated. Other accounts, particularly from the Brewer papers, suggest that it was the Klamaths. In August 1842 "A large body of the Clamoth tribe" brought "about twenty slaves" to Willamette Falls (Waller

1843). In September 1844 Klamaths were bringing slaves to Wascopam (L. Brewer, letter of Sept. 7, 1844, Canse Collection). According to Henry Brewer:

> The Clameths have been in this fall with Slaves which were soon disposed of—though we have tried yet we cannot prevent it. The Clameths take their slaves from the Shasty Indians & they in turn take of the Clameths. This is done in war. [H. Brewer, letter of Oct. 27, 1844, Canse Collection]
>
> The Shastas and Klameths, in the southern districts, have been at enmity for a long time. In their predatory incursions upon each other, they seize upon defenseless women and children, and bear them away into captivity. In some cases the males are enslaved, but the difficulty of retaining men as property prevents this result from frequent occurrence. These slaves are purchased by the more northern tribes. A horse, or six beaver skins, or two blankets, or a pair of pantaloons and a vest, will purchase a slave. [H. Brewer in Mudge 1854:25]

By the 1830s mid-Columbia River peoples, with horses and guns, were raiding southern Indians. In 1842 and 1843 Columbia River peoples are recorded as making trips to the south to barter for slaves, and by 1844 Klamaths were bringing slaves to the Columbia to trade. What was happening in the south to cause those shifting patterns is not known with certainty but may be surmised. The Klamaths were apparently becoming enriched with horses and perhaps guns, and at the same time they were gaining the edge over their less-well-supplied neighbors. In the 1840s the victims were "Shastas," a term that might include either true Shastas of the mid-Klamath drainage, Takelmas of the upper Rogue, or both. Ransom, the emancipated Wascopam slave (chap. 5), was a Shasta; Paul Kane painted a "Chasty" slave at Fort Vancouver in 1847. In later years, when the supply of Shastas was exhausted, Klamath slave raiders turned their attention to their southeastern neighbors, the Achumawis (Pit Rivers), whom they raided until the early 1860s (Gatschet 1890:lix–lx, 19–26). Klamaths traded slaves in that time period at an "intertribal mart" at Yainax Butte (Layton 1981).

On the topic of Klamath slave raids, Theodore Stern quotes the Klamath chief Chiloquin:

> When the Snakes [Paiutes who had horses] made war on us that made us keen to fight other Indians and we made war without provocation on the Pit Rivers, Shastas and Rogue Rivers, but they never made willing war on us. Those wars lasted a great many years. We found we could make money by war, for we sold the provisions and property captured for horses and other things we needed. It was like soldiers nowadays who fight for money. We made war because we made money by it and we

rather got to like it anyhow. The Snakes provoked us to make war on them. [1956:240]

The diffusion of horses and guns has been correlated with a southern expansion of Sahaptin peoples (Ray et al. 1938). The same processes may have resulted in analogous ethnic dislocations in south-central Oregon (such as the upper Rogue drainage [see Dixon 1907:387]).

Perkins mentions two characteristics of Klamath hostilities, scalping and the use of arrow poison, that merit further discussion. Both practices were typical of southern Columbia Plateau peoples, as they were of the Indians of the Great Plains (Ray 1942:151, 226). In California, however, their distribution was concentrated in the northeast segment only (Voegelin 1942:72, 111). That distribution suggests a relatively late introduction to the Klamath and their neighbors, with a source in the Columbia Plateau. On the Plateau itself, a significant cluster of traits characteristic of larger-scale Plains-type warfare is assumed to have entered the area following the introduction of the horse in the early eighteenth century (Ray 1939:35-52). On the Northwest Coast, scalping and the other elements of the Plains warfare complex never appeared. People on the Coast took heads, not scalps, and their style of warfare was qualitatively unique (Drucker 1965:75-82; Ferguson 1984).

# 8

## Imposed Culture Change:
## Elijah White's Law Code

The preceding examples of change differ qualitatively from the type of change to be discussed in this chapter. Most of the changes treated in chapter 7 resulted from the introduction of material things—cattle, crops, clothing, guns— associated with Euroamerican culture, into Indian cultures. In some cases the changes those new things produced were limited to simple substitutions (for example, clothing), in other cases there were internal barriers to adoption (crops), and in yet other cases the new things caused widespread systemic change (guns). All those changes occurred naturally, as the result of give and take between donor and recipient cultures. They were in a sense volitional, and once the new things established a fit with the native systems, they were accepted with minimal resistance.

In late 1842 a new kind of change was introduced. It involved nonmaterial things—laws, sanctions, and ideas—that pertained to a different, more diffuse level of Indian culture. As has been discussed earlier, Pacific Northwest social relations worked on the level of kin relations. There were minimally developed governmental institutions—chiefs were essentially family heads and had little true authority. Disputes were handled largely within and among kin units of varying size, with restitution of balance a guiding principal. Although there were mechanisms of social control, there were no discrete judicial institutions and no legal code. The system worked well by itself. But it was quite different from and fundamentally incompatible with the system with which the Euroamerican traders and missionaries were familiar, and which was followed by the American settlers who would begin arriving in large numbers in 1843.

There was some precedent for Sub-Indian Agent Elijah White's law code, although given the available information, it is difficult to know how extensive or important it was in pre-1842 Plateau cultures. Anthropologist Thomas Garth (1965) maintained that the "Plateau Whipping Complex" resembled the system of punishment among the Spanish colonies of the Southwest and must have diffused from there very early in the contact period. But there are no solid ethnohistorical references to punitive whipping on the Plateau until the late 1830s. Ethnographically, whipping has been recorded in two contexts: as a form of "hardening" useful especially in preparation for spirit quests, and as

159

punishment for unruly children. Whipping as punishment for adult transgressors was probably an innovation introduced in the early contact period.

Henry Perkins first mentioned whipping in a letter of December 24, 1839: "Wamcutsul and his people were going to tie me today and whip me, because I would not sell them an axe for six dozen salmon" (Canse Collection). There are a few other references of that sort in the same year from the pens of Thomas Farnham and Henry Spalding (Garth 1965:145). After the imposition of White's law code, whipping as a punishment by Indians is mentioned often in the missionary letters. On August 13, 1843, Perkins said it was used on those who did not observe the Sabbath (Appendix 1, Doc. 5). Perkins was threatened a second time with the whip on August 19, 1843, for interfering with slave trading ("Journal," Appendix 1, Doc. 5).

The system was most likely introduced by the Hudson's Bay Company. Fort Nez Percés head Pierre Pambrun stated that he had "introduced a code of laws" among the natives following his arrival in 1832. A letter of John McLoughlin dated November 28, 1837, says: "The chiefs were in the habit of flogging, at our suggesting, those who stole, etc., and by which in a great measure, they had put a stop to these evil practices" (cited in Drury 1973, 1: 277). Pambrun claimed the code punished "all the crimes denounced by the Christian faith" (Irving 1837:259), but that probably overstates the case. It was that precedent that White followed and developed in 1842.

White's law code, however, was not encouraged by "suggesting" but was enforced; it did not gradually establish a fit with the native system but was superimposed upon it, resulting in inevitable conflicts and contradictions. The 1842 law code created considerable systemic disruption within the Indian cultures affected by it and resulted in confusion and resentment that eventually contributed to a backlash against those who forced it upon its unwilling subjects.

A biographical sketch of White appears in Appendix 3. The Perkinses had known him for some time—he accompanied Elvira to Oregon on the *Diana* in 1837 and was at Willamette Mission throughout Henry's 1837–38 stay. Unlike most of the other members of the Oregon Mission, the Perkinses apparently did not take sides in his battle with Jason Lee. There is little in their papers that indicates unhappiness with either man. White was on the East Coast during most of 1841 and 1842, and when he returned in September of the latter year, he had the title Sub-Indian Agent for Oregon: appointed by the secretary of war, he was the first U.S. government official to hold office in Oregon—which at that time was still legally jointly occupied with Britain.

Most of White's activities in 1842–44 took place upstream from Wascopam, at Fort Nez Percés, Waiilatpu, and Lapwai, and are hence outside the scope of this book. But because White's law code had region-wide effects, and because Henry Perkins was a member of White's May 1843 interior excursion, a brief discussion is in order. Details on White the Indian agent may be found in Allen (1850:177-93, 213-17), G. Hines (1850:142-91), Josephy (1965:226-33), and Drury (1973, 2:20-25).

## The Law Code and Its Aftermath

The burning of the grist mill at Waiilatpu and the evacuation of Narcissa Whitman to Wascopam prompted White's first trip to the interior, from late November to December 1842. At Lapwai he introduced the law code, as follows:

Art. 1. Whoever wilfully takes life shall be hung.

Art. 2. Whoever burns a dwelling-house shall be hung.

Art. 3. Whoever burns an out-building shall be imprisoned six months, receive fifty lashes, and pay all damages.

Art. 4. Whoever carelessly burns a house, or any property, shall pay damages.

Art. 5. If any one enter a dwelling, without permission of the occupant, the chiefs shall punish him as they think proper. public rooms are excepted.

Art. 6. If any one steal he shall pay back twofold; and if it be the value of a beaver skin or less, he shall receive twenty-five lashes; and if the value is over a beaver skin, he shall pay back twofold, and receive fifty lashes.

Art. 7. If any one take a horse and ride it, without permission, or take any article and use it, without liberty, he shall pay for the use of it, and receive from twenty to fifty lashes, as the chief shall direct.

Art. 8. If any one enter a field, and injure the crops, or throw down the fence, so that cattle or horses go in and do damage, he shall pay all damages, and receive twenty-five lashes for every offense.

Art. 9. Those only may keep dogs who travel or live among the game; if a dog kill a lamb, calf, or any domestic animal, the owner shall pay the damage and kill the dog.

Art. 10. If an Indian raise a gun or other weapon against a white man, it shall be reported to the chiefs, and they shall punish him. If a white person do the same to an Indian, it shall be reported to Dr. White, and he shall redress it.

Art. 11. If any Indian break these laws, he shall be punished by his chiefs, if a white man break them, he shall be reported to the agent, and be punished at his instance. [Allen 1850:189-90]

In addition to the code, White appointed several whippers, who were to enforce the laws, and designated Ellice as the sole recognized chief of all the Nez Perce peoples.

White returned to Wascopam and was there for Christmas 1842. Curiously, only one member of the Wascopam Mission, Henry Brewer, wrote down anything about the first interior trip:

> Dr White has returned to this country & holds the office of "Indian Agent" for Oregon Territory. . . . He with Mr [Thomas] McKay, Br [Cornelius] Rogers . . . & others have recently visited us & have been far into the interior to instruct the different tribes in their intercourse with the whites, give them law to some extent, etc. . . . we are much pleased with him as a gentleman & christian. [H. Brewer, letter of Jan. 2, 1843, Canse Collection]

Troubles started brewing among the upriver peoples almost immediately after White's departure. One of the sons of Piupiumaksmaks, the most influential of the Walla Walla chiefs, got into a fracas with a Hudson's Bay Company employee at Fort Nez Percés over a piece of wood. Piupiumaksmaks (plate 17) promptly appeared at the fort. "Then ensued a long conversation about Dr. White's laws, wherein if an Indian struck a white man he would be flogged & if a white man struck an Indian he would also be flogged" (McKinlay 1911:371). The laws, of course, did not address that precise issue, but they did (in articles 10 and 11) suggest equal punishment of White and Indian for like offenses. The problem was that, for the Whites, punishment was to be meted out by Dr. White, who had dubious authority over Americans in the area and none over Hudson's Bay Company employees. The Indian desire for balance and equal treatment was not to be satisfied: the post head refused to punish his employee, there was a standoff, and Piupiumaksmaks departed in high dudgeon. After the intervention of Tawatoy, Five Crows, and the chief's other son, Elijah Hedding, followed by some more unpleasantness, the incident was settled with an exchange of gifts (a more purely Indian way of settling disputes) (McKinlay 1911:372-74).

But the Walla Walla chief's discontent did not stop here. Shortly after that incident an apparently distraught Piupiumaksmaks appeared at Wascopam Mission to confer with the visiting Jason Lee:

> The Wallawalla Chief, (Elijah Heddings Father,) called on me with several of his people. They were very anxious to know whether Dr. White, and ourselves, are the same. They said that we sunday Chiefs; had been long with them, and they had been accustomed to hear us; and they were anxious to know whether this new thing that Dr. White was bringing in, was the same, or not. They asked the following, and many other questions. "If white men sleep with our women by stealth, is it right for us to tie them up and whip them?" We referred them to Dr. White for an answer. They wished also to know what effect did the coming of so many

white people into the country would ultimately have on them? Whether their condition would be made better, or worse, by the whites? I told them that depended much upon themselves; if they imitated our industry, and adopted our habits; that their poverty would disappear and they would have things, as well as we. [J. Lee, comments dated Feb. 3, 1843, letter of Mar. 27, 1843, Archives of the Pacific Northwest Conference]

While at the mission, Piupiumaksmaks also attempted to settle a dispute involving the theft of a cow by a nephew of his ("Elijah's cousin") more than six months earlier (Brewer 1986:75). Again according to Jason Lee:

[February 3:] One who gave us a horse came here last summer, and forcibly took a heifer from our band and drove her away. I scolded the man severely, for stealing the heifer. he would not allow that it was stealing, but only exchanging property.

[February 10:] The Wallawalla Chief came again with the man who took the cow, and wished to have the business settled at once. I insisted on having the cow returned as the first step. They seemed unwilling to promise to do it. I am fully satisfied, that all gifts of Indians are emphatically Indian gifts, That they, invariably, expect, and are not satisfied unless they receive more value than they give, where they make a present. [J. Lee, letter of Mar. 27, 1843, Archives of the Pacific Northwest Conference]

To the missionaries, the taking of the heifer constituted theft, punishable under White's law code. To the Indians it was merely delayed reciprocity for the previous present of a horse. It may well be that Piupiumaksmaks was testing the Methodists, to see whether they would adhere to White's code or whether a settlement would have to be made on different terms, as had been the case at Fort Nez Percés. The incident was not resolved until May 25, 1843, when White met with the aggrieved Walla Walla and agreed that for every horse given Lee, a cow should be received in exchange (G. Hines 1850:183).

By now Piupiumaksmaks must have begun to realize that White and his law code did not speak to all White people and that there were indeed different tribes of Whites. So who did White speak for? Maybe it was the King George men at Vancouver, or maybe it was the Americans who were rumored to be coming overland. He next traveled to Hudson's Bay Company headquarters at Fort Vancouver to find out. Here the "hias" (great) doctor allayed his fears and addressed the rumors

that the whites would come in the summer, and kill them all off. . . . Dr McLaughlin said he had nothing to do in a war with the Indians; that he did not believe the Americans designed to attack them, and that, if the Americans did go to war with the Indians, the Hudson's Bay Company would not assist them. [G. Hines 1850:165]

Piupiumaksmaks returned home with the news and, according to Hines, "the Indians became more calm" (G. Hines 1850:165).

The calm must not have lasted very long, however, because by early April the Plateau missionaries detected more unease among the Indians. Daniel Lee's "Dalles Journal" entry for April 10, 1843, read: "We regret that Dr White does not intend to visit the Indians as he engaged to do this Spring. This will make a bad impression on them and quite destroy their confidence in him" (Archives of the Oregon-Idaho Conference). On April 14 Narcissa Whitman, one of the persons for whose safety White had devised his Indian code, wrote:

> The agent is quite ignorant of Indian character and especially the character of the Kaiuses.... Language like this has been told them, and at the meeting last fall, "that if you do not make laws and protect the whites and their property, we will put you in the way of doing it." They consider this a declaration to fight and they have prepared accordingly.... Mr McKinlay has brought word to the Kaiuses from Dr. McLoughlin that the British do not intend to make war on them. This relieves them greatly. [1894:161]

At approximately the same time White received a letter from Henry Perkins. The letter itself has not survived, but according to Gustavus Hines, it said

> that the Wascopam and Walla-Walla Indians had communicated to him ... that the Indians are very much exasperated against the whites in consequence of so many of the latter coming into their country, to destroy their game, and take away their lands; that the Nez Perces dispatched one of their chiefs last winter on snow shoes, to visit the Indians in the buffalo country east of Fort Hall, for the purpose of exciting them to cut off the party that it is expected Dr. Whitman will bring back with him to settle the Nez Perce country; that the Indians are endeavoring to form a general coalition for the purpose of destroying all the Boston people: that it is not good to kill a part of them, and leave the rest, but that every one of them must be destroyed. [G. Hines 1850:143-44]

Brewer also wrote to the agent, reiterated the rumors of war, and requested that White meet with the Indians (G. Hines 1850:147).[1]

White therefore assembled a party of four, including Gustavus Hines and "his Indian boy" Sampson (Wilder), and left Willamette on April 25. At Vancouver they hired a party of seven Wascopam Indians to guide them upstream, and on May 4 they arrived at Wascopam (G. Hines 1850:148- 56).

Here White parleyed with twenty Indians (apparently Nez Perces), including several "chiefs," concerning the law code:

> The chiefs had found much difficulty in enforcing the laws. . . . The chiefs appointed through Dr. White were desirous that these regulations should continue, evidently because they placed the people under their absolute control. . . . But the other influential men who were not in office . . . said they had been whipped a good many times, and had got nothing for it . . . they were willing it should continue, provided they were to receive blankets, shirts, and pants, as a reward for being whipped . . . the Doctor . . . wished them to understand that they need not expect pay for being flogged, when they deserved it. They laughed heartily at the idea, and dispersed. [G. Hines 1850:157]

As the party was without an interpreter (Cornelius Rogers, who had served in that capacity in the fall, having drowned in February), Henry Perkins was engaged to translate.

There is nothing in the surviving Perkins documents about what transpired during the ensuing trip to Waiilatpu. All information comes from other sources, particularly Hines and Narcissa Whitman. The latter noted their arrival at Waiilatpu:

> Dr. White arrived on the 9th accompanied by Mr Perkins who is to act as Interpreter & Rev Mr. Hinds [sic] of the Methodist Mission. He quite took us by surprise as we had heard several times that he was not coming. (indeed Doct McLoughlin was quite unwilling that he should come) He sent word to the Kaiuse to have them assemble immediately. Mr Perkins went himself to the Utilla to invite Tauatau. . . . It may be that the Kaius will by this time find themselves prepared to . . . farming & adopting those laws . . . —Mr. Perkins thinks not however—A great difficulty will be in electing a High Chief—Tauatau and Pahat-Koko seem to be the only ones on the list. [N. Whitman, letter of May 18, 1843, in Hulbert and Hulbert 1938:305]

The selection of Perkins as interpreter was probably a good choice— besides being fluent in Sahaptin, he was apparently on good terms with both the Cayuse and the Walla Walla peoples. Perkins served as personal emissary to both Tawatoy and Piupiumaksmaks: his encounters with both men, described in detail by Hines, appear in Appendix 3.

At the meeting of the Cayuses and the Walla Wallas with White on May 23, Piupiumaksmaks was finally able to question the author of the law code that had caused him so much confusion and trouble. According to Hines,

> he rose and said: "I have a message to you. Where are these laws from? Are they from God or from the earth? I would that you might say they were from God. But I think they are from the earth, because, from what I know of white man, they do not honor these laws."
>
> In answer to this, the people were informed that the laws were recognized by God, and imposed on men in all civilized countries. Yellow Serpent [Piupiumaksmaks] was pleased with the explanation, and said that it was according to the instructions he had received from others, and he was very glad to learn that it was so, because many of his people had been angry with him when he had whipped them for crime, and had told him that God would send him to hell for it, and he was glad to know that it was pleasing to God. [1850:179]

More deliberations, the selection of a Cayuse chief, a slaughter and feast of two oxen, and speeches by Perkins, Hines, Tawatoy, his brother the new chief, Piupiumaksmaks, and various Nez Perce worthies followed, and the meeting was adjourned.

On June 1 Brewer recorded:

> Dr White, Br Perkins & Br Hines have just returned from the upper country some misunderstanding that existed between the Nez Perces, Cayuses & the Dr have been settled to the satisfaction of both parties, their visit was quite opportune. [H. Brewer, letter of June 1, 1843, Canse Collection]

Temporarily, at least, things appeared to be smoothed over. But the laws were intact, and more incidents arising from their interpretation would follow. The patience of the Indians was also to be tested by other events: in fall 1843, the return of Marcus Whitman and the arrival of the 1,000- strong overland migration, and in 1844, on the heels of Perkins's departure, the dysentery epidemic and first reports of Elijah Hedding's murder in California. All those added salt to a still-festering wound.

## The Cockstock-Sciats Affair

Two more examples of the effects of the new legal system are recorded in Perkins documents. The first example is very complex and involves a clash between the superimposed rule of law and the native concepts of reciprocity, kinship obligations, and slavery. There was a sequence of unfortunate and mishandled events, most involving White. The entire sequence might be referred to as the Cockstock-Sciats affair.

The first incident occurred at Oregon City in April 1843, a month before White's second trip to the interior. Winslow Anderson, the African American who had worked as a carpenter at Wascopam, had hired a Molala Indian to work for him for a year and had promised to pay him with a horse (Allen 1850: 233). Before the Indian had finished his work, Anderson sold the specified horse to someone else, so the Molala, Cockstock, feeling aggrieved, helped himself to another steed. Anderson accused him of theft and reported him to Dr. White. Because horse theft was one of White's punishable transgressions, the agent sent a posse after Cockstock. According to Hines (G. Hines 1850: 144–46), the Indians tried to make amends by offering (after the fact) another horse in exchange, but by that time the damage had been done. Cockstock remained at large.

The next month, in the interior, White introduced his law code to the Cayuses, the Walla Wallas, and the Wascopam area peoples. One of the whippers appointed by White during that second trip was named Sciats (it is unclear whether he was Sahaptin or Chinookan). Three months later, Sciats got in an argument with Henry Perkins over slave trading, entered his house, and attempted to whip him. The incident is fully reported in Perkins's August 19, 1843, journal entry (Appendix 1, Doc. 5) and by Brewer in Mudge (1854: 46–48). Nearly six weeks afterward, on October 8, Dr. White arranged for Sciats to be punished. The transgressions included White's article 5, "enter[ing] a dwelling, without permission of the occupant," and article 10, which prohibited an Indian from "rais[ing] a gun or other weapon against a white man" (Allen 1850:189–90). Jason Lee was present at the sentencing.

> Attended the trial of the man who a few weeks since tied Bro. Perkins an account of which you will receive from him. In the mean time he had been to Bro. P. and made his confession and received his forgiveness and on this account he seemed to claim exemtion [sic] from all trial, but Dr. White and the chiefs, were resolved to investigate the subject. At first he tried to make out what he had before stated to Bro. P. Viz. that he had been instigated to it by others, but this was shown to be a mere excuse and at length he owned that it was his own heart alone that instigated him to do it. After much talk it [was] determined by the Chiefs and Dr. white that he should be publicly whipped, and he was taken out forthwith and received 25 lashes. [J. Lee, diary, entry for Oct. 8, 1843, Archives of the Pacific Northwest Conference]

Elsewhere, Lee stated, "Mr. Perkins interceded for the prisoner and was anxious that he should be pardoned, but it was thought that prudence required an example" (Brosnan 1932:217).

The two incidents so far may appear not to be related, but in fact they were. Cockstock was "connected with the Klackamas Indians by marriage" (G. Hines 1850:144) and at The Dalles as well, where Sciats was "one of his connexions" (Allen 1850:234). The public humiliation of his "connexion" caused Cockstock to (in White's words)

> take fire afresh, and in November last came with a slave to my house, with the avowed object of shooting me at once; but finding me absent, after a close search in every part of the house, he commenced smashing the windows, lights, sash, and all, of my house and office, with the breech of his gun; and it is but just to say, he did his work most effectually, not leaving a sound window in either. [Allen 1850:234]

One month after that, White parleyed with a band of fifteen Molalas and Klamaths; on their way home, the Indians were massacred by Cockstock and his party. Throughout the winter, Cockstock continued "making threats against the settlers" (specifics not reported), and White put a price of $100 on his head. On March fourth, in broad daylight, Cockstock and six men entered Oregon City, "rode from house to house, showing their loaded pistols," and then crossed the river to Willamette village. When they recrossed the river, the settlers were waiting. A fracas ensued, and, according to White, "a mulatto man ran up, named Winslow Anderson, and despatched Cockstock, by breaking in his skull with the barrel of his rifle." Three Whites were wounded, of whom two died. The Indians, with two hurt, retreated to the heights above the city, where they took potshots at the citizens and then fled.

But the affair did not end here. On February 16, 1844, while he was "penning these lines," White found himself

> completely surrounded by at least seventy Indians . . . armed to the teeth, and painted horribly . . . just down from the Dalles of the Columbia, many of them professed relatives of the deceased [Cockstock], on their way to the falls of the Willamette, to demand an explanation, or, in other words, to extort a present for the loss of their brother. . . . I told them we had lost two valuable innocent men, and they but one; and should our people learn that I had given them presents, without their giving me two blankets for one, they must expect nothing but the hottest displeasure from the whites. After much deliberation among themselves, they with one voice concluded to leave the whole matter to my discretion. I at once decided to give the poor Indian widow two blankets, a dress, and handkerchief, believing the

moral influence better than to make presents to the chief or tribe, and to receive nothing at their hands. To this proposition they most cheerfully consented, and have now left, having asked for and obtained from me a written certificate, stating that the matter had been amicably settled. It is to be hoped that the matter will here end. [Allen 1850:233, 237]

For once, White seems to have handled the affair correctly, for no more problems followed. He had, of course, reverted to Indian custom by noting that two Whites had died for the Indians' one and by giving presents to the aggrieved. There is no evidence that he pursued the fugitives, who under his code should have been hanged.

Sciats, as it turned out, would suffer further indignities related to the law code. Article 8 stated that anyone whose cattle or horses "injure the crops" of another "shall pay all damages, and receive from twenty to fifty lashes." As recorded in a letter of Henry Brewer dated January 27, 1846:

"Sept 2 [1845]. Sciats one of our chief men came to my house very early & demanded a shirt, for the damage my cattle had done to his corn. I had before told him I feared the result so long as he would not build him a house near his field to watch his crops. . . . I told him plainly I could not give him a shirt. upon receiveing this piece of information he became very angry & stamped about the floor & looked about for something on which to spite his vengeance, he cast his eyes on . . . the clock. . . . I very soon took my position between him & the clock with my hatchet in my hand, (as I had been to work with my hatchet I did not lay it down) I took hold of him & put him out of doors—here he became cool & promised to do better if I would let him go, but I told him *no* we would go over to Br Waller's & as there was no law here we would make some & have him whipped forthwith. . . . Sciats again became very angry & said "Have I no gun at my house?" . . . He flew to the shore in great haste. . . . Now what is to be done, he may return with his loaded gun in a few moments. . . . The neighboring Indians gathered around, some loaded their guns & said if Sciats should come near they would shoot him The day passed off & no Sciats appeared—early next morning he went to Br Waller & requested him to come with himself to me & intercede for him, he confessed his fault & asked my forgivness & promised in future to do better I could but forgive him seeing he had humbled himself & I told him to ask forgiveness from god. We shook hands & parted in peace. [H. Brewer, letter of Jan. 27, 1846, Western Americana Collection; revised version in Mudge 1854:48]

Sciats, as chief whipper, certainly had White's law code in mind when he approached Brewer. Brewer either did not make the connection or chose to overlook it. In any case, it was a demeaning experience for Sciats and a demonstration to him that the law code that had been used to punish him, an Indian, was not equally applicable to Whites.

## Inheritance

Yet another example of the effects of a superimposed legal system concerns patterns of inheritance following a death. In his December 24, 1843, journal entry, Perkins describes the usual aboriginal procedure when a man died:

> The brothers generally divide, or if there are none, the nearest male relatives ... the strongest generally gets the most, & oftentimes all, so that the poor wife, & fatherless children are turned upon the world naked, & dependent upon the charity of their friends. [Appendix 1, Doc. 5]

The first part of that description is essentially accurate, but the rest is marred by unfortunate bias. Throughout the Plateau and southern Northwest Coast, among societies that emphasized descent in the male line, it was common procedure that a deceased man's relatives would receive the bulk of his property. Widows, however, in such cultures, were not actually "turned upon the world naked," although such might seem to be the case to observers used to a different system of property distribution after death. The widow had, in fact, at least two potential ways to turn: she might, reflecting the opposite facet of patrilineal group unity, fall back upon her own family for support, or, on the other hand, remain a part of her husband's family by marrying one of his close male relatives, such as his brother, or his father's son. The latter practice, called the levirate, is an institutionalized practice that has a wide cross-cultural occurrence. It is reported ethnographically as a normal mode for both Chinookans and Sahaptins.

Perkins, presented with the bare facts of property distribution, probably jumped to a conclusion about the future state of the widow. Other White observers were wont to do the same. Elijah White, confronted with a similar situation at Wascopam in August 1844, imposed a solution upon the Indians that was consistent with White practice. White observed what was apparently an early version of the contemporary funeral "give-away" and memorial, in which gifts were dispensed to all present, with more to respected elders (Eugene Hunn, personal communication, 1982-93). White gives the impression that cattle and horses were among those gifts, but that is not contemporary practice (Kathrine French, personal communication, 1989-93). It is very unlikely that, as he claims, the "males of the family" received only "a small share," and simply untrue that the females became "destitute . . .

slaves of the tribe." But such assertions make Dr. White's imposed "solution" appear more palatable.

> The agent spent a fortnight with Perkins and Brewer, during which the Indian chief died, leaving a large property in herds, horses, etc. Immediately after the demise of an individual it is customary for the head men of the tribe to assemble and distribute among themselves his possessions, excepting a small share for the males of the family, leaving the females destitute, to become the slaves of the tribe. Learning from Mr. Brewer that they were already convened, and that the only remaining relatives of the deceased were a wife and three daughters, the doctor repaired to the place of meeting, determined, if possible, to break up the cruel practice. . . . The people assembled, before whome the "white chief" arose, and spoke of their calamity in losing so great a warrior, and told them that he would relate to them what would be done in his own country at a similar event. That at the death of a man, three or five of the wisest men among the people would meet to say how his property should be disposed of. He asked them if they thought this was a good law? They talked awhile among themselves, and then through the chief, replied, "it is good." "Then," said the speaker, "if you would please my great chief, who sent me here, choose five of your wisest men, and let them say what shall be done with your brother's possessions." Some time was occupied in making this, to them new arrangement, and then the chief announced that their visitor and four others were elected, using as a reason for his appointment that they would not know how to proceed without his assistance and directions. He then stated to them in what high estimation the women in his country were held and as examples cited to them the mission ladies, with whom they were acquainted. He told them that one-third was given to the wife, and the residue to the children, either sons or daughters, and that no portion was received by the chiefs unless they gave a full equivalent in return. He saw this caused some demur, and said he did not know how the law would suit his good friends, but that they would retire and consult on the matter, and then the people should know the result. The committee then went into privy council, constituting Mr. Brewer their secretary, the old chief first remarking that the course his brother had marked out was very difficult, as it was opposed to their customs, and those of their fathers, besides, some of the property had already been given away. On asking if they had a right to recall it, after some deliberation, it was decided they had, and it was restored. Finally, it all ended as Dr. White wished, the widow and daughters receiving the whole. [Allen 1850:278-79]

# 9

## Religious Change before the Missions

Besides preserving a significant amount of information about aboriginal religion, the Wascopam documents contain much information on the process of religious change among the natives. It is probably safe to say that at the beginning of the nineteenth century the religious systems of the middle-Columbia region were "pristine"—at least in the sense that they had not incorporated any elements from Christianity. Three-quarters of a century later, however, the situation had changed dramatically. What happened was not a simple matter of conversion, or replacement of native religious systems by those of the White invaders, but a more complex process that involved some replacement, some retention, and a great deal of recombination of constituent elements from native and introduced systems into configurations that were different from both of their parents. New religions—including *šmuxala's* religion, the *Wáašat,* the Feather (Pom-Pom) religion, and the Indian Shaker Church—took shape and coalesced in the second half of the century, generally under the leadership or influence of one or a number of Indian prophets. The grounds for that change were laid in the first half of the century, when White contact brought changes that undermined the old ways and when Christianity was introduced to the Plateau. The missionizing efforts of Perkins and Lee were crucial elements in that complex and intriguing process. They brought Christian elements to the Indians in a form that was both comprehensible and emotionally satisfying to them, at a time when their cultures were in need of innovating stimulation and open to receive it.

### Epidemics and Religion

There were many reasons, of course, for that receptivity. One that was emphasized by Perkins and has been discussed by later anthropological theorists deserves special mention. That was the effect of introduced diseases and resultant depopulation on religious change. In his first *Christian Advocate and Journal* report Perkins stated:

> The great plague, or sickness, eight or nine years previous, had greatly lessened their numbers, and in a manner dispirited them. At the same time they were led to believe that this dreadful mortality was through the

172

influence of the white traders: they therefore stood in awe of all white men, and looked upon them as yielding a secret power which was to them incomprehensible; while a few looked upon it as rather a punishment sent from Heaven on account of their former atrocities. But, from whatever cause, there had been peace among them for several years, and they were in a state, therefore, to give attention to the message of salvation. [Appendix 1, Doc. 2]

The "great plague" of course, was the fever and ague epidemic, which had first appeared in The Dalles area in 1831. Population decline in the Wascopam circuit area, as noted earlier, may have been as high as 71 percent (chap. 2).

Recorded Indian traditions on the origin of fever and ague uniformly attribute it to two American vessels, the *Owyhee* and the *Convoy*, which were anchored in the Wappato Valley area for a year until their departure in late July 1830. In the early 1830s the role of mosquitoes in malarial transmission was not known, and the Whites and Indians of the focal area of the disease had different theories concerning its origins. The Whites attributed it to swamp gases (mal–aria); the Indians blamed it on the malevolent powers of hostile White traders. The recorded Indian traditions fall in two classes. The first has John Dominis, captain of the *Owyhee*, uncorking a bottle and letting the disease out (see, e.g., J. Lee 1841; D. Lee and Frost 1844:108);[1] the second associates the disease with survey sticks ("power sticks") left in the river by the American vessels (see, e.g., a letter dated Sept. 3, 1854, in Tappan 1854). There is some indication that the Hudson's Bay Company people, in direct competition with the American ships over the Indian trade, planted or encouraged belief in the first version.

Anthropologist David Aberle's deprivation theory on the origins of contact-period nativistic cults is similar to Perkins's hypothesis. Aberle suggests that four kinds of White-induced deprivation contributed to a process that led to a proliferation of native prophets and emergent religions during the nineteenth century. The four forms of deprivation are

1. "a general worsening of the condition of the tribe, perceptible to its members,"
2. "exposure to new wants which cannot be satisfied,"
3. "differential shift of status of the tribe," and
4. "ill-understood information . . . of a strange materially and magically powerful group." [1959:79–80]

Number 1 includes epidemic depopulation; number 2, exposure to new material goods; number 3, a shift in the balance of power in the region (for example, the "pax H.B.C."); and number 4, beliefs such as the Indian theories on the origin of the fever and ague. Perkins—an eyewitness observer and a participant in the religious changes of the mid-nineteenth century—cites both numbers 1 and 4 of Aberle's forms of deprivation.

In "Wonderful Work of God. . . ." Perkins restates his theory: "These natives are ripe for the gospel. They are fast passing away; they know it, and they are ready to lay hold of any hope on which their desponding minds may rest" (Appendix 1, Doc. 3). Rephrased in anthropological terms, Perkins's statements suggest that among the middle-Columbia Indians of the early 1840s there was a definite need for new systems and rituals that would help explain and cope with the unprecedented effects of White contact. The actual process of religious change, which had begun in the early decades of the century, picked up steam during the 1830s and 1840s and began to take definite form following the later deprivations (war, removal to reservations) of the 1850s.

## Introduction of Christian Elements to the Columbia Plateau

Since 1935, when Leslie Spier wrote *The Prophet Dance of the Northwest and Its Derivatives*, it has been general knowledge in anthropological circles that elements of Christianity were introduced to the Columbia Plateau well before the arrival of the first missionaries in 1835. After several decades of ensuing scholarship, it is possible to separate the skeins of the complex web of influences that constituted that process. Chronologized, those influences constitute at least four separate layers, as follows: layer 1: indirect influences, 1793–1830; layer 2: direct influences from Hudson's Bay Company traders and Christianized Indians, 1831–35; layer 3: missionization, 1836–47; and layer 4: missionary withdrawal and rise of nativistic religions, 1848 and after. The first two are discussed here; missionary effects are considered in chapter 10; for the rise of nativistic religions see Mooney (1896), Spier (1935), DuBois (1938), C. Miller (1985), and Ruby and Brown (1989).

### Layer 1: Indirect Influences, 1793–1830

Events and changes during the first period are still vague. Spier maintained that there was an aboriginal ritual, which he termed the Prophet Dance, which, with later changes and accretions, formed the basis of the nativistic religions of the second half of the nineteenth century. In its germinal form, the Prophet Dance included a prophet, who visited the land of the dead in some form of altered psychological state and returned with a message; an association with disruptive natural phenomena and an attempt, through ritual action, to rectify the upset; and a dance in a circle performed by all members of the local group (Suttles 1957: 353). Spier (1935:8, 55) gives several examples of intensive dancing associated with a volcanic explosion and ash fall during the late eighteenth century. Other important events in the late eighteenth century that were disruptive (or potentially so) on the Columbia Plateau included (1) a smallpox epidemic, dated variously between 1775 and 1781, followed by a second in 1801-02 (Boyd 1994b); and (2) the first passage of Whites through the Plateau region (Alexander Mackenzie, in central British Columbia, in 1793) and rumors of their presence on the peripheries of the region (Walker 1969).

It is likely that some Plateau Indians had known of the existence of White people since the middle of the eighteenth century, when their annual horseback treks to hunt bison in the Great Plains brought them into contact with Indians who had seen such beings firsthand. Thus it is not surprising that Sahaptian and Upper Chinookan traditions tell of a prophet who foresaw the arrival of the Whites (see, e.g., Kuykendall n.d.; Sapir 1909:229-31; Walker 1968:34-36).

In the Wishram version an old man described the new things the Whites would bring and introduced a dance that lasted day and night (Sapir 1909:229-31). Lewis and Clark may have met that prophet (or one like him) and viewed a form of the circle dance near the mouth of the Walla Walla on April 28, 1806. They reported:

> The whole assemblage of indians about 350 men women and Children Sung and danced at the Same time. most of them danced in the Same place they Stood and mearly jumped up to the time of their musick. Some of the men who were esteemed most brave entered the Space around which the main body were formed in Solid Column and danced in a Circular manner Side wise. . . . One of their party who made himself the most Conspicuous Charecter in the dance and Songs, we were told was a Medesene man & could foretell things. that he had told of our Comeing into their Country and was now about to Consult his God the moon if what we Said was the truth etc. etc. [1988:180-81]

Land-based fur-trading posts, which brought people with Christian backgrounds into regular contact with Indians, appeared in the second decade of the nineteenth century. Astoria (later Fort George) was established in 1811, various northern-Plateau posts in 1807 and after, and Nez Percés at the mouth of the Walla Walla in 1818 (see chapter 1). Records from Astoria are very good up to 1814; for the later years of that decade they are virtually nonexistent.

In the summer of 1811 an Indian prophetess traveled down the Columbia from Spokan to Astoria and then back again, leaving rumors of upcoming events among peoples along her route. That was the Kutenai female berdache Kocomenepeca and her "wife," whose story is preserved in the records of fur-company employees Gabriel Franchere, Alexander Ross, and David Thompson (Schaeffer 1965). Her exact message to the Indians appears to have

varied with local circumstances. At The Cascades, she threatened the people
with disease. According to David Thompson:

> Four men addressed me; saying . . . is it true that the white men have
> brought with them the Small Pox to destroy us; and also two men of
> enormous size, who are on their way to us, overturning the Ground, and
> burning all the Villages and Lodges underneath it: is this true and are we
> all soon to die[?]. I told them not to be alarmed, for the White Men who
> had arrived had not brought the Small Pox, and the Natives were strong
> to live, and every evening were dancing and singing; and pointing to the
> skies, said, you ought to know that the great Spirit is the only Master of
> the ground. . . . At all which they appeared much pleased. [1962:367]

Upstream on the Columbia, according to Ross, Kocomenepeca promised
wealth:

> They showed the Indians an old letter . . . and told them that they had been
> sent by the great white chief, with a message . . . that gifts, consisting of
> goods and implements of all kinds, were forthwith to be poured in upon
> them; that the great white chief knew their wants, and was just about to
> supply them with everything their hearts could desire. [Ross 1849:144-
> 45]

Ross implies that the prophetess used her stories to extort goods from the
Indians.

Spier suggests that the prophecies of Kocomenepeca spread throughout
the Columbia and Fraser Plateaus and contributed to the rise of nativistic
religions in the latter area (1935:25-29). There seems to be some evidence that
that was the case on the middle Columbia as well. In 1934 Cora DuBois (1938:
8-9) collected three accounts from Klickitats and Cascades on the origin of
the *Wáašat* religion that, collectively, appear to refer to Kocomenepeca.
Although all three tales apparently conflate separate events from the early
nineteenth century, they nevertheless contain important information. Mary
Lane's story is particularly interesting.

> A woman on the Columbia River . . . died and came back to life and told
> all she had seen. She said a people with white hair and skin and eyes were
> coming. She said they had different materials to work with, different
> clothing, different food that they would give the Indians. They all got
> excited like Seventh Day Adventists. They sang and danced all day and
> all night. They went crazy. They burned or threw in the river all their
> things. They destroyed everything because the whites were coming to
> give them everything. [DuBois 1938:8-9]

That passage may contain a native memory of what Perkins labeled the time "before missionaries were sent to this country" when the Indians "burnt" the "great body of" their "pat-ash." Although such an act of destruction may seem odd, it is well attested in the anthropological literature as a usual feature of *cargo cults*. The latter, best known from New Guinea, normally arise in the initial stages of acculturation, preceding direct contact with Whites but following introduction or knowledge of some items of material culture (see, e.g., Worsley 1957).

Kocomenepeca spoke with some downstream traders in Cree, which she must have learned in the north. Crees (whose homeland is the Canadian Shield) were occasional visitors to the upper Fraser as early as 1793, when Alexander Mackenzie (1970:318) passed through the area. A second group of eastern Indians whose influence on the Plateau is well established were Iroquois, (specifically, Catholic Mohawks from Quebec), who established a colony near the headwaters of the Columbia sometime during the second decade of the nineteenth century (Frisch 1978). Several, including the well-known Ignace Lamoose, intermarried among the Flatheads and introduced elements of Christianity to them. According to Bishop Rosati on October 20, 1839:

> Twenty-three years ago [1816] two Indians of the Iroquois mission left their native country, Canada, with twenty-five other warriors, and went to settle in a country situated between the Rocky Mountains and the Pacific Ocean. That country is inhabited by infidel nations, especially by those the French call Tetes Plates. They married there and were incorporated into the Indian nation. As they were well instructed in the Catholic religion . . . they have continued to practice it as much as it was in their power, and have taught it to their wives and children. Their zeal went even further; becoming apostles, they have sown the first seeds of Catholicity in the midst of the infidel nations among whom they live. [Rosati in Blanchet 1932:94-95]

Exactly what elements of Christianity the Iroquois introduced is not clear.[2] One concept that certainly entered the Plateau religious system at that time was, as Perkins put it "some idea of a God, the common Father of all" (Appendix 1, Doc. 2). That religious personage is first mentioned by Perkins on April 4, 1838, as "Sah-ha-le-tice" (Chinook Jargon) or "the chief above." As "the great Chief above" he is noted twice in "Wonderful Work of God. . . ."

Some form of that name, "the Great Chief Above" in the vernacular, or its Jargon equivalent *sáxali tayí*, had a wide distribution in the Northwest in later years (Suttles 1957:377-81). Its earliest attestation in the ethnohistorical literature dates from 1822. In that year, Hudson's Bay Company trader Archibald McDonald, newly assigned to Spokan House, met Indians who "were addressing devotions to the sun as 'Master of Life'" (Chance 1973:76). Three years later Hudson's Bay Company Governor Sir George Simpson, who was touring the Columbia Department, received two delegations of Indians at the fort, one from Thompson's River, the other from Nez Perces country, inquiring about the "Master of Life." With reference to the latter visit, Simpson stated on April 9, 1825:

> Two Nez Perces Chiefs arrived to see me from a distance of between 2 & 300 Miles; my fame has spread far and Wide and my speeches are handed Camp to Camp throughout the Country; some of them have it that I am one of the "Master of Life's Sons" sent to see "if their hearts are good," and others that I am his "War Chief" with bad Medicine if their hearts are bad. [Merk 1931:132, 136]

The Thompson's River chief requested "Messengers from the Master of Life" (missionaries, most likely). The next extant mention of the "Master of Life" is in the (Hudson's Bay Company) "Fort Colvile Journal," June 8, 1830 ("he thought I might like the 'Great Master of Life,' have the power of seeing into his heart").[3] On October 10, Indians were "praying to the Great master of Life." It is obvious that by 1825 the concept of the Christian God had become part of the Plateau belief system, present among peoples from both the far northwest (Nlaka'pamux) and southeast (Nez Perces) of the region. The quotations above suggest that the concept was accompanied by a belief in a Son of God or Messiah concept, prayer to the deity, and some knowledge of Christian functionaries (missionaries).

*Layer 2: Direct Influences from Hudson's Bay Company Traders and Christianized Indians*

Sir George Simpson's 1825 interview at Spokan resulted in his sending sons of "The Spokan & Flat Head [*sic*] Chiefs" to Hudson's Bay Company headquarters at Red River (Manitoba) for schooling. The boys were named Spokan Garry and Kootenay Pelly. They were gone for four years, returning to the Plateau in the summer of 1829. After a winter in the west, in May 1830 they returned to Red River, joined by Spokan Berens, Kootenay Collins, Cayuse Halket, and the Nez Perces Pitt and Ellice. Of those seven individuals the two Kutenais and Spokan Berens died early and had no influence on their people. Spokan Garry returned home in 1831 and became important in subsequent Plateau history. Cayuse Halket returned in 1833 and taught his people until his death in 1837. The Nez Perces Pitt and Ellice returned the same year; Pitt died in 1839, but Ellice remained an important influence among his people until well into the reservation period (Jessett 1960).

Jessett, the biographer of Spokan Garry, describes Garry's influence as follows:

> Garry set up residence in the village across the river from the abandoned [1827] Spokane House. Here he built a tule-mat building. With a bell that had been given him, Garry called his tribe together on Sundays so that he could teach them what he knew about the Christian religion. . . . Garry taught his people to conduct a simple service of prayers and hymns each morning and evening, based upon the Daily Offices in the book of Common Prayer, to say grace at meals, to keep the Ten Commandments, and explained them according to the catechism of the Church of England. He emphasized brotherly love, peaceful behavior and humility. He taught them to follow a simple formula of worship and to say Amen at the end of prayers. For group use he taught them the Lord's Prayer. [1960:42]

The return of Garry in May 1831 was followed in October of that year by the "Macedonian Call" of Nez Perces and Flatheads to Saint Louis (chap. 1). It is surprising that Garry is mentioned only a few times in the Wascopam papers, and then not in a religious context. The missionaries were apparently unaware of his influence.

What Perkins does mention, however, is the influence of White traders on Indian religious beliefs and practices. This appears in at least three contexts: (1) on March 25, 1838, he states that "the white people . . . in passing . . . have told them . . . how wicked it is to kill and steal, and what a good Being God is" (Appendix 1, Doc. 1); (2) on December 13, 1839, at Claticut, he says, "They had formerly worshipped by dancing . . . a religion the traders had taught them" (Appendix 1, Doc. 3); and (3) in the "History of the Oregon Mission: Part One" he reports:

> The light they had received from time to time from the traders and others had been enough to give them some idea of a God, the common Father of all, and that he would be sought unto by them for temporal favors. . . . A few . . . used a sort of prayer. . . . They had some notion of a future state of retribution. these were evidently recent notions. [Appendix 1, Doc. 2]

David Chance, who has studied contemporary Hudson's Bay Company records from the upper Columbia, states that "the overall religious influence of the Company has been underrated" (1973:77) Extant records from at least two Hudson's Bay Company forts on the Plateau, Colvile and Nez Percés, indicate that Chance's assessment is correct.

The principal at Fort Colvile was Charles Heron. In the "Fort Colvile Journal," under the date of July 10, 1830, he stated, "From the little instruction I have given them on religious matters, they have become perfect saints." And in an April 1831 letter he gave specifics: (1) they had been taught, "every chief is parson to his tribe," (2) there were regular Sunday services and "family service, morning and evening, throughout the week," (3) the chiefs led "prayers to the Master of Life," there was grace before meals, and (4) some kind of moral code, including a belief in punishment after death for transgressions, had been introduced. Heron stated that "since this reformation" the Colvile people had become "the very best Indians I have ever seen" (Glazebrook 1938:71).[4]

The journal for Fort Colvile is extant until April 1831; the first entries in the Nez Percés journal date from May of that year. That important document records events at a very significant juncture in the history of the middle Columbia. Downstream the fever and ague was about to enter its second deadly season, and at the fort itself the Indians were holding Sunday dances with great regularity. It appears that Sunday dancing was a recent innovation; according to Meredith Gairdner, who witnessed one at the fort in May 1835, they had been introduced "about five years" earlier (1841:257).

One of the first entries in the Nez Percés journal states, "We have instructed them in the forms of religion" (McGillivray and Kittson 1831-32). Details are not given, but it is clear that, as at Colvile, chiefs led the Sunday services. Most of the dances were held outside the fort walls, and one entry states, "The men put up the Indians' Flag Staff"—the first historic mention of the central pole that was an important feature in later Plateau nativistic religions, such as šmúxala's (see Hunn 1990:253) and the Feather religions (Mooney 1896; DuBois 1938).

The journal covers a time span of ten months (forty-three weeks). During that time twenty-four Sunday dances were recorded. Between August 28 and November 6 there were dances every Sunday, with one exception. That period corresponds exactly with the time span when fever fatalities downstream and isolated cases at the fort are mentioned in the journal. A few entries note the Indians' fear of the disease. The pattern *suggests* a connection—that the Indians may have been dancing to protect themselves from the disease. At other times of the year, dancing was irregular.

At this juncture we should introduce two important Indian accounts from the early twentieth century, from the Wishram Martin Spidish and from Wasco Jim (Ie-keep-swah). Spidish related that shortly following the appearance of "fever" (smallpox, according to Spidish, but more likely fever and ague, which was epidemic at Vancouver in summer 1830, and upstream to The Dalles in summer 1831):

The big chiefs decided to go to Ft. Vancouver. . . . Some white religious men were [there]. They gave the Indians a piece of cardboard like the

> page on a calendar. It had holes punched in it. They taught the Indians the
> days of the weeks. On Friday they were told to get all dressed up and
> confess.... These trips were the beginning of the understanding about
> Sunday. [DuBois 1938:10]

Ie-keep-swah's account discusses the beginnings of the Pom-pom religion
and attributes it to the revelations of The Dalles chief Tilki, mentioned earlier
(chap. 4).

> Wat-til-ki was first man to find the Pom-pom, the Dreamer Religion;
> first to bring it to the Wascos. Wat-til-ki died; laid four suns, four nights
> on his robe-bed. Then on fifth sun he wakes up. He sings! he sings! he
> sings! He talks about what he has seen; what he has heard when dead.
> People come hear him talk; hear him sing. He gives them the instructions;
> what to do. Gives this as he had received it. The people listen; they begin
> to dance on their knees. Lots of Injuns. Come from all around. Warriors,
> hunters, medicine men. All come. Women and children there to hear and
> see. They cry! cry! cry! They cry and mourn! They feel bad[ly] for what
> is coming.
>
> Wat-til-ki tells them of a White people who are to come; how
> everything will be changed; how the roots will be destroyed, eaten by
> strange animals brought by the White-faced people. How the Injun will
> be like children among the strangers; who swarming, will replace him in
> his own lands. Tells how the Red people will grow poorer and weaker;
> weaker and die. Die because of diseases brought by the strange people.
> How the Injun will lay dead like drift wood along the shores of the
> nChe-wana; how the death-huts can no longer hold the bodies of the fast
> passing tribes. [McWhorter n.d.: "Vision of Wat-til-ki," file 1514]

Assigning dates to orally transmitted memories is dangerous, but there are
a few anchored dates in the above two accounts that allow us to pin them down.
First, the years for fever [and ague] were 1830 and following on the lower
Columbia and 1831 and after in The Dalles area. What we know about Tilki
includes his presence at the time of the temporary Dalles-area trading posts in
1829-30 and his visit to the Reverend Samuel Parker at Vancouver in February
1836, when he was told to stop dancing on Sunday. Putting the two accounts
together yields this plausible reconstruction: In late 1830, following the
closure of the Hudson's Bay Company's Dalles outpost and the first outbreak
of fever and ague in the vicinity of Fort Vancouver, upriver chiefs visited the
fort. There were no professional religious men at Vancouver at the time, but
the Hudson's Bay Company officials gave the Indians a calendar and told them
they should observe Sunday. At about the same time at Fort Nez Percés,
Hudson's Bay Company officials were also starting to teach local Indians

rudiments of Christianity. Returning to The Dalles, Tilki (who may have had a spell of fever himself) "died" and received a "prophecy" of impending disease and destruction. It should be noted that all the dire predictions that Tilki is supposed to have given are perfectly understandable in terms of what was happening in Vancouver at the time. Tilki's remedy harkened back to the old Prophet Dance tradition of the Plateau; his innovation was to schedule the dances on Sundays. As noted above, there was a flurry of Sunday dancing around Fort Nez Percés in late summer 1831 when fever and ague made its first inroads in The Dalles area. This is, of course, only a reconstruction. But it is consistent with both the historic texts and oral tradition, and, if true, lends support to Aberle's deprivation hypothesis.

In March 1832, Pierre Pambrun took over as head of Fort Nez Percés. Two sources—his son Andrew's memoirs (1978) and Washington Irving's *The Adventures of Captain Bonneville. . . .* (1837)—state that he took an active role in instructing the Indians in the elements of Christianity. Andrew Pambrun recalled:

> Each winter father taught one chief the Lords Prayer, which had been translated into Indian, and every Sunday the Indians collected, when the chief chanted the prayer, and danced in cadence. This was quite novel to the Indian who took quite an interest and soon learned the prayer, then the Apostle's Creed was taught the same way. He also gave to each chief a card, on which was tallied the number of days he should be absent, and come in to trade. [1978:34-35]

In April 1834 Pambrun told Benjamin Bonneville that he "had been at some pains to introduce the Christian religion in the Roman Catholic form, among them" and that he had also introduced a "code of laws. All the crimes denounced by the Christian faith met with severe punishment among them" (Irving 1837:259).

Several contemporary sources confirm Pambrun's role. When Jason Lee first met the Walla Wallas on August 29, 1834, he stated:

> The chief of the Walla Walla tribe was there and he showed me some old papers with scraps of writing on them and a calendar showing the day of the month with Sunday distinctly marked—written—I presume by some gentlemen of the H.B. Company. . . . They have prayer on Sunday forenoon and run horses and dance in the a m [*sic:* p.m. is intended]. In short their religion amounts to nothing more than a sort of Catholic mummery taught them by the traders. [1916:255-56]

Similar statements on the influence of "a Roman Catholic trader" or "the superintendent of W.W." were made by Narcissa Whitman (e.g., entry of Jan.

2, 1837, 1963:123) and Samuel Parker (entry of June 25, 1837, 1936:127).

The above citations give an idea of what the traders taught the Indians. In addition, there are several descriptive accounts of Indian Sunday services witnessed by Whites between 1832 and 1836. Those include Nez Perces (in 1832, Irving 1837:82), "Skynses" (in August 1834, Irving 1837:343), Teninos (in January 1835, Wyeth 1899:247-48), Walla Wallas (in May 1835, Gairdner 1841:257), and Cayuses (July 1836, Townsend 1839:240). Common elements in those accounts include Sunday observance, ceremonies led by a chief, prayer with responsive amens, hymns, exhortation by the chief, and some form of weekday worship. The two most complete descriptions come from Irving, among the Skins (north-bank Columbia Sahaptin), observed in August 1834 (Sunday worship) and from Townsend's account of the Cayuses' July 26, 1836, weekday worship:

> Sunday is invariably kept sacred. . . . They will not raise their camp on that day, unless in extreme cases of danger of hunger: neither will they hunt, nor fish, nor trade, nor perform any kind of labor on that day. A part of it is passed in prayer and religious ceremonies. Some chief, who is generally at the same time what is called a "medicine man," assembles the community. After invoking blessings from the Deity, he addresses the assemblage; exhorting them to good conduct. . . . Prayers and exhortations are also made early in the morning, on week days. . . . On all occasions, the bystanders listen with profound attention, and at the end of every sentence respond one word in unison; apparently equivalent to an amen. . . . With these religious services . . . the tribes mingle some of their old Indian ceremonials; such as dancing to the cadence of a song or ballad; which is generally done in a large lodge, provided for the purpose. [Irving 1837:343-44]

> Divine service, or family worship . . . is their invariable practice twice every twenty-four hours, at sunrise . . . and after supper . . . all the indians belonging to the village assembled in our lodge . . . squatted on the ground, and the *clerk* (a sort of sub-chief) gave notice that the deity would now be addressed. Immediately the whole audience rose to their knees, and the chief supplicated for about ten minutes in a very solemn, but low tone of voice, at the conclusion of which an amen was pronounced by the whole company, in a loud, swelling sort of groan. Three hymns were then sung, several of the individuals present leading in rotation, and at the conclusion of each another amen. The chief then pronounced a short exhortation, occupying about fifteen minutes, which was repeated by the clerk at his elbow in a voice loud enough to be heard by the whole assembly. At the conclusion of this, each person rose, and . . . departed. [Townsend 1839:240]

Irving's last statement indicates that those new Christian practices were being accreted to an older base that centered on ceremonial dancing.

## Meeting the Missionaries: 1835–36

The above accounts demonstrate that by the time the first missionaries arrived in the Columbia Basin in 1835, many Christian elements had been introduced and the process of blending with native beliefs and rituals was already under way. The Indians, moreover, were eager to learn more. They had been told that there were religious specialists east of the mountains and had sent emissaries to request them. When bona fide missionaries began to appear in the region they were approached by Indians and questioned about particulars. At the Green River rendezvous in August 1835, a Nez Perce chief came up to Marcus Whitman and "said that he had heard something about the worship of God from the traders but he did not understand it, it had only reached his ears; he desired to be taught so that it might sink deep into his inward parts" (Hulbert and Hulbert 1936:155). At Fort Nez Percés itself, on October 9, 1836, Henry Spalding stated:

Sabbath . . . greatly astonished at their eagerness to learn something about god. . . . Frequent visits to our tent to inquire about God, how they should pray, what should be their position, whether they should stand or kneel; what they should say, and whether they should pray together or by themselves; and many other like questions. [1837:427]

Moreover, that willingness to learn was not limited to the acquisition of new elements. The Indians were willing to revise and drop older practices if necessary. That is patently clear from Samuel Parker's February 14, 1836, interview with The Dalles chiefs at Fort Vancouver.

The first chief . . . from the La Dalles [probably Tilki, see chap. 4] . . . said a white man gave them a flag, and told them to set it up on a pole, on Sundays, and meet and pray, sing their songs, and dance around the pole bearing the flag; and they had done so a long time. He wished to know if this was right. I told him it was right to meet and pray, and sing, and talk about God, but dance on the Sabbath was very wrong, and would offend God. I added further, that they needed some person to teach them the right way to worship God and to be saved. He was affected, and kneeled down, and with tears in his eyes said, if you must go away, do send us some one to teach us the right way to serve God. We will now throw away what the man said to us about dancing. [Parker 1838:254–56]

And from March 1, 1836:

> One of the La Dalles chiefs stated to my friend Mr. T.[ownsend] that they
> had changed their mode of worship; they do not now dance on the
> Sabbath, as they used to do, but they meet and sing, and pray. [Parker
> 1838:254–56]

In January 1840, during the Great Revival at Wishram village, Perkins cleared
the "rubbish" from and held services in an abandoned "cellar, dug some years
ago, when dancing was in vogue, and capable of containing the entire village"
(Appendix 1, Doc. 3). The quotation from Parker appears to indicate when and
why it was abandoned.

# 10
## Methodist Missionary Methods and Effects

Chapter 9 described the milieu in which the new missionaries found themselves when they arrived at Wascopam in March 1838. The Indians of the area had been introduced to several elements of Christianity, which they had adopted into their culture, and they were eager to learn more. With the arrival of Marcus Whitman, Henry Spalding, Henry Perkins, and Daniel Lee, the Cayuses, Nez Perces, Columbia Sahaptins, and Kiksht-speaking Chinookans had each acquired a full-time religious specialist, whose job it was to teach the specifics of the Christian belief system and the procedures of the most important Christian rituals.

That was easier said than done. The English-speaking Christians had no ready-made means of communicating their complex messages to the Indians. Eventually all of the above-named missionaries became proficient in the local language, and Spalding and Perkins became adept. But until they could sermonize in the vernacular, they had to communicate via less efficient means. All used interpreters. Perkins used Chinook Jargon, which many of his flock understood. Spalding displayed pictures along with his sermons. All of those methods were picked up and developed by Catholic missionaries when they arrived in the field two years later.

### Ladders

Spalding's pictures are especially interesting because they were a source of what would become, in Catholic hands, a most effective pedagogical device: the Catholic Ladder. According to Spalding himself, in January 1836:

> My manner of preaching is as follows. We have represented in paintings several events recorded in the Scriptures, such as the passage through the Red sea, the crucifixion of Christ, etc. These I explain first to my crier. I then go over with the subject to the people, the crier correcting my language and carrying out my history. But this only forms a starting point for these inquiring minds. They return to their tents, and sometimes spend the whole night in perfecting what they but poorly understood on the Sabbath. If one is to leave camp for some distant part of the country, my crier and the paintings are sent for, and the whole night spent in going

over with the subjects to prepare himself to instruct others. Several are already preaching in different parts of the nation. I am frequently astonished at the correctness and rapidity with which several will go through with many events recorded in the Scriptures. [H. Spalding 1837]

The paintings, carried long distances, must have been effective. Spokan Garry received some and took them to his people. In June 1837 Spalding received a delegation of four north-Plateau Indians "to receive religious instruction." At least one, a Spokan "chief," came especially to see the man who had made the paintings and request more for himself that he might learn as well (H. Spalding 1839:300-301).

Spalding's paintings undoubtedly served as a model for the Catholic variations that followed. In 1839, at Cowlitz Mission, Father Norbert Blanchet devised the Sahale Stick, which presented the major events in Catholic history carved onto a piece of wood. Combining Spalding's visual images with an object reminiscent of the shaman's or "power" stick, the Sahale Stick was immediately popular and was carried by the Catholic missionaries north to the Indians of Puget Sound (Whitehead 1981).

The Sahale Stick was an improvement over Spalding's pictures, as it allowed presentation of a chronology of events. But because it was difficult and time-consuming to make, in late 1839 Blanchet and Modest Demers devised a paper version. It was immediately put to use on the southern front, among the Klickitat and Cascades Indians of eastern Clark County, who had been effectively proselytized by Daniel Lee and Perkins during the 1839-40 revival. Perkins (Appendix 1, Doc. 4) gives a succinct and understandably biased description of the major elements of the Catholic Ladder in his second *Christian Advocate and Journal* report . A more complete description may be found in Clarence Bagley's *Early Catholic Missions in Old Oregon* (1932: 120-22).

To summarize: between 1837 and 1839 Northwest missionaries developed at least three kinds of visual aids to help in their instruction of the Indians: Spalding's pictures, Blanchet's Sahale Stick, and Blanchet and Demers's Catholic Ladder. But the innovation did not stop here. Sometime in early 1840 Daniel Lee devised what became known as the Protestant Ladder, which depicted religious history as interpreted by the Methodists. It may have been as early as February, when Lee was in direct competition with Father Demers and his ladder at Fort Vancouver ("This is a warfare for spiritual weapons" [D. Lee, letter of Mar. 2, 1840, Canse Collection]). It was probably in use at the April 1840 Kowelapse Camp Meeting. Here, according to Lee, "the great and most important facts of revelation were spread out before them in a connected chain, beginning with accounts of the creation . . . [followed by 15 more lines of events]" (D. Lee and Frost 1844:191–92).

The Oregon Historical Society holds a Protestant Ladder that appears to be in Daniel Lee's handwriting. A comparison with the Catholic Ladder reveals the following similarities and differences: Both ladders read from the bottom up. Ascending horizontal lines represent centuries. Individuals and events are introduced chronologically and seem to fall into three major periods: the Old Testament, Jesus and the New Testament, and the Reformation to the present. The Protestant Ladder provides more information and has more pictures. Although Perkins states that the Catholic Ladder has Luther going to hell, it doesn't show in extant versions; Lee's Protestant Ladder, however, obviously has a priest (the Pope?) dropping off the chart and into the fire.

The competing ladders appeared again at Clackamas in an 1841 dispute over Indian souls between Blanchet and Waller (Waller, diary, Alvan Waller Collection; Landerholm 1956). Alvan Waller, to his dismay, found Catholic Ladders at The Cascades in 1842 and among the Yakamas in 1845 (Waller, diary, Alvan Waller Collection).

## Linguistics

A continuing theme in the Wascopam papers concerns Henry Perkins's attempts to learn, transcribe, and make translations into the Walla Walla (Columbia Sahaptin) language. The impetus for those efforts was the instructions given to Perkins and Daniel Lee by Jason Lee in his letter of April 25, 1838 (Daniel Lee Collection); the models were the systems devised by Henry Spalding for the Nez Perces and, indirectly, by the Hawaiian missionaries for their flock. Perkins was singular among the Methodists of the Oregon Mission in his linguistic efforts: he preached in Sahaptin, compiled a Sahaptin speller, and translated portions of the Bible into Sahaptin; all the other Methodists preached in Chinook Jargon and made only tentative attempts to transcribe the native vernacular. If Perkins's speller had been published at the Lapwai Press in 1840 as planned, it would have been one of the earliest printed works in the Pacific Northwest.

The process of learning and transcribing Sahaptin was gradual and extended throughout Perkins's tenure at the mission. In January 1839 he gave his first sermon in Sahaptin; by August he had translated some hymns; his speller was finished by August 1840; in early 1844 he was translating the Bible. Perkins's efforts were aided by the presence of Siminese, a "boy in my family from [the Walla Walla] tribe," and after June 1840, by Henry Brewer, whose presence allowed Perkins to spend more time on his linguistic work.

*Chinook Jargon*

In the early nineteenth century Chinook Jargon was the usual means of communication between Whites and natives throughout the lower Columbia drainage. Perkins's most complete statement on the Jargon appears in his September 1843 *Christian Advocate and Journal* report. He terms it a "philological curiosity . . . a sad mixture . . . [not] a real language" (Appendix 1, Doc. 2). In Perkins's time, Chinook Jargon was composed of a few hundred words, drawn especially from the native languages Chinook, Chehalis, and Nootka as well as English and French, with a Chinookan grammar. It was the common means of communication between White traders and Indians and the initial (and all too often only) language used in sermons by missionaries. It was an adequate vehicle for conveying simple messages but deficient when it came to communicating abstract thoughts and shades of meaning. By the late nineteenth century, however, it had spread from its focal area on the lower Columbia throughout the Northwest, it had become more complex, and—in a few Indian communities—it appears to have assumed a first-language status. Although there have been many studies of Chinook Jargon, one of the best remains Horatio Hale's "An International Idiom. . . ." (1890), which is based on information collected by Hale in 1841, when he was part of Charles Wilkes's United States Exploring Expedition. It describes the Jargon as it existed in Perkins's time.

Perkins states that the Jargon "began first to be put together by the early fur traders." That was apparently the consensus among Perkins's missionary contemporaries who had any linguistic expertise (see, e.g., D. Lee and Frost 1844:153; Demers 1871:8) as well as among the earliest scholarly writers on Jargon (e.g., Gibbs 1863:vi; Hale 1890:4). In more recent years, however, there has been a division of opinion among linguists as to whether the Jargon had a precontact equivalent or was totally a result of the contact situation.[1] The arguments are diverse and complex and include, in favor of postcontact origins, the simplicity and flexibility of Jargon lexicon and grammar, the importance of White trade as a stimulus, early statements on trade-period origin (as above), and the presence of postcontact multiethnic communities. Those who support the precontact existence of Chinook Jargon point to the phonological and syntactic similarity of Jargon to native languages; the possible precontact stimuli, including aboriginal trade patterns, slaving, intermarriage, seasonal movement, and ceremonial contexts; the presence of Jargon phrases in very early documents (e.g., Lewis and Clark's); and the existence of numerous languages in a limited geographic area (summarized from Samarin 1986). As of 1994 it is possible to say that the English, French, and Nootkan lexical layers were postcontact additions and that they were incorporated into Jargon naturally, as a result of increasing White-Indian contacts on the lower river. It is clear that Jargon was not, as Perkins implies, an invention of the Whites, but a purely indigenous development (Hajda, Zenk and Boyd 1988). What is still unclear, however, is whether there was anything like it (a simplified Chinookan?) in use on the lower river before initial contact in 1792.

By Perkins's day Jargon had expanded beyond its function as a trade language and was being used as a day-to-day mode of communication in at least two lower Columbia settlements, Fort Vancouver and the French Prairie. What those two communities had in common was the multiethnic and multilinguistic nature of their populations. According to Hale:

> The place at which the Jargon is most in use is at Fort Vancouver. At this establishment five languages are spoken by about five hundred persons, namely, the English, the Canadian French, the Chinook, the Cree, and the Hawaiian. . . . Besides these five languages, there are many others, the Chehalis, Wallawalla, Calapooya, Nisqually, etc. which are daily heard from the natives who visit the Fort for the purpose of trading. Among all these persons there are very few who understand more than two languages, and many who speak only their own. The general communication is therefore, maintained chiefly by means of the Jargon, which may be said to be the prevailing idiom. There are Canadians and half-breeds who have married Chinook women, and can only converse with their wives in this speech; and it is the fact, strange as it may seem, that many young children are growing up to whom the factitious language is really the mother-tongue, and who speak it with more readiness and perfection than any other. [1890:19-20]

That mix, of course, was duplicated in other Northwest trading posts, most of which did not have (at least in the early period) Jargon available to serve as a medium of communication. The French Prairie population was drawn mostly from Fort Vancouver, from which it differed chiefly in percentages of ethnic groups.

In the mid-1830s missionaries added a new element to that mix. The function of Jargon expanded beyond trade and daily communication among peoples of varying mother tongues to include a pedagogical role as well. Easily learned and familiar to a larger proportion of an audience than any single native tongue, it became by default the favored language for sermonizing and teaching religious classes to Indians (Blanchet in Landerholm 1956:169) even though, as Daniel Lee said, it was a notoriously "imperfect medium of communication" for expressing religious concepts (D. Lee and Frost 1844:153).

Those missionaries who used the Jargon "as is" could not have given very effective sermons. But the Jargon could be and was enlarged and improved by others. The Methodist Reverend Alvan Waller was one of those who used it, apparently without improvement, throughout his career. After six years in the field, his typical Sunday was as follows:

> usual . . . Sabbath . . . Metting with the Natives at ten o'clock. . . . I generally give them as nearly as I can in the Jargon . . . the sense of a chapter, or part of a chapter. . . . This is first interpreted by one Indian into the Chinook language and then by another into the Walla Walla language. [Waller, letter of Apr. 27, 1846, Archives of the Pacific Northwest Conference]

It would be very difficult, needless to say, to translate and convey the meaning of a biblical chapter in a tongue of about 300 words. Translating from that linguistic shorthand into third languages would compound the problem. Certainly the Indian interpreters added considerable meaning in their translations of the generalized, colorless Jargon words, and we can be sure that that added meaning was more congruent with native belief systems than it was with biblical writ.

The Catholic Father Modeste Demers, unlike Waller, appears to have gone beyond simple use and molded and modified that very flexible medium to serve his own purposes.

> The Indians were gathered twice a day in the forenoon and in the evening. Rev. M. Demers, who had learned the Chinook jargon in three or four weeks, was their teacher. Later, in January [1839], having translated the *Sign of the Cross*, the *Our Father* and the *Hail Mary,* into that dialect, he taught them to these poor Indians. In February, he succeeded in composing some beautiful hymns in the same dialect. [Blanchet 1932:57]

Demers was the author of the first Jargon dictionary, assembled in 1838-39. French Catholic missionaries, more than any other group, were responsible for capturing the heretofore verbal speech form in writing and introducing it to many Indian populations in Washington and British Columbia. The lexicon grew from 200-300 words in Perkins's time (Hale's 1841 count was 252, 14 percent French) (1890) to 485 in Gibbs's dictionary (19% French) (1863); Gill's dictionary (1891) had more than 660 words.

## Learning "Walla Walla"

The most effective way of transmitting the Holy Word, of course, was in the local vernacular. Most of the interior missionaries, members of the American Board of Commissioners for Foreign Missions, learned the local Indian language. That was true of Whitman and Spalding at Waiilatpu and Lapwai (Nez Perce), and of Walker at Tshimakain (Spokan). But Indian languages were difficult, full of unusual and hard-to-pronounce sounds (note Elvira Perkins's comments on Chinookan, chap. 2). In the area where Chinook Jargon was current, missionized by Methodists and (after 1838) Catholics, the situation was different. As Gibbs stated, Jargon's prevalence and easy acquisition "tended greatly to hinder the acquirement of the original Indian language" (1863:vii). Among the Methodists, Perkins was the only missionary who thoroughly learned and used the vernacular.

The first time Perkins felt comfortable enough to use Sahaptin in his sermons was in mid-January 1839, at Fort Vancouver. His maiden sermon, surprisingly, was to "Clickatats" (letter of Jan. 16, 1839, Canse Collection), who would have found his Columbia River version of Sahaptin dialectically different. In June Elvira reported that he was sermonizing "in the Wallawallah language" at Wascopam (E. Perkins, letter of June 1839, Western Americana Collection). By fall he had "laid aside the Jargon altogether" and "made several hymns in Walla Walla, which pleases my people very much" (H. Perkins, letter of Aug. 4, 1839, Canse Collection).

By 1840 both Henry Perkins and Daniel Lee had made considerable progress in their respective languages. In mid-1840, as Lee was canoeing to Clatsop to meet the *Lausanne,* Silas Smith recalled:

> Mr. Lee had a crew of Wasco indians, his converts. He and Mr. Perkins . . . had translated some of those good old hymns, like "Greenville," "Watchman" and perhaps some others into the Wasco language, and the converts would sing these pieces in their native tongue, chanting sometimes as they rowed. Wherever we stopped religious services were held. [Silas Smith 1899]

In a letter of August 22, 1840, Henry Brewer stated:

> Br D. Lee . . . is learning the Chenook & intends to publish a spelling book soon & commence teaching. Br Perkins . . . has learned the Walla Walla language, & preaches without an interpreter. He has written a spelling book & goes to Fort Walla Walla to get it printed next fall. [Canse Collection]

The earliest printing press in Oregon was set up at Henry Spalding's Lapwai Mission on May 16, 1839. The press was brought from Hawaii by C. O. Hall.[2] The first book printed on the press was Spalding's Nez Perce speller, set to print on May 24, 1839 (see Ballou 1922 for details.). As there is no record of a printing press at "Walla Walla" (Fort Nez Percés), it is probably the Lapwai press to which Brewer refers.

Daniel Lee's "Vocabulary of the Dalles Indian Language," dated 1840, survives (Archives of the Pacific Northwest Conference), but it is, unfortunately, incomplete. Lee provides partial word lists for words beginning with certain letters (a, i, k) on certain subjects (men's clothing, land, water, etc.) and a few pages of adjectives and phrases, but there are many pages showing English words only, with no Chinookan equivalents, and still more left blank. It is, nevertheless, an important linguistic document. Some samples of Chinookan phrases and a translation of the Lord's Prayer appear in Lee's *Ten Years in Oregon* (D. Lee and Frost 1844).

Apparently, none of Perkins's Walla Walla writings survive. They were not printed, as the following passage indicates. Some of the translations (copies?) were left behind with Brewer and Waller, and it is possible others were taken by the Perkinses home to Maine. Inquiries to various New England depositories have proved fruitless. That is indeed a shame, as Perkins labored mightily on his translations and knew the language very well. The magnitude of our loss is indicated in a later Brewer letter:

> Br Perkins is now translating the scriptures into the Wallawalla language, he is now in the miracles of our Savior "Ni-toh-la" and averages 20 verses per day. We all feel encouraged to think that the time will ere long come when this poor people can read the holy scriptures in their own tongue. . . . We now give ourselves up to the language all we can & feel more interested than formerly—at the Indian meeting I know enough of the language to keep the thread of the discourse. Another thing is we are treated with more respect than formerly. . . . Br Perkins finds it quite difficult to translate some passages but the more he translates the better he can succeed. . . . L[aura] is now printing with a pen Br P's translations. O how much we need a printer & press. I hope the time will come when we shall have one. it is a slow business with a pen. [H. Brewer, letter of Jan. 1, 1844, Canse Collection]

Henry Perkins took his translating very seriously, as his requests for help in finding the proper native words for biblical categories show. In the 1843-44 journal, he asked Secretary Pitman's advice on the proper word for *prophet;* early in 1844 he wrote to Marcus Whitman for help finding equivalents for the English words *spirit* and *living.* Whitman, in response, commiserated and gave an example of his own from Northeast Sahaptin:

> I find a difficulty in the native language in finding words sufficiently expressive, for example "Thou shalt not make unto thee any graven image," for every form of making—whether by graving, carving or otherwise,—have a separate form of expression. [M. Whitman, letter of Mar. 26, 1844, Canse Collection]

In autumn 1844, before his departure from the field, Perkins questioned the new superintendent of the Oregon Mission, George Gary, about the possibility of Church support for continued linguistic study and publication of his Walla Walla texts. Gary's response follows:

Br Perkins has done much in learning and arranging the WallaWalla language. But upon the practicability of making many translations into it; and printing these translations, I am not able to give my opinion or advice . . . should the question come before the board, a correspondence with him may be of use. [Gary, diary, entry for Sept. 9, 1844, Archives of the Pacific Northwest Conference]

The last statement on the Walla Walla texts comes from Henry Brewer, on October 27, 1844, shortly after Perkins's departure for Vancouver.

Br Waller will do all he can but he does not know the language sufficient to read Br Perkins' translation of the scriptures; the burden of the school rests on me. . . . Br Perkins had made a spelling book, which I shall copy from. [H. Brewer, letter of Canse Collection]

The sole linguistic items we have from Brewer's pen are contained in the two passages below, from letters of March 31, 1842 (Walla Walla), and August 7, 1843 (Chinookan), respectively.

We are now learning Walla Walla language. it is much prettier & smoother language than the Waskopam. A few nouns I will give. Wins (Man) Iat (Woman) Meanas (Child) Enow (Young Man) Wapsene (Young Woman) Cose (Horse) Moosmoosin (Cattle) Hookhook (Swine) Looloquas (Milk) Tapas (pine) Tsonieps (Oak) Nuso (Salmon) Itilo (Wheat) Stinostino (potatoes) Alice (Bread) etc. etc. [H. Brewer, letter of Mar. 31, 1842,[3] Canse Collection]

I would like to say something to Herbert [Brewer's nephew] about the little Indian boys. . . . I sometimes give them little things & they say "Etokte mika Mr Brewer" (You are very good Mr Brewer) they have no word in their language equivalent to I thank. But they say, you have a good heart to give me things. . . . The fathers of some of the little boys come to me & say my little boy has no name. Mr Brewer will you name him? I have named one David another Moses, Peter, Joseph, Simeon, Julia, Dinah etc. But I have named none Herbert, but think I may by & by.

We had a little school for some of the boys last winter & expect to have another next, but we have no books only as we make them something like this

| Alka     | Alma      | Kaskas | Kautan | Tukli |
|----------|-----------|--------|--------|-------|
| by & by  | in future | child  | horse  | house |
| Waskan   | Kanatskan | Wilih  | etc.   |       |
| box      | oak       | Land   |        |       |

I have given you enough for a [sample?] but I presume you canot pronounce these words aright for they are spelled & pronounced not after the English language but after the indian language. Notice how we spell the Brewer in this Indian language Blua. Indians cannot sound r we use l in the room of r, u is sounded like oo, a like r, thus we have the word as before spelt Blua. but enough of this. I hope Herbert is a good boy & minds his father & mother goes to school learns his book & is very happy in the Sabbath school. [H. Brewer, letter of Aug. 7, 1843,[4] Canse Collection]

Perkins's corpus of Sahaptin works included at least a 35-page grammar, a 1,000-1,200-word vocabulary, a spelling book for school children, various hymns, and translations of an undetermined portion of both the Old and New Testaments. Unless copies of those are located, the earliest extant Sahaptin texts are Oblate Father Casimir Chirouse's manuscript dictionaries and grammars of Walla Walla and Yakama, which date from the late 1840s and early 1850s.

## The Role of Revivals and Camp Meetings

Although the Christian message was transmitted to the middle-Columbia Indians via several mechanisms (pictures and ladders, Chinook Jargon, translators, and first-person sermonizing in the vernacular), missionization, if it was to be successful, had to pass on more than just words. Using Perkins's own term, it had to transmit the "religious experience": the excitement, the motivation that drives religious movements. Missionization in the Pacific Northwest also provoked a subtle change in the style of religious expression: from an experience that was essentially personal and individual to one that was communal and standardized. Henry Perkins, more than any of his missionary counterparts, had a tool that was remarkably effective in transfusing what Emile Durkheim would recognize as the "communal experience" into Northwest native religions. It was the religious revival.

Henry Perkins had experienced his first revival at Monmouth, Maine, in mid-1837. Jason Lee, too, had been infected by that communal excitement, at Stanstead, Ontario, in 1826 (Brosnan 1932:24-26). And several Oregon missionaries (for example, Daniel Lee and all members of the First and Second Reinforcements of 1837) had seen firsthand the enduring ten-year Hawaiian revival.

The role of revivals and camp meetings in early Oregon history is a neglected topic. Perusal of the Methodist mission documents shows that those gatherings were extremely important, not only to the mission itself, but to the growing population of settlers and to many of the Indians of the lower Columbia drainage as well. There were several held during the time of Henry Perkins's tenure in Oregon. The Willamette Revival of 1838-39 was the first, followed by the Wascopam Revival of 1839-40. Camp meetings were held in the Wascopam circuit in April and October 1840 and in early spring 1842. There was a camp meeting in the Tualatin Valley in August 1843. Each meeting brought together usually disparate social entities in a way that emphasized their oneness of purpose, generated and channeled emotions in a way that promoted enthusiasm and continuity, and, in the case of Indian-White gatherings, provided a context for the entry and combination of ideas into new and useful configurations. Camp meetings, indeed, were germinal socioreligious phenomena of a type that has been discussed by sociologists and anthropologists of religion such as Emile Durkheim, Max Weber, Anthony Wallace, and Victor Turner.[5]

The camp meeting is a peculiarly American phenomenon, intimately connected with the frontier. The best source on the topic is Charles Johnson's *The Frontier Camp Meeting* (1955), on which the following discussion is based. Although there were some precedents, the first camp meetings in America appeared suddenly, without prior planning, on the Kentucky and Tennessee frontier in 1800. According to Johnson, they resulted from a combination of a religious trend to "continuous outdoor service" plus a new element of camping in tents on meeting grounds (1955:36). On the frontier church buildings were not large enough to hold very many people, and there were too few dwellings to lodge all attendees. When normally scattered and isolated frontier people were brought together in large numbers for a lengthy period of time in a potentially emotional setting, the result was a celebratory atmosphere and release of pent-up feelings in forms that no one anticipated.

The Great Revival of 1800 began at Red River, Kentucky, in June and continued at Gasper River in July. Camp meetings spread throughout the trans-Appalachian west and to the East Coast in the five-year period that has been called the Second Great Awakening (1800-1805). The 1800 Kentucky meetings were dominated by a Presbyterian, James McGready, who preached a doctrine of "new birth," but Baptists and Methodists also participated, sometimes in concert. The former two denominations eventually dropped out, and camp meetings became, by 1825, a Methodist institution. Prominent Methodists such as Francis Asbury and William McKendree (names that appear frequently in the Oregon Mission records) promoted camp meetings as an effective means of proselytization. And indeed they were. The Methodists added 100,000 new members between 1802 and 1811, more than doubling their ranks (C. Johnson 1955:85).

The "most fabulous" of all camp meetings occurred at Cane Ridge, Kentucky, in August 1801. Some of the earlier meetings were truly phenomenal in size—from 3,000 to 20,000 participants and up to thirty preachers. Common themes of sermons in the early years were "universal redemption, free and full salvation, justification by faith, regeneration by the Holy Ghost, and the joy of a living religion" (C. Johnson 1955:55). But participation was quite democratic and by no means limited to passive listening. Group singing of hymns was popular, and the movement spawned a batch of new songs and hymnals. Lay attendees, if so moved, could rise to "exhort" (speak) on their own religious experiences, and there were many spontaneous demonstrations of faith, sometimes all at once. One observer noted, "People were differently exercised all over the ground, some exhorting, some shouting, some praying, and some crying for mercy, while others lay as dead men on the ground" (C. Johnson 1955:57).

The latter phrase refers to the most common of a number of psychic conditions experienced by attendees in the height of religious excitement, the "falling exercise." "With a piercing scream, the affected individual would fall like a log on the floor, earth, or mud, and appear as dead" (C. Johnson 1955: 57). Sometimes breathing became labored and the body cold; the state might last up to an hour; up to 800 at a single camp meeting might be so affected. Another condition was the "jerking exercise," in which the head, and sometimes the whole body, jerked violently forward and back. Johnson mentions other less common conditions, including the "rolling, dancing, running, singing, laughing, and barking exercises."

In later years the unbridled emotion of the earliest meetings lessened, and camp meetings became more standardized and structured. The layout of the meeting took several forms, but most common was a circle of tents. The preacher spoke from a simply made pulpit; there was generally an altar in front where individual "mourners" might present themselves. In the audience, the sexes were separated, with men on the left and women on the right. Four days of meetings (Friday through Monday) were usual. Rules of order became common after the first decade. Johnson quotes Nathan Bangs on the usual Methodist format in the 1830s (1955:91–92). All arose at five o'clock, had "family prayer," and breakfasted at six. Sermons were held three times daily, at ten, three, and seven, according to Bangs, though eight, eleven, and three is also mentioned as a sermon schedule. The middle sermon was the most important of the day. Between sermons there were "prayer meetings, singing, and exhortation." Everyone (except a guard) was to attend sermons; no talking, moving around, or smoking was allowed. Everyone was to be in bed by ten; there was a night watchman. The rules were administered by a committee.

From Wascopam, Henry Brewer's manuscript "Camp Meetings" (revised in Mudge 1854:32–34) describes the format of the October 1840 camp meeting. Daniel Lee gives a short outline of the April 1840 meeting in D. Lee and Frost (1844:90–92) (see pp. 204–5). Excerpts from the former are printed below:

### Camp meetings

The spot chosen for our camp meeting was a clean spot of prairie about three miles below our station. . . . About 30 brush tents were erected by the Indians around our ground, no seats were prepared we did not need any. The Indians are so accustomed to sit on the ground that this is their easiest position. . . . At this meeting no pulpit stand was prepared, the congregation being so low it was not necessary. About 500 Indians were on the camp-ground. the following was the order of the meeting which was promptly obeyed, unlike any other meeting of the kind I ever attended, every one appeared interested.

1 Prayer meetings in the tents
2 Secret Prayer
3 Breakfast
4 Public preaching when all assemble on the prairie
5 Secret Prayer
6 Public Preaching
7 Secret Prayer
8 dinner
9 Preaching
10 Secret prayer
11 Supper
12 Prayer meetings & exhortations in the tents

At the close of the second discourse on the Sabbath the Rev Mr [Jason] L[ee], who was with us at this meeting baptized 130 persons, & administered the sacrament to over 400 mostly adults. This meeting was truly a solemn & interesting season to us all. the Lord was with us of a truth to comfort & bless us all. [H. Brewer, "Camp meetings," Western Americana Collection]

It appears that the Methodist missionaries carried the camp-meeting format virtually intact from their homes in the eastern states to the Pacific Northwest. The camp-meeting pattern was, in many ways, similar to aboriginal Northwest ceremonials. And, in both broad outline and specific pattern elements, it seems to have influenced the nativistic religions that sprang up on the Columbia Plateau in the 1850s and later.

## The "Wonderful Work of God"

Perkins's report (Appendix 1, Doc. 3) is a near-complete documentation of the 1839–40 Wascopam Revival. There are, however, a few additional details in contemporary letters and in Daniel Lee's *Ten Years in Oregon* (D. Lee and Frost 1844), which are included here.

Following Perkins's "day of salvation," the first half of November saw the conversion of the Indian doctor Tumsowit, the beginning of the requests from Indians, and the intensive proselytization that marked the start of the revival. Daniel Lee was absent at Willamette during all that time, and when he arrived at Wascopam after the fifteenth, he was incredulous at what Perkins told him:

> When he [the writer] arrived, Mr. Perkins met him at the shore, and told him that a gracious work was begun among the natives. Of this he had strong doubts, and could not assent till the proof appeared. . . . Mr. Perkins was found labouring zealously night and day, going from lodge to lodge, praying and exhorting, holding prayer meetings and preaching. . . . Large numbers of the natives attended the meetings as earnest hearers, and several had begun to pray. [D. Lee and Frost 1844:182–83]

Lee was convinced and rapidly became caught up in the exhilaration of the moment. The "object and aim" of the two men was "now one—the salvation of the souls around us; and we desired no higher employment than to serve them as the heirs of eternal life" (D. Lee and Frost 1844:183).

Lee gives a more complete account of the prayer meeting of the twenty sinners.

> Some time after my return from Walamet, there being about twenty souls, men and women, in deep distress on account of their sins, and apparently near the kingdom, we met in a special prayer meeting, where few except those were present. Here was earnest, united praying, and the "kingdom of heaven was taken by violence." More than half the number gave evidence of a happy change. Their agitated hearts felt an unknown peace, a joyful smile sat on their faces, and their lips praised the name of Jesus. "Micah Jesus Christs e-toke-te!—Thou, Jesus Christ, art good!" "Cupet mi-cah mi-mah e-toke-te.—Thou alone art good!"—"Can-nu-it e-toke-te!—Certainly thou art good!" "Jesus good!" "Jesus good!" [D. Lee and Frost 1844:184]

On the following page Lee gives a second (English) example of an Indian prayer.

On November 27 Elvira Perkins wrote a hurried note to Mary Walker, which said:

> I have time to write you only a line. . . . We find at the present time our hands and our hearts full. The Lord is pouring out his Spirit in an abundant measure on our Indians. Quite a number give very satisfactory evidence of conversion and nearly all are earnestly [?] inquiring after Jesus Christ and so eager are the[y] for instruction and prayers that we can hardly find time to eat or sleep. . . . I should be very glad to give you a detailed account of the great work God is doing among us but can only say that he is doing more than we ever thought of asking or thinking possible. May your station and all those of the others share and the work spread throughout the length and breadth of the land. [E. Perkins, letter of Nov. 27, 1839, Western Americana Collection]

The intense activity continued through December. On December 17, when Lee, Wright, and Tumsowit started down the Columbia Gorge, the Perkinses were left alone again. On Christmas Eve Henry decided that he would keep a journal of his daily activities, copies of which he would now and then send downstream to Daniel. Records for three days, December 24-26, were received. The excerpts below give an idea of the hectic pace of activities in that busy time.

[December 24]
1. Rose at four . . . and enjoyed a good season of private devotion.
2. About 5, had a prayer meeting with the boys and others, and attended to their instruction
3. Reading the scriptures and prayers with my wife.
4. Public prayers at daylight in the chapel.
5. From prayers to breakfast. Had a prayer meeting with the women, a comforting encouraging season. . . .
6. Read Mr. Wesley's life & Rode about eight miles to visit some people down river opposite Claticut. Found them very stupid. Chuckalukete accompanied me. . . . Returned at sunset, having ridden 15 or 16 miles.

Christmas 1839
1st. Devotion. Rather weary in body from the labors of yesterday.
2nd Spend an hour conversing with Elvira on Redemption, considering it a fit subject for the day . . . found our ideas on the subject very vague and undefined. Postponed the subject. . . .
3rd Family prayer and instruction
4th Public prayers in the chapel. . . .
5th A long conversation with Yacooter and others on the origin of Christmas. . . .

6 Made some arrangements for forming a Society of those who are giving evidence of a change of heart—about thirty in all here, and about 11 at the little village, making in all about 40 who I think, are seeking eternal life. 7 Visited the village, while Elvira met the youg women apart at the mission house. . . .
8 Prayers, visits, and a blessed season of retirement. Felt in conversing with god a fulness of love,—no sins, no fear, but *love* and *peace,* with a small share of joy.
9 Chukalulete [*sic*] came in, and after conversation with him, we joined in prayer with and for him. . . . Have been reviewing the work of God in this place, and around us. How wondrous, how wondrous! I gladly dedicate the remainder of my days to the Lord.

Dec. 26, 1839
1. From four to five as usual. How much better is communion than sleep.
2. From five to six in conversation [with Elvira?] on the great question "Why did Christ die?" . . .
3. After prayers and breakfast, selected a crew and embarked for Claticut. We arrived about noon, which makes me think it fifteen miles distant. Found the village in expectation of me. Read your letter, which was timely. . . . After reading your letter, I retired into the "raceground" for meditation and prayer.
At twilight met the people. Gave them a talk and had a prayer meeting. Twenty-five or thirty prayed, our number—(five) included. Gave them another talk. Was pleased with their behavior, very eager for instruction. As we had no tent, we kindled a little fire on the sand, by which we ate our supper, and after we had prayed, I wrapped myself up in my buffalo robe, and lay down in an empty canoe, where I slept till morning. [H. Perkins, letter of Dec. 24, 1839, Canse Collection]

The next day Perkins was at Cutcatalk, and then home. The letter he received from Daniel Lee on the twenty-sixth was not, in all probability, what Perkins had expected. It was an admonitory note warning him to slow down. Lee was concerned for his health: Perkins should get enough rest; he should eat regularly; he need not preside at all exercises—Elvira Perkins and the converts could help.

I should think your soul had declared war with your body, with a fair prospect of demolishing the same "earthen vessel." A house divided against itself can not stand. let the soul and body materially support each other. [D. Lee, letter of Dec. 25, 1839, Canse Collection]

Henry Perkins's response was courteous: "Thank you for your excellent advice respecting my health." He had cut out tea, and when he got less than six hours of sleep, he made it up the next night by going to bed earlier. But he would continue rising at four. The most obvious result of Lee's admonition was that Henry Perkins stopped sending him detailed accounts of his activities.

Daniel Lee's draft of *Ten Years in Oregon* contains the following information on his late December–early January activities in the Columbia River Gorge:

> My preaching, was the Simple Story—of the gospel—Christ crucified to take away our Sins and give us peace,—and many repented like the Ninvites, from the least to the greatest, and like the Samaritans gave heed with one consent to the things they heard.
>
> In these villages Six in number, there were Supposed to be about 475 Souls. A class was organized in each. ["Ten Years in Oregon," partial draft, Archives of the Oregon-Idaho Conference]

There is more information on Lee's activities at Vancouver in his letter of January 15. He, Wright, and Tumsowit had arrived on the tenth. Following are his activities for the twelfth:

> Sabbath 12th. 1. Met the Clicatats. 2 Preached in the Hall on "how shall we escape if we neglect so great salvation?" It was a time of deep feeling. 3rd. Spoke to the Cascade Indians, and felt much assisted. 4th. Met the Clicitats again, at sundown. 5 Attended br. Wright's meeting with the men at 6 p.m. 6th. Preached in the Hall at 9, on "and as he reasoned of righteousness, temperance, and judgment to come, Felix trembled," etc. It was a solemn season. [D. Lee, letter of Jan. 15, 1840, Canse Collection]

Wright, as noted earlier, "preached with power" to "the Company's servants," who were "beginning to be alarmed." The effects spread to the gentlemen as well. According to Lee:

> Mr. Douglas and Mr Ermatinson [*sic*] feel keenly. Dr. Tolmie seemed not far from the Kingdom. I have spent considerable time with him today in discoursing on justification. My own soul was blest, and we had a good season together in prayer. I believe he will soon be joined to the Lord. [D. Lee, letter of Jan. 15, 1840, Canse Collection]

"Mr. Douglas" was James Douglas, lately in charge of the fort while McLoughlin was in London. "Ermatinson" was Francis Ermatinger, a chief trader. Dr. William Tolmie was the fort physician.

In the letter, Lee was also optimistic about the local band of Klickitats. "I have held meetings with the Clicatats morning and evening, and several have begun to pray. I look for a great work ere long among them." In *Ten Years in Oregon*, speaking in retrospect, he stated:

The writer's labours among the Indians at Vancouver were not attended with as much success as above the Cascades. . . . Night and day, from house to house, he preached unto them Jesus. They then heard, and never before, the simple, pure truths of the gospel; and that, as a people, they will ever again hear them, is not probable, for there are influences thrown around them, which cut off the approach of truth. [D. Lee and Frost 1844: 188]

In early February Perkins traveled downstream to Vancouver, where he met Lee, and then returned to Wascopam. Lee's draft of *Ten Years in Oregon* states that he "visited and instructed the converts in the villages above The Cascades" ("Ten Years in Oregon," partial draft, Archives of the Oregon-Idaho Conference). Lee himself started upstream in early March. On his way back he

visited all the villages above the Cascades. . . . and found them in a prosperous state, "walking in the truth." Having been previously instructed in the nature and design of the ordinance of baptism, they were most of them now baptized, both adults and children. Who could "forbid water" that they should be baptized? Especially when, according to Scripture example, they might have been admitted to that ordinance on the day in which they first believed. The season was one of great joy to the writer; and the happiness of these poor yet simple believers was another proof of the power of the gospel to triumph over the deepest degradation and the most abject destitution. [D. Lee and Frost 1844:189]

Baptism was similarly administered to "a large number" of the Indians at Wascopam and "about two hundred and fifty souls" at Wishram, where both Lee and Perkins "held several meetings in public" and "visited and prayed from lodge to lodge." Following that joint endeavor, the two split ranks again. Henry Perkins, accompanied by Elvira Perkins, revisited the six Gorge villages (H. Perkins, letter of spring 1840 [dated spring 1839], Canse Collection; D. Lee, "Ten Years in Oregon," partial draft, Archives of the Oregon-Idaho Conference); Lee, along with two converts from Wascopam (probably Tumsowit and Yacooetar) and one from Wishram, went to the two interior villages of the Klickitats. That was the first time those settlements (which could be either *nakipanik* [Husum] and *xaɫxa'ywaša* [BZ Corner] on the White Salmon [Ray 1936] or *waka'yk-as* and *xwa'ɫxway* up the Klickitat River [Eugene Hunn, personal communication, 1982-93]), "numbering more than two hundred souls"—had been contacted, though they certainly had heard of the missionary activities through the regular Indian communication network.

Here he [Lee] saw such a readiness to hear and to follow the teachings of the gospel as had not been surpassed in any other place. The old, the middle-aged, and the young, even little children, received it as the most joyous tidings that ever saluted their ears; and their earnest prayers and confessions told how fully they believed it was the word of the Great Spirit, given both to govern them and to save them. Never did the writer enjoy his work more than while engaged among these poor red men in preaching, and exhorting, and praying for their salvation. That numbers of them were converted there was no room for him to doubt. [D. Lee and Frost 1844:190]

## April 1840 Camp Meeting

Then, in April 1840, an eight-day camp meeting was held at Kowelapse, just downstream from Wascopam. There are only two extant descriptions: one in Perkins's first *Christian Advocate and Journal* report (Appendix 1, Doc. 2); the second in Lee's *Ten Years in Oregon*, draft and published versions (D. Lee, "Ten Years in Oregon," partial draft, Archives of the Oregon-Idaho Conference); D. Lee and Frost 1844). Perkins says, "the number of natives in attendance was not large," but Lee claims "about twelve hundred were present." Perkins's account is a mere four sentences; Lee's, reproduced below, is two and one-half pages. The reasons for that discrepancy are not clear but may be political. The detail that Lee gives plus the corroboration of his numbers by Brewer (who arrived two months later) suggest that his account is accurate. Perkins's probable downgrading of the event may relate to Jason Lee's skepticism about its effects (see below). Daniel Lee's account follows:

At this meeting about twelve hundred were present from the villages along the river, from the Cascades, from Wishham and Caclasco, and from the neighbouring Walla–wallahs, and the Clickatats. The spot . . . about six miles below the Dalls, and three miles from the mission house, at a place called Cow–e–laps . . . was chosen in the open plain, bounded on one side by a ridge of rocks, at the foot of which the writer pitched his tent, while on either hand were ranged the wigwams of the natives, gradually rounding in a circle, meeting in front, and enclosing an area of half an acre. The wigwams were made of willow poles set in the ground in a circular or oblong form, inclining toward the centre at an angle of fifty degrees, and enclosed with mats of grass, having an opening at the top, and a door at each end, with a fire in the middle, and sometimes two fires, when the tenement was long, and then it was occupied by a large number, perhaps thirty. When it was completed, the tops of the poles were the most prominent elevation of our city, which had grown up in a day. The good order observed throughout the whole meeting was never surpassed in an assembly of such numbers, and which continued so long together. At daylight they were awakened by the sound of a trumpet, and soon after engaged, first in singing, and then in prayer, in their houses. Then followed the washing of hands and faces, after which they took breakfast. For public exercises they were called together three or four times during the day, the women and men apart, with a space of four or five yards intervening, sitting on the ground, sometimes with a mat or a bearskin spread beneath them, and a blanket or skin or mat over their shoulders; presenting a dense mass of black heads and sunburnt faces, altering between adults, and babes, and little children, withered old age, and gray heads, remnants of other days! and—The pencil drops. The company beggars description! To know, the reader must see. [D. Lee and Frost 1844:189-91]

Our teaching was Substantially a rehearsal of the Bible truths we had already taught them—We took up the most important facts of Revelation—in a connected chain—from the creation down—great truths, which they heard with the deepest interest—and which they would repeat again & again—among themselves—when again at home, in their different Villages—and lodges and in their different languages. Wanting a written language they depend So much on Memory that it becomes quite perfect—and frequent repetition makes it perfect. [D. Lee, "Ten Years in Oregon," partial draft, Archives of the Oregon-Idaho Conference]

In the intervals of public worship they withdrew some distance from the ground and engaged in prayer alone. Prayers in their houses in the evening closed the day. Thus the time was employed till the ensuing sabbath, our meeting having continued from Monday, when the communion was administered to several hundreds. . . . Thus ended a day that the writer will long remember with thankfulness to the God of love that he was ever permitted to see it; and he expects to meet precious souls, with whom he enjoyed that communion, in the kingdom of heaven, and will ever pray in hope of that event. [D. Lee and Frost 1844:192]

One thousand (H. Brewer, letter of Aug. 22, 1840, Canse Collection) to twelve hundred natives is not a small number when one considers that the total estimated population of Upper Chinookans at that time was fifteen hundred, and that of the entire Wascopam circuit (most of the above with some Sahaptins) sixteen hundred (see chap. 2). It may be assumed that between November 1839 and April 1840 most of the population of the circuit experienced two, in some cases three, periods of intense religious instruction. The peoples of the river villages between The Cascades and The Dalles were visited at least four times, by either Daniel Lee or Henry Perkins. The intensity of those experiences and the number of contacts in the winter of 1839-40 should have left some impression on aboriginal religious beliefs and practices.

*Summer 1840*

During the summer of 1840, while Daniel Lee was busy with affairs down-stream, Henry continued his round of visits to local villages. A letter dated June 2 describes a five-day circuit to settlements at Wishram, Waiam, "the Fishery" (Tumwater), Attachak *(aɬaxačak)*, and among "Mesulsul's people" (the latter not identified). Excerpts follow:

> May 30, Wishram:[6]
> With Tumsowit visited all the people from house to house, and inquired into their state more particularly. The men appeared very well generally, but the women from their excessive labors [at this season] do not pray as much. One of them had fallen into a snare of the devil, and has no longer any place with us. Neither has Tilke's son.

> May 31, Waiam:
> Spent the whole day visiting from house to house. I judge there were about one hundred in all, every one of which I visited, and talked with many of them, and I think about sixty individuals joined with me in prayer in the course of the day. Most of them prayed frequently, and appeared to be earnestly striving to find the straight gate. . . .

> June 3:
> This was as pleasant a voyage as I have ever made in Oregon. The Lord vouchsafed His presence with us, and gave it favor in the eyes of the people. Our bretheren and sisters got along very well every where, remarkably well. I find the more frequently we visit them, the better for our influence, and theirs too. [H. Perkins, June 2, 1840, Canse Collection]

Two weeks later the Perkinses were at The Cascades, where they met newly arrived members of the Great Reinforcement—including the Brewers and the Babcocks and Daniel Lee's new wife, the former Maria Ware, married to him at Vancouver on the eleventh by Jason Lee—all of whom would join them at Wascopam. On June 21 Daniel Lee (with Joseph Frost) preached to The Cascades people, while "Perkins went below the Cascades and preached." On June 24 the party arrived at Wascopam; on the twenty-eighth Lee and Brewer visited Wishram, where the former "talked to two congregations" (Brewer 1986:60–62). In early July Perkins traveled to "Tilkume . . . Wiam, Wisham, and Claticut," as well as other places (letter of July 11, 1840, Canse Collection). Through the next month the usual pattern was for Perkins and Lee to absent themselves on Sundays to visit the scattered Indian settlements (H. Brewer, letter of Aug. 14, 1840, Canse Collection). From August 12 through October 2 Perkins was gone on a visit to Willamette (H. Perkins, letters of Sept. [no day indicated] and Sept. 12, 1840, Canse Collection; Brewer 1986:63–64).

## October 1840 Camp Meeting

Following Perkins's return, plans were made for a second camp meeting, to be held concurrently with Jason Lee's anticipated visit. Between October 4 and 8 Daniel Lee and Perkins traveled to Wishram, and Perkins went to Waiam and "down the river" to invite Indians to attend. On the tenth people began to assemble at Kowelapse, and on the eleventh Jason Lee arrived for his first visit in a year and a half (Brewer 1986:64).

The October camp meeting is described in several sources (J. Lee 1841; D. Lee and Frost 1844:245; Mudge 1854:32–33; Brewer 1986:65). About thirty willow brush tents were erected, occupied by between 300 and 500 Indians. The following excerpts are from Jason Lee's journal:

October 14:

After singing and prayer in the houses, the males retired upon one side of the campground, and the females on the other, for private prayer. Then followed breakfast—that over the trumpet sounded and all assembled and seated themselves in the center of the ground, the men on the one side, the women on the other. The preaching was in the jargon, interpreted by one man in the Wascopan, and by another into the Wallawalla. They listened with great interest, and with as much solemnity as I have ever seen; and the word seemed to take effect. Prayer meetings in the evening lively and interesting. Hundreds of fervent, and I trust, effectual prayers, were sent up to the throne by those who a few months since were in total darkness.

October 15:

The chief exhorted the people this morning, with great earnestness, to take heed to the things which they had heard, and not let them slip, but practice them in their lives. These Indians are extremely poor, many of them not having clothes and skins enough, all told, to cover their persons from the falling rain, and yet they sit most patiently to listen to words which are able to make them wise unto salvation. [J. Lee 1841]

The meeting was apparently held at a poor time. Though the "Waskopam Indians had returned from getting berries" (Brewer 1986:65), "many" were "in the mountains gathering nuts," and "Nearly half being destitute of food, were obliged to leave before the exercises were closed" (J. Lee 1841). Nevertheless, as Perkins noted, around 400 natives participated in Holy Communion, and Lee baptized more than 100 Walla Wallas.

Both Brewer, who was new to Oregon, and Jason Lee, who was not accustomed to such large numbers of apparently interested Indians, were impressed with that assemblage:

Glorious were the manifestations of the divine power! Shouts of praise ascended from hundreds of new-born souls, and experienced believers rejoiced in God's quickening grace. [Brewer in Mudge 1854:33]

Thank the Lord for the happiness with which He is filling my soul. I had rather be a laboring, suffering missionary in Oregon than to fill the presidential chair, or sway the most potent scepter in the old world. [J. Lee 1841]

Neither Perkins nor Daniel Lee, with the much livelier and better-attended Wascopam Revival and April camp meeting behind them, thought very much of the October meeting. In what was to became a common theme in their later writings, both of the Wascopam missionaries expressed doubt about the long-term effects of temporary bursts of emotion and ritual activity.

There was not to be another camp meeting in the Wascopam circuit for another fifteen months. But in the interim, the evangelical fervor spread east. The Nez Perces at Lapwai experienced their own revival:

I held a protracted meeting in Oct of 9 days. Perhaps 3000 attended regularly. We trust a few found the Saviour. 7 have been examined as candidates for admission into the church. Our Saturday inquiry meeting is attended by about 50, Tuesday prayer meeting the same, sabbath school over 100, sabbath congregation about 500. [H. Spalding 1842]

## March 1842 Camp Meeting

In late March 1842 the last recorded camp meeting was held at Wascopam. Like the October 1840 meeting, it paled in comparison to the great meeting of April 1840. Again, neither Perkins nor Lee was impressed. Henry Brewer's account, from his letter dated March 31, is the most complete report:

Our camp-meeting commenced the 21. & closed the 28 inst. The Lord was with us in great mercy. We had long prayed for the outpouring of his spirit among the people. At this meeting we saw happy results; many who were lukewarm & careless were stirred up and awakened. My own soul drank largely of the blessing; in going from tent to tent striving to show them the blessed way, my heart was much blessed. O it blessed to see Indian converts pray & praise the Lord. I can no more doubt their conversion, than my own, they gave such clear & demonstrative proof that Christ Jesus was in them the hope of Glory. I asked one how he felt, he said "happy, happy" the Holy Spirit given him was like food to his soul. I asked another, he said "when I came to this camp meeting my heart was ponanico—(that is blind, dark) I prayed my heart felt like a stone. I prayed again, & again I felt a little better, & now my heart is all light. I am glad I am happy" this is the substance of what many said. . . . April 6. I have risen at 3 o clock this morn to write more. The good work goes on among the people, meetings are held daily among them. A few usually attend with us in our little social meetings, although they do not understand, yet they feel, & pray in their own language. Last Sunday evening the Lord so filled us as to cause us to rejoice with joy unspeakable. we had a shout of the king in the camp of Israel. [H. Brewer, letter of Mar. 31, 1842, Canse Collection]

An edited version of Brewer's account appears in Mudge (1854:33–34). Daniel Lee's résumé of the meeting, from his draft narrative for *Ten Years in Oregon,* states:

The numbers attending were not large—Yet it was a time of great blessing—Some who had wandered away returned. Some remained steadfast while others were as unstable as water—Their goodness as morning cloud evanesent.—Alas, christendom itself is full of backsliders. [Archives of the Oregon-Idaho Conference]

## Methodist Missionaries' Contributions

Catholic missionization among Pacific Northwest Indians was relatively successful. Blanchet and his cohorts were aggressive and energetic, the Catholic Ladder was an effective instrument of proselytization, and the Indians were taken with the Catholic emphasis on ritual. The Catholic influence on the Indian Shaker Church of Puget Sound is quite obvious (Amoss 1990).

The influence of the Methodist missionaries of Wascopam has been overlooked by later researchers, mostly because of the inaccessibility of records. Especially during the period of Perkins's tenure, 1838–44, the impact on the Indians was strong.

The effectiveness of the Wascopam Mission was a result of many factors. One was the character of its two principals, Perkins and Lee—enthusiastic, energetic, and committed to the missionary cause. Another was the receptivity of the Indian cultures of the middle Columbia to religious change. Diminished by disease and beginning to feel the onslaught of new things and ideas, they were ready for a message and a ritual that would help them cope and feel optimistic about the future. Also important was the broad similarity of many aspects of frontier Methodism with aboriginal religious systems, including an emphasis on communal religious experience and individual spiritual rebirth. Finally, Perkins and Lee presented their message in a form that was not coercive and superimposed, that allowed the Indians to select what was relevant and not destructive to their own system. Although the Wascopam interlude was historically brief, it was broad based and well received. After Perkins's departure in 1844 and the closing of Wascopam Mission three years later, the Indians of the Wascopam circuit were left with an enlarged repertoire of Christian elements and a strong impetus (if not enthusiasm) to use them in whatever ways were most useful to them.

Much of that has been discussed in previous pages. Here we will review the process of missionization in the circuit, with an emphasis on the infusion of structure and organization, and discuss some of the particulars of the Methodist message, as revealed in the Perkins and Wascopam papers.

*Timing of Revivals*

The compatibility of frontier Methodism with Indian religious ceremonialism expressed itself in some very interesting ways. One was timing. The aboriginal sacred season in the Pacific Northwest was in mid-winter— December and January. Spirit-sings and ceremonials were held in rotation, for five-day spans, at the houses of ranking individuals in each winter village. The Methodists, unlike their Presbyterian brethren, celebrated Christmas with communal gatherings and held a Watch Night on New Year's eve. The Willamette Revival of 1838–39 and the Wascopam Revival of 1839–40 both occurred during the normal time of religious celebration both for Indians (Chinookans, Sahaptins, or Kalapuyas) and for the Methodist newcomers.

To a lesser extent, the timing of the three recorded Dalles-area camp meetings was also significant. All were convened on dates when Indians were congregated in restricted areas, at significant junctures in their seasonal rounds. To hold meetings at such times was merely common sense on the part of the missionaries, but it was fortuitous as well. The two spring camp meetings were held in early April 1840 and on March 31, 1842. As Perkins notes, that was near the end of the lean period of late winter and early spring; Lee stated that the day after the 1840 meeting "all the Indians scattered to their various quarters to engage in removing to their fishing grounds against the arrival of the salmon" (D. Lee and Frost 1844:192). On the Christian side, the two spring camp meetings came during the season of Lent and Easter; on the Indian side they were close to the usual timing of the first salmon ceremony (see chap. 6).

The one recorded early-autumn camp meeting (October 13–19, 1840) was probably held to coincide with the visit of Jason Lee, but it also took place at a time when it was likely that a sizeable number of Indians would be present locally. The October camp meeting immediately followed the return of the Wasco Indians from the Mount Adams huckleberry fields and preceded their retreat into their pit dwellings for the winter. In contemporary *Wáašat* religion, the berry festival precedes the huckleberry harvest, usually in August.

The Christian ceremonial calendar was introduced to mid-Columbia natives from Catholic sources as well. Bonneville stated that both the Skins and Nez Perces "had a rude calendar of the fasts and festivals of the Romish Church" (Irving 1837:83, 344), all undoubtedly introduced by Pierre Pambrun. Contemporary Sahaptin-speaking peoples celebrate several calendrical first fruit rites. Of them, only the first salmon ceremony is attested from the prereservation period. The others were an important part of *Šmúxala's* religion, the forerunner of the modern *Wáašat* church of the southern Plateau. Current first fruits ceremonies include, in addition to the berry festival, the root feast, held just before the root harvest (principally *Lomatium canbyi* and bitterroot) in early April, and, among a few groups, a rite celebrating the first greens *(Lomatium grayi—latitlatit—*or Indian celery) in late February (Hunn 1981).

There is also a similarity in the lengths of aboriginal winter ceremonials and Methodist revivals. Five was the ritual number on the Plateau, and single rounds of spirit dancing usually lasted five days and nights (Ray 1942:249). The Willamette Revival lasted four days and nights. The Wascopam Revival was composed of several meetings at winter villages: the lengthiest stay at any one village was a week (Claticut and Wishram). The October 1840 and March 1842 camp meetings both lasted one week.

There were also parallels in the roles of Henry Perkins and Daniel Lee in the revivals to the roles of leading men in the winter ceremonies. As noted earlier, Tumsowit and Yacooetar (shaman and war chief) accompanied Perkins and Lee on most of their initial visits to outlying villages during the Great Revival. In the winter ceremonies, leading men hosted gatherings and might be prominent performers. The Indians probably identified Perkins and Lee as two more leading men, but from the White tribe. Leading men also utilized speakers, as we have seen. Perkins's and Lee's interpreters (when they had them) were functional equivalents. Prominent men in the Indian culture were respected, and the people listened closely to what they had to say. From the accounts presented here, it appears that the Indians of the Wascopam circuit responded to Perkins and Lee in a similar way.

## Experiencing Religion and Converts

The mode of experiencing religion at Indian winter ceremonies and Methodist camp meetings was very similar. Although the Indian form emphasized song and dance and public performances, and the Methodist emphasized sermonizing, exhortation, and song, both were communal in nature, characterized by several meaning-laden activities, and compacted into a restricted, marathon period of time that produced heightened emotional states. And each promoted individual religious experiences. In the Indians' case, the heightened emotional atmosphere encouraged each participant to enter a state in which he was in communion with his personal guardian spirit and could act out his spirit songs and dances or, in extreme cases, perform unusual ceremonial acts. The Methodist camp meeting encouraged its participants to release their pent-up feelings, confess their sins, and in general give themselves up to the charged atmosphere of their surroundings, in which they might feel a surge of emotion, which was interpreted as a spiritual rebirth. Of all the missionary denominations in the Northwest of the late 1830s and 1840s—Catholic, Presbyterian, Congregational, Methodist—only the Methodists shared with their charges such an emphasis on the communal and individual religious experience.

That similarity is obvious in the conversion experiences of the Willamette Revival participants. White and Indian expressions were similar in form, although the Indian expressions were probably grounded more in indigenous tradition than in any Christian teaching. In the case of the Wascopam Revival the Indian element is obvious. Tumsowit's conversion—with his retreat to the "rocks and hills"—smacks of a spirit quest. Yacooetar's conversion lasted four or five evenings. And the Wishram conversions mix the liminal states of a funeral, spirit acquisition, and Methodist conversion indistinguishably into one experience. Although the Christianizing elements of those initial experiences were certainly much less than the missionaries wanted or perceived, there is no doubt that, in many cases, in a certain limited sense, the conversions were real. Both Tumsowit and Yacooetar certainly perceived what they were going through as a Christian experience and were henceforth more willing to accept elements of Christian doctrine and practice. In the early stages of the Christian experience they both became exhorters and teachers and helped transmit Perkins's and Lee's message to others, although in later years both "backslid" considerably.

The Wascopam Revival, in many of its particulars, resembles the initial stages of what anthropologist and student of religion Anthony Wallace calls a "revitalization process" (1970). In Wallace's scheme, a new code of belief is introduced to a people experiencing considerable cultural stress; it offers a new "goal culture" and is preached to others "in an evangelistic spirit"; converts are made, with initial experiences "ranging from the mazeway resynthesis characteristic of the prophet, and the hysterical conviction of the 'true believer,' to the calculated expediency of the opportunist"; the converts separate into two groups, disciples and followers (1970:192-93). Beyond that point, there may be formation of a formal organization, further spread, and eventual cultural transformation.

In early 1840 the "Wonderful Work of God" had not progressed to those later stages. There is, in fact, no evidence that it ever did. But it appears that the Wascopam Revival had at least reached the stage of initial acceptance. The repeated conversion experiences and appearance of exhorters argue that a need was being met and that a message, however incompletely or imperfectly understood, had found a conduit into an alien culture. The fact that the momentum was not carried on to later stages resulted from many factors, including, in particular, historical and personal circumstances that made it difficult for the missionaries to sustain their effort and logistic and linguistic difficulties in transmitting the message to its audience.

## Organization

During the "Wonderful Work of God" Perkins and Lee did attempt to infuse some organization (at the local level) into the movement and lay the foundations of a nascent church. At Clemiaksuc 100 converts were "formed into classes, appointed leaders"; at Nenootletete 75–80, at Scaltape 28 or 30, and at The Cascades 28 or 31 were "put into classes" (higher figures from D. Lee, letter, Jan. 15, 1840, Canse Collection). In addition Perkins established the "first native church in Oregon" on December 31 at Wascopam, with 200 members, and in January at Wishram 260 were "taken into society" (an apparent reference to the organization of classes) (Appendix 1, Doc. 3).

In March 1840, emigrant Robert Shortess witnessed one of those local organizations in action, at a village on the Deschutes:

> During the previous winter a revival had been going on, and 1,000 natives had, according to a report sent to the board of missions, been hopefully converted. While stopping at this village, I had an opportunity of seeing some of the effects. Each morning and evening the village was called together at the chief's lodge to hold a prayer meeting. The exercises were as usual on such occasions. At the close, the chief would say to the writer, interrogatively, "Tants ta token" (good people). Being answered in the affirmative, he went on to tell of the change from sin to righteousness wrought in them through the instructions of the missionaries, and concluded by asking for tobacco to treat his people to a smoke all around. [Shortess 1955:111]

That organization seems not to have persisted. Classes and church are never again mentioned during Perkins's tenure at Wascopam. In 1846 Alvan Waller stated:

> formerly there were some classes formed as I have in my travels seen in the hands of different individuals old papers with a number of persons names on them, in the form of a class-paper. But as near as I could ascertain no distinction was made, polygamist and all. . . . I have formed no classes, for the reason that I have not been able to satisfy myself who

it wold be safe to admit or unite in Church fellowship. [Waller, letter, Apr. 27, 1846, Archives of the Pacific Northwest Conference]

## The Methodist Message

What was the content of the Wascopam missionaries' message? That, it turns out, is an elusive question. In their correspondence, Perkins and Lee never explicitly address the question. The subjects of sermons are mentioned occasionally in passing, never more. We would have a better idea if Perkins's Walla Walla transcriptions had been preserved. Without good records, it is possible to make only a few tentative statements.

One important limitation on the amount and kind of information that was transmitted has been mentioned before: Chinook Jargon, the normal vehicle of sermonizing in the first few years of the Wascopam Mission, was capable of conveying only limited amounts of information. A jargon is not a language, and a great deal more meaning was lost in translation than would have been if there had been direct translation from English to Sahaptin or Upper Chinookan, for instance. The role of the missionaries' speakers was also important. Translating sermons from Jargon to the native vernacular left much room for elaboration by those individuals, and it is probable that they "filled in the blanks" with information that was consistent with their own backgrounds and that of their audiences.

The Protestant Ladder would have been a useful adjunct to the sermons. There is no evidence that Henry Perkins used that nonverbal medium, however. Chances are that it was most often used by its originator, Daniel Lee, as an adjunct to his Jargon sermons among Upper Chinookan-speaking Indians of the western (Columbia Gorge) portion of the circuit. The ladder transmitted the basics of Christian history, including the Creation, the Flood, Moses and his laws, the Messiah and his Resurrection, the disciples, the Reformation, and so on. Many of those stories, in forms that made them comprehensible to Northwest native peoples, worked their ways into the oral traditions and have been preserved, in the local vernaculars, in several myth and folklore collections.

### THE RESURRECTION AND THE SECOND COMING

One story that was definitely retold time and again by the Wascopam missionaries was the story of the Resurrection of Christ. As a major biblical event, it was depicted on both the Catholic and Protestant Ladders. It seems to have been a frequent theme with first-time audiences. During the Wascopam Revival it was presented by Daniel Lee (through Tumsowit) at Claticut and by Perkins (through Yacooetar) at Wishram. If, as Perkins claimed, most of his students could "repeat from memory the history of Christ," they certainly were familiar with the Resurrection.

Alvan Waller, Perkins's successor, told the story of the Resurrection often. During his April 1845 trip through the Yakama country, he related it at least four times: on the thirteenth at a camp of 200 east of The Dalles, on the twenty-fifth at Cappilli's village, on the twenty-seventh at *k̓amáyaqan* and his brother's villages, and on the thirtieth at Owhi and Ti–i–ish's camp. Waller commonly told the story at funerals, as in this account dated January 24, 1847:

> I have often assisted them in interring their dead, and with feelings never to be described listened to their hideous and pitiful wailings, and have tried with the doctrine of the Resurrection to discipate [*sic*] the gloom which hangs upon their minds in reference to their departed friends. In this I have felt an unexpressable happiness, especially when attending the funeral obsequies of their infant children. [Waller, letter, Feb. 3, 1847, Archives of the Pacific Northwest Conference]

Deaths, particularly of infants and very young children, were frequent in the 1840s. It was that cohort that provided much of the target population of the whooping cough, dysentery, and measles outbreaks of 1843, 1844, and 1847. A promise of rebirth would be a very seductive message to a people who were bereaved as often as the Indians of the middle Columbia in the 1840s. Repeated often and answering to a profound psychic need, it is not surprising that the Resurrection theme entered the collective consciousness of the Indians of the Wascopam circuit.

One of the strongest statements about the Second Coming in the Bible is contained in 1 Thessalonians 4–5, the subject of Perkins's December 17, 1843, services. The important passages are reproduced below.

> 5:2. For yourselves know perfectly that the day of the Lord so cometh as a thief in the night.
> 5:3. For when they shall say, Peace and safety; then sudden destruction cometh upon them, as travail upon a woman with child; and they shall not escape.
> 5:4. But ye, brethren, are not in darkness, that that day should overtake you as a thief.
> 5:5. Ye are all the children of light, and the children of the day: we are not of the night, nor of darkness.
> 5:6. Therefore let us not sleep, as do others; but let us watch and be sober.
> 4:14. For if we believe that Jesus died and rose again, even so them also which sleep in Jesus will God bring with him.
> 4:16. For the Lord himself shall descend from heaven with a shout, with

the voice of the archangel, and with the trump of God: and the dead in
Christ shall rise first:
4:17. Then we which are alive and remain shall be caught up together
with them in the clouds to meet the Lord in the air: and so shall we ever
be with the Lord. [KJV]

Here we have, with the Resurrection and Second Coming, the destruction of
evil persons, the rising of the dead, and the millennium in which all believers,
dead and alive, are united with God in a golden age. Those are potent themes
and appear with little modification in several Northwest nativistic religions.
Like the "aged doctor" *atníxlúidix* (Appendix 1, Doc. 3), Indian prophets such
as the Wanapam *šmúxala* (*Wáašat* religion) and the Paiute Wovoka (Ghost
Dance) had certainly been introduced to the lessons in the Pauline epistles.

Sometime after the missionary period and before the appearance of
*šmúxala* and several secondary Plateau prophets, the Tenino Sahaptins had
a prophet of their own, Dla'upac, whose message of death and rebirth was
obviously inspired by Christian doctrine. According to George Murdock's
field notes, Dla'upac was "dead" for five days, and then "came to life" again,
with a millennial message:

> In [his] song, the boy predicted the end of the world either by flood or by
> fire, just as once before, long ago, it had been burned up. He advised the
> Indians to prepare to meet xwamipama (God) [$x^w$aami-pamá 'above,
> high up' in CR Sahaptin]. He predicted that all the dead would come to
> life, would be resuscitated, just before the destruction of the world."
> Tenino mythology adds force to this interpretation of the end. The world
> has been completely destroyed twice before, the second time by a great
> flood. When the water subsided and land appeared at the beginning of the
> present (third) world, twelve supernaturals appeared who established the
> rites basic to the Smohollah cult. [Murdock in Spier 1935:21–22]

THE GADARENE

Comparing the original versions of biblical stories with the native versions
reprinted in the collections listed above is a useful way to detect underlying
themes and prominent characteristics of Indian cultures. That is a project in
itself (e.g., Ramsey 1983: chap. 10). Here, working from the other direction,
we can examine a biblical tale mentioned by Perkins himself and discuss how
it might have been interpreted by an Indian audience. The example is the
account of the Gadarene (Mark 5:1–20), which Perkins cites in his August 26,
1843, discussion of translation difficulties. The major passages of the story are
reproduced below:

1. And they came over unto the other side of the sea, into the country of the Gadarenes.

2. And when he [Jesus] was come out of the ship, immediately there met him out of the tombs a man with an unclean spirit,

3. Who had his dwelling among the tombs; and no man could bind him, no, not with chains:

5. And always, night and day, he was in the mountains, and in the tombs, crying, and cutting himself with stones.

6. But when he saw Jesus afar off, he ran and worshipped him.

8. For he said unto him, Come out of the man, thou unclean spirit.

9. And he asked him, What is thy name? And he answered, saying, My name is Legion, for we are many.

11. Now there was there nigh unto the mountains a great herd of swine feeding.

12. And all the devils besought him, saying, Send us into the swine, that we may enter into them.

13. And forthwith Jesus gave them leave. And the unclean spirits went out, and entered into the swine: and the herd ran violently down a steep place into the sea, (they were about two thousand;) and were choked in the sea. [King James Version]

The Indians would likely ascribe all three unusual behaviors of the Gadarene (living in the mountains, frequenting cemeteries, and self-mutilation with stones) to possession by spirits, but other than that common element, they would be confused by the juxtaposition. Frequenting cemeteries was exceedingly dangerous because of the presence of ghosts; it was virtually unheard of in Indian culture. Only professional corpse handlers, who had spirits that could deal with ghosts, ever set foot in such places, and then only temporarily. Anyone who dwelt among the tombs must be either crazy or possessed by a spirit more powerful than any the Indians knew. If that behavior was bizarre, spending time "in the mountains" certainly was not. It was a normal part of the spirit quest and in no way odd or "unclean." Cutting oneself with stones, the usual behavior of one possessed by a skep spirit, was indeed extreme behavior, but it was a recognized part of Indian culture and not necessarily undesirable, because the scars conveyed great prestige. One might want to exorcise a spirit that induced him to live in cemeteries, but why get rid of a spirit that had been obtained on a night and day quest in the mountains? Without a guardian spirit, one would become very sick indeed! The skep spirit could be dangerous to its owner and yet give power and prestige: exorcising it might make sense, but then again might not. The act of exorcism and transferral of spirits, as Perkins notes in his text, were perfectly consistent with Indian culture (Jesus would be a "powerful shaman"!). And of course, Indians were only recently familiar with swine (those few that were kept at the mission) and would not necessarily understand the association with uncleanness in the biblical sense. On the whole, in the Indian eye, that parable is both heavy with meaning and fraught with contradictions. It would be a very difficult pill to swallow. One begins to appreciate the problems Perkins was faced with.[7]

## Beyond and after the Mission

The teachings of the Methodists extended beyond the villages of the Wascopam circuit. In some cases, even a tentative contact left an impression on the Indians. That seems to have been the case among the Klickitats, who occupied the backcountry of what is now Skamania County.

In his second *Christian Advocate and Journal* report, Perkins made the interesting statement that

> Some of the Klihatats . . . who had been baptized by brother Lee, have moved off in various directions; so that to this day we have never seen them together. We have met one here and there, and . . . learn[ed] that a few kept up the forms of religion, particularly praying, but most of them "had even forgotten," as they said, "how to pray!" [Appendix 1, Doc. 4]

During the Great Revival, Lee had visited two interior Klickitat winter villages. In the warm season of the year Klickitat winter villages disbanded, and small family groups went in different directions in search of food. Numbers congregated at the appropriate season at fishing sites along the Columbia at the camas grounds near Glenwood and at the huckleberry grounds near Mount Adams (Norton, Boyd, and Hunn 1983). That annual pattern of separation, scatter, and congregation into units of varying composition was eminently suited to the spread of new ideas and the blending with old.

In the summer of 1853 George Gibbs met some of Lee's converts at Chequoss prairie in interior Skamania County:

> No systematic attempt has, it is believed, been made to convert the Klickitats to Christianity, although many individuals have come in contact with missionaries of some denomination. Several of these, at Chequoss, have had instruction from the Rev. Jason [*sic*] Lee, and others formerly at the Dalles. The old chief, Towetoks, preserved a paper on which some one had made a sort of calendar, or record of the days of the week. He expressed great anxiety lest, as it was nearly worn out, he should be unable to distinguish the Sundays, and requested Mr. Gibbs to prepare him a new one. He added that he was in great fear of death, and constantly "talked to the Chief above." [Gibbs 1854:426]

One of the forerunners of the Feather religion was a Klickitat from Husum, Lishwailit. According to DuBois (1938:16-18), he was born during the 1820s and received his vision when a "young man," probably sometime during the life span of the Wascopam Mission.

The impact of the Methodists was felt among peoples upstream from The Dalles as well. In 1860 the Presbyterian Reverend E. R. Geary recorded:

> About twenty miles east of The Dalles [near contemporary Maryhill] . . . we entered the lodge of . . . Elippama. He was in feeble health, but impressively venerable in appearance. . . . He said (in the Jargon) that we both had one God; that he talked with that God every day. . . . Who told you, said I, of the great God you worship every day? The priest, was his reply; and immediately hurrying to the corner of the lodge he drew out a carefully folded buffalo robe from beneath a number of other packages. Within this was a dressed deer skin, then that of a badger, then a piece of bright blue cloth enwrapping a small book. Holding it up, he exclaimed, "This is God's book; the priest gave it to me." I of course concluded him to be a Catholic, and that the book was a volume of devotion. On opening the book, however, I was surprised to find it one of the early publications of the American Sunday School Union. He evidently thought it the Bible, and I did nothing to destroy the innocent illusion. I now asked the name of the priest. His prompt reply was "Jason Lee." [sic: probably Daniel]. Light at once broke on the mystery. "Many years before," he told me, "he had heard Jason Lee talk first to the Indians and then to God"—that is, I suppose, preach and pray, and he had talked to that God ever since. The book was restored to its wrappings and place. To the Indian it seemed a "holy of holies." [H. Hines 1899:272-73]

The Wascopam papers record the presence of Klamaths at The Dalles. In 1873, one of them recalled such a visit:

> Link River Jo . . . said that thirty years ago, when he traveled to the Columbia river, good men told him about the Holy Spirit that was to come to the whole world and visit its remotest parts. When he came back from the Dalles he told his people about it but found them groping in perfect darkness. They were killing and murdering each other and he tried to tell them about the mission of the Holy Spirit preached by the white man, who, they said, would bring peace on earth among all men. They would not believe him and told him he lied. [Clarke in Stern 1956:233]

In 1871, on the Yakama Reservation, George Paul, one of the (Methodist) Reverend James Wilbur's converts, also recalled Wascopam:

> A long time ago, when Lee and Perkins (missionaries) came to the Dalles, the older Indians were like dead; they woke up, but the old Indians are

almost gone. Mr. Wilbur came here and woke us up as Perkins did the others. . . . Our hearts are glad. [Brunot 1871:548]

The Reverend Harvey Hines, who served at The Dalles from 1856 on, stated:

Since 1870 the writer has personally known at least a score of the converts of this wonderful revival who were yet steadfast in the faith and experience of the Gospel. In 1898, fifty-seven years after, some are [still] holding "the beginning of their confidence steadfast unto the end." [H. Hines 1899:168, 170 (reorganized for clarity)]

And finally, more than sixty years after the fact, the Yakama White Swan recalled the October 1840 camp meeting:

It seems to me the missionary used strong words when he opened the Bible to speak to the Indians. While Lee was preaching the Indian chiefs sat smoking, not caring about hearing the Gospel. Three or four days while he was preaching all women and chiefs felt different, just like something had melted and hot had come down, and then threw away their tomahawks and war bonnets and fall down and ask God to forgive them. 'People were surprised to see what kind of spirit came down, and they looked at each other and all saw the tears that ran down each other's faces and then they all fell down and worshiped God. [Grubbs 1908]

**Plate 1.** Two views of the Wascopam Mission, 1849. TOP: View from the north. Sketch probably by Osborne Cross; from Cross, "A Report . . . of the March of the . . . Mounted Riflemen" (1850). BOTTOM: View from the south, inside the compound. Painting by William Tappan. Photos courtesy Oregon Historical Society, Portland.

**Plate 2.** Panorama of The Cascades, 1849. TOP: "Commencement ... of The Cascade or Great Falls of the Columbia River." BOTTOM: "Continuation ... of The Cascade ...", from Osborne Cross, "A Report ... of the March of the ... Mounted Riflemen" (1850). Courtesy Oregon Historical Society.

**Plate 3.** The Dalles, 1853. Engraved from a drawing by John Mix Stanley; from I. I. Stevens, *Narrative and Final Report of Explorations for . . . a Pacific Railroad* (1859). Apparently looks downstream from the head of Five Mile Rapids. Courtesy Oregon Historical Society, Portland.

**Plate 4.** Tamakoun's flat-headed son. Sketch by Joseph Drayton, 1841. An engraving based on this sketch appears in Charles Wilkes, *Narrative of the United States Exploring Expedition* (vol. 4, 1844), where it is misidentified as coming from "Niculuita" (*nixlúidix*), instead of The Cascades. Courtesy Smithsonian Institution Archives, Washington, D.C.

A Cascade Chief

**Plate 5.** Tamakoun. Watercolor by Paul Kane, 1847. Throughout the missionary period, Tamakoun was head man at The Cascades. He was in his early thirties when this painting was made. Courtesy Royal Ontario Museum, Toronto.

**Plate 6.** "Mountain Landscape with Indians." Painting by John Mix Stanley, a romantic artist of the Hudson Valley School. Stanley visited the middle Columbia twice, in 1847-48 and in 1853; this painting was probably completed in a studio, based on his field sketches, after his return east. It shows Mount Hood from what is most likely one of the settlements in the Hood River and White Salmon area, but the exact location is not known, and it may be a composite. This is the only known surviving depiction of a mid-nineteenth-century Upper Chinookan settlement. Courtesy Detroit Institute of Fine Arts.

**Plate 7.** Indian dip netter at The Cascades. Watercolor by Paul Kane, July 1847. Courtesy Stark Museum of Art, Orange, Texas.

**Plate 8.** Autumn fishing camp at Celilo. Painting by James Everett Stuart, October 1884. Courtesy Oregon Historical Society, Portland.

**Plate 9.** Salmon dry-house at The Dalles. Based on a drawing by James Drayton; from Charles Wilkes, *Narrative of the United States Exploring Expedition* (vol. 4, 1844). Courtesy Oregon Historical Society, Portland.

**Plate 10.** Chinookan bowman at the Green River rendezvous. Painting by Alfred Jacob Miller, 1837. Few Chinookans traveled to the summer mountain rendezvous, where Plateau and Plains Indians and mountain men met to trade furs. This young man holds an elk-horn bow. Courtesy Walters Art Gallery, Baltimore, Maryland.

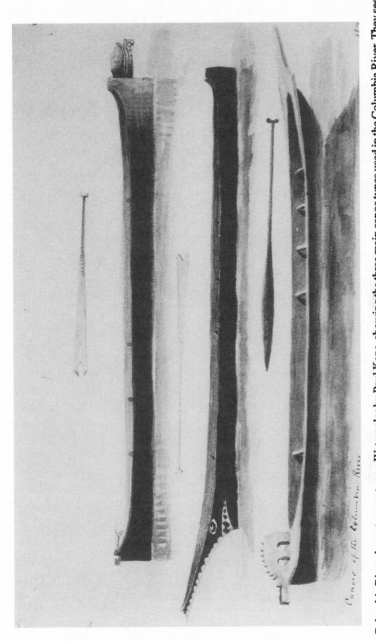

*Canoes of the Columbia River*

**Plate 11.** Columbia River dugout canoe types. Watercolor by Paul Kane, showing the three main canoe types used in the Columbia River. They seem to correspond (top to bottom) to Lewis and Clark's sea-going "Kilamox" canoe, the large "Chinook" canoe found up to the Klickitat River, and the medium-sized canoe found up to The Dalles. Courtesy Stark Museum of Art, Orange, Texas.

**Plate 12.** Chinookan girl with shell bandeau. Sketch by Paul Kane at Fort Vancouver, 1847. Courtesy Royal Ontario Museum, Toronto.

**Plate 13.** Chinookan Indian with flattened head. Watercolor by Paul Kane at Clackamas, February 1847. Courtesy Stark Museum of Art, Orange, Texas.

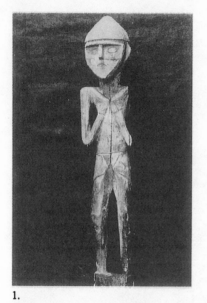

1.

2.

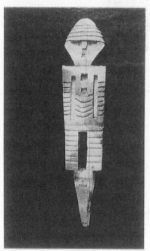

3.

4.

**Plate 14.** Grave figures from the Memaloose Islands. The first three of these figures were collected in 1882 from "Tum-wa-ta, Memaluse Rock" (probably Grave Island), and the fourth from Upper Memaloose in 1905. Numbers 1 and 2 are just over a foot high, of cedar, with "traces of red, white, black paint." Number 3 is 8 1/4 inches high, of maple; number 4 is a foot high, of cedar (Wingert 1949: plates 59, 60). Numbers 1-3 courtesy Department Library Services, American Museum of Natural History, New York; number 4 courtesy Field Museum of Natural History, Chicago.

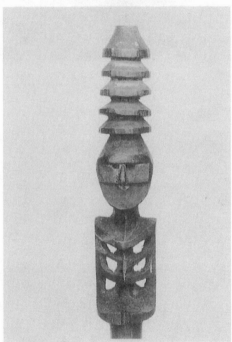

**Plate 15.** Shaman's wands from The Dalles. The photos show the upper part of the "tamnous sticks," 28 inches long, made of ash, with "traces of red paint on the upper part" (Wingert 1949: plate 62). Courtesy Field Museum of Natural History, Chicago.

**Plate 16.** Zoomorphic stone mortars from near *nixlúidix*. The flat mortar is basalt and represents a beaver; the other is granite, shaped as a turtle. Courtesy Oregon Archaeological Society, Portland, and Emory Strong Collection, Columbia Gorge Interpretive Center, Stevenson, Washington.

**Plate 17.** Piupiumaksmaks, Walla Walla chief. Painting by Paul Kane, late July 1847. He was about fifty when this painting was made. Courtesy Royal Ontario Museum, Toronto.

# Appendix 1
# Original Documents

## Autobiography: Chapter 7
Wascopam, Spring 1838

*The first selection from Perkins's manuscript autobiography describes the establishment of the Methodist Mission at The Dalles (Wascopam). The inclusive dates are March 14–April 4, 1838. The text is based on the first typewritten version of the autobiography, submitted by Perkins's granddaughter Grace Albee to Rev. John Canse in 1934; brackets [ ] enclose additions to the text from Albee's more complete 1952 version (see Introduction).*

### Founding a New Station with Dan Lee at the Dalles

The Indians of the Willamette valley were few in number, and so demoralized by contact with the Canadian French who had settled among them that no mission purely Indian was practicable. We therefore decided to proceed up the Columbia beyond the Cascade Mountains, and wherever we should find enough Indians and a location suitable, pitch our tents, and await further instruction from the Superintendent, Reverend Jason Lee. Of course I could not take my wife on such an exploring expedition as this, and into an entirely unknown region.

We obtained two wooden canoes of unequal size, one carrying three men, baggage and provisions, and the other a little larger. As I was the smallest man I took the smaller canoe, and loaded her nearly to the water's edge. Mr. Daniel Lee took the bulk of the supplies needed for starting the mission,—tools, implements of husbandry, cooking utensils, seeds, and a supply of goods to trade for provisions.

We bade good-bye to our Oregon friends on the fourteenth of March, eighteen thirty-eight, and proceeded down the Willamette River a distance of fifty miles. From the mission to the falls, where Oregon City now stands, the river ran swiftly within high banks, for the most part lightly wooded. Below the falls its course was irregular [and its width varies according to the varying character of the country], sometimes running in a narrow channel, along high rocky banks, sometimes smoothly and peacefully among low green islands, spreading out into a low shallow basin, and finally—dividing itself into two equal streams,—ran along the willow shores of a large delta.

We took the eastern channel, which brought us a little below Fort Vancouver. For an account of the voyage [from this point upward], I quote from a journal kept for the benefit of my wife, whom I left with Mr. Leslie.

*Wascopam Village, March 21, 1838.*

My Dear Elvira,

Through the goodness of God we arrived safely at this place [at two o'clock this after noon], it being just a week since we left the Willamette.

We left Vancouver Saturday night, a little before sunset with two deeply laden canoes and six Indians, including an old chief named Marnicoon, to whom I am much indebted for the watchful and fatherly care he has had over me. He took charge of the canoe in which I sailed, and from his knowledge of the Indians, the navigation of the river, and everything connected with the voyage, a better companion I could not have had. On the whole we had the finest company of Indians I have seen.

On leaving Vancouver I could hardly restrain my tears. I felt that I was going for the first time beyond the pale of civilization, with but one with whom I could converse in English. I do not know that the prospect of earthly gain would have inclined me to proceed, but calling to remembrance the perishing Indians, I at once took courage, and in a little while began to feel quite cheerful.

We went on till dark, and stopped [for the night] at the saw mill, eight or nine miles[, more or less,] from the fort. [The Indians encamped on the shore, and Brother Lee and I slept in a small empty house built, I believe, for the purpose of entertaining such voyageurs as these.]

We were refreshed on Sabbath morning, and after breakfast and prayers, the day being fine, concluded to proceed on our way slowly, [as the best way we could spend the day,] and after a little while, the wind blowing softly, hoisted sail, and went forward rapidly and pleasantly, we in the mean time reading and singing. We passed little land capable of cultivation, the river being hemmed in on either side by huge granite rocks, rising ever and anon to a formidable mountain. Some of the cliffs ran up from the river perpendicularly several hundred feet. Sunday night we got a little rain, and having no tarpulin to cover them, some of our articles got wet. Monday morning [the rain having ceased,] we embarked, and the wind blew so hard that we could just keep our canoes from filling. But we scud along close to the shore at a rapid rate until afternoon, when we reached the foot of the rapids, which were very bad for about four miles before reaching the Cascades, [or great falls.] Here Brother Lee and I disembarked, and the Indians took the canoes, while we travelled on shore. We hired, also, several Indians[, residents at the Falls,] to assist us by. We met with no accidents except the filling of my canoe in passing a rapid, and the wetting of our flour, wheat, sugar and various other things, but were thankful to get by with so little loss. By dark we had everything over the portages, and ourselves secure in our tent.

We met at the portages three loads of our Dalles or Wascopam Indians, going with dry salmon and acorns to the Fort to trade, and among them their chief, Wamcutta. Wamcutta [and his people] was very glad to see us, having heard we were coming, and offered to accompany us, and build houses [for us] if we desired it. He was dressed in the French style, and over all a large buffalo skin. We made him a small present, and passed on.

The falls of the Columbia have nothing of the sublime, being only an irregular rush of water over a rocky channel. [The rocks are dark granite.] The portage is rather rough, and about half a mile in length. The rapids are in a ten fold degree worse to pass than the falls, and take much longer. On the whole it is most dangerous navigating them with loaded canoes. There is some fine mountain scenery around the falls, and indeed most of the way up the river. Abundance of snow lies on the hills, which sends many a stream leaping and roaring to the river, sometimes over a precipice of fifty feet.

Tuesday we embarked about eight o'clock, with a fine, fair wind blowing, which lasted all day, and brought us on our way very pleasantly. About two thirds of the distance up we passed several villages of Indian[s which were all on some salmon creek. Towards night, we overtook some Indian] hunters, who had been out for some time, killing and drying venison. There were eight or ten canoes, heavily laden. Marnicoon went on shore, and purchased four large cuts, which I think was the best venison I ever tasted. They kill the deer, cut it up in large pieces, build a large fire, build a scaffolding of poles over and lay on the meat until smoked and dried. Last night we were visited at our camp by some Indians on horseback, who talked with our people a long time.

The hills around our encampment are very high and beautifully green, even to their tops. Along the margin of the river were a few willows, poplars and pines, with here and there a creek, skirted with firs. [Scarcely any driftwood was to be seen anywhere on the river.]

This morning we had to ply our paddles, there being no wind, [and we were threatened with rain, but after a while the clouds broke away], and we had a good day. The land we passed to-day has not been so barren [as formerly]. It has been very broken, but covered with verdure, just high enough for grazing. [We passed one beautiful spot by the name of Claticut on the north side of the river where was quite a village of Indians and plenty of horses grazing. It only wanted a few English houses to make it an enchanting spot.] As we sailed along the country became more pleasant, and Indian encampments more numerous. We at length arrived at this place, the name of which I have placed at the head of this letter.

We are encamped by the side of a good stream of water, which is large enough for a good mill or two, and which divides in two a good intervale, extending from here to the Dalles, about one mile, and down the river about the same, and varying from half a mile to a quarter in width, according to the winding of the river, and with soil like your richest prairies.

A few rods distant[, on the stream before mentioned,] is Wascopam village, containing fifteen good houses, built of boards and mats, the best I have seen, containing, I suppose, from a hundred to a hundred and fifty inhabitants, who are permanent residents. They are good looking, and the adults very well clothed for Indians. All along the prairie the Indians congregate in the salmon season from other parts, so we shall have an abundance of company. They have plenty of dried salmon, and catch, at present plenty of [excellent] salmon [trout] in the stream, besides.

They had heard of our coming and as soon as our canoes touched shore about fifty came out to meet us. Mr. Birney used to have a trading house here, and the Indians suppos[ing] we had come for the same purpose[, were therefore loud in their joy on our arrival and hastened to show us all the land, the wood for building, and the horses for hauling it, and were all ready to turn out and work for us, as they did for Mr. Birney. But you know what the Indians mean, by offering to do and give.] When asked what Mr. Birney gave them for helping him build, they said "Oh, a plenty of shirts, blankets, trousers, jackets and tobacco". But alas, we are not blessed with the same supplies [as he, and we know not, therefore, how to receive their offers. Were we as rich as the Hudson Bay Company, we could get along very well.]

Just above the intervale where we [and the Indians] are there is a fine table land which is about a hundred feet high, and extends from the stream of water to the Dalles, parallel with the intervale, and extending to the hills which bound it on the east, from a hundred to a hundred and fifty rods, probably of very rich soil. [On the border which overlooks the low intervale and river, we have concluded to build.] This tableland is bounded on the back by hills resembling those opposite the mission house [at Willamette], only some of them are well wooded with oak and pine[. Pine on] their tops, and oak on their sides [and in the vales. About a hundred and fifty rods from where we intend to build] there is the finest grove of oaks I have [seen in the country. I mean their picturesque beauty. There are, I should think, some] five hundred of them, in fine rich soil[, w]here the grass is three or four feet high, and the ground is covered with acorns, which the Indians eat or trade. This grove is at the extreme end of the wooded land. All, beyond is grazing land, which at present is beautifully green.

We have had a supper of stewed ducks and chocolate [or cocoa]. We have gone through the ceremony of smoking with all the principal men of the village, [sung and prayed] and now all is safe and still, I will commit myself to Somnus.

Thursday morning a fine day. Thermometer at the back of the tent at freezing point,—plenty of frost and a little wind. The Indians are all around the tent, of all sizes, and both clothed and naked, some on foot and some on horses. We sang and prayed with them, I in English, and Mr. Lee in the jargon, a mixture of English, French and Indian. During prayers not a word was spoken by any of them, but they uncovered their heads [and] listened attentively till all was finished, after which our old friend Marnicoon[, the chief before spoken of,] voluntarily interpreted it in the Chinook tongue.

The Indians brought us three nice salmon trout this morning, and two last evening, so we had a luxurious breakfast. After such a fatiguing voyage, everything relishes well. We are drying our things, this morning, and preparing to decamp, and explore the length and breadth of this land.

Thursday. P. M. We have returned from our excursion, and are prepared to speak of the country for several miles around. We traced the stream of water which flows up by us among the hills, and find it comes from Mt. Hood. From the hills above us we have a full view of that mountain, and also on the north side of the Columbia of Mt. Helena, and also a good view of the country north and east for about fifty miles. [The country back of us towards Mt. Hood is well wooded with pine and oak equally intermixed.] Mt. Hood lies to the southwest a distance of about thirty or forty miles, in a direct line to Willamette.

From a view of the country I should think that the journey might be made by land very easily in three days with horses. The country abounds with grass and the horses are very fat. If we only had oxen we could begin to plough at once, but as it is we can make only a small garden, which we intend to commence at once, as our seed was wet by the filling of the canoes, and we fear it will spoil if not planted.

We shall always have wood enough at hand for building, fencing and burning; the pine, however, is nearly all small, from a foot to fifteen inches in diameter, the oak the same.

## Indian Visitors

Our tent is thronged with Indians and horses. The men are lying down around the tent in scores. At present we are enjoying a visit from a great Cayuse chief by the pretty name of Tu-e-tas-o-mittle-cum. He is in our tent, sitting with our old chief and Brother Lee, and I am sitting facing them, and having a long serious talk on many subjects[, so I have to talk and write at the same time.]

Tuetasomittlecum would put to shame any of your down country chiefs. For dignity of manner and appearance he is exceeded by no Indian I have yet seen. He has a neat underdress of white blanket, trimmed with blue and perfectly clean—moccasins—, —a cap,—and over all a pale red robe, fringed [and colored] with various figures, and made with a large cape. The robe is covered nearly half with various beads. [Several other chiefs have visited us from various quarters with whom we have smoked in token of friendship.]

March 23, 1838. Have sent off two canoes to Vancouver for provisions. Talked a great deal with the Indians, traded some, written a few letters, made a grindstone-crank, sharpened some of our tools, staked out a site for a house, and commenced a garden.

March 24, 1838. This morning removed our tent and all our things near the place where we intend to build, which occupied us all the forenoon. This afternoon we received a visit from a young chief [who came] from the other side of the river. About a dozen old men came with him, and in token of friendship we smoked with them, and had a long talk under the oak in front of our tent. He said his people were two hundred—old men, forty old women and a great many young people. [Received also a visit from a party of young Indians who came on horses.] About 4 P. M. Dr. McLoughlin came and talked with the Indians, and Brother Lee went with him to the Dalles. In his absence, I worked in the garden, accompanied by one of the principal men of the village and his two sons. [The old man used the spade very well, while his boys collected and burned the weeds.] We dug up and prepared one large bed in which we sowed parsnip and cabbage seed. [While we were at work many Indians came around and were very much pleased to see me plant the seed.] The old man's name is Canicissa. Another old man by the name of Tumsowit, who is one of the fathers of the village, is much interested in our welfare, and tries to help us.

This evening several Indians came and supped with us,—who belong far up in the interior, and who are acquainted with Brothers Whitman and Spaulding. One of them had a testament of which he was very proud. He stayed with us till after prayers, sang with us, and when we prayed knelt down. Before eating I observed that he stopped and uttered a few words in his own tongue.

The Indians have a beautiful green about a quarter of a mile from here, where all the men of the village resort occasionally for a game of ball. About a dozen sally forth on the green, strip off their clothes, pile them in the centre, and commence the game like so many boys. One thing is remarkable about these Indians, their women remain constantly at home. Not one, I believe, has been near our tent, and indeed, unless you go to their houses are not to be seen.

While I have been writing this, the wolves have been howling around. So closes the week.

Sabbath, March 25. This is the first of the kind we have passed on this soil, and one which we shall long remember, [as shown in] the following letter written to my wife the same day.

My dear Elvira,

How are you this morning? I suppose just now you are preparing to attend meeting at the mission house. That privilege is denied me, but we are going soon to meet our people at the village, where we told them to assemble.

I feel much happier here than at the Willamette, and think you will, too. The Indians are far, far superior in intelligence to the Calapooyas [at your place]. They all appear friendly, and talk very rationally on religious subjects, even now. [They sometimes begin of their own accord and tell how wicked it is to kill and steal, and what a good Being God is, which the white people have told them in passing up and down the river. We have much to encourage us here. You know I am not sanguine, but certainly the Indians promise much.]

George does our cooking very well, and is very useful. He is building him a house in the Sandwich Islands fashion, and has got one side covered with grass. The scenery around here you will admire, I think. [This morning I walked out about sunrise, and the birds were singing most delightfully.]

Sabbath evening. I now sit down to continue my letter. We attended meeting in the village at 11 a. m. Brother Lee spoke to forty, mostly old men, in the jargon, and old Canacissa interpreted it [for them] in the Chenook. We conducted our meeting in the usual form. The Indians joined us in the singing, and all kneeled when we prayed. Not one of the women was at the meeting. We cannot tell why.

We are told there are forty-seven in the village, residents, but many are away, now.

It was a great satisfaction to me to kneel down in the midst of forty Indians for the first time, and commend their souls to God, who looketh on mankind as his children, and who cares for the red man as well as white. I looked forward to the time when they would publicly unite their prayers with mine. I just begin to feel I am a missionary, and an increasing attachment to the work. May the Lord hasten the day when

'Peoples and tribes of every tongue
Dwell on His love with sweetest song.'

It has been raining this evening, and is rather cold. We are comfortable, however.

Monday, March 26, 1838. This day have been making a garden, and have succeeded in getting in most of our seeds. Canicissa and Tumsowit worked with us all day and have labored faithfully. Some twenty Indians were around a great part of the day [looking on], and if we had spades and hoes, and something to give them for their work, we should be at no loss for laborers, but as it is we have only a few tools, and very little provision, so that it is impossible for us to avail ourselves of their help. We find [them ready to work for pay, but] an Indian will not work for nothing, and I know not who would.

Tuesday, 27. This morning dug out our spring, which we think will afford us water most of the year. Went out and cut some axe handles, handled our pickaxe and stone hammer, worked some in our garden and set two men digging.

About 11 a.m. after some debate, concluded to build a small 'stone castle', for our present accomodation as a home, and in time of war for protection, to stand parallel with the sun, and face an oak tree. After considerable labor and mature deliberation we succeeded in laying the north-east corner stone on the 28th day of March, at precisely 12.M I would explain that this formidable 'castle' was a low, irregular stone wall, two or three feet high, to form an enclosure, first—for our tent, which we pitched in the back, and secondly—for a kind of dining room,—a few feet square,—which we covered with boughs, and thirdly—for a kitchen, which was bounded on one side by a large rock, against which we built our fire, and which was for the most part left open, so we might not be annoyed by smoke. Here we stayed till fall[, when we got into our house].

At dinner we had a discussion over some mouldy bread, as to what were the feelings of the various races of beings which inhabited it, as we dipped it into the hot soup. [This p.m. have been rolling stones down hill for our castle wall.] Have eaten three ducks to day, each duck being made into soup, serving a meal for five of us.

George has been bringing timber to build a 'hotel' for the entertainment of guests. He thinks he will have it up in a week or two, besides doing the cooking. I would explain that George was a Hawaian, who had spent some time with us the first year of the mission, and was very useful in helping us build.

I now make extracts from a letter written to my wife the last of March.

My dear Elvira,

It is Saturday night, and I am quite tired, and I suppose you are, too. I have been [at work] in the woods all day, cutting and hewing timber for a house. I came home very hungry, and have done justice to a very good partridge soup, and the last of the bread you made, which was very mouldy, but while I am writing this, Brother Lee has been baking some more, and has just brought me a hot cake spread with butter,—of which we have plenty,—and wished me to guess how he baked it, which I guess was in the ashes, from its appearance.

We had a Walla Walla chief to tea,—who resided near Dr. Whitman this past season,—and who prays and sings quite well. Twenty or thirty of his people are encamped within two rods of us, and they are making plenty of noise.

We are making use of every opportunity of collecting the language. There are two languages spoken here, [the Walla and the Chenook,] but there is no similarity between them. The Chinook is the harder [to speak and] to learn, but is more frequently used here than the other, the Walla Walla. I have collected about 200 words of it.

The nights are quite cold yet,—a basin froze over at the door of our tent. We shall have a beautiful view of Mt. St. Helena from our tent, and by going a few rods, of Mt. Hood.

Sunday, April 1, 1838. This morning was quite cold. I rose early, [and took a walk] and wrote and read till meeting time, when the people assembled back of our tent. There were more than 60 [50] men in attendance, most of them past middle age. About half of them were from the Dalles, just above us, the rest were our villagers.

Brother Lee and I sat under an oak tree, and the Indians arranged themselves on each side of us. The most profound attention was given by all. Poor souls! They have remained in darkness all their lives, when they might, if Christians had done their duty, have been rejoicing in the knowledge of God. I never loved the Indians half so well,—never felt so much interested as among these. I could not refrain from tears when beholding them, and commending them to the mercy of God.

A young chief from the Dalles slept in our tent last night—of a very pleasing demeanor. His name is Celest [Celetee. He came to spend the Sabbath with us]. I have made him a present of a testament, which he is perusing as attentively as if he understood it all. [I tell Brother Lee he will make a preacher yet. He interests us very much.] He was here two nights ago, and when he and his people encamped for the night, they sang the tune of 'Greenville' very correctly. Before sleeping, they joined in praying in their own tongue. [Tell us not that the adult Indians are to be neglected, or that they must be farmers and mechanics before being converted.] Such things [as I have witnessed] encourage my soul to pray and labor. The fields are white, ready for harvest.

The next letter I find written to my wife was

April 4, 1838. Wednesday morning we dismissed our visitors, and went into the woods, and hewed timber. Yesterday we worked hewing in the forenoon, and in the afternoon Marnicoon arrived from the fort with our canoe and provisions. In company with him came our Indian chief, Wamcutta, and of course we had to receive him in accordance with the scripture injunction 'Honor to whom honor is due.' He took tea with us, and after tea we talked with him a long time, explaining to him the object of our coming. He seems friendly. [He cannot understand the "Jargon", and therefore we are under the necessity of talking through an interpreter.]

This morning we were informed that the villagers were to have a council at the chief's house, and eat with him, and he was going to give them a talk, and so today has been a holiday, and we have used it accordingly. After breakfast Wamcutta furnished us with two good looking horses, and we started on another exploring expedition. In the forenoon we went to the hills north of Mt. Hood, and examined the timber, which we found to be very good and abundant.

A finer mill privilege I do not think is to be found than the little stream which passes our place affords. The name of the stream is 'Hois'. We are going to petition for a new saw mill, grist mill, a miller, carpenter, blacksmith, physician, school master and farmer.

After dinner, we next proceeded to the Dalles. It is only fifteen minutes ride to the foot of them, where we dismounted, and went to examine the rocks [from which they catch their salmon. An old Indian named Canissa accompanied us and we clambered over the rocks] along the margin of the river, about a mile to the top of the Lower Dalles. The whole river is here compressed into a channel of a few rods in width, and rushes down very swiftly. On going thus far, we found ourselves very tired, and concluded to return and visit the Upper Dalles, several miles distant, another day.

Opposite the Lower Dalles is a village of some 25 or 30 good houses, where a young chief named Tucknawack [Pucknawuck] resides. He was here yesterday, and we got him a bag of potatoes [and some peas] to plant, but, poor fellow, I think his well meant efforts to teach his people agriculture will not be successful unless he comes to our place, as we could not see any land around the Dalles fit for cultivation. [He is a very intelligent young man and promises much eventually.]

Canicissa showed us the rock from which he caught salmon. He said that a long time ago, Sah–ha–le–tice [Sah–Ha–Li–Tice] (literally the chief above), told him to fish there, and he would catch plenty of salmon. Be that as it may,—I believe he has been pretty successful.

On the whole, we had a pretty good holiday, and this evening finds us writing in our tent, while the moon is shining most beautifully. We have just been wishing you were here, and concluded it would have been best to have brought you along [with us,] and that you would have been able to take care of yourself, and us, too.

Brother Lee is writing an address to the churches, which I hope will make them take hold and help us. This location, I think, promises much more for the Indians than does the Willamette. It is healthy, its natural advantages are as good, and its fishery will sustain all the expense that will be needed for the civilization of the Indians, if taken hold of by friends of the mission. We think 8 men with their wives are needed here immediately, and several thousands of dollars expended for goods for the Indians.

We went into some houses today at the Dalles, and seeing the children naked, and the adults not much better, we asked them why they did not clothe themselves. 'Oh', they said, 'we are very poor. We have no skins, and no clothes. If you will come and trade with us, we will give you salmon, and you will give us clothes, and we will clothe ourselves.' We saw their predicament and ours, too. [The Lord have mercy on those who are hoarding their thousands in the land of plenty.] Yesterday Tumsowit showed me his ragged pants, and begged a little piece of cloth and some thread to mend them. I had not a patch [to give him], but I gave him one of the little bags you had made us and told him to cut it up and mend his clothes, which he did.

My heart is pained from day to day on account of our poverty. Our bretheren have sent us here to behold wretchedness, without the means to relieve it. [A few days ago I went to the house of one of the men who has been at work for us, and is a good wood chopper, to take him with me into the woods, and seeing him come with me without any clothes, I told him to go and put on his trousers. He said 'One of my men has gone after a horse and I have lent him my trousers and have nothing else to wear.' You may imagine my feelings. I told him to return to his house and I would see him again, for I did not want him to work in the hot sun naked. The next morning I carried him a shirt and set him to work. His name is Hanecunewitt.] Here we are, with provisions for ourselves only, a few blankets and shirts to buy horses with, a few knives, and a few little trinkets for trade[, and this is the way we are going to civilize the Indians]. We could set the whole village to work digging up the land, cutting timber, or anything else they could do[, but when they come begging for work what shall we say? We tell them only that we are very poor, and have nothing to work with].

Their fire wood they [have to] bring on their backs or on horses a long way, because they have not axes to cut that which is only a few rods distant. They wish to buy from us, but we have none to part with. They want tools to manufacture various articles, such as saw and draw shave, but we have none to sell. What fools they must think we are, to come here to teach them to work, and not a tool to put into their hands, even when they desire to purchase them honorably!

I think we can have access to at least one thousand Indians here. The women have to labor like slaves. Every day we see them out beside their houses, sitting almost naked [on the ground,] in the wind and the sun, manufacturing large coarse mats, on which to dry [and in which to preserve] the[ir] salmon. They are as untiring at it as the Virginia slaves; while at another season of the year they are out on the hills, and prairies, getting berries and roots for winter provisions. We saw some in our ride, bright looking young women on the sides of the hills, toiling in the cold wind, almost starved, I might say, digging up the ground for roots. But my heart is full.

Well may the female sex rejoice that Christianity has been introduced into the world, Christianity which raises woman to the dignity of her sex! I would that American females could have their sisters of this land portrayed to them in all their wretchedness, methinks some of their prayers for the success of the mission would cease, or their purses would open. Most of the Indians are bareheaded and they would be glad to wear the little bags you make [us on their heads], if we would let them, but we tell them they do not become them, and we will make something better.

The foregoing extracts from my letters will convey our situation the first two weeks of our stay, and the difficulties under which we commenced our new Mission.

# Appendix 1

## History of the Oregon Mission: Part One

Wascopam, Spring 1838

*Christian Advocate and Journal,*
September 13, 1843

*This short report on the beginnings of Wascopam Mission was published in the Methodist magazine the* Christian Advocate and Journal, *September 13, 1843. It was Perkins's second* Advocate *report (the first, on the 1839–40 Wascopam Revival, had appeared in October 1840). The "History of the Oregon Mission: Part One" recalled events from March 1838 to fall 1839. Brackets [ ] enclose additions to the* Christian Advocate and Journal *text from the typewritten manuscript version submitted by Perkins's granddaughter Grace Albee to Rev. John Canse.*

To the Corresponding Secretary of the Missionary Society of the M. E. Church.

Wascopam, March 21, 1843.
Dear Brother—It is now about three years since I penned a communication to your worthy predecessor upon the state of religion at this station, and of a work of grace then in progress among the natives along this river.[1] As that communication was of such a character as to excite considerable interest among the friends of the Oregon mission, I have thought perhaps some anxiety would be felt by them to learn particulars respecting the *continuance* of that work which then appeared so promising, and *the history of our operations since;* as also *a view of our present state and prospects.* These particulars I would cheerfully give, were I certified that they had not been given already, by one whose proper business it is to make all such reports [the Superintendent, Jason Lee]. Being entirely ignorant of what has been written from time to time, I feel a delicacy about saying any thing to the public; and I have therefore

233

concluded to say what I have to say to you alone, as a private individual. In this manner, too, I can write more freely and fully than if I were writing for general circulation, or for publication.

I take it for granted that you feel an interest in all that relates to the missionary work, and are doing all you can to spread the missionary spirit through the high places of the Church. I trust, therefore, the simple details I am about to give of missionary work, and missionary life, will be of some service to you.

That I cannot give you as cheering an account of the state of the work now as formerly, arises not from any unwillingness so to do, but solely from the facts in the case, and our friends must be willing to hear the truth, whether cheering or otherwise.

I arrived in this country, as you may recollect, in company with Rev. David Leslie, in the fall of 1837, as a part of the second reinforcement. My first winter was spent upon the Willamette.

In the spring of 1838 Rev. Daniel Lee and myself were sent to commence a station among the natives of this place. It is just five years to-day since we landed here in order to survey the ground, and ascertain the situation and disposition of the Indians. It is a little short of five years since we held our first meeting among them, and began to sow in their hearts the seed of heavenly truth.

The only language by which we could communicate with each other was what might be justly called a philological curiosity—a sad mixture of French, English, and corrupted Indian words, culled from the various dialects of the lower waters of the Columbia. This strange language, or "jargon," as we generally call it here, began first to be put together by the early fur-traders. Year by year additions were naturally made of words from each of these languages, as they were caught up by one or the other party, until it became the current medium through which all business between the whites and Indians was transacted. Consisting of only 2 or 300 words, the veriest stranger, after the attention and observation of a few months, could converse in it with tolerable facility. It came at length to be spoken between the French and American settlers upon the Willamette. As a matter of course the first missionaries sent out by our Board readily took it up, and once in use it was scarcely possible to lay it aside; and considering the very early period in which they were incumbered with an English school; the almost constant sickness with which they were visited; the labors, cares, and anxieties of their first years in the country, it was impossible to substitute a better.

Previous to our arrival among the people of this place quite a number of them, by intercourse with the fur-traders, had rendered themselves familiar with this "jargon," to use a common word again; and this, of course, for the present, was a direct and easy mode of communication between us. But, while it brought us into immediate contact with the native mind, it became a very formidable barrier in the way of our acquiring their real language. For, first, the people themselves constantly addressed us in it, and thereby fastened upon us the habit of using it; and, second, having a language at hand with which we were familiar, (an Indian language, too,) we did not exert ourselves in the study of the real languages spoken around us, as we should have done if the one of which I am speaking had not existed. I have judged these remarks necessary, that you might have a proper view of our situation in the commencement of our labors here. After tarrying two weeks, and being fully satisfied of the pacific disposition of the natives, and their readiness to receive instruction, I left Brother Lee and one Hawaiian, and proceeded to Willamette for my wife. Through the kindness of Dr. White[, the physician of the Willamette mission,] I also obtained the services of a [mulatto] man, then in his employ, Winslow Anderson, formerly of Boston, for the term of one year.

We had now two families to provide for—our own and Anderson's; and it was no small undertaking to think of the transportation of all our luggage for 150 [100] miles,[2] in small Indian canoes. We succeeded, however, in getting our families and stores all up in safety. By this time the spring was far advanced, and it was extremely hot. As we had no house, we pitched our tent [under the branching oaks,] and began our work—building, of course, to screen ourselves as soon as possible from the scorching rays of a summer sun. The work of building to persons in our situation, however, was not a trifling labor. For first, a team was wanting to draw the timber. Instead of this, we were under the necessity of employing a large gang of natives to drag it together by means of long ropes, a stick at a time. To their praise too it should be said, that this was done *gratuitously;* but *the only thing* ever done for us by them in this way.

[The house we built was twenty by thirty feet, and was made of pine trees, hewed on two sides, and dovetailed at the ends, and the seams corked with moss. It was divided into two rooms below, one for general reception and housework, the other for sleeping. It stood directly facing the river.

Having erected the walls of our house, the next thing was to get boards for the window frames, doors, floors, etc. It was plain we could not transport them from the Hudson Bay Company's mill, ninety miles below us. So the only thing we could do was to saw them ourselves out of pitch pine trees, getting one good log from each tree.]

To obtain shingle timber we went to the mountains for the red fir, and packed our shingles home upon horses, a distance of ten or twelve miles.

Having obtained from the H. B. Company another Hawaiian, we set the two to work with the pit saw,[3] and was thus able to obtain a few rough boards for flooring, partitions, doors, &c. Our chimney we constructed of wood, stone, and clay.

But we could hardly begin to build before brother Lee was obliged to make a voyage to Fort Vancouver for barrels and salt, in order to secure a stock of salmon for our families and laborers, during the ensuing winter. The labor and care attendant upon such a cargo, for nearly 100 miles, against the strong summer current of the Columbia, you can hardly conceive. And then the trading and curing of 15 or 18 barrels of fish was an additional drawback upon our time; so that it was nearly midsummer before we were ready to give our time to the main job, the mission house. In the mean time we erected a small house of rough logs for the family of Anderson, and covered it with bark of cedar, which we hired the natives to bring from the mountains.

We then found, what we have found all along since, that whatever is done among Indians must be done at an infinite expense of patience, care, and trouble. Our interruptions were constant. Parties of Indians from all parts of the surrounding country were every day coming and going, so that, had we had no other employment but that of waiting upon them, our time would have been fully occupied. You can form but a little idea of the begging habits of Indians. It would have been a strange thing indeed for one to pay us a visit without begging for something—either some victuals, a knife, an awl, handkerchief, soap, thread, or needle; and stranger still, to have him go away quietly and pleasantly after being denied. It had been the custom, time out of mind, for all white travelers to pay their way along by little presents of this nature; and we, of course, were expected to conform to the laws custom had established.

It was not until the early part of August, I think, that we exchanged our tent for the lower part of the mission house, the roof not being as yet on. It was but a shell, as you can well imagine; but it was a great relief, especially to Mrs. Perkins, whose health at that time was very feeble, to get under such a shelter as this afforded. Brother Lee, at the same time, pitched his tent upon a portion of the chamber floor which we had previously laid.

We now had to think of getting some stock; and our only way was to penetrate through the woods and mountains to the farm at Willamette. This was by no means a light undertaking. The journey had been made only by an Indian here and there, at long intervals, and there was scarcely the remains of a trail much of the way, and abundance of windfalls and underbrush to encounter. But we could not think of sustaining ourselves without cultivation, and to cultivate we must have cattle, and this was our only alternative. As a preparatory step, brother Lee was obliged to proceed to the H. B. Company's Fort at Wallawalla, distant over 100 miles, for horses. Horses were then cheap, eight dollars a-piece, (beaver at eleven shillings,) and we obtained twenty: a surprising number, you may think, for our business; but not so. An Indian poney [grass-fed horses] can stand but few days hard riding, and then a fresh one is required.

[In the early part of September] Brother Lee started for the Willamette with ten of them, and four natives [in order to make a trail, and] to obtain, if possible, what we so much needed. They took provisions only for six days, supposing from the distance that in that time they might reach the Clakamas River, and obtain further supplies: but, owing to the ignorance of their guide, after traveling four or five days, they were completely bewildered, having lost all signs of the trail. What added to the distress of their situation was, they were short of food. After making what progress they could for several days, their way almost hedged up by large wind-falls, and finding no grass, day after day, some of their horses could go no further One they were obliged to shoot to prevent themselves from starvation, and three others perished in a little while from fatigue and hunger. At length, after fifteen days of intense labor and anxiety, they succeeded in finding their way out upon the waters of the Clakamas; a small stream which discharges itself into the Willamette just below the falls. Here they found some Indians, and were right glad to obtain once more something to allay the pangs of hunger. But two horses ever got back to the station; for those which were not lost were so completely tired out that they had to be left at Willamette. After obtaining some fresh horses, and men, and an experienced guide, brother Lee started back with ten California heifers, and four young steers—so wild, however, that they could only be driven by men on horseback. By slow marches they were enabled to prosecute the return journey without any further disaster, except the tiring again of a portion of their horses.

Before their arrival I was obliged to leave for the Willamette, with my family, to obtain medical assistance: in hopes, however, to be able to reach the station again before winter. But in this I was disappointed.

[On my arrival at the mission, I found there was not a room to be had where I could shelter my wife, who was on the eve of confinement. Dr. White, who had just got into an unfinished house, offered me the privilege of fitting up a chamber, if I could procure the lumber. As there was no other way than to saw it by hand, I rigged up a place, got my logs, and taking hold of the pitsaw, with the help of another man, soon had boards enough to run a partition from one side of the roof to the other, and got my wife sheltered the day before I received into my arms my first born child. He was a fine child, a boy, and we named him Henry Johnson, after his grandfather, who had practiced law in Clinton, Maine. The Doctor and his estimable wife were so kind to us during our stay, and we were all comfortable.]

[Nevertheless] my anxiety induced me, with my wife still in feeble health, and a young child but five weeks old, to make an attempt as late as December.

Traveling at this season of the year upon the Columbia is very cold, not to say dangerous; and the chance of reaching home a bare possibility. [By January the river was usually closed by ice.]

But after arriving at Fort Vancouver, and learning that some boats were there, lying at a point of the river some fifteen miles distant, carrying supplies for the interior, we were inspired with fresh courage to proceed.

The Hudson Bay Company having given us leave to take passage in their boats, provided they were able to ascend the river, we immediately proceeded to join them. It was now past the middle of the month, and the east wind had set in, as usual, with great violence. Already the boats had been in waiting somewhat more than a week, and the gale was in no wise abated when we joined them. We could hardly keep our tent from blowing away, and it began to be bitter cold. We were four boats in all, and deeply laden with goods. Mr. M'Kay, father of the three lads who accompanied Mr. J. Lee to the states a few years ago, was in charge, and his kindness in this time of trial we gratefully remember. Such was the violence of the gale, that it was with difficulty a fire could be kept, and our little babe suffered exceedingly. At length we met with a sad disaster. One night, one of the boats, which had been turned up to dry, was taken by a gust of wind, and carried some ten or twelve rods completely clear of the earth, and with such violence, that its fall caused its complete destruction.

By this time the water below us, a small basin separated from the rest of the river by an island of sand, and protected from the wind by a high bluff of rocks, had frozen completely over. We of course began to think of getting back [to the fort] as quickly as we could. The only way now left, was to carry back all the goods to where the river was open, a distance of a mile or more; so that it was yet a long time ere we were ready to embark, a whole week from the first that we were obliged to endure this inclement weather, and we were glad once more to accept the hospitality of the Fort.

[We arrived at Vancouver in time to enjoy a comfortable Christmas dinner.] Nearly two months elapsed before we were able to get to our station. It was during this interval that I made another visit to the mission at Willamette to attend a watch-meeting, of which, and the revival that attended it, I suppose you have seen extended accounts from others.[4]

I arrived at Wascopam, I believe, about the middle of February. I had left here the first day of October, and all this long interval brother Lee had been sole occupier of the lonely mission-house, except as he was daily thronged with the Indians; and it was a time of rejoicing with both of us when we were permitted to meet once more.

By this time I had acquired a ready use of the common "jargon," and was able to take my turn with brother Lee upon the sabbath, in giving what little instruction we could. Nothing occurred of any particular interest of a religious nature this winter, nor had we much reason to expect it. Our heads and hands too were so constantly full of secular business, that but now and then we could give a moment's time to the acquisition of the native language [real language of the people].

And now as this second spring opened, we had to turn our attention to the making of a farm. Thus far we had been obliged to keep our canoes constantly going, to and from Willamette and Fort Vancouver for supplies, and at such expense as could not well be longer afforded. We began therefore with "breaking in," as it is called, our cattle, rigging out harnesses, yokes, plough, harrow, cart, and various farming utensils, with which we were unprovided. Fences also had to be built, and the only material for them being heavy pitch pine timber, it cost a great deal of labor with our yet wild oxen and horses to get it together. And then how would our old farmers at home have laughed, to see our efforts with our half-ox, half-horse team, at breaking up! However, by dint of labor and perseverance, we got over some twenty acres in the course of the spring, and sowed it with peas and wheat; and did what we could at planting corn, potatoes, beans, *et cetera*. The land was so poorly broken that we could not promise ourselves much, but we had done the best we could [we knew it would be better each succeeding year].

Seed being all in, and Anderson's time having expired, he left us once more to ourselves. Our house as yet was but half-finished, and the summer had to be spent in making it comfortable, and various other work, such as one could only know by being on the spot, and such as a stranger to missionary life could never appreciate.

Early this spring I had turned my attention to the acquisition of the Wallawalla language, and made some little progress. Having a boy in my family from this tribe, I could obtain, as I had leisure, a word here and there, until I could converse about common things with tolerable facility. It was also a happy circumstance, that scarcely any of this tribe had obtained a knowledge of the "jargon," to which I have alluded, and being unable to address me in any other than their own tongue, we soon got in the way of understanding each other. Brother Lee also turned his attention to the Chinook tongue.

Such was my progress in the Wallawalla by the fall of this year, that I began to give instruction in it on the sabbath to a portion of that tribe—very imperfectly, however, of course. Nor would I advocate such an early use of foreign tongues to make known those important truths which are the subjects of revelation.

[As the language could not be represented by our English alphabet, I was obliged to construct a new one, with a revised system of orthography, somewhat resembling that used by the Sandwich Island missionaries. With this system well understood, a native would have found no difficulty in reading his own language. As we had no immediate prospect of a printing press, I commenced a system of pen printing. My object was to furnish the natives as soon as possible with some simple Scripture lessons which they themselves could use, and which we could refer to as authority in our teaching.]

Our farming business turned out worse than we had expected. Of our wheat and peas, *we barely recovered our seed.* About an acre of corn, which promised well, was entirely taken off by the natives as soon as it was in the milk, and altogether without our knowledge or suspicion. So completely was the field stripped in the course of a few days, that not a dozen ears could be found out of the whole! Some of our potatoes shared the same fate; so that after a whole season of hard labor, we were still dependent upon transportation for supplies.

It would be a hard task to count up all the voyages we made during the first two years of our stay for this purpose: sometimes one, and sometimes the other of us—and you will recollect, that the shortest time for a trip to Willamette and back was about three weeks—more frequently a whole month: and then the great perplexity of settling with the crews; this was the most dreaded of any part of it. It was almost always impossible to render them any *satisfactory* equivalent for their labor. Indeed, without drawing upon the Hudson Bay Company for goods we never should have been able to obtain help from them at all. In those days the pay of a native for a trip to the Willamette Settlement, (about one hundred and fifty miles,) was one shirt, one fathom of English [green] baize, handkerchief, knife, awl, needle, gunworm, flint, [bell,] pint dipper, [twelve or] fifteen or twenty loads of ammunition, [and some provision]. I would remark here, that since the multiplication of whites in the country, and the increased call for native help, the pay of an Indian is more than doubled. [We usually had from five to ten of them with us, and two canoes of twenty or thirty bushels capacity.]

We have come now in our history to the fall of 1839, the period of the reformation. What the natives were previous to this you have already doubtless formed some idea. The greatest, or, at least, the most glaring vices among them were lying, stealing, and fornication[, and this last was carried on to such an extent that I doubt if there was a woman grown who had not known man.] Fighting and bloodshed had been mostly put an end to through the influence and exertions of humane gentlemen of the Hudson Bay Company. The great plague, or sickness, eight or nine years previous, had greatly lessened their numbers, and in a manner dispirited them. At the same time they were led to believe that this dreadful mortality was through the influence of the white traders: they therefore stood in awe of all white men, and looked upon them as wielding a secret power, which was to them incomprehensible; while a few looked upon it as rather a punishment sent from Heaven on account of their former atrocities. But from whatever cause, there had been peace among them for several years, and they were in a state, therefore, to give attention to the message of salvation. The light they had received from time to time from the traders and others had been enough to give them some idea of a God, the common Father of all, and that he would be sought unto by them for temporal favors. In consequence, a few were to be found who used a sort of prayer for success in their hunting excursions and the like. They had some notion of a future state of retribution. These were evidently recent notions. Their *fathers* had no such light.

Their common legends ascribed the creation of most things with which they are acquainted, to Talipaz, [the Chinook name of] the common prairie wolf. Their tales about this strange [itinerant] being are amusing, and to a lover of tales might be very interesting. There is scarcely a stone or hill along the river but possesses to them some interest, as having been the scene of some strange exploit of old Talipaz. Thus, for example, a long line of perpendicular rocks, running along the base of a hill upon the river, is no other than a party of Indians, who, being on their way to make war upon a neighboring tribe, were by chance met by Talipaz, and for their folly converted into their present trap rock state, to teach a lesson to coming generation! But I shall weary your patience by...

[In the early days of the mission, we used to point to the sun and visible creation, and ask "who made these things," and they would always answer "Clomas", (don't know) and with a look that seemed to say it was a subject on which they had never thought. As to the idea of a universal Father of the human race who made and loved them, they had, up to this time when we visited them no knowledge whatever. This was the good news or the gospel especially entrusted to us. Alas that during the time we had been among them that Saviour's love had been felt so little in our hearts! We had a form of religion, it is true. We had maintained an intellectual conviction of spiritual realities, but these realities did not possess us and overwhelm us.

We felt a compassionate love and tender interest for the Indians, but it was fast waning. For the first few months we were among them they were on their good behavior. They wished to be considered our dearest friends. They expected great things of us, but at length the advantages did not appear. Our supplies were insignificant, our medicines we did not know how to use. At length their clandestine appropriations of our corn and potatoes told us what we were to expect. We were alarmed. Brother Lee was going down to the settlement for supplies, and had decided to procure a stock of arms. As all Indians went armed, with bows and arrows or knives, I got into the habit of wearing a pistol myself. But all this was soon to be changed. How this was brought about I will relate. We had been considering the necessity of having some place where we could assemble the natives and children; to accomplish this purpose we resolved to build an additional house on our little square of the same dimensions as the one we now occupied.]

# Appendix 1

## Wonderful Work of God among the Indians of the Oregon Territory

*Perkins's description of the 1839–40 Wascopam Revival is the best known of his writings. It was originally published in the* Christian Advocate and Journal *15. no. 9 (October 14, 1840):1. It was republished separately by the Tract Society of the Methodist Episcopal Church (New York: n.d.) and also appeared in W. P. Strickland's* History of the Missions of the Methodist Episcopal Church *(1850:120–59).*

*Another, longer version is included in Grace Albee's 1952 transcription of her grandfather's papers (see Introduction). The composite reprinted below is based upon the 1840* Advocate *article, with supplementary passages (in brackets [ ]) included from the 1952 typescript. The title ("Wonderful Work of God . . . ") comes from the Tract Society reprint.*

Joyful tidings. Upward of five hundred native
Indians converted to the Christian faith!

Who that reads the following cheering account will grudge to contribute to the support of the Oregon mission! Let it be remembered, however, that funds are much needed just now to enable the society to prosecute its evangelizing plans as extensively and vigorously as the pressing wants of the heathen demand.

To the Corresponding Secretary of the Missionary Society of
the M. E. Church.

Journal of H. K. W. Perkins.

Very Dear Sir,—Knowing the deep interest which the friends of missions

ORIGINAL DOCUMENTS

feel in the success of the Gospel in this country, the large sums which have been expended, and the many prayers which are daily offered to God for this object, I deem it will be highly gratifying to them to hear that God has begun to pour his Spirit out upon us, and that there has been a glorious work advancing the past winter among the Chinook tribe for one hundred miles along the Columbia, and that some hundreds of them have turned to the Lord, and have become a spiritual Church of praying souls. The work has been gradual, but very powerful. It commenced at this station, as follows.

## Chapter I

About the beginning of Sept. last, there arrived at this station three men, travelers, from the United States, via the Rocky Mountains, bound they knew not whither, but seeking a better country—not the heavenly, for they were all prayerless souls. Yet they had not always been so, or at least not all of them, as will be seen hereafter. Their names were Benjamin Wright, David Dutton, and Peter Lawson.

Being about to put up a large building for the convenience of giving instruction to the natives, [we proposed to them the job, and asked if one of them could do the carpentering. One of them who seemed to be the leader, stepped forward,—a man of middle age, and declared himself to be a master workman at the business, and after consulting his companions, said they would all turn in and put up a house if we desired it. Making a bargain with them on the spot,—they threw off their saddles, secured their baggage, turned their horses loose, and were ready for work. The foreman said his name was Benjamin Wright.

The next morning we proceeded to the woods, and commenced felling trees. It was decided to build a Spanish wattled house, a story and a half in height. First were laid the sills, and in these were inserted posts of the desired height, about three feet apart, and capped with beams corresponding to the sills. Between the posts were inserted short sticks of wood, a few inches apart, to give firmness to the filling of mud, of which the walls were to be composed.

It was a dirty job throughout, but the men worked with a will, and the Indians collected grass, and mixed clay, and soon the walls were completed, and we let the two younger men depart. We had the chimney to build, and various things to do before the house could be occupied, but Mr. Wright and myself undertook to do the remainder, while Brother Lee prepared himself for his trip down country for supplies.

It was while Mr. Wright and myself were on the roof of the house topping the chimney, that he remarked to me "You are nothing but Congregationalists," meaning, as I understood him, that we missionaries were a set of formalists. This was the estimation in which we held the Congregationalist bretheren of that day. They had the form, but not the power of godliness. These remarks went home to my heart as true—as far as I was concerned, and led to a course of earnest thought. Our new laborers we had looked on with suspicion, not knowing how they would relish our religious exercises. We knew nothing of them, nor they of us, and we were backward in making advances.]

After some days, the uncommon pensiveness, or rather sadness—for he was always pensive—of Mr. Wright, awakened suspicion in our mind that he had known something of disappointment, or sorrow of some kind, we hardly knew what, and hardly dared to make inquiries. Particularly at family worship this feeling of restless sorrow was more particularly visible—not in his eye, for this was usually closed or turned away at such seasons, but in his manner—the tardy step, the suppressed sigh, the tremulous voice, all, all told too plainly what it was the wish of the man to conceal. Reader, if one should ever ponder these lines,—*it was the guilt of an unfaithful messenger of Heaven!*

[The whole matter was soon plain, for one evening we questioned him as to his former course of life, and he reluctantly confessed that for many years he had been a circuit rider in the Methodist Episcopal Church. But such was the reluctance with which he made the confession, and such was the sorrow that seemed to overwhelm him at the bare mention of it, that we forebore. He begged us not to make him known, and intimated to us the distraction that filled his mind. For several days I hardly dared to speak to him. There was a mysterious something about the man that told us this was not a common case. He seldom spoke unless spoken to, and then as if fearful of betraying himself.

I at length ventured to ask him to pray. The first attempt was accompanied by such deep feeling, such fervor and unction as quite surprised us; such feelings as are begotten in the soul by a deep sense of guilt, past unfaithfulness, and present mercy.]

Many weary months had passed, months of deep anguish such only as an unfaithful minister can feel, since he had laid aside that commission his Lord had given him to execute. In the mean time he had tried the world; the paltry trash of wealth flowed into his hand in abundance, but happiness was not in it; riches came and went, came and went, until his weary spirit loathed the pursuit; and now came the struggle, whether he should return to God and duty, or persist in the heart-sickening chase. Undecided, ashamed, bewildered, he sought to fly the abodes of men. With a wild tumultuous storm raging in his bosom, he mounted his horse to travel he hardly knew whither.

At length, thinking that happiness might possibly be found by exchanging the shores of the Atlantic for those of the Pacific, he joined a small company who, like himself, were in pursuit of happiness, and boldly ventured across the Rocky Mountains, [and only halted to do what he considered necessary work

at our station.] The voice of prayer and praise awakened in his breast that class
of feelings which he could not well conceal. The secret and irresistible wish
arose in his soul to regain that peace and happiness which he had lost.

But then he was no private individual. He again felt that "wo" which had
followed his soul fourteen years before to follow him if he preached not the
Gospel. He knew his duty, and he knew that to return to that duty was his only
path to the favor of God. The struggle was hard. The tempter came with
overwhelming violence; he was on the very borders of despair. He at length
resolved, though feeling extreme weakness, to take again the hallowed cross,
and, come what would, never to hide again his Lord's command. He humbly
requested the privilege of testifying in his Master's name. The privilege was
granted, and by discharging this duty, his peace of mind returned. Not as in
past days, but such a taste as only induced him constantly to apply to the same
great source. Brother Lee, finding it necessary at this time, for the supply of
our temporal wants, to make a voyage to Willamette, left us on the 16th of
October, with our house about half completed; Dutton and Lawson leaving us
about the same time, I was left alone with brother Wright.

Soon after we were left alone we concluded, for the improvement of our
minds and our advancement in the spiritual life, to deliver a sermon before
each other every evening before our fireside, my wife being the only one
besides who could understand English, and accordingly commenced with all
the formality due to an audience. These exercises were greatly blessed to us
and as we unfolded to each other the Gospel duties and privileges, we were led
to seek more and more an entire conformity to Christ.[1] Seeing us so earnestly
engaged from day to day in the services of religion, the attention of some of
the natives was arrested, and they began to attend with us, although as mere
spectators, for they understood none of these things. At length their curiosity
arose to such a pitch that a few of them begged of me to explain to them in their
own language what we discoursed to each other.

We had constantly preached to them from the commencement of our
mission among them, but without effect, they being entirely indifferent to
Gospel truth. I now commenced explaining to them, at the close of every
sermon the leading truths which we had discussed, and we now saw, for the
first time, that these truths produced a seriousness among them [and their
interest seemed to increase every evening.

At length they complained because we spoke to them last, and desired us
to reverse the order, which we did, and after I had given them a talk in their own
tongue, I dismissed them, and then went on to speak in English, but we found
them unwilling to leave, and they insisted on staying till our meeting ended,
which sometimes was at a very late hour.]

## Chapter II

[These religious exercises were so blessed to us that] we now began to wrestle for all the fulness of the Gospel blessings, even for the "sanctification of soul, body, and spirit." This great blessing I obtained at the Monmouth camp meeting in 1836, but after going again to my station, (Mercer, Me.,) I enjoyed it only a few weeks. It then gave me such happiness that the impression of it never left me; and in all my backslidings since, I have ever looked back to those few weeks when I enjoyed this fullness of love as the happiest portion of my life—it was heaven below.[2] There was but one on my station who professed to enjoy it, and she being an unmarried female, I could have no counsel or instruction, which I so much needed at that time. The valuable works of Wesley and Fletcher were not then in my possession, nor was I thoroughly acquainted with the doctrine of holiness. My inexperienced feet were, therefore, soon turned out of the way; and, yielding to the reasonings of Satan, I soon lost the witnessing Spirit, and fell into darkness—such darkness as might be felt. This was the commencement of that long and painful season of distraction and doubt, which arrived only to a crisis at the Sandwich Islands, on my way to this country, in 1837. The darkness was only heightened when I fled to books for help; and what was worse still, not to those calculated to throw light on the subject, but such as served to darken counsel by words without knowledge.

But this is not the place for a history of my experience. Suffice it to say, that from the time of my losing this blessing, in 1836, to this period, however much I had at times enjoyed of religion, the loss of this left

"An aching void
The world could never fill."

Feeling at this time that the good Spirit was present, and feeling how unprepared I was to engage in the work of saving souls, I was led to cry mightily to God for [a clean heart and a full baptism of the Spirit.] For several days I was extremely tempted and buffeted; and although it seemed sometimes very near, I was afraid, but continued to strive, and pray, and preach, though I saw more and more my unfitness for any religious duty.

Monday, the 28th of October, was my day of salvation; but notwithstanding this it was a day of severe trial. In the evening, [I retired as usual to the woods to pray] [but] I was in such darkness that I could not pray. I was brought to a crisis. I felt willing to give up all for the prize, but to exercise faith in God *now* seemed impossible. I felt my need, but I thought not now, not just yet—my heart is too hard—too dark. I knew not what to say. My heart stood still, until unawares I found myself on my way again to the house. But I resolved to neglect no duty, blessed or not; I therefore took my Bible, and discoursed as well as I was able in Indian and English, and [our meeting closed. I had not obtained what I wanted.] I felt weary, and concluded I had better give over striving for that evening at least.

[My wife, I think, proposed another prayer. I knelt in a corner of the room], and fell into a train of thought on my then present situation. I felt the time had come when I must be blessed or give over the struggle.

What was in the way? It was *unbelief.* But why was it I could not believe? I ran over once more in my mind the promises. Who, thought I, has made these promises to me? A man—an impotent being? ["]No; Jehovah [.—the same yesterday, to-day, and forever."] I could doubt no more. My soul was in an instant overwhelmed with shame, under a sense of past unbelief. I saw the promises in a new light—the words of Him who could not lie—the great God—myself a poor worm of the dust. I was abashed, humbled; the great deep of my soul was broken up. I burst into a flood of tears—a moment more, and I was enabled to cast myself on the mercy of God in his promises, and the tumultuous feelings of my soul subsided, and I found myself calmly and firmly trusting in Christ my Saviour—whom I now felt to be a glorious Saviour—able to cleanse from all sin; yes, I felt that he had spoken a second time, "Be clean." My every breath seemed prayer and praise alternately. I felt so weak and helpless, that I dare hardly move from my knees, for fear I should again grieve the Spirit. It was a late hour, yet I scarcely dared sleep lest I should lose my hold of my Saviour. I slept less than usual, and awoke at an early hour in a tranquil, praying frame.

## Chapter III

Feeling that I had now received the Lord's anointing, my first inquiry was, What can I do for him who has done so much for me? After praying for direction, I proceeded to the Indian [village, went into the first hut I came to, and sat down. As usual the Indians asked me what I had come for, and I frankly told them to talk about their souls. After some time spent in conversation with them, I went to the house of a noted gambler. He, and many of the villagers had been gambling for more than a week, and I supposed he intended to gamble that day. I expostulated with him to stop gambling, and commence praying. He appeared affected, and said he would.

In about an hour, an Indian informed me that the people were gambling as usual. I dropped my work, and hastened to the camp. The gamblers had secreted themselves in a grove of willows near the river. As I approached, the game was going on in high glee. They formed a ring, in number about twenty-five. Stepping into the midst of them, I began to expostulate with them.

Finding them beginning to waver, I pulled off my coat and fell on my knees, entreating God to destroy the works of the Devil. I sat down near the pile of clothes which it was the object of the game to win, and told them that each man would better get his clothes and go home. They promised to disperse when the game was out, and wished me to sit down and oversee it. To this I would not consent, but told them I would retire to a clump of willows, and pray for them. In a few minutes the gambling stopped, and I knew by their angry voices that they were quarrelling over the stakes. As the tumult moved toward me, I rose from my knees, and hastened among them. They were preparing for a fight. Two were in a dreadful rage, and one was stripping for a knock down.

I walked up to the most violent one, and patting him on the shoulder entreated him to stop, and tell me the cause of the quarrel. "My cap, my very fine cap, that fellow has taken it!" He gave him a blow in the mouth. "Stop," I said, "here is my cap", pulling off my own. "No, no!" he said. "My cap is a very fine one, not like this." The Indians around began to pull me, wishing me not to interfere, for they wanted to see the fight. I still insisted in offering my cap, which he finally took.

His opponent now started for home, and I supposed the fray had ended, but in a few minutes he returned with a knife, and running upon his foe, tried to rip him up, when the man took to his heels, but was overtaken, and the conflict renewed.

The Indian with the knife returned to us almost exhausted with rage. Gaining breath a little, he evinced his intention of attacking me. The Indians, seeing this, placed himself between us,—and after walking around several times with looks of rage fixed on me, seeing no way of coming at me, he silently returned to his home.

I then tied a handkerchief on my head and started for home. As I passed the village there was a general rush to know the cause, and where my cap was. I told them I had given it away to prevent a fight. They stared and wondered, telling me my cap was very valuable. I made no reply, but passed on, rejoicing in spirit that I had the privilege of giving away my cap in a good cause, as well as that God had answered my prayers in the cause of the gamblers, and that my presence had probably saved the life of a fellow creature. Many of the Indians followed me to the house, some sharply rebuking me for giving away my cap, saying that they never knew of any of the French chiefs to do such a thing.

It was not long before one of the principal men of the village came hastening up the road with my cap in his hand, and the Indian to whom I had given it following him. They came into the house,—and the chief, fixing a severe look on me, wished to know if I had given the Indian my cap. I said "yes, I did not want them to fight about a cap". After telling me that he had settled the difficulty, and obtained for the man his "very fine cap," which proved to be an old hat, he gave me my cap back, telling me I should not give it away for nothing. "But you," he said,—"I know not but if an Indian should come and ask you to give him your little son here, you would do it." "Yes," thought I, "if God spared not His own son for us, we should not withhold even our children, if a good cause required us to sacrifice them."]

About this time some of the natives began to pray. The first individual who was so wrought upon by the Holy Spirit so as to betake himself to this duty was an old Indian doctor, who lives within half a mile of the mission house, by name Tumsowit, a little free-hearted, jovial old man, but, in consequence of his profession, a man of some consequence; for the title of doctor always gives weight to character either in the civilized or barbarous world. At first the old man thought praying to be an art, and most happy was he when he could string together some ten or twelve sentences in the manner in which I used them, and his inquiry seemed to be how he should increase his stock of words. He therefore lost no opportunity of praying and attending prayer.

But now a storm of persecution opened upon him, for all his people contended that he did not pray correctly, and used words which I did not, and I was called upon to decide the question, which gave me a fine opportunity of explaining to him and them fully the nature of prayer—that God looks not at the words, but the heart.

Seeing the old man anxious to be taught the right way, I lost no opportunity of impressing on his mind the corruptions of the natural heart, and the necessity of a thorough change. Brother W. and I often took him with us in private to pray; and feeling that God alone could teach him effectually, we often plead before the Lord for his conversion. As he was the only one for some time who showed a deep feeling, we took in him a peculiar interest.

It was not long before conviction was deeply wrought in his soul, and his only desire seemed to be to escape the wrath to come, and lay hold on eternal life. After praying a week or more, he entirely forsook his family, and what time he did not spend with us at the mission house was spent alone among the rocks and hills on his knees. When our meetings were over for the night he would lie down on the chamber floor, and pray sometimes for half an hour, or until nature was exhausted, and sink to rest, and in the morning at an early hour leave his bed for the woods. Every day for a fortnight his convictions seemed to increase. For a whole week I do not know that he once visited his people or his wives, (he had three,) and his sighs, and tears, and prayers, told his deep penitence. He used almost constantly to watch for us when we retired for our secret devotions, that he might have the privilege of praying with us; and often, when we would be engaged in the woods, not suspecting any one near, the old man would make his appearance, and, kneeling beside us, would pour out his soul with strong cries, and sometimes tears, to Him who was able to save. At length, after a fortnight spent in this manner, God, who is rich in mercy, turned his mourning into joy. This took place at the close of one of our little meetings, while we were engaged in prayer and supplication for this same object. His joy on this occasion was not great, but the change was immediately observable. He was a new man.

His care and concern for himself now in a great measure ceased, and immediately his soul went out in strong desires for the salvation of others. The next day he began to exhort individually those with whom he met to break off their sins.

The work now spread. Others commenced seeking the Lord by prayer and supplication; and such were the number of inquirers, that I was obliged to lay aside all business, and devote myself day and night to the great work.

Our house now being so far complete as to permit us to assemble in it, we forsook our former place of assembly, which had become too small for the congregation which attended, and henceforth met in the new hall, 30 by 20 feet. This too was soon filled, and on the sabbath to overflowing.

At this juncture brother Lee arrived, and was astonished to see the change which had taken place during his absence of five weeks.

Previous to this, as our time was devoted in the evenings to praying with the Indians, and giving instruction to the mourners, we had established five o'clock meetings in the morning, and had our English exercises at that hour. Brother Lee now joined us, and our meetings increased in interest. Some twenty were now under conviction, of each sex about an equal number.

The most interesting case was that of one of the chief men of the village, whose Indian name is Yacooetar. This interesting native stands unique among his tribe for one singularity—his parents did not flatten his head. He is a stout, well-built man, with a high, full forehead, and such a countenance as would command respect in any nation. Proud, haughty, fearless,—"a brave" among his tribe—it was hardly to be expected that he would be among the first who should become followers of a meek and lowly Master. But God can abase the proud, and give humility.

This man lived in the same house with Tumsowit, and for a time was his bitterest opposer. They now met to pray together, as did many more, while old prejudices were forgotten.

For a time he said but little, but sat and heard with deep attention. Evening after evening he was the first to come, the last to go away. In the morning, too, while the other villagers were locked in slumber, he would steal from his bed and make his way to the mission house. Seeing him thus attentive, I asked him one morning how it happened that he arose so much earlier than formerly. "Why," said he, "I cannot sleep. When I go home and lie down, I think of what you tell us, and I cannot sleep. I sleep a little and then I dream that I am in meeting, and my heart is all the time talking over what you say. My heart was formerly asleep, I see, but it is now awake." He soon after this began to pray; and his convictions of sin increased, until he was led to give his heart to God.

The evening of his conversion will long be fresh in my memory. It was an evening of the power of God. Our kitchen was crowded with sinners inquiring what they should do to be saved, and our souls were unusually drawn out in prayer. The powers of darkness seemed to tremble before the power of a present God. It was some such season as those often described by the Methodist fathers. I was kneeling by Yacooetar's side. His strong heart bowed—he prayed, unconscious, it seemed, of all that was passing around him. He plead before that God who has said, "Draw nigh unto me and I will draw nigh unto you." God was there—his heart yielded—he trusted—the struggle was gone—his soul was at peace. His thoughts now turned upon his wife and daughter, who were both present; and going and kneeling by their side, he exhorted them to pray, while his own spirit arose in prayer for God's blessing upon them.

On this and three or four of the following evenings the power of God was wonderfully displayed, and we have reason to believe fifteen or twenty passed from death unto life.

These were days of rejoicing with us, and many of the poor natives will doubtless recur to them from the blissful seats of heaven, as the commencement of their journey thither.

Mrs. Perkins now took upon herself the charge of the females, meeting and praying with numbers of them every day, and the good work spread rapidly among them.

The sound of prayer was now as common among the rocks and hills of Wascopam as the shining of the sun. It was usually first heard about four o'clock, which we made our hour of rising, and it was continued sometimes until near midnight.

I will add a short account of one more individual conversion, which must suffice. This I relate of Tumeocool, another of the chief men of the village, and who resides only a few rods from our door. He is called "the one-eyed chief," as he is blind of one eye. He has generally acted as our interpreter, and of course is more intelligent than most of the village. Being a very dispassionate man, it was several weeks before his attention was aroused to a sense of his condition; but when this conviction of himself as a sinner was brought home to his heart by the agency of the Holy Spirit, he no longer delayed.

After attentively attending on the means of grace for some time, and seeing his people becoming changed, he commenced in earnest seeking the Lord. One morning at public prayers, seeing his deep concern, I requested him to pray. This he did at some length, and with much feeling. After prayers I took him with me to the wood. Passing along I asked him how he felt. "O," said he, "my heart is very small, and very sorrowful. Yesterday I prayed most all day out behind that hill." pointing to a distant hill, "but my heart is still bad." I told him God alone could change it, and of what Jesus had done to make him happy; and, kneeling down, exhorted him to give his heart immediately to God, and he would find relief. It was a hallowed spot. We felt God to be there; and ere we arose from our knees his poor benighted soul was filled with light and love, and we returned to the house filled with joy. Since that time he has ever appeared like a pious, humble Christian.

## Chapter IV
*The work spreads—Brothers Lee and Wright's travels, &c.*

It was not to be expected that these things would remain a secret, or that such a work would be confined to one small village. The love of God shed abroad in the heart is a flame which cannot be hid.

An Indian tribe is like a great family, every member connected with another; and as all the members of a family feel a mutual interest, so with all the members of any one tribe.

As soon, therefore, as the love of God was shed abroad in the hearts of a few at this village, these social ties were immediately tested, and they were for going off directly to tell their relatives in the neighboring villages "what great things the Lord had done for them."

This was especially the case with Tumsowit. Having a large circle of relatives in the neighboring villages, his soul could hardly contain itself in Wascopam; nor did it have occasion to long, for as the work became more general, we concluded it would be best for us to separate, and extend the work as fast as possible. Having fully made up our minds on the subject, brothers Lee and Wright, with Tumsowit and several of the converts, left me on the 17th Dec., 1839, [for a preaching tour down the Columbia].

[They] proceeded down the river about ten miles, to a small village called by the natives Claticut. They arrived in the evening, and proceeded to an old man's house, by the name of Papeus. Their errand was anticipated, and the old man, calling his people around him, to the number of 50 or more, anxiously waited to hear the talk of "the Great Chief above," (their name for the Deity,) [Brother Lee discoursed to them in the "jargon", and Tumsowit prayed in the language of the people.

To have one of their number pray in his own tongue of course awakened a great deal of interest.] It was the first time that many of them had heard a Gospel sermon; and as they had heard what strange things God was doing at Wascopam, and seeing before them their "brothers" recently made happy, and earnestly engaged in this new way of worshipping "the Great Chief," (they had formerly worshipped by dancing—a religion the traders had taught them,) some of them were much affected. There is nothing like living witnesses to give edge to truth.

The brethren resumed their labours at 5 o'clock the next morning, and continued their meetings through the day. A man having died the night previous, half the village was in mourning, which gave the brethren an opportunity of showing these poor benighted souls their relations to death and eternity, and of preaching unto them "Jesus and the resurrection." Tumsowit was now in his element, and labored powerfully in exhortation and prayer.

The evening was a time of the overwhelming power of God. Many cried aloud for mercy, and conviction seemed general; and after the public exercises were over, many retired and poured out their souls in secret. The next day was spent in the same way, preaching and visiting from house to house, and holding prayer meetings with the mourners; for their mourning for the dead was now taken up in mourning for themselves, as sinners. This third evening was a time of still deeper feeling than any before, and the cry for mercy was general. Like the Ninevites, they repented from the greatest to the least, and ere their meeting closed, which was continued to a late hour, many, it was believed, were born of the Spirit. Day and night the sound of prayer was now heard in every direction,—in the houses, the woods, and prairies. The few following days which were spent there witnessed the same things. Men, women, and even little children, were alike affected. One little boy in relating in his simple artless way, the change he felt in his heart, said, "I feel now very light. I can run very fast; and if I have to bring water now, I shall not be tired." The secret of it all was, *the mighty workings of the Spirit of God.* Monday 22d brother W. returned to Wascopam, informing us what great things God was doing, which greatly strengthened our hands. Wednesday, having spent one week at this village, and having joined nearly one hundred in society, the brethren thought it expedient to pursue their voyage still farther, and accordingly dropped down the river about 15 miles, to two other villages, situated on opposite sides of the river, and containing about 140 inhabitants.

They pitched their tent before the largest village, called Clemiaksuc, and commenced their labours as they had done at Claticut. The same power here attended their labours as at the former village. Their meetings were continued, with but little intermission, day and night. Brother Lee says he related to them the simple story of the Gospel—the history of Him who was manifested to take away our sin and as it happened to Philip [Jesus] while preaching at Samaria, that "they all gave heed to those things, from the least to the greatest," so it was here, but not without some opposition the first few days. One Indian doctor, ("sorcerer," he would have been called in Paul's day,) in particular, used his arts to hinder the work, but the power of God soon made *him* tremble even, and sue for mercy.

In one of their meetings, brother W. relates, one woman was so affected that she fell to the ground, and lay two hours as one dead, insomuch that many said, "She is dead," and then coming to herself, praised God aloud for what he had done for her soul. This was in the evening. The next day she went into the woods for secret prayer, and was so overcome by the power of God, that she lay on the ground nearly all day, unable to return to her house. She was a woman of influence and respectability, and continues to walk in the narrow way. At another time, while the brethren were wrestling in prayer in their tent, there happened to arrive two strangers, one of them an Indian doctor, who, after remaining a short time, were so convicted that they fell on their knees and cried for mercy; and ere they ceased praying, which was continued about two hours, one of them was set at liberty. Such were the wonderful displays of divine power from day to day. They tarried at these two villages 10 days, during which time it was judged 100 turned to the Lord. These they formed into classes, appointing leaders, and passed on to another village, 3 [ten] miles below, called Nenootletete. About 100 Indians were congregated here, to whom they preached the word. Being so near the other villages, they had knowledge of all that had been passing there, and were in anxious expectation to witness the same things, though they hardly knew what to make of them.

Such was the power displayed at the first meeting with them, that there was a general and simultaneous crying for mercy. The next, being sabbath, was a time of power, and a day of salvation to many souls. The interest was indeed universal and as they all desired it, brother Lee put them all into classes, to the number of 75 or 80. [all the adult population professed conversion.]

The brethren called next at a small village, 3 miles further down, containing 30 souls. Here the word was attended with such success, that out of this number they joined 28 in society. They found no more Indians until they reached "the cascades," a distance of about 20 miles. Here were about 40, in winter quarters, and they tarried with them one day and two nights. Here they met with some opposition in consequence of Roman Catholic influence having been felt among them, the priest being beforehand in giving his instructions. The good seed, however, took effect in many of their hearts, and two classes, numbering 27, were formed. I have since visited them, and much of the opposition I find has vanished, and the little classes were unmolested, and striving to walk in the fear of God. [I visited all these villages soon after, and the work seemed genuine.]

Being strengthened and greatly encouraged, they now resolved to push the conquest farther, and embarked for Fort Vancouver, distant some 40 miles. They now entered on a new field, quite different from that in which they had been laboring, and one which presented many difficulties. For, besides the soul-destroying influence of this large trading establishment, they had Roman Catholicism to contend with, but knowing the Gospel commission to be, "Go ye into all the world, and preach the Gospel to every creature," they could not hesitate, but went boldly forward, preaching the Gospel to all who would hear it, whether whites or Indians, until the 21st of January, 1840, when brother Wright concluded to leave brother Lee at Vancouver to prosecute his labours, and pay a short visit to the Willamette settlement. His first discourse was delivered at a saw-mill, where 4 or 5 white men were at work, and was attended with visible displays of divine power. One man, a Mr. Gale, born somewhere in the vicinity of Washington, (D. C.,) was so wrought upon that he cried aloud for mercy, and has since found pardon in the blood of Jesus. He then passed on, and preached once at the mission, and finding some laborers at work on the mission hospital, he tarried with them a few days, and his labors were blessed to the awakening of several of them, who have since sought and obtained the pearl of great price. His visit was short, and he returned to Vancouver on the 7th of Feb., and found brother Lee enjoying considerable prosperity in his labors among the natives, but none among the white population. Truly did Christ say, "How hardly shall they that have riches enter into the kingdom of God." It was hardly to be expected, such are the fascinations of wealth, that these rich men of the Hon. H. B. Company would engage in seeking that which, if obtained, requires us to renounce the world and become followers of him who had not where to lay his head.

They, however, treated the brethren as they always have our missionaries, with a generous hospitality, and afforded them every facility in their power for prosecuting their work; and you will please credit to John M'Laughlin, Esq., the present governor of this fort, the sum of $44, as a donation to our mission.

February 13th I had the happiness of meeting once more with brother Lee, at Vancouver, and spent the sabbath with him. Found him in health, and strong in the Lord; rejoicing for all that he had seen of the wonders of redeeming grace, and finding him still determined to occupy all the ground he had explored in this lower region. We again parted, commending each other to the grace of God. When I returned to Wascopam, brother W. arrived soon after me, and is still with us, although expecting, in a few weeks, to leave the country.

## Chapter V
### Progress of the work—
### Reception of the Gospel at Wishham, &c.

Since the departure of brother Lee, in December, my time has been almost wholly devoted to travelling from village to village, preaching, catechizing, and taking the oversight of the classes as far as the Cascades, a distance of 50 miles—embracing more than 500 souls, and classes to the number of 30. Mrs. Perkins has had the principal care of this station, the females especially, and has devoted many of her evenings in my absence to the instruction of the boys in Scripture history.

[During the two months absence of Bretheren Lee and Wright my own labors were very arduous. I left the station week days mostly in my wife's care and with Yacooeter visited from village to village all that the bretheren had visited, and besides preaching, gave them catechetical instruction. Having but the barest rudiments of Christianity, it required great care and painstaking, but I found everywhere the utmost docility to learn.]

[Poligamy was the worst question involved, and a more puzzling one could hardly be conceived. We taught, of course, that Christianity allowed but one wife to each man, but which one of two, three, or half a dozen should be repudiated? The old mother, who had born the burden of the day, and brought up a large family, or the middle aged one with several young children to be looked after, or the blooming young bride, just enjoying her honeymoon? Each one seemed to have peculiar claims on the husband and father. If the youngest were turned off, she was no longer marriageable, having already been a wife, and was in danger of becoming a waif in the community, and open to many temptations. The oldest had claims to pity and the kindest consideration, and where should she go if put out of her husband's shelter? And the new born babes should be provided for, any way. For a time we had to let things be, only stipulating that if a man had one wife, he should take no other during her lifetime. Plurality of wives we found a curse to the natives, as it has been a curse everywhere, not excepting Old Testament times; always leading to heart burns, strife, jealousy, making the wigwam often a Hell on earth, and almost enough to drive a man from his home forever.]

Notwithstanding my absence from this station, the work has spread and deepened here in many hearts. [During my visits to the villages down river, I did not cease caring for our home station, but generally returned in time to preach on the Sabbath.] Nearly the whole village, for a time, seemed deeply affected, and their attention on the means constant, and on the sabbath there was usually a great flocking from the villages around[, so that our new hall would not accomodate the multitudes who wished to hear, and I had to hold meetings out of doors in the coldest winter weather.] I have sometimes detained them for two hours, sitting on the cold, wet ground, listening to the words of eternal life, without their appearing weary, many of them nearly naked too. [It was affecting to witness the desire of the aged to receive instructions.] Several aged females of more than threescore years, have traveled more than 2 miles to prayers, through the severest weather this winter, [with scarcely a rag of clothing,] and it is truly soul-cheering to witness their desire for instruction, as indeed of most of the natives. They are now pretty well acquainted with the historical parts of the Bible, at this station, and can repeat from memory the history of Christ, as found in the Gospels, as accurately as one in ten of Christians in civilized lands.

[On the last night of the year eighteen thirty-nine, I held a watch-meeting in the hall,—or chapel—we called it. The house was crowded, and I took this opportunity of forming the first native church in Oregon. I explained to them its rules, questioned them on their individual experience, and united in fellowship forty persons. I subsequently took the names of others, till their number swelled to two hundred.]

On the 10th of Jan., of the present year [eighteen forty], I paid a visit to a large village which stands at the head of the Chinook tribe, at the head of the Dalles, called, by the natives, Wishham, (the Wishram of W. Irving—see his "Astoria,") and preached to them for the first time the Gospel. I arrived thither with Yacooetar in the evening, and the first night was spent in preparing me a lodge of sticks and mats, which I set up within 20 rods of the village.

The first night scarcely any one came to see us, or took any notice of us, and I therefore caused it to be proclaimed that I would meet them at my lodge at the hour of sunrise in the morning. Morning came, and the hour of sunrise, but out of a village of 300 souls but one man made his appearance, the people alleging it was too cold to meet out of doors.

I therefore looked round for a meeting-house, and at last found one where I least suspected it. It was a large cellar, dug some years ago, when dancing was in vogue, and capable of containing the whole village. [It was very damp, and as one of the villagers had been murdered in it a short time before, it was deserted, and looked upon much as a haunted castle of former times. Many a time it had rung with the sound of the dance, and I was fully persuaded that henceforth it would ring with prayer and praise. The chief man of the village said he would not go there because blood had been spilt there.] Making a clearance of the rubbish which had collected in it, and flooring it with mats, I called the people together here about 10 A. M., and commenced my labors. The congregation was small, consisting of a few men and boys, and about 25 women. In the afternoon the congregation was increased. The next day, Wednesday, it was doubled; Thursday, about 200; and Friday nearly the whole village. I never saw such wretched objects in one congregation before, and probably there never was a village more degraded. My bowels yearned over them. Long, long had been their night; and while I stood before them with the Bible in my hand, you may be assured I felt it an unspeakable privilege.

O, I would that my brethren in the ministry at home knew what a blessed privilege it is to preach the Gospel to the heathen; then methinks more of them would volunteer in this work.

Naked, squalid, ugly featured, blind, halt, and lame [they came]. How truly does the Scripture say of the heathen, "*Destruction* and *misery* are in their ways." I now endeavored to show them the way of peace, by pointing them to Him who has made peace for us by his cross. [Every sermon was received with a deep interest. I gave them simple Bible truths, with scarcely note or comment.] After preaching to them for 2 days, they seemed to awake as from a dream. Satan's whole empire felt the shock. I expected it would be so.

Friday was a cold, rainy day, but a blessed day to many souls. At the hour of twilight I walked out to find a retired spot, where I might give vent to the feelings of my soul, but this was impossible without traveling a long distance, for the rocks and prairie for half a mile around rang with prayer. I should judge there were 50 engaged in such wrestling that the sound might have been heard afar off. Their secret chamber, nature's own temple; and although it rained and hailed, and the ground was covered with snow, many of them struggled half an hour. I was much moved in thinking of the change which had taken place in 4 days; but the Gospel was to them *the power of God to salvation,* because it was believed.

In the evening I met the men at one of the largest houses, and enjoyed a season of conference. The house could convene about 80, almost the whole of whom spoke very feelingly of their past wretchedness and darkness, and their great joy that they now had heard the words of the Great Chief above to them. Several testified that their hearts had become very light since they had begun to pray, and 8 or 10 said they were filled with peace while they were out in the prairie that evening. How many were justified I could not tell, but many, I was sure, would be, as sure as that God hears the prayer of penitence. They all seemed to feel a deep abhorrence of their past situation, and expressed, over and over again, their determination henceforth to serve God. Will not many prayers be offered by the friends of the poor heathen, that the Lord will give assisting grace?

I called at one house where was an aged doctor, who had seen nearly a hundred years. He remembered the visit of Clarke and Lewis, and described their dress, and the general sensation produced on them by their unexpected appearance, and the trinkets they brought with them. His appearance and conversation interested me much. He seemed a relic of former days—a voice from the past. A whole century he had stood and seen his people rise and fall around him, and many a time had he shed the bitter tear for his comrades, while he had seen the oblivious wave of death close over them, and not one ray of light cast athwart the gloom, and no voice to direct him, or them, to a glorious immortality, where friends may meet again. My heart arose in silent praise to Him who had spared his life to hear, like Simeon, of Jesus, and what was more interesting still to me, was, that I could give him the Gospel now through one of his own countrymen. "Tell him," said I to Yacooetar, "of Jesus." Yacooetar commenced—gave an account of his birth—his life—his conversations with his disciples—his instructions;—but when he came to tell of his sufferings and death, "Ah! ah!" the old man would exclaim, at every few sentences, and seemed all eye and ear. Yacooetar then told him of his resurrection, and the charge he had given to his disciples, to give his talk to all the world, and tell them to throw away their bad hearts and come to him—of his ascension, and the pouring out of the Spirit on the day of pentecost—and then told him of the scenes of a future judgment, and the final destiny of the righteous and wicked after death. When he had finished, (and they were both by this time very much excited,) "Ah!" exclaimed the old man, with a loud voice, "this is the talk I want to hear;" and then turning to me, he tried to express his thankfulness that I had come to tell him of these things, and then taking a poker and pulling the coals from the fire, "There!" he exclaimed, "you have come just so, to pull me out of the fire." The old man then joined us in prayer, and has since that time been like a true seeker of the pearl of great price. He prays regularly with his family from day to day, and, so far as I know, walks worthy of the Gospel.

Saturday my appointments called me away from this interesting village. I have several times since visited it, and find that in this place "the kingdom of heaven is like leaven which a woman took and hid in three measures of meal." The work has ever since been spreading and deepening. The Lord has raised up several powerful exhorters there; one especially, who is a Walla-walla, (the tribe adjoining.) I have seen him exhort until the sweat rolled down his animated face like rain.

The last time that I was there was on the 15th inst., when I spent one night only, but it was a feast to my soul. Almost every man, woman, and child in the village leads a life of prayer, and seems anxiously striving to enter in at "the strait gate." I have taken into society there 260. This is the Lord's doing, and it is marvelous in our eyes. I am anxiously waiting the return of brother Lee to give them the ordinances.

O ye friends of missions, and ye who profess to be followers of Him "who went about doing good," in behalf of these heathen I bespeak your prayers. Think of their wretched situation without the Gospel; think what yours must have been; then think of them *with* the Gospel: while it brings life and immortality to light, it at the same time is to them the power of God to salvation. O pray, then! Raise your voices to almighty God, that he may send forth more laborers into the harvest; and if He calls to any one of you to engage in this blessed work, say, "Here am I, send me."

I observed that Wishham stood at the head of the Chinook tribe. They are scattered along the banks of the Columbia river, from this place to its mouth, a distance of about 200 miles, [they had their little villages. Before the appearance of the whites were a numerous and powerful people. Our mission embraced only those who lived above Fort Vancouver, including about one thousand souls. These had now nearly all become praying Indians, with quite a number of the Walla Walla tribe.] The Indian population, however, below Fort Vancouver, is very sparse. The few who are left make their rendezvous at Fort George, or what was formerly "Astoria." They are living there in a most wretched state, as will be seen by the following letter, written by Mr. James Birnie, a gentleman of the H. B. Company, who is at present in charge of that post. It was written in answer to some inquiries made by brother Lee.

*Fort George, Feb.* 27, 1840

"My Dear Sir,—The Indians about this quarter are the most abandoned and profligate set of people you will find on the Columbia. Their numbers have been on the decrease for the last 20 years. The causes are venerea, abortions, and infanticide. Both men and women think nothing of destroying their offspring. A case of this kind happened the other day. After the child was born, the father declared it was not his, and ordered the mother to throw it into the river, which she did, without thinking any thing more about it.

"The numbers of the Chinooks about here last year were as follows: 75 men, 88 women, 69 children, and 58 slaves. The Clatsops are about the same number, but the Killimuks are more numerous. There are other small tribes in the vicinity.

"I am, &c., James Birnie."

I here draw my account of the great work which has been going on among the Chinook tribe to a close. You have the facts before you, and may judge, in some sort, of the divine power which has been displayed. This work has not been of man, but such as to hide pride from man; and while we acknowledge "the help that is done in the earth, the Lord himself is the doer of it." Let us unite in giving him the glory.

## Chapter VI
### *The Walla-wallas.*

Soon after the commencement of our station at this place, my attention was turned to this interesting tribe of Indians. [The Walla Wallas extended up river from the Dalles to Fort Walla Walla, a distance of one hundred miles. At or near this place, the principal chief resided. His name was Peu peu muchmuks, which means Yellow bird. They had their villages, also, on all the small streams which flow into the Columbia from the south.] Owing to the great call for manual labour in the commencement of our mission, our numerous voyages, &c., I was prevented from turning my attention to the acquisition of their language until last summer. During the summer and first part of the fall I made this my principal business, and made good proficiency. I have reduced it somewhat to system, and have been for several months conversing in it. I find it extremely simple and regular. I now preach in it without an interpreter. [As I was the only one who had made a study of their language, the labor of evangelizing devolved mainly on me.

As they could be reached only by horseback riding, this tribe not using canoes to any great extent, it cost me many hard journeys, and much exposure. I could carry on my horse only my overcoat and blanket, and had to camp down wherever night overtook me. Sleeping thus on the ground, I found little rest, and the morning found me sore and unrefreshed. But it was a labor of love, and I enjoyed it.]

I travelled among this tribe considerably last summer, but principally with a view to facilitate the acquisition of the language, by cutting myself off from all intercourse with any other. As the work has progressed so rapidly among the other tribe, and called for such constant labor, I have almost wholly neglected the Walla-wallas. A short time since I labored one week with them, and had the happiness of seeing many of them become deeply interested in the truths of the gospel. In consequence of this visit there has been of late considerable excitement, and it is a time of general expectation among them. I am anxiously waiting the return of brother Lee, that I may resume my labours among them. The fact is, these natives are ripe for the Gospel. They are fast passing away; they know it, and they are ready to lay hold of any hope on which their desponding minds may rest. The following incident will serve to show the desire they feel for instruction.

One of our exhorters at Wishham paying a visit to one of their villages the other day, the chief men inquired where Mr. Perkins was, that he did not come to visit them; and being informed how I was engaged, they desired him to make inquiries whether I was going to visit them or not; and if not, begged that he would come and spend a few days with them, to teach them how to pray.

I am now done. Deeply sensible that Christ is all, and anxiously desiring to see yet greater displays of his mercy among these tribes of the west, I remain, reverend and dear sir, your son in the Gospel,

H. K. W. Perkins

*Wascopam, Columbia river,* March 31, 1840.

# Appendix 1

## DOCUMENT 4

## History of the Oregon Mission: Part Two
### Wascopam, Spring 1838

Christian Advocate and Journal,
September 20, 1843

*Perkins's "History of the Oregon Mission" was printed in the Christian Advocate and Journal in two parts, on September 13 and 20, 1843. The first installment is reprinted as Document 2 of Appendix 1. Part 2, reprinted here, covers events from late 1840 through 1842.*

Toward fall [1840], having a desire to see our superintendent, and also to form a personal acquaintance with the brethren and sisters recently from the United States, I took a trip with my family to Willamette. It was the sickly season of the year, and most deeply were we called to repent of the visit. After seeing our friends, and about the time we were ready to leave, one of my Indians began to show symptoms of the prevailing fever. He was able, however, to work a little, and we set off down the Willamette. The heat was intense, and the poor sick native was obliged to lie down in the bottom of the canoe in great distress. When we reached our evening encampment he was burning with a high fever. We were far from any house, and lodged upon the sand. I gave him a portion of calomel, and gave strict charge to his companions that he should be kept from the use of cold water. The darkness, and damp, chill miasma of the Willamette soon closed over us, and under their cover the poor fellow, being unable to endure the pains of fever longer, crawled to the river's brink, and tried to allay the burning inward heat by large draughts from the running stream. His companions had knowledge of this, but out of sleepiness or laziness were unwilling to give any alarm. In the morning, as might have been expected, our patient was a picture of disease and distress. We were obliged, however, to proceed, and by noon had nearly reached some houses at the Lower Settlement of the Willamette, when the violence of his pains obliged us to put ashore, to find a shelter under the shade of some low willows. In a few minutes violent retchings of the stomach commenced, accompanied, at intervals, with short spasms, and in less than an hour he lay stretched upon the grass before us a frightful corpse! After wrapping it in blankets, we left the body, and proceeded to the nearest house to get some help to inter it. Pitching my tent upon the bank of the river, upon the borders of a farm, and leaving it in charge of Mrs. P., and having obtained some spades, and the company of a kind-hearted Frenchman, we proceeded back to the sad duty of burying. Transporting him across the river, to the foot of some heavy firs, we made his grave, and heaping upon it a mound of logs, to prevent its disturbance by wolves and panthers, we left him to his long repose.

That night another of my Indians was attacked in the same manner. We were therefore obliged to lie in camp, and obtain the services of a physician, Dr. William J. Bailey, since gone to the United States. My little boy, too, had chills of the ague, and my wife showed every symptom of approaching disease. In spite of all our medicine and attention the native grew worse; and not knowing how it would go with my wife and child, I concluded to go on a little further to the Land encampment, near Mr. Thomas M'Kay's, that in case of emergency we might obtain a shelter in his house. Here we again encamped, and Mrs. Perkins and my only remaining Indian were both brought down with the ague and fever. All the help I could get to assist me in attending upon all these was a native servant of one of the French settlers.

At length my second man died, in the same manner as the former, and we buried him in an old Indian graveyard, where scores of the poor Calapooewas had lain their bones before him. Being unable to bear up any longer under my constant labor, watching, and anxiety, I became at length the last victim of the disease. My wife by this time had partially recovered, and my little boy was convalescent. I now agreed with Dr. Bailey to take the remaining Indian into his own house, several miles distant, and endeavor, if *possible,* to save his life, well knowing that if none escaped to go home to their friends, and make the matter straight with them, the property of the mission at Wascopam must be the sacrifice. You will not readily understand this, of course, and I will give you a case in point, to explain to you the grounds of my fear.

I have elsewhere said, that in the early days of our mission at the Dalls we had a boy from the tribe of the Wallawallas. He was of a large family, and had many friends. He served us faithfully about two years, when we were under the necessity of parting with him, and he returned to his people. This was in the spring. The summer following he was attacked with a bilious inflammatory fever, and died. We had set very much by the boy, and we had good reason to believe that during his stay with us he experienced a change of heart. I procured his interment a short distance from the mission house. The father was frantic with grief. The supposed cause of his death was the "watait," their name for the secret influence of their "medicine men." Their reasons for supposing this were,—the envy with which he would be looked upon by them from his connection with us, and his own opinion on his death-bed, that he was suffering under the pains of this invisible agent. When his death was announced, I was, therefore, called upon to render to his family some remuneration. Such a claim of course we rejected. The consequence was, that in a few days we lost the best horse in our band, and his relatives were only prevented from committing other acts of violence by a fear of what might be the consequences.

But to return to my story. Thus far we had kept in our tent, in order to attend to better advantage upon the sick native; but being released from this care, and Mr. M'Kay kindly vacating his own sleeping room for us, we took up lodgings within doors, until we were so far recovered as to be able to proceed toward home. Our sick Indian we had to leave behind; and through the care and attention of Dr. and Mrs. Bailey he slowly recovered, and we settled with the relatives of the deceased without any great trouble, although the excitement was very strong.

Dr. White leaving the country just at this time, our physician, Dr. Babcock, was called to fill his place at Willamette. He had been with us just long enough to get a little acquainted with the people, and gain in a manner their confidence, before he was thus under the necessity of leaving them. This was peculiarly unfortunate, as for a long time we had taken upon us to supply the people under our care with medicine; and the calls had become so numerous that attention to them generally required half of *one's* time. And from this burden, by the coming of a physician, we had looked to be relieved. Besides, there were many cases of disease among the natives where the services of an able physician would save the life of the sufferer, but for which, with our limited knowledge, we could find no remedy. But this was not the most urgent reason why we wanted a physician for the natives. By not having one a greater evil exists among them than the loss of a few, or even many lives. I mean the juggling—the *constant shameless juggling* of a large class of "medicine men," so called, and medicine women too. So long as this wretched system of superstition is kept up among them it seems almost impossible to free them from the long train of their former superstitious practices. I might fill sheets, were I so disposed, with simple details of the numerous evils suffered in consequence of the toleration of these sons of Simon Magus that would make your heart ache.

One scene, which I accidentally witnessed, will never be erased from my memory. I allude to the putting to death of an infant. Astonishing! you are ready to cry out. What, do the Indians, then, put to death their own children? Yes; but more commonly they hire some juggler to do it for them, which was the case in the present instance. The victim was a little child only a few days old, and I happened to enter the lodge just as the murderous deed was about to be performed. On entering I observed nothing unusual in the appearance of the family circle, except that an earnest conversation was going on between the father and one of these falsely styled doctors. The child was sleeping quietly in its mother's arms. In a few minutes this fiend of a man seated himself by the side of it, and coolly feeling of its little body, at length thrust his hand inside of its covering of skin, in the direction of its stomach, and the conversation went on as usual. I observed the movement, but still suspected nothing, only I supposed he might be going to perform upon it some act of the common jugglery. After a few minutes my attention was again called by a half-suppressed cry from the mother—when, lo, the child was dead! The man had strangled it! Its little face was turned black, with a slight froth at the mouth, and its breath gone for ever. You may judge of my feelings—myself a father.

But why this dreadful deed? The *present* and *immediate* cause was, doubtless, the slight *pay* with which such deeds of darkness are rewarded. But the more *distant* one will not be so apparent to you. The child after its birth had been rather disposed to cry, and was somewhat troublesome, when, as usual, one of these conjurors was called to reveal the cause. After some act of divination, it was ascertained that there was a malformation of the stomach. Upon further questioning the parents it appeared, by the confession of the *father,* that some time previous to its birth he had been so thoughtless as to wash himself, by going into one of the small native bathing houses. This explained at once the whole matter. The formation of the child's stomach corresponded precisely to the formation of this bathing house!

You smile. Nay, it is no cause for laughter to see the immortal mind of man so sunk in stupidity and darkness. Upon this wonderful discovery, the next step is to advise the poor unfortunate parents to have their infant destroyed; as to protract its life under these circumstances would be useless—and the fatal deed is done. We hardly know which most deserves our pity, the blind, credulous parents, or the dark-hearted, wily magician. The present undertaker was a few years ago a slave, but by such acts of deception and sagacity has arisen to be the owner of considerable property, and an object of terror to the little community in which he moves.

Soon after my arrival from the Willamette we called another camp meeting [October 1840]. At this meeting our superintendent was present, and of which I suppose he has given you an account. It was not very fully attended, nor so interesting as the first. This might be accounted for from the fact that there was not so much of the spirit of religion among us as formerly. There was much, too, of unrepented sin among the people. And here I might repeat what I have said in substance before, that many of the natives have such low ideas of the nature of transgression, that they never feel on account of it as deeply as we do; and an act of licentiousness, lying, or sabbath breaking, seems but little to disturb them. Brother Lee administered the holy sacrament to several hundreds, who appeared sincerely endeavoring to serve God, according to the light they possessed, and quite a number were baptized, chiefly people of the Wallawalla tribe. How many of these were *sincere* in taking upon them a profession of piety, or how far grace had operated upon their hearts, we of course could not tell. In too many instances, however, their goodness has proved to be like the morning cloud and early dew, and they have "endured but for a time."

Through the fall of this year I endeavored to reorganize the classes, and take account of the number who were still trying to serve God. I did not do any thing, however, with the people below the Cascades. Pretty soon after brother Lee had left them the previous winter, they were pretty much all drawn away by the Roman Catholic priests, crosses and beads placed upon their necks, and such doctrines inculcated upon them as led them to behold us, and all other Protestants, with pity and contempt. Large papers were drawn up for them, containing, in symbolical language, the history of the world and Christianity, and representing *Papacy* as beginning with the apostles, and extending down in a straight line to the cecession of Luther and his associates. His cesession from the main body of the church was represented to them under the figure of a crooked path leading from a large straight road, which was called the road of the Roman Catholics, and the only road that extended to heaven. Luther, of course, went to hell; and all who do not join the Roman Catholic Church are his followers, and will also inevitably go there too. This, with various other arts, had the desired effect. So afraid have they since been of our doctrines that we cannot even get a hearing from them. Some of the Slihatats in that region, who did not join the Roman Catholics, and who had been baptized by brother Lee, have moved off in various directions; so that to this day we have never seen them together. We have met one here and there, and upon inquiry of these, we could only learn that a few kept up the forms of religion, particularly praying, but that most of them had even "forgotten," as they said, "how to pray!"

While I was engaged in this manner brother Lee made a trip to Willamette, with his family. He himself visited us soon after, but returned again in the early part of February [1841], and did not arrive again at the station until June following. I also made a visit to the Willamette about New-year's but was absent from the circuit only twelve days. During the winter I was pretty much confined to the station. Very many of the Nezperces, Kaius, and Wallawalla Indians made their camp in the vicinity, and we were very much encouraged to look for a religious movement among them. Nothing, however, very important occurred; and early in February I made a short visit to Dr. Whitman's station, at Waiiletpu, on the Wallawalla River, some 135 miles distant. I had it then in my mind to visit the United States as soon as spring should open, and wished first to acquaint myself with the plans and operations of our Presbyterian brethren, which might be of advantage at some future day. My brethren strongly remonstrating against such a movement, I was induced to give it up.

You may be led to inquire, What could make you think of leaving the work at such a time, and coming home to the United States? To this I reply,—A conviction of duty, based upon what I then viewed to be a call from God. To express it in few words—from an attentive perusal of the Scriptures, experience, and observation, I was led to believe that the standard of practical piety by the great majority of professed Christians was placed far below where it ought to be; that consequently very many of the visible Church were indulging delusive hopes of heaven and happiness. Among these I could recognize a large number of my past acquaintances in my native land; and I doubted not but the fact would hold good of the generality of my countrymen whom I had not known. With these views I felt my soul moved to proclaim in their ears what I conceived to be the whole truth in their case, and so entirely did these things possess my mind, that my interest in the work in this country was very much diminished, or rather swallowed up, in the interest I felt for the friends in my own. For several months I felt no rest in my mind, and suffered severely in my health on account of the constant pressure of this subject; and to cut short what little I have to say on this subject at present, I will only add, that I have not found much rest yet.

Being unwilling to take any step without the consent of my brethren, and finding the desire so strong in their minds for my continuance among them, I proceeded to make another tour around the circuit, taking my family with me. This was in April. During this trip exposure and anxiety of mind brought upon me again the ague and fever, and I was able to do but little more missionary work before the arrival of brother Lee and his family, who, as I have said before, arrived in June. Mr. David Carter, who a little before had been married to Miss Orpha Lankton, accompanied brother Lee, and with his excellent wife remained with us through the warm season. During this time he put us up a good barn frame, which we covered with boards the following winter, and which has been of great service in our farming operations. I would remark here, that since the arrival of our farmer, brother Brewer, we have been released from the care of laboring in this line of business; and by his valuable services are likewise released from many other burdens of a secular nature. We have many thanks to render to our friends for sending us out such a help. We hope he will be spared a long time to the Oregon mission.

The fall before last [1841] we commenced building a house of worship for the natives. It is built of logs, a good shingle roof, and the gable ends covered with boards. In the lower part are set six good windows. The length of it is 40 by 30 feet in breadth. It is not yet finished, i. e., furnished with floors and seats, but we have met the people in it through the past winter, and for the most part it has been pretty well filled with attentive hearers. The natives settled around us this winter have been far more numerous than heretofore. I should judge that in the circle of a mile there have been 500 persons, old and young.

The Nezperces, Kaius, and Wallawalla people have also visited us as usual. They make their camp here, on account of the abundance of dried salmon which is to be obtained from our people. The principal unpleasant thing arising from this is, they are too severe in their exactions of this powerless people, and leave them toward spring almost entirely destitute of the means of subsistence. Indeed, the hunting tribes around consider the fishers along the river as their humble servants, and there is no end of their acts of injustice and oppression toward them.

Last fall [1842] brother Lee and brother Brewer, with their families, made a visit to the Willamette. Brother Lee was absent about two months and a half.

I have not yet mentioned that we had another camp meeting early last spring, which was a great blessing to us all. The number of the natives in attendance was not large. This arose partly from a scarcity of provisions. Many at the time were literally starving, or just gaining a meagre subsistence from their daily employment of root-digging, which at this early season afforded the bare means of sustaining life. Soon after the camp meeting, brother Jason Lee and David Leslie paid us a visit. They were too late, however, to see the people, who had gone after their spring provisions.

At this visit I was advised by brother Lee to set about the acquisition of the Chinook language; or spend at least one year in obtaining a knowledge of its principles, that so I might be prepared to advance my knowledge of it by way of travel and direct ministerial labor. This step seemed very necessary; for, 1st. I had as yet given *all* my attention to the Wallawalla, neglecting the other purposely, in order to facilitate my knowledge of this. 2d. The interests of the people demanded that something should be done as soon as possible in the way of books and schools. 3d. From the extent of the Chinook tribe, that language being spoken by some fifteen hundred individuals, including the Indians at brother Waller's station, at the Falls of the Wallamette, we could not think of making any other than their own language an organ of conveying to them instruction. The Wallawalla would not do, of course, as there is no more affinity between it and the Chinook than between the English and Chinook. And, moreover, the people themselves are averse to all such amalgamation.

The "jargon" could never answer as a *written* language; and however we have thus far used it in conveying oral instruction, no one would ever think of printing a book in it. The only way, therefore, to get along, is, to have *a thorough knowledge of the languages of both the Wallawalla and Chinook.* The fact is, we are just between the two tribes; we have as much to do with one people as the other. Our congregation here through the winter is composed of each, about an equal number; and to have books for one people, and not the other, would certainly place us in a very unpleasant situation, from their extreme jealousy; and although we have a sufficient knowledge of the Wallawalla to commence among them native schools, if we had the means of printing books, yet we have plainly seen we could not do it without starting one in Chinook at the same time. The Chinook is a singularly difficult language to acquire, worse still to pronounce, and thus far, to our knowledge, it has never been thoroughly learned by any one, except one of the tribe. It is a curious circumstance, that while the Wallawalla and Slikatak are spoken with facility by numbers of the Chinooks, that not one of the former of these tribes, to my knowledge, can speak the Chinook readily. It is very harsh, uncouth, and guttural, and all other Indians seem to avoid using it when they can possibly get along without it.

# Appendix 1

## DOCUMENT 5

## 1843–1844 Journal

*Perkins's heretofore unpublished 1843–44 journal exists in two parts: book 1 (covering the period between August 13 and October 23, 1843) and book 2 (December 4, 1843, to March 19, 1844). The ellipses (. . .) indicate sections without ethnographic content that have been deleted from this printing.*

### Book 1

Dear Bro. Pittman—[1]
The thought occurred to me while riding to my last appointment, of keeping a sort of Diary, or Journal of my labours & travels, of which I could occasionally send you a transcript; & thus while it would give you a general & somewhat particular view of missionary life in Oregon, you might possibly gather from it a few incidents for your "Missionary Notices".[2]— Of course you would not expect to find much that would be striking, in the common, every day routine of affairs, but I flatter myself that there would be considerable to amuse you, & beguile an hour here & there of relaxation from the arduous & perplexing business of your Station. But without detaining you further with preliminary remarks, I will begin, by giving you a concise history of my last excursion: which for regularity's sake, I shall call—

### A Sabbath at Waiam.

Waiam is an Indian village upon the southern shore of the third great fall of the Columbia. It is about ten miles from our Station, up river. It contains, at the present time, some four hundred inhabitants; being the largest village in the Walla Walla tribe. Two other small villages immediately below, contain about two hundred more; making in all, at this great fishery, 600. You must not suppose, however, that these villages are permanent; for in three months, should you pay a visit to these same falls, you might look in vain for villages,

271

or even a place to shelter your head. The only objects of attraction here are the excellent salmon, which are taken about three months in a year. The fall of water here is generally about 20 feet, & the facilities for fishing are unsurpassed by any other in the country. The river, instead of rushing over in one unbroken sheet, as is usual, where there are falls, is split up into an immense number of little channels, & tumbles down in a variety of irregular, & beautiful cascades across the entire river; which is, at this place, at least half a mile in width. During the early part of summer, however, the water rises to such a degree as to cover the obstructions of the river, & give it an unbroken passage.

I arrived here Saturday evening a little before sunset, & after the usual salutations, took my pencil, & a scrip of paper, & went to my work of translating until dark. The bell (a common cow bell) was now rung around the village to call the people to their evening devotions.[3] In two or three minutes we had collected around us about 150, as near as I could judge, seated in several large unbroken circles around two fires. Several of the principal men of the village, & two or three women joined in prayer, one after another, with much solemnity, & some feeling. I gave them a short discourse, & after singing, & joining with several more of them in prayer, we retired: they to their houses, & I to a sand bank a little out of the village, where, among a few dried tuffts of wild sage,[4] silent, & alone, I deposited myself upon a black bear-skin, pulled my blanket over me, & slept sweetly until morning.

### Sunday Aug. 13 "

A little after sun-rise, we assembled in the same manner as in the evening, & passed through pretty much the same exercises.

As the sun ascended the heavens, it became oppressively hot, with not a breath of wind, & the large smooth flinty pebbles every where scattered around us, served as so many reflectors of its fiery beams. The stench of decaying fish, & the thousand nameless offals of an Indian village, too, became more & more intolerable: but there was no retreating. The mat-covered area for the drying of the salmon, & which we denominate in this country a "house", was our only asylum. Under such a covering, with scores of drying salmon on either hand, we assembled about 10 A.M. for the worship of our Common Father. Numbers coming in from the adjacent villages, our little congregation might amount in the whole to about 300. These seated themselves in a circle upon the ground, the women forming one side of the ring, & the men the other. In the center was spread a rush-mat, covered with a bear-skin, appointed for the "preacher's stand." I had prepared for the occasion a translation of the ten commandments, as put down in the 20" chap. of Exodus. The principal object I had in view in doing this, was to call their attention to the *fourth,* which enjoins the observance of the Sabbath. The proper observance of the holy Sabbath in this country appears to be the hardest of all things to establish, & perhaps it is so in all heathen countries. The trifling objects of temporal gain, & sensual gratification, outweigh in the minds of the natives every other motive, & they rush on to transgression with a thoughtlessness, which is very trying to the missionary. Recently, however, the leading men of Waiam have made vigorous exertions to put a stop to this sin. Quite a number, who persisted in fishing on this holy day, have been taken up, & publicly whipped: & the rest so severely threatened, that but few have the hardihood to persist in the practice. During the forenoon services, a few ventured out with their nets, but the Chief having sent a man to inform them of the new regulations, & to threaten them, they retired, & kept quiet through the day.

In the afternoon we had for a subject of discourse primitive christianity, as portrayed in the first three chapters of the Acts. The interest manifested was an encouraging indication, that the time is not far distant when this people will reap in all their fullness, the unspeakable blessings of the gospel.

In the evening, after partaking with the chief, & his family, of a boiled salmon, followed by a dessert of hazel nuts, & choke-cherries, we assembled for the fourth time, & enjoyed a season of singing & prayer. Having my stand between two fires, which had to be kept burning to light the house, & hemmed in by so many people, I was nearly suffocated with the heat, & so oppressed, & fatigued with the labors of the day, that as soon as the services were concluded, I went out of doors, & flinging myself down upon the low, cedar-bark roof of the chief's lodge, with a large bundle of flags[5] below me, to prevent my rolling to the ground, I fell into a sound slumber, & continued in this situation all night. I awoke in the morning somewhat chilly, & but partially rested, but although I had had neither my coat, nor blanket, I took no cold, & received no perceptible injury.

## *Monday 14"*

Very much depressed—horse gone—wandered off somewhere among the hills. Had morning service as usual—lectured the people on lying —gave them the story of Ananias & Sapphira:[6]—About 100 present—The men briskly engaged in fishing. After breakfasting on boiled salmon without salt, employed my time in getting additional light upon the meaning of sundry Walla-Walla words connected with my translations until noon. No horse—sent an additional man to hunt him. Visited some of the families in the village to observe their employments—Women busy in dressing & curing salmon—The old men lying about here, & there like spaniels—some sleeping, some vacantly gazing at the various employments going on, & some smoking their stone pipes. About an equal number of large & small dogs in the same posture, but abundantly more annoyed by certain small insects, perceptible here & there in very nimble gymnastic exercise. Alas, these creatures[7] are not the smallest annoyance of an Indian Missionary.

But to keep to my subject. My horse came in season to enable me to reach home a little before sun-set, & so after a thorough ablution & change of dress, I enjoyed the luxury of sitting down quietly in my study, with a couple of natives, & spending the rest of the evening endeavouring to make out a translation of the Lord's Prayer.

## A.M.  15"

Finished a translation of the Lords prayer—not however to my satisfaction. It is certainly a most difficult piece of composition to put into an Indian language: It is multum in parvo.[8] The ideas expressed in those two petitions—"Thy Kingdom come, thy will be done" etc comprehend matter enough for a sermon. I have been sadly perplexed to know what language to use—And then again "Thy name be hallowed." The natives have but one word for "hallowed" or sacred, & this is applied in such a manner, that I have had doubts about using it in conjunction with the name of our Heavenly Father. For instance, the "tu–a–ti–ma"—or medicine men— as they are sometimes called by the whites—practice a sort of invocatory ceremony on the first arrival of the salmon in the spring. Before any of the common people are permitted to boil, or even to cut the flesh of the salmon transversly for any purpose, the "tu–a–ti"—medicine man of the village, assembles the people, & after invoking the "Tah" or the particular spirit which presides over the salmon, & who they suppose can make it a prosperous year, or otherwise, takes a fish just caught, & wrings off its head. The blood, which flows from the fish, he catches in a basin, or small dish, & sets it aside. He then cuts the salmon transversly into small pieces, & boils. The way is thus opened for any one else to do the same. Joy & rejoicing circulate through the village, & the people now boil & eat to their hearts content.

But I wish to call your attention to the *blood.* This is considered to be "aut–ni"—or as we should say sacred, or hallowed, or sanctified—i.e. it is sacredly set apart, & carefully garded for five days, when it is carried out, waved in the direction in which they wish the fish to run, & then carefully poured into the water. This is but one example of the use of the word. The verb shap,a,aut,sha of which autni is the adjective form, is also used for to *prohibit.* Now if I knew the ideal meaning of the original word which we translate hallowed previously to its being used in the sacred writings, I could pass some judgment upon the propriety of using the Indian word under consideration. The idea which any word naturally conveys to their minds, & the associations with which it is connected, I find we cannot be too intimately acquainted with in conveying religious instruction to the natives. I would like much your advice on the subject.

### Tues P.M. 15" Aug.

Commenced a formal translation of the gospel according to St. Matthew, & nearly finished the genealogical part of it.

### 16"

Continued my translation, with studies connected with it. Slow progress—spent much time upon the 18" verse, & collecting facts with regard to the natives' espousing their wives, & in finding their word for "espouse"—A history of their espousals, & marriages, I must give you some other time.

### 17"

Spent the day much as yesterday. Was puzzled to know what to call a *prophet.* The word occurs for the first time in the 22" verse. Donnegan[9] makes the word, as used by the Greeks to mean—"One who interprets the words of a person under the effects of supernatural influence." Also "a soothsayer" & even "a forerunner, or herald".

Now the natives have their soothsayers or "tu–a–ti–ma" & their heralds or "sap–a–wanp–tlam–a" & their newsbearers or "tai–mu–tlam–a." The first, I think it will not do to use, as it would carry the idea that it was an Indian conjurer—The second designates a man, such as I use every sabbath to proclaim my words to the people, & which we sometimes term "a crier". This would do better, & I am inclined to use it. God's herald, or crier! What was a prophet but this? What but this was John the Babtist [*sic*]? What are all prophets, ministers &c but instructors of the people at second hand? God first gives to us, & we give to the people. What say you to this word?

The canoe which carried Bro. Daniel Lee down river has returned, & by it we receive the inteligence that he has arrived safely at Astoria, & expects to be out of the Columbia in a few days. Brs. Frost, & Babcock with their families accompany him. This departure takes a large number from our Missionary circle. May we have more abundantly of His presence who "hath chosen the weak things of this world to confound the things which are mighty, & things that are not, to bring to nought things that are."

### 18"

Translated a few verses of the 2nd chapter of Matthew, wrote & read the remainder of the day.

### 19"

People moving to the mountains for berries. They obtain at this season the large mountain huckleberry. The berry month is to the natives like one great holy-day. It always succeeds to the fishing months. The young, the middle-aged, & the aged, share alike in the release which is thus afforded them from the burning rocks, & sands of the fisheries, & the pent up life they are obliged to endure while procuring their winter provisions. Before leaving for the mountains, however, they carefully secrete all their salmon, by covering it up in the ground: which is generally done near where they intend to have their winter quarters. They are usually absent on these excursions, from four, to six weeks; during which, each family lays in, for winter use, four or five pecks of nice dried berries. These they mix from time to time with pounded salmon, & a good portion of salmon oil, & thus is prepared one of the best dishes of which an Indian can boast.

But a scene presented itself to-day, of which I doubt not you would have been an interested spectator. It was an attempt of one of the principal men of the village to "tie me up" for preaching abolitionism.

About the middle of the afternoon, I was informed, that a large party was forming in the village to go to the Tlamath country, to purchase slaves. A party composed of individuals from this, & the Kaius, & Walla Walla tribes, had been out in the Spring, & brought in fourteen: mostly young women, & boys—captives of the Chas–ti tribe. The prime cost of the slaves, was a horse for each, or about ten dollars, while slaves stand upon the Columbia at more than double this price. We had no knowledge of the designs of the party in the Spring, & all we could do, was to remonstrate with them on their return upon the wickedness of their course. This, some resented, & would not be convinced that the traffick in slaves was "a moral evil". The 100 per cent profit being too much to get over by argument. Doctor White our Indian Agent—being here at the time of their arrival, strongly interested himself to break up all future traffick in this way. He even went so far as to make propositions to redeem them, & send the poor creatures back to their own country. These propositions on the part of the slave-dealers were coldly listened to, but we had flattered ourselves that we had so far established a moral influence against the trade, that no more would go forward for the present. But in this, the result has shown we were mistaken. But a few days since, one of these same slaves was sold for 5 large blankets, worth four dollars apiece, & about eight dollars in Indian money beside: & about the same time, another, the amount for which I have not heard. The additional knowledge of their proceedings to day, was two [sic] much to bear in silence. I therefore laid down my pen, & sallied out to find, & remonstrate with those who were carrying forward this business.

Whatever I might be in the United States of America, in Oregon I am "an immediate abolitionist.["][10] I have seen so much of this sickening business, that my soul revolts at the idea of its contin[uance] for a time however short.

I went out, as I said, to try to break up, if possible, the party. Happily I had not to go far, to find some of them, & among them the one who had been most recently engaged in the sale of a slave. During the discussion which ensued, which lasted about half an hour, & during which the slavery advocates exhibited more of anger, than argument, I was convinced that the sentiments of the party were responded to by the people generally, & it was a business which they could not easily be induced to relinquish. News of my interference, in the matter, soon flew to the head man of the party, & I had but just reached my house, & sat down, before in he rushed, with a whip in one hand, & a rope in the other, & coming fiercely up to me, proceeded to put the rope around my hands, & also around my legs. Being entirely ignorant of his intentions, I was at first a little alarmed; but recovering myself, I remonstrated with him upon what he was about to do, & demanded his reasons for it. To this, he replied in a torrent of abuse, & in his turn demanded what right I had to interfere in the slavery business. "Slaves" said he "are our money, as dollars are yours. You have no more right to tell us to throw away our slaves, than we have to tell you to throw away your dollars. Where shall we get our food if we liberate our slaves? Who will procure it for us? Give us property—feed us & clothe us, & we will relinquish slavery. Till you do this *we never will relinquish it.* The French, & English may do this, but *we* are a different people. If your people come & shoot us, we never will relinquish it—If I should be cut up in small pieces, I never will relinquish it. It is *bad* for you to talk to us. It is your duty to keep *still.* Are the canes corn, that I can go & supply myself? Or can I find peas upon the willows? All of you Americans are *liars*—we wish to be *left alone.* Mr Lee has gone, & left us, we are glad: if you would go also we would be glad. You have food, you have clothing, but you will not feed nor clothe *us.* Before you came among us we were fearless, & strong: our hearts were upon our trade—we had many slaves, & our property increased. Your words have made us fearful. We have listened to you, we have prayed, we have lost our interest in our trade—we have been growing poor. You have deceived us ten years—you are a liar" &c &c.

During the pauses of this speech—of which I have put down but a small part—several other natives took an interested part. One slave-holder, in particular, who is otherwise one of the most respectable men in the village, labored hard to convince me that it was altogether a *necessary* thing to hold slaves. "My children" said he "arise in the morning—they are hungry— they call to a couple of slaves & send them off after food. My children sit down & wait. By & by the slaves return, & bring them some breakfast & they eat. Who would get my children food if I had no slaves? "Besides" added he "why should we put away our slaves? They are our *brethren, & sisters*—we *love them*—They are not dogs, & horses that we should turn them off to take care of themselves. We do not call them *slaves* to their *faces*—If we want them to do any thing, we say Brother, do this, or Sister, do that."[11] Of course I am too modest to give my own arguments which I advanced in opposition to all this, but I flatter myself, that the cause of emancipation lost nothing by this little mobocratic assemblage. But now for a few *facts* to put by the side of Mr Bearcap's[12] assertion that they *love* their slaves, & consider them their *brethren & sisters*. I have seen slavery in Brazil, Chili, & also in that worst of all the dens of slavery, the city of Lima, (Peru) but slavery there, bears no comparison to *Indian Slavery*. The blacks of those countries, are lords in comparison of the poor, naked, filthy Chas–tis who are obliged to administer to the wants of the great lordly salmon-eaters along this river. If any thing would rouse your pity, it would be to see one of these poor wretches, in the hottest summer days, outside the door of an Indian lodge, sitting upon a cast-off oil-soaked buffaloe skin.[13] You can recognize beneath the soot, & oil, which covers the entire surface of the body, a strong, athletic young woman. Her hair, which never felt a comb, hangs over her face & shoulders, completely matted together with oil & dirt, & swarming with vermin. Her only covering is a piece of deer-skin girded with strings of the same, around the loins. As she sits & yawns, or stretches herself upon the ground, she busies herself in deliberately extricating the pilferers from her hair, & placing them between her teeth. At length overcome with enui, she is for a while released from her misery by sweet sleep. From this however she is soon aroused by a shrill voice calling from the inside of the lodge—Sister— bring me some water! She slowly rouses herself up, & handing a dish of water to her lounging mistress, retires again to her former place & former employment. The night finds her there, the morning finds her there, each succeeding hour of the holy sabbath finds her *there*. Poor wretched slave! At length the winter comes—the cold sweeping blasts whistle around, & she is at length permitted to enter, & sit inside the lodge door-way. She knows this is her station for the coming winter. Here she is to remain, to execute the commands of her unfeeling masters, & mistresses. Day or night she must go, for if she refuses, she knows she must feel the whip, poker, or whatever comes to hand. To keep her from freezing & thus having her disabled from service, she is permitted, through the cold months, the use of some of the cast-off skins of the family. For food, she eats what she can get, which is generally the poorest salmon, or the leavings of the children. Life cannot be long sustained in this manner, & consequently her term of service expires in a few years. But we come now to the closing scene. The family at length perceive that something is the matter with their slave—she refuses to eat. But little notice at first is taken of it, as she knows not to complain. At length the change in her appearance arouses the family to the startling fact, that they are going to lose the labors of their faithful servant. What is to be done? Done!

why, "she must not die in the house"! This would be to pollute it, according to an Indian's idea, & so she is removed, on an old mat, to the little underground out-house. This is a little oven-like sellar, where the women manufacture their rush-mats in the winter.[14] Here she is left—to die. After lingering here days, or weeks, as the case may be, she is discovered by some one to be *dead.* A person is at length sent to convey her away. Putting a rope around her neck, she is dragged forth like a dead dog, and—shall I write it?—actually thrown to the dogs! The wolves sometimes of a night share the carcase with them. Sometimes, however, it is but just to say, a delicacy of feeling, causes the corpse to be dragged to the river & thrown in, to become food at length to the greedy vultures. . . .

But to return.—The people at length retired. I took the rope from my legs, & handed it back to its owner, who at length went as he came, to pursue his dark schemes of traffick in human souls & bodies. Whilst upon the subject of slavery, I will mention some of the transactions of the last year, & which will also reveal to you some of its concomitant evils. I would not dwell upon these dark scenes, but that you may know something of the difficulties with which you, & with you the church, & friends of missions will have to contend, in subduing the Indians & bringing them to Christ.

About one year since, two of the Indians of this village started on an expedition to the Tlamath country, to buy, as they said, beaver skins; but, in fact, to trade slaves, as the event proved. It so happened that a little previously to their arrival, one of the Tlamaths had been clandestinely killed by a camp of their enemies somewhere in the neighborhood. The murderers in the mean time had escaped, & with the rest of the party, the whole making a large camp—were lying within half a days ride of the Tlamath village. The friends of the deceased were meditating how they might revenge themselves, & obtain blood for blood. They have no guns in that part of the country, & their enemies could arm themselves with bows, & arrows, as well as they. It would be dangerous to make an attempt upon the whole encampment, & might lead to the loss of more blood than they would obtain. In the midst of their deliberations our two Waskopam Indians arrived. They were armed with rifles. The thought now presented itself to the Tlamaths of employing one or both of these men to obtain the proposed revenge, which they supposed, with their rifles, they might easily do, & thus prevent the risks of a general war. One of the men was at length induced to engage in this undertaking. The price offered for the scalp of an enemy, was a young woman—a relative of the deceased Tlamath. The arrangements were accordingly made, & the prospective warrior having received his new bride, (He had a wife, & family at Waskopam, & another still at Wishham) set off early in the morning with his fellow traveller to find the camp of the enemy. After riding over hill & dale for several hours, they came in sight of the camp. The village was posted behind a little hill, around which was spread out an open plain, dotted here & there with trees & shrubbery. Our hero disdaining to reconnoiter, & flushed with the hope of success, rode directly up in view of the villagers, deliberately dismounted, & levelling his rifle, awaited the sallying forth of the enemy: intending, as they came out, to shoot down his man & be off. The villagers were not so reckless of life as to place themselves immediately in the way of being cut down. They rushed forth, indeed, but not as he had fondly anticipated. After discovering his situation they placed themselves so as to surround him, & cut off all possibility of retreat, & at the same time so as to be out of the way of his rifle ball. As they closed around, he fired, but missed his enemy. He loaded his rifle again, & fired, but with the same success. His enemies in the mean time were not idle—their poisoned arrows flew around him thick & fast, & at length pierced his body in various directions. It was like being bit by so many rattlesnakes.[15] But a moment more, & his scalp was in the hands of his enemies. His companion, who witness[ed] this combat, made the best of his liberty in flight from the field, & having purchased a couple of slaves, returned to tell the tidings to the afflicted family of the deceased. The Waskopam people took the affair into consideration, & their judgment was, that as the blood of one of their people had been shed through the means of the Tlamaths, that it was but just that one of the Tlamaths should die in return, & therefore it was advisable to make out a war party, & make the demand upon them. To this I objected, & finally dissuaded them from the measure. Subsequently, the Tlamath woman was brought to this village, & became the property of the brother of the deceased, & a settlement concluded between the two tribes.

We have tried in vain to obtain the release of this poor unfortunate woman, & have her returned to her people. Her owner—who is a middle-aged man, with a wife, & family—asserts, that if the woman goes back, a Tlamath must die. She still forms a part of his family, but is very brutally treated.

O this polygamy! This passion for a plurality of wives! Life, property, every thing is risked for this, & in the attainment of their object, consanguinity, delicacy, honour, all are set aside. It is common for a man to put off two of his daughters to the same person, & that too in some instances before they are even marriageable. Last year, a man not far from this took to wife a little girl, apparently not more than six years of age, & this summer he obtained from the parents her older sister, perhaps 12 years of age, as a second wife!

*Property* is the chief consideration with the parents in disposing of their daughters. The man who bids the highest usually takes them, whether he be an old man, or a young man, a knave, or a fool; whether he have half a dozen other wives, or none at all—& this, not for *property's sake*—as there is a pretty equal *exchange* of property between the parties contracting—but, as it would appear, just for appearance'[s] sake. It is the *quantity of property exchanged* at their marriage, you will observe, which *marks their grade in society.* For the first girls in the country, the quantity of exchange is ten horses, guns, blankets, kettles & Indian money, amounting in the whole perhaps—$200.00. Common girls about half that amt. or one hundred dollars, & the coarser ones, two or three old horses, an old kettle, blanket, guns & a few other small articles. Women that have once had husbands go for about half-price. Repudiated wives for little, or nothing; but whatever is received for *them,* must be received by the man from whom she has been put away, & is rather considered as a quit claim feel. *There are no old maids.* Chastity is not carried so far as this in heathen countries—at least I have not yet found an instance of it.

### *Sabbath 20"*

Rode to the fishery, about three miles distant, & preached to the few who still remain there, not exceeding 30 I think, & in the afternoon met a few in the chapel at home. The departures last week for the mountains have left us almost alone.

### *Monday 21"*

Spent this day in my study, principally in writing. Finished reading the "Life of bishop Emory."[16]... [Perkins's excursus of his readings is deleted.]

### *22" 23d 24" Translating as usual.*

Finished reading Cecils memoirs of the Revd John Newton. . . .

### *25"*

Translating goes on slowly—got through 16 verses to day. Found some difficulty in rendering into Indian the 16" verse of the 4" Chap of matthew. Have thought that the idea of the natives with regard to the "Shadow of death" might be as near the original as Dr Clark's, in his observations upon this place. I shall put it down for you, any way, & if you adopt it, I shall have the praise of going beyond the Doctor.

"Shadow of death"—The natives say, when their friends die, that a shadow comes over the world—every thing in it to them looks dark, & it is a long time before the sun shines, or the world appears as bright as before. This "skesh", or shadow, they term "The shadow of death".[17] This to my mind is beautiful. In a region where death was constantly making its ravages, the people would constantly sit under such a shadow. How cheering then to them the glorious light of the gospel, piercing this shadow, & revealing to the mourners "life & immortality"! How cheering to all such Galilees of the Gentiles would such a light be "springing up"! How desirable to see all these murky shadows lifted from off the whole world! O let us pray, & labour for this.

## 26"

Have at last got through with the first four chapters of Matthew. A task which has occupied all my leisure time from the study of the language for a fortnight. But I wish I had some one to consult who has had experience in this business. In translating the 24" verse of the 4" Chap. to day I have been met with the same difficulty which has often occupied my thoughts heretofore. What shall I say concerning those who it is said "were possessed with devils"? or, the demoniacs? The opinions of the Greeks, Romans, & Jews, with regard to evil spirits, or demons, formerly, appear to have been almost precisely what the opinions of these Indians are now. I know not how to account for it. What a Greek would have called a demon, the Indians call a "skep" (pronounced scape) The "skep" they suppose to be the spirit of some dead person, which after the death of the person, wanders about invisibly, and is capable of entering into the bodies of the living. When this is the case, the person either gradually pines away, & dies, without any perceptable cause, or becomes frantic, & insane. Numerous instances of this kind the Indians mention, in which the "skepi" or demoniac, has wandered about in the snow, wild & naked, in the severe winter weather. Sometimes mangling his body with a knife in the most shocking manner, & subsisting upon the raw flesh of dogs, & such offals as here & there could be found. You ask the Indians what the matter was with such persons, & they will answer "skep-i pau-a-cha—skepi-in pu-kui-a." i.e. they were bedemoned,—wrought upon by the spirits of the dead. What is singular too, the "skep-ma" are all bad—they are all evil geniuses. It sometimes is the case, that one becomes released from the influence of the "skep", but when this happens it is always by the interference of some spirit of an opposite character. Such a spirit usually appears to them in a dream, or vision, under some form, generally of some human person, or some beast, & from the influence of this supernatural visitor the person recovers. One of the first things however which the man does, on his recovery, is to make in wood, or other material, the likeness of this supernatural visitor: & hence their "pat-ash" or gods. These formerly were very numerous. Some are still to be found among them, but the great body of them were burnt on the first introduction of the Gospel among them. This was some years before missionaries were sent to this country, & hence but few records of those days have been preserved. These "pat-ash" are never exhibited to strangers. Wherever they are possessed, they are preserved in the safest, & most secret manner possible. Hence we had lived several years here, before we were aware that any thing of the kind had an existence among them. Indeed we felt quite sure, that whatever else the Indians of Oregon had been guilty of, they had never been guilty of *idolatry*. Formerly they used to carry their gods about their persons, when they were particularly in danger, as in battle, & sickness, but this practice is now generally laid aside.

To give you even a meager idea of their Mythology, would require more time than I can well spare, but I will make a beginning.

In the first place, then, you will bear in mind, that all the creatures which now cover the face of the earth, are in reality *people*. The fly, the hawk, the eagle; the toad, the snake, the turtle, the wolf, the bear, &c. They are not simply insects, reptiles, birds, & beasts. They are the remains of past generations of *men, & women*. Each of these creatures, a few of which I have named, are the vehicles of the spirits of men who have lived in past ages, according to their *former characters*. Great warriors e.g. inhabit the wolf, the bear, the eagle, & in fine the whole class of birds, & beasts of *prey;* & manifest themselves also in what is great, & terrible in nature such as thunder, wind &c, & these spirits in their turn become the guardians of the living, or at least they become so connected with them, that they can have their interference when in particular danger. The general name of these spirits, or saviors are called by the natives "Tah" (plural "Tahma") & appear to be, in the minds of the natives, a distinct class from the "Skepma" or demons, for while the "Skepma" are only evil, & never appear but for evil purposes, the "Tahma" appear as succourers, & interest themselves for their favourites in times of danger & distress. For instance one's "tah" is the "Thunder Spirit". He goes into battle, & is wounded. His friends bear him home to his lodge—His life seems to hang quivering—his relations begin their notes of lamentation over him—& think, alas, he has no "tah", & in that case there is no hope. At length he so far recovers himself as to call for his god, or sacred things, the representations of the "Thunder Spirit". They are pulled out from some secret deposit, & hung up in sight of the wounded man, who now begins his song of invocation. The countenances of his friends now brighten with hope—In a little while—if successful in his conjuration—the heavens are covered with blackness, the thunder begins to roll, & the rain comes hastening on apace. The dying man is now safe. He deliberately squeses [*sic*] the blood from his wound, drinks freely of the descending torrents, & in a few days walks abroad, the fear, & wonder of the neighborhood! It is the same if his "tah" is the bear, or wolf. In this case, the sacred parts are the claws of the former, & the tail of the latter. These "pat–ash" or visible representations of the "tah–ma" or invisible spirits, are always kept at hand, & sometimes worn upon the person, i.e. the more common class of the pat–ash, for they are of various degrees of sacredness: some of the lowest order being simply a sort of charm, or warder of[f] of evil, or procurers of good luck in their various pursuits. They strongly remind one of the "holy cross" of the

Roman Catholics. These "pat–ash", like the metal crosses of our Catholic friends, are always buried with the body of its possessor—for notwithstanding all such charms, amulets, talismans &c heathen, as well as Romanists *die*, & their gods perish with them.

O how much better is the trust of the enlightened, happy christian! While the poor dark-minded Indian, & the semi-christian Catholic, have their "tahs" & their "intercessors", how different is the state of that man who has "the God of Jacob" for his help! How different, I again exclaim is the situation of the enlightened, happy christian!

But there are comparatively few "tahma" which are even professed to be *saviours from death, & danger.* The more common are such as give them success in their particular business in life. A man is a hunter, for instance. The support of himself & family depends on his success in the chase. But from some cause or other he has hunted day after day in vain—not a deer is to be found in all the prairies. He returns at length to his wife & famishing children, weary, & dejected. If he is so fortunate as to have a "tah" there is still hope for them. He commences his song invocatory of the spirit who presides over the game, & perhaps spends the live long night in tiresome incantations. But it is his last resort. His children must have meat or die. he therefore gives his body no rest, & the morning finds him early on his way to the woods, & prairies flushed with new hope, & vigor. The game were never so plenty in the world. he can shoot as many fine fat deer as he pleases, & before the sun descends behind the western hills, his house is filled with the finest venison! Such are Indian tales.

But it is not every one who is so fortunate as to have a "tah". The process for obtaining communion with these invisible spirits is a tedious one, & what some are too imbecile, & delicate, & withal *unbelieving* to attempt. The usual method is this. While quite young, mere boys, they are instructed by their parents in these things, & after receiving directions how to proceed are sent off, of a dark, cold, or stormy night, to the woods, & mountains, in some parts of which, they are taught to expect that a "tah" of some kind will make its appearance to them—i.e. if they are to be objects of *favour*—if not, all the waiting, & watching in the world would not bring a spirit. There they must tarry, alone, & unprotected, perhaps filled with fears, & shivering with cold, night after night, for several nights in succession, or until some bird, beast, or reptile is shown to them. This, whatever it be which is seen at such times, gives them to understand what their future guardian will be, or what their future fortune. You will recollect that these beasts, or birds, are represented to them *supernaturally.* Sometimes the beast speaks, & sometimes it is silent. If the appearance of a bear is presented to them, they are thenceforth known to be taken under the protection of some *warrior spirit*, & may expect succour in battle: & a string of this animals claws are forthwith procured, & hung around the neck, as a sacred talisman.

If it be any particular bird, this, accordingly becomes their guardian; & its feathers are accordingly procured, & hung to the hair, or cap, as a sure warder off of evils.

Sometimes a "tah" appears to a person *unexpectedly* without any such previous pains-taking to put himself in the way of one. To give an instance. A few days ago an Indian told me that when a boy, wandering in the prairie one day, the appearance of a man was presented to him holding in his clenched teeth an arrow. After standing before him some minutes, he addressed him, & informed him that he was an Indian from another part of the country, & had been shot with an arrow so, & so. A moment more, & who should it be but a little prairie wolf,[18] which immediately ran away & disappeared! He ran home to his father, wrapped himself up in his skin, & for a long time was so affected that he could not eat, or take any diversion. At last he related to his father what he had seen, who replied that it was a "tah", & the ghost's holding the arrow between his teeth, with which he had been shot, was a sign that he would never be killed with an arrow.

Sometimes a "tah" appears to a person in a dream & shows him his future fortune. If he has placed before him a large pile of "ahshahs", (Indian money) it is certain, that in a little while by some means or other, he will come in possession of the same; & so of other things.

In addition to all these, they have their signs, & omens, pretty much the same as country people in the States. e.g. A man takes his net & goes to fish: if he sees a hawk plunge into the water, & bring up a fish, it is to him a sign of "good luck", & such like things too numerous to mention. You can see, however, by what little I have put down, that we dwell in the strong holds of heathenism. Paul might well exclaim here "I perceive that in all things ye are too superstitious." But you will ask. What is all this to the subject of demoniacal possession? Pardon me—I have written on unawares.—I was translating the 24" verse of the 4" Chap. of Matthew,[19] which asserts that they brought to him "those that were possessed with devils"—or more litterally "demoniacs". (See Greek Testament) The difficulty in bringing such things before the people I find to be this—it is placing in their hands an argument in favour of *present demoniacal possession,* which I know not how to get over. A native will tell you that such & such persons are labouring under the influence of the spirits of some dead persons, & will die. You can see nothing in their case but the common symptoms of hypochondria, insanity, or monomania. The Indian, in spite of your medical disquisitions, philosophising &c still persists in telling you that they are demons or "skepma" who have possession. Moreover the sick men positively affirm that it is so, or, perhaps, that there are a "legion" at work upon them, as the Gadarene in Mark. Now what will you reply to him? If you admit that there *was* such a thing as demoniacal possession in the time of Our Saviour you can hardly satisfy an Indian that there is not such a thing *now.* at least I have not arguments conclusive on this subject to satisfy either him, or myself.

You are aware, I suppose, that the reasoning in Dr Jahn's[20] celebrated work on "Biblical Archaeology, now so generally put into the hands of Biblical students, is greatly in favour of the position that these persons were merely afflicted with epilepsy, melancholy, or madness—in the ordinary way. If you have any good work on the opposite side of the question I should be much obliged if you would send it to me.

## *Sabbath 27" 1843*

Had an interesting time to day at Waiam—congregation large, & attentive. Read to them a chapter of my translation—the first time in Oregon that I have been able to give the people a whole chapter of the Word of God. O, when will they be able to read it themselves! The work among this people is but just now *begun.* The whole process of education is still to be gone through with. The preaching of the gospel has done much, but much still is left *undone.*

Alas, who is there left to engage in this work! On each side of us there is a large tribe of Indians. The Chinuks (pronounced Che–nooks) on one hand, & the Wallawallas on the other; with languages entirely distinct from each other, & feelings almost equally so. Each strongly prejudiced against the other, & ready to catch at any thing as an occasion of offence. There is at length left but *one missionary for both.* Is this as it should be? Is this the way that the tribes of Oregon are to be converted? After the toils, & labours of five years, & just as we have got into a condition to sustain ourselves comfortably by a long process of manual labour, & just as we have acquired in a tolerable degree their language, so as to get into their minds, & form some just idea of the dark depths of heathen degradations, are we to turn from them, & give them up? Then of whose hand will their blood be required? In view of so many of our brethren's leaving, we are ashamed to ask the church for more missionaries. But I hardly know why we should be. If one set of men go into the field, & after a fair trial find themselves unprepared to accomplish the work, I know not why, as they retire, that another class should not be tried.

We want, at least, *in each language, two men.* Will any body deny this? Men who are *well versed in the principles of language* i.e. men who have not only *tried* to get, but who have *succeeded in acquiring a foreign tongue.* Not only this, but men who are sure that they have an *ear* that can *readily distinguish sounds.* Many men can acquire language from *paper,* whose labours are almost lost in endeavouring to acquire by the *ear, unwritten languages.* Once more, we want men *whose organs will readily yield to the pronunciations of foreign tongues.* Experience shows that it is quite useless to send men to communicate the gospel in a foreign tongue, whose vocal organs will not admit of the use of that tongue. I speak not by way of *complaint.* I know that it is hard finding men, who have the *proper qualifications,* who are *willing* to engage in the labours of an *Indian Mission.* . . .

But few men can be found, who have sufficient strength of mind to sustain for any considerable length of time the burden of missionary labours *alone*—In heathen countries, if any where in the world, the christian needs *society.* It is not *weakness* in him, that his mind *sinks* if he does not have it—It is *nature*—it is just what we should expect of any one in like circumstances—Take a carpenter out of any of your large ship-yards in N. York & send him into the forest with one or two men, to build a ship:—furnish him with tools, & the means of gaining subsistance. Tell him—that as he has not much help—he must get along for a few years as well as he can; examine the timber, put his tools in order, & look out the best place for building, et cetera. Now does any one suppose that your ships-carpenter will have the same feelings that he had in the large ship-yard, laboring with scores of his fellow trades-men? Certainly not. . . .

So with the missionary. Place him *alone,* with a *great* work before him, & render that work uncertain of accomplishment by the fewness of the men, & means placed at his disposal, & he will certainly sink in his mind, & feelings, & be rendered incapable of performing as much labour as he would have done with proper encouragement.

But you will naturally ask—"Have we not sent men enough to Oregon to supply each tribe with a sufficient number of Missionaries?" I answer, we have no reason to complain perhaps for want of *numbers.* Neither shall I *complain* any way. But will simply state as a fact, that *no tribe as yet* has been supplied with *proper labourers.* By a *proper labourer,* I mean one, who is both *able* & *willing* to do the *work assigned him.* It is notorious in the history of this Mission thus far, that those who have appeared to be *able* to labour, have not been willing, & those on the other hand who have appeared *willing* have not been able for *want of suitable qualifications,* & thus, after a trial of several years, the tribes of Natives, even along the broad Columbia, have little, or no prospect from any men *now* in the field, of ever being permitted to hear in their *own tongues* the soul subdueing strains of the gospel, or permitted to scan for themselves the blessed pages of divine inspiration. Any man of common forethought must see, that unless a new state of things is speedily entered upon, that our labours among the tribes of this country are destined, & that at *no distant day to terminate in bitter disappointment.*

28th Br Brewer leaves us to day for the Willamette with 30 bushels of wheat to be ground at Vancouver mill, which is nearly one hundred miles distant. He will be gone probably 3 weeks. I dread the loneliness consequent upon his absence.

### Sept 8"

Some time has elapsed since I laid away my diary:, for I have such constant employment for my pen in translating, revising, copying &c that I have been too tired to employ it in journalizing. I will not conceal it from you, either, that since Br Brewer's departure I have been too much the prey of melancholy feelings to be in a mood to interest my friends by the writing of composition. Melancholy is one of the many things which peculiarly unfits *me* for labours among the heathen. Very few feel the loss of, or the need of, good society as I do. This almost constant incarceration causes the sharpest pains of self-denial which I have to endure. . . .

One cause of depression of late has been the state of my poor people. The ague, & billious fever has for a few weeks been making fearful ravages. They are scattered about here, & there, & are taken sick, & die in a few days. Some one comes with the news that such an one is sick, & pretty soon another follows, & informs of his or her death. News of the death of two came yesterday: one of them long known as a very wicked man, & of late a slave-holder, & slave-dealer. He owned three slaves when he died. Poor man! He used to say when exhorted to reform, that he should die just as quick if he prayed, as if he did not; & *now* it is *too late*.

"What day, what hour, but knocks at human hearts."

### Sept 16th

Since last writing I have been down river about 25 miles to visit the sick, & dying—was occupied most of three days—returned only last evening. O what would I give to see this poor benighted people laying aside their superstitious juglery[21] over the sick. But alas, this will never be, until we can give them something better. Of medicine we have a small assortment, but alas, for my poor people I know but little of the nature of it. It is painful to me to see a fellow creature writhing in pain, or burning with fever, groaning, gasping, & dying without knowing how to afford the least relief. How much good a *humble devoted* physician might do among this poor people. O, we want Howards[22] for missionaries. . .

*18th*

Translating as usual. Have bin engaged of late in writing a small grammar of the Walla Walla language, both for my own benefit, & the benefit of those who may come after me.

*20th Sept.*

By improving the hours of relaxation from study, for a few weeks past, I have at length written out in a convenient form for use, observations on every part of the WallaWalla language.

They occupy 35 pages of 6 inch square paper, & have been the result of months, & years of patient, & attentive observation. After this, the worst part of the labour, in acquiring the Walla Walla language to any one who may wish to learn it, is over. I have also written a small Vocabulary, containing a thousand or twelve hundred of the most common words of this language, but have not found time, as yet, to arrange it alphabetically, which will require the whole to be copied.

*Friday 22*

Br Brewer has at length returned from the Willamette, & brings the cheering inteligence that the work of God is still going on in the Willamette Settlement. Mr Pettygrove & wife, recently from N. York are among the late converts.

"God moves in a mysterious way, his wonders to perform." These people after withstanding all the light, warnings, & invitations of the gospel for years in their own favoured land, come here, where the gospel has just begun to sound the light just begun to shine, & the truth finds way to their hearts, & results in their immediate conversion.

25" Br Brewer very sick with fever—symptoms alarming—severe pain in his head—whole system very much disturbed—taken last evening.

26th Br Brewer much worse—pain in his head almost insupportable—fever very high—no sleep.

3 O clock P.M. Have been under the necessity of doing what I never had courage to do before viz. that of using the lancet. Took a pint & a half of blood from Br Brewer's arm, & gave 15 gr. of Calomel.[23]

5 P.M. Gave a dose of Castor oil, & applied a blister[24] to the back of the neck.

## 27th

Br Brewer finds slight relief—but no sleep—fever very high.
5 P.M. Slight remission—pain in the head abated, but not gone—great weakness.

## 28th

Br Brewer has been much the same to day as yesterday. Slight remission again this evening—weakness increasing—hardly know what to do next—it is useless to send for a physician as one could hardly be got here, before the fever will arrive at its crisis, & Br B. live, or die. Indeed we have no one to send for, but Dr White our Indian Agent, & we know not where he may be.

## 29th

Dr White very unexpectedly arrived at this Station this morning before we were up, on his way to the Interior—a very providential arrival indeed. Thus man's extremity, is God's opportunity. No one had told him that Br. B. was sick, & no one knew he was near. We have prevailed on the Doctor to spend the day with us. 5 P.M. Under Dr. W's treatment to day Br. B. has manifestly improved, has had a more perfect remission of fever, with a copious sweat. We feel very *very* much relieved from what has been to us, a *painful suspense*.

## 30th

Dr. W. Leaves us this morning: with an addition however to our little fund of medical knowledge, & little brighter hopes than when he found us. . . . [Perkins's entries on the 1843 migration begin here. As they contain information that is marginal to Indian affairs, they have been deleted from this printing.]

Saturday night.—Thus one week has passed, & nothing done in the way of translating. Br Brewer has shared much of my attention, & the secular business of the Mission the rest of it. We have dug up our potatoes this week, & housed them: being unable to look after them as we ought, from the pressure of other business, a great many of them have been taken off by the Natives. I should judge, at least 50 bushels. This is very trying, but we can not help ourselves. The chiefs here have but little authority, & the people do pretty much as they please. As soon as we commence digging, the people come in from every direction, & throng the field—from one to two hundred constantly stand, or sit around, & each one is pretty sure to carry away *some* when leaving. All manner of manoevering is resorted to, to accomplish their purpose. In one instance three or four men came from a distant village, & tarrying at the station till midnight, loaded their horses from the potatoe field, & returned home. And after our potatoes, corn, & other vegetables are gathered, the natives will hang around for days, & weeks, sometimes, just to beg. It seems as if they would gladly get from us, if they could, the last mouthful of provision we have. This is a *sad* picture, but true to life.

### *Sabbath Oct 1"*

Religious services at the Station as usual. Br Brewer convalescent. Evening. . . .

### *9th*

Have had up for trial to day the Indian who attempted to tie me, a few weeks ago. Was sorry to have the poor fellow flogged, but perhaps it has been the best course that could have been pursued with him. The Indians highly approved of it. Indeed, the natives appear very much awed, by seeing so many white people coming through their country just now.

### *Monday 23d. . . .*

By letters just received from you to the Revd J. Lee, we learn that you have made it our duty to keep "diaries" to be transmitted to you by every opportunity. So you will please accept this as a specimen. I must now close. You see where we are, & what we are doing. May the Lord bless you in your arduous work, & bring us all finally to his heavenly kingdom. Excuse the carelessness with which much of this has been written &

Believe me Dear Sir
Respectfully Yours
H.K.W. Perkins

# Book 2

Wascopam Dec. 4 1843

Dear Bro. Pitman,

In my last communication to you, which I sent by the Brig Palace [sic: Pallas], some two months since, I informed you that we were thronged with emigrants, which were passing us by hundreds & that in the consequent disarrangement of our regular missionary business I should be under the necessity of laying aside my pen for a time. I would now inform you that the noise, bustle, & hurry of emigrating companies has quietly subsided, & I am once more the retired occupant of a study, & have resumed my business of translating. . . .

More recently, we have had the pleasure of an acquaintance with Lieut. J.C. Fremont who had been here on a topographical survey for Government, with a party of 25 or 30 men. He left us a few days since to return, via the Clamat Lake south. An Indian boy, who has been a member of my family about four years, being very desirous of visiting the States, I have committed him to Mr Fremont's care. He is an enterprising lad & I hope the journey may prove beneficial to him. But I suppose you will be more interested in hearing how the missionary work goes on. I will say then that it is now Saturday night. A week has elapsed since I commenced this communication. I have scarcely laid down my pen since monday morning, except for meals, & sleep. I have translated (including some copy which I had before) & printed with my pen, in a little book which I have prepared, one hundred & ten verses of the gospels. The plan I have hit upon to convey the gospel histories to the natives is that of Dodd-ridge as printed in his Family Expositor.[25] His plan of harmonizing the gospels, & giving all in connected lessons, has many advantages for the natives, as it prevents all apparent contradiction, & makes but *one* story, which is more easily remembered, & saves them from many perplexities. His Paraphrase also is very beneficial to the translator in conducting to the sense of the original. By the help of this, & Clark's Com, with Wesleys Notes, & Campbell's Gospels[26] I suppose one may come near enough to the sense for all common purposes of translation. I print all, with my pen, as fast as I get it translated to my satisfaction, that I may more easily read from it to the natives, & that it may serve for a copy to those who may wish to print from it, should I be taken away, & also to serve for my pocket testament which I may always have about me in travelling, from which to select texts, & subjects for discourse. I have constantly with me an engaged assistant, a native, whose services I obtain for about 3 or 4 dollars per month.[27] Sometimes I admit another, but generally he is the only inmate beside myself of my study. If I have calls from others of the natives, they remain in the sitting room, to which they always have free access, until I can wait upon them. In addition, I have two native lads, who have been trained to do most of the kitchen work such as cooking, washing, cutting the wood, & bringing the water.[28] These, beside their board, which is considerable, cost me 6 or 7 dollars per month. The natives are settled arou[n]d us within short distances, so that we have no want for neighbours, such as they are. What is wanting in them, we must try, & make up. The past week the Kaius, & WallaWallas have been moving in. Several lodges have been put up within a hundred yards of our door. This is the month when the Kaius, WallaWallas & Nez Perces make their yearly gathering here, to pass the winter. The former of these are the elite of the country. They are few in number but exert a very great influence. They are a brave, & enterprising people, & command a great deal of respect from the surrounding tribes. The Nez–perces through the indefatiguable labors of Mr. & Mrs Spalding, are ahead of them in learning, & are more cultivated in their manners, but have less of a spirit of independance, & a fewer number of noted men. The Wallawallas being more stationary, & abundantly supplied with provisions from their fisheries, have far less enterprise than either of the others. The Chinuks are still behind these in point of civilization. Indeed there seems to be a regular diminution of enterprise among the Indian tribes as one descends the Columbia, owing much undoubtedly to climate, & different modes of living.

## Saobath Dec 10" 1843

Met the natives about 11 A.M. & read & explained to them the visit of the angel to Mary & her subsequent history to the birth of our Saviour, including also the naming of the child Jesus. About 150 were present who listened with considerable interest.

The naming of a child among the natives here is attended with a great deal of ceremony. The time when this is attended to varies according to the circumstances of the parents, but it is generally I believe during the first year of the childs life. A grand feast is always made, or *was,* rather, formerly, & a great deal of property given away. The relatives on the father's & mother's side are generally collected, & supper being served up, before it is partaken of the ceremony takes place.

An old man is always selected for a herald or crier & when all things are ready, the mother of the child to be named presents to him a fathom of "ahshahs" (Indian money) which is a sign for him to arise. The old man therefore rises, & publishes with a loud voice, "I have received this present." He then inquires for the name of the child, & having received it he again cries "Hear ye earth, water, & fire; ye heaven, sun moon & stars: ye clouds, & trees, & rocks, & all creatures in air earth, & sea, (naming over the things of the animate & inanimate creation in regular order) and all ye people, old men & old women, young men & maidens, & ye children this name." He then goes on to say from whom the name is derived, from such a relation, who was such a man or woman, & who died so & so, & on pronouncing the name, the whole company repepeat [sic] it simultaneously. Sometimes the child takes the name of a living relation, friend or aquaintance, but should that friend or relation die the name ceases, & he who took the name must find another as it is not customary to call the name of a person that is dead, for a long time after his decease. After the naming is over, presents are distributed according to the circumstances of the parents to all the company present, giving to each according to their dignity. Generally 3 or 4 large dressed elk skins are cut into small pieces, each large enough to sole a pair of moccasins; & these being all distributed, a quantity of "ahshahs" i.e. Indian money is then brought forward, & strings of this, of perhaps a foot in length each, are also distributed. Besides these presents, any one of the company has a right to ask for such an article as he is needy of, & at such times custom demands that he receive it, even to the last shirt the father has, or the only knife or gun. After every thing else is given away the old ladies call for the rush mats, which the mother distributes among them, & so the party breaks up.

This feast is called in Wálawála Pam–a wa–nicht pam–a ti–kuat–at or The feast of the naming.

Closely connected with this ceremony, & which formerly could not be omitted without great disgrace to the family, is that of boring the ears, & nose of the infant. This also is generally attended to during the first year of the child's life. This business is always performed during the morning twilight. The ceremony is generally performed by some one of their aged female jugglers. The child, as usual is bound to its little board or cradle, & in this situation the old woman receives it, & places it upon her knees. She then mutters over it in a low half-whisper voice, a sort of prayer or incantation, & then taking a needle, (formerly a sharp bone) she perforates successively each of the ears, & nose. If the ears are hard to be perforated, or if the child cries, or if much blood follows the operation, it is a bad sign, & the child will be short-lived, & vice versa. This feast is called Pam–a si–akt pam–a ti–kuat–at—The feast of the boring.

I have here adverted to these ceremonies of the natives as my subject seemed to call them up, & if preserved may be interesting to some one, & all such customs which they have formerly had seem destined to be veiled in oblivion in a few years, as the manners, & customs of the whites are gradually introduced. Even now, these ceremonies are fast being laid aside. At 12 O. clock we had our usual English services. Preached from 1 Thess. V. 6.[29]

Immed[i]ately at the close of the English services we met the natives & had for subjects good old Simeon, & Phanuel's daughter.[30] In the evening we had a prayer-meeting. As this is the standing order of our Sabbath exercises it will not be necessary for me to be particular in naming them hereafter.

## Sabbath 17[31]

Translated this week 76 verses. Ill health has prevented me from applying myself as closely to study as heretofore. Religious exercises to day as usual. Gave the natives that portion of the gospel history which includes, the visit of the wise men to the Saviour, the flight into Egypt, slaying of the infants, & Joseph's settlement at Nazareth. In the afternoon added some account of the ministry of John, his preaching, & instructions to the people.

## Sat 23d

Much company this week—a fresh arrival of Kaiuses. Have got through with 100 verses however of very interesting matter. viz. the conversations of Christ with Nicodemas, & the Samaritan woman. Some of the principal men of the Kaius have taken up a pretty permanent abode in my study. So eager have they been to learn, that they have scarcely left it except for meals & sleep during the week. They sit around my table & seem to drink in every sentence, with such eagerness as contributes very much to my encouragement.

## Sabbath 24 "

Had an interesting season with the people to day. Congregation very large & attentive—their interest seems to be very much increasing in the truths of the gospel. Had for subject the baptism, & temptation of Christ, & the visit of the priests & Levites to John, inquiring after his character, & the reasons for his ministry; & Johns subsequent testimony of Christ as the Lamb of God which taketh away the sin of the world. Have attended two funerals within a few days—one, of an infant belonging to a Walawala, & the other of an infant belonging to the Kaius tribe. I always feel a peculiar satisfaction in committing these little ones to their mother earth. I know their spirits are up on high, & forever hence beyond the contamination of heathenism. One of them was brought by the parents for interment some 25 miles. I felt to sympathise with them, because they were a young couple, & this was their only child: the mother seemed scarce out of her teens, & she appeared as though she deeply felt this separation from the first, & only child of her bosom, & I felt peculiarly happy in soothing their troubled minds with the precious truths of that gospel, which reveals to us our separated babes as always beholding the face of our heavenly Father. It seems a wise arrangement of Divine providence that so great a proportion of the heathen die while in a state of infancy. We should have a great many funerals to attend if we could furnish the means for interments. Our way of burying requires a coffin, which we are seldom able to furnish for want of boards, hence the natives, as a general thing, continue their own way of intering, which on the whole I consider very good. There are two ways of burying among the natives here, each tribe having its own way. The Chinuks bury their dead by placing them in low flat roofed houses, built expressly for this purpose generally on some island. There are three islands in the Columbia in this vicinity, which are expressly devoted to this purpose. These islands are considered "autni", or sacred, & are never visited by any except the tlchacha kutkutlama or those whose express business it is to bury the dead. The most noted of these islands is situated in the lower part of the Dalls, or great rapids, about three miles distant from us. It has been several years since I visited it, as it is hard of access, & as I said before, the common people can hardly be induced to approach it. There were then, some 8 or 10 of these houses standing, some of them in pretty good repair. They were all constructed in the same manner, & generally about 10 feet square, & 6 or 7 feet high, the walls of split cedar, & the roofs of bark of the same. The one which I visited, & which we may take as a sample, was arranged inside, the same as a dwelling—On one side was what the natives call the "simas" or sleeping place, & on the other a vacant space. The "simas" is a low scaffold of cedar boards supported by small poles, laid upon short upright posts, firmly set in the ground. The "simas" contained a large number of bodies piled upon each other, much the same as corded wood, each body being snugly wrapped in dressed elk skin; those which were more recently dead, lying uppermost. Beneath the "simas", & around the walls of the apartment, were promiscuous heaps of mouldering bones, in different states of preservation; arms, legs, & skulls of numerous individuals all commingling, & all alike unconscious at last in whose society found. In one corner I noticed, what might once have been some voyager's provision chest, & which contained, as I found upon inquiry, the bones of a noted chief. A splendid mausoleum, could not hold them more snugly [or afford the departed more consolation]. Had I opend this box, or almost any one of these bundles of crumbling bones, I should have found an abundance of Indian treasure; such as beads, shells, copper, & brass coins, knives, spoons, & all kinds of trinkets, the product of many a day of anxious thought, & care to the once haughty & fortunate possessor, but now alas forever useless.

Great attention is paid to the dead by the near relations while the relations live, but time at length veils their memory in oblivion, & they sink one after another in the crumbling mass. The hig[h]er classes of the natives at death, are arrayed in their best dresses, profusely ornamented, & wrapped, first in new blankets, & then in elk skins. After the lapse of one year, the corpse is taken out, & the bones cleansed, & if the relatives are able to afford it, wrapped in new blankets, & fresh skins. A certain class of old men perform this business, & for which they generaly receive large pay. Formerly, the natives had a practice of sacrificing a large amount of property, such as guns, bows, & arrows, kettles, axes, & whatever was valuable to the owner while living, & these were all wrapped together with the body; but this is now very much laid aside. The Walawalas have a different way of disposing of their dead. Their burying places are large underground vaults, generally at the foot of a rocky hill, where they may easily be covered with stones. These vaults are very difficult of access, requiring much labour to remove the stones by which they are concealed, & which would render a stranger entirely ignorant of their existance. Sometimes they become lost to the family itself, especially if they are in the vicinity of drifting sands. A burying place belonging to a village on the Columbia about 8 miles above this has been completely lost in this way. They point to the spot where lie the bones of the forefathers, but nothing is seen but immense heaps of these shifting sands beyond the power of removal.

The stones & earth being removed, the bodies are found empaled in boards of split cedar, in the manner of a "cache" & as in the former instance which I have mentioned, in different states of preservation. Each family has a separate vault which contains the bones of its progenitors from time immemorial. In this manner every fresh victim in the family line is "laid unto its fathers". A small pole is usually set up after a fresh interment over the place—having tied to it a small strip of scarlet cloth, which I presume however, is a modern practice, introduced by the traders. It is remarkable that whatever offerings were formerly made to the dead, of arms, & furniture, were always first rendered useless to the living. If it were a gun, it was first *broken*, & then laid with the corpse. If a dish, or kettle, it must first have a hole broken through it. Horses were formerly slain upon the spot when the person was buried, & I am sorry to add human victims also. The fate of a poor young woman a few miles from this is still fresh in the minds of the present inhabitants of this village. She was unfortunately a slave, & her master, a young man, was accidentally drowned in the great rapids just above here. His death was deeply felt by the family, & in their darkness they concluded that they could not do better for him, now that he was gone, than to send his faithful female servant after him. They accordingly led her to the point of the rock from which her master had fallen & hurled her into the boiling current.

The property of the deceased goes to the most influential of the relatives, whether they be near or distant. The wife is hardly considered an heiress to her husband's estate, neither are the children allowed a part, if they happen to be young. The brothers generally divide, or if there are none, the next nearest male relatives, & so rapacious are they, as I said before, that the strongest generally gets the most, & oftentimes all, so that the poor wife, & fatherless children are turned upon the world naked, & dependant on the charity of their friends. This distribution of the property is made immediately on the death of the individual, & in the presence of the dead body. In the same manner all quarrels with the deceased are settled. If any one has inflicted wounds or blows on him while living, or if any one has been known to be his public enemy he now brings some present, & deposites it with the relatives, & the remembrance of it perishes. Should no such settlement be made, this is the time for vengeance, & woe to him who falls in the way of the frantic relatives. Their vengeance is more frequently wreaked on the poor jugglers, who, the natives are of opinion are the secret cause of almost all the deaths which occur. Some one of these is selected whom they suppose is the murderer, & unless he secretes himself, is shot, or butchered in some way. Such murders are but little thought of by the common people. Ind[e]ed they look for them constantly on the death of every person of any note. A large number have thus been killed in this vicinity since our settlement at this place. Two have been shot now, within a month, very near us, one on the death of a young man, & the other on the death of an infant.

It is hard telling what notions the natives have formerly had of a future state of existance; their mythology, however, & their legends, & traditions, all lead us to the conclusion that they believed in the *immateriality,* & *immortality* of the soul, thus placing themselves in the scale of inteligence far above a certain class of our own countrymen. . . .

[Several pages of what amounts to a sermon on the missionary effort follow.]


## Dec 25 Christmas

Translating, & instructing as usual. All the members of our little circle met together at dusk, & partook of a Christmas supper, & spent a long evening in singing, conversation, & prayer. We missed the society of our Dear Brother & Sister Lee, but hope they were far happier in the enjoyment of society elswhere. Truly we are in an isolated situation, & we never feel it more, than when some such season as this occurs . . .


## Sabbath Dec 31

Services as usual among the natives. Had a good deal of liberty in explaining to them the third chapter of John's gospel, & showing them the love which God the Father had to us in giving his only Son to die for our sins. In the afternoon gave them the circumstances, & causes of John Baptist's death, & endeavored to point out faithfully the evils of *adultery* which is such a crying sin among them. I trust the good seed will not all be lost. " " Have translated 74 verses this week & given a good deal of private instruction to visitors, & others. . . .

## Jan. 1, 1844

Felt fresh courage in commencing anew our labours among the natives. Believe the feeling is general among all the members of the station. The ground is covered for the first time this season with snow. Have all enjoyed a social season this evening at Br. Brewers. Have reason to render many thanks to Heaven, that the New Year finds us all in such good health, & with such bright prospects.

## Sabbath Jan. 7"

Met the people as usual about 11 A.M. & instructed them until night with the exception of a short intermission. Read to them from my translation the visit of Christ to Samaria, conversation at Jacobs well, his arrival in Galilee, & his cure of the nobleman's son at Capernaum with his subsequent visit to Nazareth, & shameful treatment there. Also his calling of Peter Andrew James & John to the discipleship with the miraculous draught of fishes, their entrance from thence into Capernaum, casting out of a demon, & cure of Simon's wife's mother. Have spent much time the past week in the study of Longking's Notes on the gospels,[32] & comparing his harmony with that of Doddridge. . . .

## Sat. 13'

Two weeks of the new year has passed, but nothing particularly worthy of note has occured. Have proceeded much as usual in my translation. The weather has been pretty cold, & we have been more than usually crowded in the house with the natives, who are always glad to avail themselves of our fires. To render this a little less annoying we get our morning meal before it is fairly light, & before the natives throng in upon us, & our evening meal we take after dark, for the same reason. Have spent much time in translating the fifth of Matthew, particularly the first 37 verses. The "beatitudes" as they are called were not particularly difficult of translation, but I have hesitated in using the word "blessed" because it is not in accordance with the ideas of a native to consider a person blessed, until he comes in possession of the blessing, whatever it be. They do not consider themselves as blessed in anticipation, but only in *participation*. This is a peculiarity in the language. Instead of using therefore the native word i auni, which is the participial form of the verb i–au–sia, to bless, & which would be the word, were the blessing spoken of already in possession, I have had to use another form, viz i–au–las, which signifies, when joined with a noun, or pronoun that the person spoken of is a *subject* for such, & such a blessing. The 21", & 22 verses I have found particularly difficult to translate, so as to satisfy myself. Indeed I cannot bring myself to believe that our translators have given us a faithful translation of our Lords words. . . .

I have, however, given a literal translation of the English.

## Sabbath 14"

Gave the people to day the first 57 verses of the 5" of Matthew which they listened to with a great deal of interest, it required however a great deal of explanation. The 22nd verse produced considerable discussion among them as I expected it would. The word "Raca" I have rendered by "am–ti–ton," which signifies among the natives, a vain, emty, rattle headed, talking fellow—One who thinks he knows every thing, & consequently is always talking, & meddling in all controversies, & every bodies' business. The words "thou fool" I have rendered by "pai–ik–nail," literally "without understanding" this is one of the most contemptuous words in the language, & is applied generally to those who are wholly given up to wickedness—one who is totaly regardless of reproof, or the usual restraints of society, & is running on headlong to ruin. The natives have both of these words in such common use, that they do not look upon it as criminal to use them: even the most moral, & religious, have not been accustomed to consider the sinfulness of putting upon each other opprobrious epithets, & to tell them that for the use of such language they are in danger of hell fire, very much astounds them. I hope it may lead them to reflection, & repentance. This is one of the hardest things to accomplish, viz to make a native feel that he *deserves punishment:* he will justify himself in the committal of the basest crimes, & if he is moral, if he has never indulged in outbreaking sins, he is so far from deserving punishment that he thinks himself deserving of great praise, & will look down upon his more openly sinning neighbour with the greatest contempt. I have frequently been reproached for receiving such, as are known to be guilty of great crimes, into my house, & especialy for administering to their necessities— such as giving them food, or medicine when sick.

Indeed there is no trait of human nature in the civilized world, & among polished society, which is not exemplified in the savage, & unpolished— the same inherent depravity fastens upon all, teaching us conclusively that the whole human race is descended from one head, & all deserving of a like doom. Man, the world over, is found with "his whole head sick, & his whole heart faint". . . .

There is a kind of Deity, if I may so speak, which men both civilized, & savage may be said to love—a Deity who in spite of all the sin, ingratitude, & unholiness of his creatures, will manifest himself only to them in love: &

compassion; who will see men trample on all his laws, serve the devil all their lives long, & die like brutes, & throw over them all at last the broad mouth of his charity, & receive them to his bosom. Such a God is unknown in Scripture History—such a God dwells not in the high palaces of eternity. The heathen love to think of such a God. I believe all the Indians of North America might be brought to the love, & worship—if I may be allowed the expression—of such a God in a very short time. . . .

[Another sermon on the Christian mission to the heathen omitted.]

### Jany. 20

The cold weather, which commenced with the new year still continues. The Columbia is at length covered with ice. But notwithstanding the weather, the Kaiuses, Nezperces, & WallaWalla's have for several days been steadily moving off, & are at length pretty much all gone—three or four lodges only are left. They return earlier than usual this year on account of the scarcity of provisions. I hope their visit to this place has not been altogether in vain as it regards their spiritual state.

### Sabbath 21"

Had a cold, dreary day for our exercises—but few out, & indeed I could not blame the people from not coming. Our Meeting house although a good log building, & well covered, has no floors, above or below, & it is so large, that we never think of warming it. Indeed we could not warm it so as to make it comfortable, even if we had stoves, or fire-places. Discoursed to them from the latter part of the 5" Chap. of Matthew. Had but one service. P.M. Preached to the Mission family in English. There is much sickness around us at present, in consequence of the whooping cough having lately been introduced into the neighbourhood by some Kaius families who contracted it in the Rocky Mountains some months ago. Some children have already died with it, & it promises to become general among the children. Mr Brewers two, & my two youngest have already taken it, & cough very severely.

### Feby 8th

By letters received from below to day, we are informed that the Superintendent of the Oregon Mission, accompanied by Revd Mr Hines & family sailed from Oregon some time in Dec. last, for the U. States. Had we heard of their death, our feelings would have been scarcely more melancholly, than they were for a few hours after hearing of this sudden, & unexpected departure. . . .
[Elaboration on the fate of the Oregon Mission omitted.]

*Sabbath Feby 11"*

Had the pleasure to day of meeting my poor people in a new, & comfortable house, which we have been gradually building for more than a year. It has been fitted up principally for a school which we have long been preparing to commence among the natives. Having had the services of a young man from the U. States for a couple of months, he, & Br Brewer have at length completed the job. It is 24 ft long by 18 wide, well floored above, & below, & furnished with benches a good desk, & black-board. Br Brewer will open a school tomorrow. One thing however we feel sadly the want of, I mean *books*. We cannot expect to do much without these, but we are convinced it is time to make a *beginning*, & teach them by means of the black-board, & such little easy lessons as we can print for them with our pens, on slips of paper. You can anticipate our difficulties.

*20"*

The spring seems to have fairly opened. We took our children out to walk yesterday & gathered up during our ramble quite a bunch of little flowers. The snow has been at no time I think more than 12 inches deep, & our storms have been far from severe. Since the middle of Dec the Thermometer has generally ranged from 25' to 35' & the lowest point to which it has fallen was only to 20' of Fahrenheit. To day Brother Brewer is getting in his spring wheat, or rather his hired man; he himself is in the School. My own time is now pretty much employed in preparing lessons for Br Brewers School. Translating gets on slowly—more time I hope by & by.

Dear Bro. It is now the 19" of March, & the time has come when we must have our letters in readiness to go to our native land. We expect the Express here tomorrow or next day, & must therefore close up our Spring's writing. I have been looking over the preceeding sheets of my journal, & am really sorry to find it so meager & uninteresting. It does not seem worth sending so far, & if it was not made my duty to transmit to you an account of my labours, I would not trouble you with a line of it. The 5th Sheet I have thrown into the fire, & have run my pen over a part of the 7" & 8th, & I would beg as a particular favour that you will make public as little of it as possible. Perhaps you can make some general report out of it, & cloth it in your own language, which will do more good, & be more acceptable to the public. I have not time to *coppy* it, & send it as I have penned it down from week to week. To send you the incidents of each day, as they have occured, I have thought would be making ourselves unnecessarily public & would swell my journal to such a length, as would make too great a bill of postage for you. I have wanted to send you a few sheets on the peculiarities of the Walawala language, but must defer it until another time for want of paper, which I am almost out of. For nearly a month past I have been engaged in preparing, a School Book to send to you to be printed as soon as possible. I hope to have it finished in time for the Express but it is rather doubtful, if not I must send it by the next earliest opportunity. Br. Brewer urges this measure, as he thinks he must have books, to go on with the School successfully. I have found it not an easy task to prepare a suitable book, it being quite a new business to me, & it will of course be in a manner imperfect. I intend to have the reading lessons to consist altogether of Scripture Stories as I flatter myself quite a number of the school will be prepared to read them readily by the time we receive the books you will print. I have therefore translated for it the first three chapters of Genesis, containing a history of the Creation & Fall of man, as the easiest & most important of any thing I could select for the first lessons.

> Dear Br Pray for us & believe me as ever
> Yours Truly
> H.K.W. Perkins

P.S. I should be obliged if you would send me by Br Lee a Hebrew grammar, & Dictionary.

# Appendix 2

## Oregon Mission
## Manuscript Sources and Locations

The following list of manuscripts written by persons involved with the Oregon Mission is provided for the convenience of individuals who wish to pursue their own research on the material covered in this book. Unless otherwise labeled, a date listed under a person's name signifies a document written by that person on that date.

The location of each item is indicated by an abbreviation, as follows:

AW    Alvan Waller Collection. Mss. 1210. Manuscripts Department. Regional Research Library. Oregon Historical Society. Portland.

OIC    Archives of the Oregon-Idaho Conference of the United Methodist Church. Willamette University. Salem, Oreg.

PNC    Archives of the Pacific Northwest Conference of the United Methodist Church. University of Puget Sound. Tacoma.

C    Canse Collection of Henry B. Brewer and Henry K. W. Perkins Papers. Washington State Historical Society. Tacoma.

DL    Daniel Lee Collection. Mss. 1211. Manuscripts Department. Regional Research Library. Oregon Historical Society. Portland.

Les    David Leslie Collection. Mss. 1216. Manuscripts Department. Regional Research Library. Oregon Historical Society. Portland.

WAC    Western Americana Collection. Beinecke Library, Yale University.


Babcock, Ira
     February 3, 1845 (PNC)

Brewer, Henry
     June 3, 1840 (C)
     August 14, 1840 (C)
     August 22, 1840 (C)

"Camp meetings" (WAC)
May 22, 1841 (C)
August 4, 1841 (C)
September 23, 1841 (C)
November 9, 1841 (C)
January 1, 1842 (C)
March 31, 1842 (C)
January 2, 1843 (C)
June 1, 1843 (C)
July 30, 1843 (C)
August 7, 1843 (C)
October 14, 1843 (C)
November 7, 1843 (C)
January 1, 1844 (C)
February 13, 1844 (C)
August 7, 1844 (AW)
September 24, 1844 (C)
September 26, 1844 (C)
October 27, 1844 (C)
April 29, 1845 (C)
January 27, 1846 (WAC)
February 25, 1846 (C)
January 1, 1847 (WAC)
March 11, 1847 (WAC)
April 26, 1847 (C)
October 6, 1847 (C)
December 7, 1848 (C)

Brewer, Laura
May 28, 1840 (C)
November 8, 1841 (C)
January 30, 1843 (C)
September 7, 1844 (C)
October 16, 1844 (C)
April 29, 1845 (C)
August 15, 1845 (C)
October 7, 1847 (C)

Gary, George
Diary (unpublished version), dated November 9, 1844, for the period July
25–November 7, 1844 (PNC)

November 5, 1844 (PNC)
May 22, 1846 (C)

Lee, Daniel
"Notebook" (March–April 1838) (DL)
December 25, 1839 (C)
January 15, 1840 (C)
March 2, 1840 (C)
July 12, 1841 (AW)
"Dalles Journal" (January 1–May 12, 1843) (OIC)
April 13, 1843 (WAC)
May 5, 1843 (PNC)
August 11, 1843 (C)
"Ten Years in Oregon," partial draft (OIC)

Lee, Jason
April 25, 1838 (DL)
March 15, 1841 (PNC)
August 10, 1842 (PNC)
March 27, 1843 (PNC)
March 30, 1843 (PNC)
August 1, 1843 (OIC)
August 12, 1843 (PNC)
Diary, October 7–14, 1843 (PNC)

Lee, Maria
"Private Journal," October 5, 1840–July 29, 1842 (DL)
February 25, 1843 (DL)

Leslie, David
March 24, 1838 (PNC)
August 10, 1841 (C)

Perkins, Elvira
July 17, 1836 (C)
December 29, 1836 (C)
November 22, 1837 (C)
May 11, 1838 (C)
December 23, 1838 (WAC)
February 15, 1839 (WAC)
June 1839 (WAC)

November 27, 1839 (WAC)
early 1843 (C)
October 4, 1843 (WAC)
February 8, 1844 (Les)
August 25, 1844 (C)
September 1, 1844 (C)
November 2, 1844 (C)
November 8, 1844 (WAC)
March 1845 (C)

Perkins, Henry
　　January 12, 1837 (C)
　　November 23, 1837 (C)
　　late September 1838 (C)
　　January 11, 1839, "An Account of a Visit 1839" [Willamette Revival]
　　　　(DL)
　　January 16, 1839 (C)
　　March 7, 1839 (WAC)
　　spring 1839 (C)
　　August 4, 1839 (C)
　　December 24, 1839 (C)
　　December 26, 1839 (C)
　　spring 1840 [reads "spring 1839"] (C)
　　June 2, 1840 (C)
　　July 11, 1840 (C)
　　September 1840 (C)
　　September 12, 1840 (C)
　　January 1, 1841 (AW)
　　July 12, 1841 (AW)
　　March 15, 1842 (PNC)
　　July 29, 1843 (PNC)
　　Journal, August 13-October 23, 1843, December 4, 1843-March 19,
　　　　1844 (PNC)
　　November 24, 1843 (C)
　　July 24, 1844 (PNC)
　　September 2, 1844 (C)
　　September 9, 1844 (PNC)
　　October 31, 1844 (C)
　　January 20, 1845 (PNC)
　　January 22, 1846 (C)

Waller, Alvan
  Diary, January 18-April 1841 (AW)
  Diary, July 25-September 12, 1844 (AW)
  April 26, 1845 (C)
  Diary, April 24-September 27, 1845 (AW)
  August 15, 1845 (PNC)
  April 27, 1846 (PNC)
  February 3, 1847 (PNC)

Whitman, Marcus
  March 26, 1844 (C)

Willson, William
  February 12, 1840 (C)

# Appendix 3
# Biographical Sketches

## Whites

### Anderson, Winslow

Also known as George Winslow (Bancroft 1886:275), he was one of the first African Americans in the Pacific Northwest. Anderson came from California with Ewing Young in 1834 (Tetlow 1969). At Wascopam he was "for a year employed in procuring lumber, overseeing three natives and one Owyhee, who were engaged in sawing boards" (D. Lee and Frost 1844: 162). Henry Perkins mentioned him in a letter of January 16, 1839 ("Love to Anderson. May the Lord convert his soul") (Canse Collection), and Elvira Perkins stated: "Our hired man, an American by birth, but not all White blood, appears to be deeply anxious about his spiritual welfare, and I hope we shall soon see him rejoicing in God" (letter of Feb. 15, 1839, Western Americana Collection).

Anderson was, of course, a free man, as there were no slaves among the strongly abolitionist missionary population of Oregon. After his year's service at Wascopam, he married a Clatsop woman and settled on Clackamas Prairie (Tetlow 1969). Here, in early 1843, Anderson had a contretemps with the Molala Indian Cockstock over a "stolen" horse (see chapter 8). On March 4, 1844, when Cockstock and a party of Indians descended upon Oregon City, there was a scuffle, two Whites were killed, and (according to Indian Agent Elijah White) "a mulatto man, named Winslow Anderson . . . despatched Cockstock by breaking in his skull with the barrel of his rifle" (Allen 1850:232).

Following the Cockstock Incident, Anderson disappears from the historical records. He may have moved to Clatsop, where one A. C. Winslow died in 1874 (Tetlow 1969).

### Babcock, Ira

Dr. Ira L. Babcock, a medical doctor from New York, arrived in Oregon on the *Lausanne* in late May 1840, as part of the Third (Great) Reinforcement. With the Brewers, he was initially assigned to Wascopam Mission, but circumstances intervened: Dr. Elijah White, who had been serving in the capacity of physician at Willamette Mission, left Oregon, and Jason Lee reassigned Babcock in his place.

While serving as doctor at Willamette, Babcock simultaneously played a crucial role in the development of government in Oregon. In 1841, as a result of confusion over the disposition of Ewing Young's estate, he was elected supreme judge, following New York state laws. He was the first chairman (1842) of the committee on the Oregon Institute. Babcock generally presided at the quasi-governmental meetings held in early 1843 and was selected as chairman of the famous Champoeg meeting of May 2, which voted in favor of forming a provisional government (Dobbs 1932:74–80).

Babcock was not present at the July 5 meeting at Champoeg, which adopted the Organic Laws, having retired to Hawaii because of his wife's ill health. He remained there until late April 1844, when he returned to Willamette and resumed his judicial duties, but not for long. George Gary, new superintendent of the Oregon Mission, having fired Jason Lee, found Babcock expendable also, and the doctor departed Oregon in November, with Henry and Elvira Perkins. He spent his last years in Ohio.

## Bailey, William

Dr. William J. Bailey was born in England in 1807 and came to California via ship in his twenties. In the summer of 1835 he traveled overland to Oregon, arriving at Willamette in July in, as observer Dr. John Townsend noted, a "most deplorable condition." His party of seven had been attacked by "Potameos" (Tututni?) Indians in southern Oregon, and three were killed. Bailey himself received numerous knife wounds and a particularly hideous tomahawk blow, "which entered the upper lip just below the nose, cutting entirely through both the upper and lower jaws and chin, and passing deep into the side of the neck, narrowly missing the large jugular vein" (Townsend 1978:218–21). The four survivors had walked from southern Oregon to Willamette Mission.

Most of Bailey's notoriety in later years resides in his marriage to Margaret Jewett, one of Perkins's shipmates on the *Peru* and author of Oregon's first "novel," *The Grains, or Passages in the Life of Ruth Rover* (1986, originally 1854), an autobiography disguised with pseudonyms. Margaret Jewett was, to put it mildly, a rigid and difficult individual, given to interpersonal misunderstandings, particularly with men. Bailey (Dr. Binney in *The Grains*) was, unfortunately, a notorious drinker. The tempestuous union lasted fifteen years, ending in divorce in 1854 (Bailey 1986:8). Bailey remarried. He died in 1876.

*Birnie, James*

James Birnie was a Scot from Aberdeen. He arrived in Oregon in 1817 and originally worked for the North West Company at Fort George. In 1824 he transferred to the Hudson's Bay Company and in 1829-30 was assigned by McLoughlin to head the temporary trading post at The Dalles. Between 1834 and 1837 he was stationed at the new Fort Simpson among the Tsimshian Indians of the Skeena River. His services were apparently valued by the company, even though Sir George Simpson gave him only a lukewarm evaluation in his "Character Book" ("Useful in the Columbia as he can make himself understood among several of the Tribes and knows the Country well; but not particularly active . . . very well paid for his Services") (Simpson 1975:202).

In 1837 he took over at Fort George. Birnie's letter of February 27, 1840, giving a Chinook census, is included in Perkins's "Wonderful Work of God. . . ." (Appendix 1, Doc. 3, chap. 5). Three months later Henry and Laura Brewer, on their arrival at Fort George, described Birnie as

> a Scotch gentleman in the employ of the H.B. Company. . . . Mr B's is the only white family residing here, he introduced us to a native wife and a very pretty family of children. Astoria consists one dwelling house made of plank, two or three out buildings, and an Indian lodge. [L. Brewer, letter of May 28, 1840, Canse Collection]

Henry Brewer added: "His wife is a half breed. They have seven children" (1986:57).

Joseph Frost and family, who also arrived with the 1840 Reinforcement, joined the Birnies on July 12; Solomon Smith, his Clatsop wife Celiast, and his family, late of French Prairie, arrived on August 9; and the Reverend William Kone arrived in the fall (Frost 1934:55, 57, 71). Although the Methodists soon departed, the Smiths and Birnies stayed. Birnie eventually settled at Cathlamet, where he was postmaster and ran a general store. He died on December 24, 1864.

*Brewer, Henry and Laura*

The Great Reinforcement of 1840 brought two valuable additions to the Wascopam staff, in the persons of Henry and Laura Brewer. The pair arrived at the mission on June 24 and did not leave until September 8, 1847, when Wascopam passed out of Methodist hands.

Henry Bridgman Brewer was about a year and a half older than Henry Perkins, with a birthdate of July 7, 1813. He was born in Wilbraham, Massachusetts, and attended Wilbraham Wesleyan Academy, where he met Laura Giddings. They married September 3, 1839 (Brewer 1986:10).

Henry had already volunteered to join the Oregon Mission by that time. In October the newlyweds left New York for an eight-month voyage to Oregon. When they arrived at Wascopam, Henry was two weeks short of his twenty-eighth birthday; Laura was probably twenty-three. Three children, Susan, Walter, and George, were born at Wascopam. After leaving Oregon the Brewers returned to Wilbraham. Laura died in 1853, Henry in 1886.

Henry Brewer's primary role at Wascopam was as farmer, although after the departures of Lee and Perkins he was forced to help Alvan Waller in his spiritual endeavors. George Gary's basically correct, though too-critical, assessment of Brewer follows:

> Bro Brewer, I judge, is an amiable man, very forbearing and accomodating in his disposition and habits; perhaps few could be found who would get along so pleasantly with the Indians as he does; but he will never be distinguished for thought and energy. [Gary, letter of May 22, 1846, Canse Collection]

Henry Perkins, for one, had great affection for the Brewers. It shows in his January 22, 1846, letter to them, written from Brewer's parents' home in Wilbraham, where Perkins was visiting, almost four months after his return to New England. In the letter, Perkins related to the Brewers what he had said about them to "Mother Brewer":

> I tell her "Bridgeman is just the man [for Oregon], that he is contented any where—that he gets along easy, and is doing some good . . . that he will probably stay his time out—that he has enough to eat and drink, and wear—needs grace more than any thing else. Is that right? . . . I tell her that [Laura] ought never to have gone to Oregon—that the country is not good enough for her—that God made her to adorn better society than she finds there. Is that right? [Canse Collection]

The Brewers' greatest legacy is their sizable correspondence from Oregon. Much of it has been published. Henry Brewer's "Log of the Lausanne" (1928), the most complete and readily accessible version of the eight-month sea voyage to Oregon, appeared in the *Oregon Historical Quarterly*, as did his journal of events at Wascopam through February 13, 1843 (edited by John Canse). Both were reprinted by Ye Galleon Press as *The Journal of Henry Bridgman Brewer* (1986), edited by Richard Seiber. *Sketches of Mission Life among the Indians of Oregon* (Mudge 1854), a collection of vignettes about life at Wascopam, was published the year after Laura's death, 1854. The author, Zachariah Mudge, edited the selections from the Brewers' papers. Although the Brewers are nowhere acknowledged in the text, the source is obvious. Originals of many of the "sketches" survive in the Canse Collection at the Washington State Historical Society in Tacoma.

The Reverend John Canse collected most of the Brewer correspondence, as well as the original "Log. . . ." and journal while at Willamette University in the 1920s. The bulk of those papers, originals as well as typescript copies, are maintained in the Canse Collection. They are a primary source for the present publication. The letters, mostly to relatives in New England, stretch from 1840 through 1847 and provide a thorough account of mission and temporal affairs in and around Wascopam. They are a good balance to the more religiously oriented papers of Perkins, Daniel Lee, and Alvan Waller. Laura Brewer, like her friend Elvira Perkins, was well educated and an astute observer. Her letters are generally better written and more informative than those of her husband.

## Carter, David, and Orpha Lankton

David Carter (1793-1849?), born in New York, lived in Indiana, Mississippi, and Missouri before becoming a Santa Fe trader and purchasing a large farm from the Indians near St. Paul. In 1836 he boarded a ship for South America, where he spent the next few years. He was in Honolulu when the Great Reinforcement arrived in May 1840 and was hired as carpenter for the Oregon Mission. Orpha Lankton (1806-1873), stewardess for the mission, was a member of the Reinforcement. They married February 16, 1841. Carter and his wife were at Wascopam by autumn 1840. He helped build both the barn and the meeting house mentioned by Perkins in his first *Christian Advocate and Journal* report. The couple left Wascopam in November 1841. Carter took his own life in 1849, and his wife remarried (Lockley 1923).

## Dutton, David

See Wright, Benjamin

## Fremont, John

Lieutenant John C. Fremont (1813-1890), the "pathfinder of the West," led three exploring expeditions in the 1840s to the Pacific Slope. The second, 1842-43, the longest and most important, was intended to complement Lieutenant Charles Wilkes's earlier (1841) expedition on the Pacific coast and strengthen the claim of the United States to that territory. Fremont had met the 1843 emigrant train in northern Colorado and then dipped south to explore the Great Salt Lake before picking up the wagon train's trail again in the upper Snake River valley (Nevins 1964:19-23). He was at Waiilatpu on October 24 and at Fort Nez Percés on the twenty-fifth and continued on horseback to Wascopam, arriving there November 4. Here Fremont left most of his party under the control of Kit Carson (who had joined him on the Arkansas River), and with six men he took an Indian canoe to Fort Vancouver to purchase supplies ("flour, peas, and tallow"). Accompanied by Peter Burnett and a few other emigrants, Fremont returned to Wascopam, arriving on November 18. Here he made plans for the return trip, and the Fremont party, augmented by horses and cattle purchased at Wascopam, departed on November 26 (Jackson and Spence 1970:556-77).

Fremont's later history was very colorful. In 1845 he led an expedition to explore the Great Basin, and in 1846 he was in California, where he supported the Bear Flag revolt and took Los Angeles for the Americans. Fremont's two months in early 1847 as civil governor of California led to a dispute and detention by Stephen Watts Kearny and culminated in his infamous court-martial, which was remitted by President Polk. He led two other exploring expeditions in the Southwest and settled on a large estate in the Sierras. Fremont was senator from California for six months in 1850-51 and the Republican nominee for president in 1856 (losing to James Buchanan). In 1861-62, during the Civil War, he was in charge of the Department of the West, in the late 1860s he was president of the Memphis and El Paso Railroad, and from 1878 through 1883 he was territorial governor of Arizona. He died in 1890 (A. Johnson and Malone 1931:19- 23).

## Frost, Joseph

Joseph Frost was born in 1806 in Rochester, New York. He arrived in Oregon in May 1840 on the *Lausanne,* part of the Great Reinforcement of fifty persons that had come together as a result of Jason Lee's 1838-39 visit to the East Coast. Frost was assigned to the mission station at Clatsop by Jason Lee in July, joined a few months later by the Reverend William Kone. Neither was happy with his station: Kone resigned within a year, and Frost left after three. He sailed for the East Coast with Daniel Lee, and the two coauthored, on their return, the important *Ten Years in Oregon* (1844), a narrative of their missionary experiences. Portions of Frost's journal at Clatsop, including the record of an exploratory venture down the Oregon coast in 1843, have been published in the *Oregon Historical Quarterly* (Frost 1934).

## George

George, the Hawaiian employed at Wascopam during the mission's first few years, may be the same as the "Kanaka" George Watson who was at Fort Vancouver between 1841 and 1843 (Kardas 1971:179). Virtually nothing else is known of him or of Rosa, the Hawaiian cook at Willamette mentioned by Perkins.

After its discovery by Captain Cook in 1788, the Kingdom of Hawaii played an important role in the fur trade, and numerous Hawaiians were employed in the Northwest (Quimby 1972). The Hudson's Bay Company, in particular, through Chief Factor McLoughlin, had several scores of them signed up at any given time. In 1842 McLoughlin requested that fifty be hired to take the places of Canadians who were leaving the company to take up farms at Willamette. More than twenty worked for various Protestant missions in the early 1840s (Duncan 1972:9- 12). Two excellent sources on Hawaiians in the early Pacific Northwest are Janice Duncan's *Minority without a Champion* (1972) and George Quimby's "Hawaiians in the Fur Trade . . ." (1972).

## Hines, Gustavus

The Reverend Gustavus Hines (1809-1873), born and raised in New York state, where he had been a circuit rider, arrived in Oregon in 1840, a member of the Great Reinforcement. He was originally assigned to a post on the Umpqua River, but when an exploratory venture showed that a mission was not feasible at that location, Hines remained at Willamette. Hines's star began to rise as Jason Lee's fell. In 1843 he was instrumental in founding the Oregon Institute (now Willamette University), and he presided at the first meeting of the Oregon Provisional Government. After Lee left, Hines helped George Gary close down the Oregon Mission. He was back in New York from 1845 until 1853, when he returned to Oregon, remaining until his death in 1873. He wrote about his experiences in *A Voyage Round the World: With a History of the Oregon Mission* (1850), and *Oregon and Its Institutions* (1868).

## Lawson, Peter

See Wright, Benjamin

## Lee, Daniel and Maria

Daniel Lee, Jason Lee's nephew and one of the two original ministers in the 1834 Oregon Mission, was selected to be co-missionary with Henry Perkins at Wascopam. For the first two years of the mission's life Daniel Lee and Henry and Elvira Perkins ran the mission by themselves. Daniel Lee was thirty-two when the mission began; Henry Perkins was twenty-three. Despite the difference in their ages, the two made a good team. After Jason Lee left for the States in April 1838, Daniel threw himself into the missionary effort. He was responsible for most of the downstream evangelization during the 1839-40 revival. After Jason's return and Daniel's marriage to Maria Ware in mid-1840, there was a decline in his efforts. His stated reason for leaving Oregon in 1843 was his wife's illness, but more important was the perceived lack of support from mission headquarters in the East. That underlying motive is very clear in Daniel's unpublished May 5, 1843, letter addressed to secretary Charles Pitman (Archives of the Pacific Northwest Conference).

Daniel Lee has not received the treatment he deserves from Oregon historians. The picture drawn by Frances Fuller Victor (Bancroft 1886:57-58) was apparently based upon the opinions of a few biased observers and simply will not bear close scrutiny.[1] That has been pointed out by Robert Loewenberg (1973, 1976a:88-94), who is one of the few to examine a respectable sample of Lee's writings and discuss his conclusions in print. The man, appearances aside, was no slouch, but earnest, intelligent, and possessed of a true missionary spirit.

Loewenberg cites, in particular, a letter by Daniel dated April 30, 1838, five days after Jason's letter of instruction to the Wascopam missionaries. It was obviously intended as a companion letter to the April 21 Henry Spalding-Marcus Whitman letter to the American Board of Commissioners for Foreign Missions (ABCFM) for reinforcements. Both letters were carried to the States by Jason Lee (Drury 1973, 1:286-92). Daniel's letter is a strong statement of his dedication to the Oregon Mission: "Oregon is ripe for the Sickle. . . . The time has come which demands something to be done on a grand Scale" (Loewenberg 1973:74). Daniel listed the personnel needs of an expanded Oregon Mission ("50 effective men"), estimated expenses and how they could be recouped through trade, and requested the total commitment of the missionary society. A strong statement.

The Reverend Harvey Hines, who was familiar with the writings of both Daniel Lee and Henry Perkins, described the two coworkers as follows:

> Mr. Lee was cool, deliberate, cautious and prudent though persistent and determined. Mr. Perkins was enthusiastic, hopeful, full of fiery zeal, and had intense spirituality. . . . Both were deeply and unwaveringly pious. . . . The superintendent [J. Lee] could not have found two men better adapted to such a work or more completely complemental [sic] of each other. [H. Hines 1899:121]

Daniel Lee is best known for his book *Ten Years in Oregon* (1844), written upon his return to the East with the Reverend Joseph Frost, formerly of the Methodist mission at Clatsop. Lee wrote all of the material dealing with Wascopam and most of the Willamette Mission section, the bulk of the book. A draft of much of Lee's portion, collected by Robert Gatke, is at Willamette University (Archives of the Oregon-Idaho Conference). Willamette also holds Lee's "Dalles Station Journal" (January 1 to May 12, 1843), as well as a few letters. Other letters are held by the Oregon Historical Society (Daniel Lee and Alvan Waller Collections), the Washington State Historical Society (Canse

Collection), Yale University (Western Americana Collection), and the University of Puget Sound (Archives of the Pacific Northwest Conference). The latter depository also holds Lee's semifinished "Vocabulary of the Dalles Indian Language" (1840).

After his departure from Oregon, Daniel Lee itinerated for a while in New England before moving to Illinois in the late forties and to Kansas in 1876 (A. Lee, "A Sketch of Daniel Lee Sent to the Wichita Eagle," Daniel Lee Collection). No one has yet attempted to bring all the Daniel Lee materials together or write an adequate biography of this important figure in the Oregon Mission.

*Lee, Jason*

Details of Jason Lee's life need not concern us here; they have been covered elsewhere. Of the many books on the subject, two are especially noteworthy: Cornelius Brosnan's *Jason Lee: Prophet of the New Oregon* (1932)— best for original source material—though it exaggerates Lee's historical contribution; and Robert Loewenberg's *Equality on the Oregon Frontier: Jason Lee and the Methodist Mission, 1834–43* (1976a), a thorough and objective analysis of the basic sources, though not easy to read. The two should be consulted in tandem. Both have been used for the following summary.

Important for our purposes here are a few basic statements about Lee in his role as superintendent of the Oregon Mission and, more specifically, his relationship to Wascopam Mission. As noted above, Lee's personal characteristics and role in Oregon history have been exaggerated ex post facto. Loewenberg quotes Bernard DeVoto as saying that Lee has become "a hard man to make out" (1976a:68). The most acute and succinct assessment of Lee by one of his contemporaries that this writer has encountered comes, surprisingly, from Margaret Smith (Perkins's shipmate to Oregon), whose perceptions of many people were tainted by personal bias. Her description of Lee is, by contrast, detached and straightforward. It points out characteristics that have been emphasized by more recent, dispassionate historians.

> The Rev. Jason Lee was a *good* man, and possessed the true missionary spirit, ardent and dauntless, but deficient in judgement. . . . His great forte was in talking. He could keep the whole body of people around him listening to his conversation and waiting for his nod, but could not set them to work or decide on any work for himself which gave him satisfaction. . . . He could not with a glance see what should be done and resolve it. . . . His mind was ever vacillating and fluctuating. . . . Mismanagement and waste both operated to the ruin of the enterprise. [Bailey 1986:137–38]

A fine person and a good man of the cloth, but a poor administrator. Loewenberg makes the same point and supports it with factual detail.

Jason Lee was present throughout the period of the Johnson-Perkins presence at Willamette Mission, so both knew him well. Elvira (Johnson) Perkins wrote two appreciative poems about him, apparently after his death in 1845. Shortly after Henry Perkins and Daniel Lee left to establish Wascopam Mission, in early April 1838, Jason Lee departed from Oregon on a trip to the East Coast that was to last over two years. During his absence David Leslie was appointed acting superintendent. It was during Leslie's tenure that Wascopam Mission became firmly established and the important revivals at Willamette and Wascopam took place. During that period of growth and prosperity Leslie, it might be noted, never visited Wascopam. Jason Lee, by contrast, was at the station on at least five occasions between 1838 and 1843, a total time of over two months.

Jason Lee married Anna Maria Pitman, one of the members of the First Reinforcement, on July 16, 1837; she died June 26, 1838, in childbirth at Willamette; Lee was remarried to Lucy Thompson July 28, 1839, in Vermont. He returned to Oregon in June 1840 with the fifty members of the Great (Third) Reinforcement. Buoyed with moral and material support from the East, the superintendent began a program of expansion, with stations at Clatsop, Nisqually, and Willamette Falls. Troubles with personnel and finances grew during 1841. On February 28, 1842, his daughter Lucy was born; on March 20 his second wife died. Lee was dismissed from his post in October 1843 and left Oregon in February 1844; he died March 12, 1845, at Stanstead, Ontario.

## Leslie, David

David Leslie, after his arrival in Oregon with the Second Reinforcement (Perkins's party) of 1837, became the father figure of the Oregon Mission. He was born in New Hampshire in 1797 and had been a minister since 1820 (Judson 1971:14). His wife Mary and three daughters (Satira, Mary, and Sarah) accompanied him to Oregon. His ties with Henry Perkins were close, and after Perkins's marriage to Elvira Johnson, the couple moved into the loft of the Leslies' home. Elvira stated that the elder couple were like "parents to us" (letter of Nov. 22, 1837, Canse Collection). When Henry first aired the possibility of returning to the East, in 1841, Leslie wrote him a stern admonitory note that, at least temporarily, seems to have put the younger man in his place (letter of Aug. 10, 1841, Canse Collection). In January 1842 Joseph Williams described Leslie as follows: "Although the old man is, in his own way, very stiff, and rigid, and self-conceited he was very kind and obliging, however to me" (1921:56). Margaret Jewett Bailey had difficulties with "Mr. Leland" (as she called him in *The Grains*) on the voyage to Oregon, though they were probably mostly of her own making.

David Leslie was, indeed, somewhat rigid. He, along with Alvan Waller, was a vocal proponent of the "civilize first, convert later" school. One of his first letters from Oregon was a plea for money to establish a "literary mission" that would teach the children of settlers (that is, his daughters) apart from the Indian children, whose "moral and physical contamination" he feared. Despite its overt motivation, that letter of March 24, 1838, has become known as the first formal request for an institution of higher learning in Oregon, and it started a process that would eventually lead to the establishment of Willamette University. Leslie's experiences in the Willamette Revival of 1838-39 convinced him that there was considerable hope for the salvation of Indian children; their elders, however, were another story ( "hard! hard!! subjects," as he put it).

Leslie's early years in Oregon were filled with personal tragedy. He barely escaped drowning in the August 1838 accident that claimed Elijah White's infant son. In December 1838 his house burned. On February 15, 1841, his first wife, Mary, died; two daughters drowned in the Willamette Falls tragedy of February 1, 1843; a third daughter, who accompanied him to Hawaii, died in September of that year (D. Lee and Frost 1844:333). Two other daughters survived. In 1844 Leslie remarried the former Adelia Judson Olley.

Leslie was acting superintendent of the Oregon Mission during Jason Lee's 1838-40 absence. During that period he played a role in the emerging Oregon political situation: he was named justice of the peace in 1839; in the same year he authored the second (Farnham) petition that requested the extension of United States dominion to Oregon territory. In 1841 he chaired two planning meetings for the provisional government and administered Ewing Young's estate. He visited Wascopam once, with Jason Lee, in the last week of April 1842 (Brewer 1986:73). Leslie was also involved in the beginnings of the Oregon Institute and was chairman of its board of trustees for nearly a quarter of a century. He was the first pastor of the Methodist Episcopal Church in Salem and the second at the Oregon City Church. He died in 1869 (Dobbs 1932:60-63).

## McKay, Thomas

There were several McKays in Oregon's early history. Thomas was a son of Alexander, who had traveled to the Pacific with Alexander MacKenzie in 1793 and was massacred by Vancouver Island Indians on the Tonquin in July 1811. His mother was the half-blood Cree Marguerite Wadin, who later married John McLoughlin, making the latter Tom's stepfather. Young Tom McKay was raised in Ontario but accompanied his father to the Columbia in 1811 as an employee of the North West Company.

Someone should make a movie (or better yet, a television miniseries) of
McKay's life between 1811 and his death in early 1850. He went from one
adventure to another and was intimately associated with much of the early
history of Oregon. Sir George Simpson's character book, written in 1832,
notes:

> [McKay] has always been employed on the most desperate service in the
> Columbia and the more desperate it is the better he likes it . . . quite a
> "blood hound" who must be kept under restraint. Possesses little
> judgement and a confirmed Liar, but a necessary evil at such a place as
> Vancouver; has not a particle of feeling or humanity in his composition.[2]
> [1975:222]

According to Henry Brewer, he

> was the terror of all the upper country Indians. In earlier days he had been
> sent, by the Hudson's Bay Company, to punish them for various
> misdemeanors. So energetically has [he] performed his commission, as
> the judge, jury, and sheriff, that his name, to the Indians, was associated
> with unerring retribution for all offenses against the white man. Though
> they feared, yet they all loved him, for he had a noble nature. [Mudge
> 1854:34]

To add to the color, Tom McKay looked the part: He limped as a result of a fall
from a horse. Frances Fuller Victor stated succinctly: "He was a tall very dark
man & strange" (Lavender 1968:265n).

David Lavender's short biography in Hafen's *The Mountain Men and the
Fur Trade of the Far West* (1968), on which the following paragraphs are
based, is the most comprehensive summary of McKay's life. Between 1812
and 1814 he was involved in various incidents, usually with Indians, on the
lower Columbia: at Champoeg, The Cascades, The Dalles, and the Yakima
valley, described with variable detail in the published works of Nor'westers
Robert Stuart, Alexander Henry, and Alexander Ross. Between 1815 and 1819
McKay was in the Red River country, where he fought on the side of the North
West Company and the Métis against the Hudson's Bay Company. By 1819
he was back on the Columbia, where he established two posts, in the Willamette Valley and at Fort Umpqua, on the river of that name. In 1824, despite his
role in the Red River wars, he transferred to the Hudson's Bay Company,
helped select the site of Fort Vancouver, and surveyed Puget Sound. Between
1826 and 1828 he was with Peter Skene Ogden in the Snake Country; in 1829
he accompanied Alexander McLeod to California.

Throughout his long tenure with the Hudson's Bay Company Tom McKay
never rose above the position of clerk. In 1832 he was placed in control of a

company farm at Scappoose, but within a year he had resettled at Champoeg. By 1834 he was off again, that time as an Indian trader in the Snake country, where he built Fort Boise (in competition with American Nathaniel Wyeth's Fort Hall). He stayed in the area through 1838.

In the interior, in 1834, McKay had his first encounter with Jason Lee, whom he guided all the way from Fort Hall to Vancouver, he helped him select the site of Willamette Mission. There were other encounters during those years as well. As Lavender states:

> He enjoyed drinking bouts with traders Bonneville and Wyeth, was generous to the Lees, impressed Townsend with his ability to mold a roughneck crew into an efficient work force, carried Narcissa Whitman's trunk for her, and leaped to the assistance of Eliza Spalding when she tumbled from her horse with one foot hung up in a stirrup. [1968:273]

By December 1838 McKay was back at Vancouver, where he led the abortive boat trip of the Perkinses back to Wascopam. Most of 1839 was apparently spent at Champoeg. In 1840 he drove more than 3,600 sheep and 661 cattle from California to Nisqually for the Hudson's Bay Company. On September 4, 1841, the members of Wilkes's overland expedition to California met and breakfasted with him at his Champoeg farm. Of that encounter, George Colvocoresses recalled:

> Mr. McKoy [is] one of the most noted individuals in this part of the country. Among the trappers, he is the hero of many a tale—and he entertained us during our stay with an account of several of his adventures with the Indians, which certainly showed him to be a man of great nerve and shrewdness. He is about forty years of age, tall, and straight, and has a countenance expressive of great firmness and daring of character. His house stands on the margin of a small stream, and answers both for a dwelling and a gristmill. [1852:274-75]

In November 1842 McKay accompanied Elijah White on his trip to the interior to introduce his code of laws to the Nez Perces (Brewer's description, above, arises from that incident).

Tom McKay had three wives and several children. In the early 1820s he married Concomly's daughter Timmee; by her he had three boys and two girls. Between 1834 and 1838, in the interior, with his first wife dead, he took up with a Nez Perce woman. On the last day of 1838, back in the west, he married Isabelle Montour.

McKay's three sons by Timmee are the best known of his offspring. They joined Jason Lee at Fort Hall in June 1838 and were taken to the East Coast. John and Alex spent some time at Wilbraham Academy, and William was enrolled at Fairfield College in upstate New York, where he earned a medical degree. In later years William was a physician at the Warm Springs and Umatilla reservations and maintained a practice in Pendleton (*Oregonian,* Jan. 3, 1893).

Tom McKay's last few years of life were also eventful. In February 1848 he led a group of volunteers in the Cayuse War. In September he guided a group of fifty wagons to California. He died at Scappoose sometime early in 1850.

## McLoughlin, John

Something should be said about the character and influence of Dr. John McLoughlin, chief factor at Fort Vancouver. A great deal has been written about this man, who for upwards of a quarter century was the most powerful non-Indian in the entire Pacific Northwest. Prior to 1843 his relationship with the Methodists of the Oregon Mission was positive. Although he was a nominal Catholic, McLoughlin gave moral and material support to capable men of the cloth, regardless of denomination. Catholics, Presbyterians, Anglicans, Methodists—all were welcome at Fort Vancouver. On an individual basis, however, there were occasional problems. McLoughlin did not suffer incompetents nor narrow-minded individuals at all well. Hence his well-known difficulties with the Reverends Herbert Beaver (Anglican) and Alvan Waller (Methodist), both rigid and doctrinaire men.

The three original members of the Wascopam Mission (Henry Perkins, Daniel Lee, Henry Brewer) all benefited from McLoughlin's hospitality and thought highly of him. Daniel Lee noted the "politeness and kind attention" that the chief factor gave him and his uncle Jason on their 1834 arrival in Oregon (D. Lee and Frost 1844:124). When illness prompted Daniel Lee to take a year's rest in Hawaii, McLoughlin provided free passage (D. Lee and Frost 1844:134). McLoughlin encouraged all missionary efforts at education; in addition to temporarily employing Cyrus Shepard as teacher at the fort and sending some fort children to Willamette to be educated, in March 1836 he and six other fort officials contributed twenty-six British pounds to the fledgling mission school (Carey, ed., 1922:243). He visited Wascopam shortly after its founding on March 24, 1838 (Appendix 1, Doc. 1), and in February 1840 the doctor gave forty-four dollars to Wascopam Mission (Appendix 1, Doc. 3). There were many other small favors of this kind. The members of the Great (1840) Reinforcement were treated with considerable hospitality at the fort. Following his arrival at Vancouver in June 1840, Henry Brewer stated, "I could say much of the kindness of Dr. McLoughlin and other gentlemen of this fort" (letter of June 3, 1840, Canse Collection). The Methodist historian Wade Barclay, summarizing the literature on that relationship, called McLoughlin "a generous benefactor of the Methodist mission" (1950:208). Henry Perkins's strong positive feelings about the chief factor surfaced in 1843 when he found out about the underhanded dealings of the Reverends Waller and Gary concerning McLoughlin's land claim at Oregon City. Gary's shoddy treatment of McLoughlin was the proximate reason for Perkins's resignation from the Oregon Mission (H. Perkins, letter of July 24, 1844, Archives of the Pacific Northwest Conference).

## Spalding, Henry

Henry Spalding (1803–1874), a Presbyterian minister, was born in New York and educated at Case Western College in Cleveland. He and his wife Eliza arrived with Marcus and Narcissa Whitman in Oregon in September 1836. Their mission, Lapwai, was located in the heart of Nez Perce territory, on the middle reaches of the Snake and Salmon Rivers. Spalding, like Perkins, learned the local native language (Nez Perce, in Spalding's case) and authored a vocabulary, grammar, and various biblical translations. It was perhaps those linguistic efforts, plus the receptiveness of Nez Perce culture to new ideas (they had incorporated a large complex of Plains culture traits in the century before the arrival of the missionaries) that explain the apparent success of Spalding in converting those people. Lapwai, as noted above (chap. 10) was the site of the first printing press in the Northwest. After the Whitman Massacre in November 1847, Spalding (who barely escaped being killed himself) and his wife abandoned the mission and moved to the Willamette Valley. In 1862 he returned to Lapwai and remained there until his death in 1874 (Drury 1958:341–53). Clifford Drury's 1958 *The Diaries and Letters of Henry H. Spalding and Asa Bowen Smith Relating to the Nez Perce Mission 1838–1842* is a comprehensive study of Spalding's career.

## White, Elijah

Elijah White, a physician from upstate New York, arrived in Oregon in late May 1837 on the *Diana*, one of the thirteen-member First Reinforcement, which also included Elvira Johnson (later Perkins). Following the return of Jason Lee with the Great Reinforcement of 1840, a battle of words broke out between Lee and White that ended in White's separation from the mission and return to the East in early 1841, where he filed complaints against Lee with the missionary board (see Robert Loewenberg's "Elijah White vs. Jason Lee: a Tale of Hard Times" [1972] for details). While in Washington, White was appointed sub-Indian agent for Oregon by the secretary of war (despite the fact that Oregon was still jointly occupied with Britain). He subsequently led the second overland immigration, numbering 114, and reappeared on the Willamette in September 1842.

White was a contentious sort and somewhat of a flimflammer. His attempts to gain influence through manipulation sometimes succeeded but more often backfired. He caused dissension in the Oregon Mission and planted seeds in the East that led to Jason Lee's dismissal as superintendent. His dubious appointment as Indian agent may have given him a degree of stature in the Willamette community, but his heavy-handed treatment of the interior Indians created a simmering confusion and resentment that contributed to the ensuing Indian wars.

It was in his capacity as Indian agent that White had his most significant interaction with Henry Perkins. Details of his two 1842–43 trips to the interior to parley with the Indians are given in chapter 8.

With his federal appointment, White was also, ipso facto, the only U.S. government official in Oregon during the early 1840s. He became an instrumental member of the legislative committee of the Oregon Provisional Government and carried the Memorial of 1845 to the U.S. Congress.

White's *Ten Years in Oregon* (Allen 1850) (a separate work from D. Lee and Frost's volume of the same name) summarizes many of his activities. Its content, as might be expected, is slanted in his favor and should be read in tandem with other works. He returned to Oregon by 1850 but eventually settled in San Francisco, where he was interviewed by H. H. Bancroft in 1878. At that time, in his early seventies, Bancroft found him "exceedingly affable . . . and well preserved, though how much of him was padding, and what was the true color of his well-dyed hair and whiskers, I cannot say" (1886:291n).

## Whitman, Marcus and Narcissa

Marcus Whitman first entered Northwest history in 1835, when, as a young physician, he traveled with Samuel Parker of the American Board of Commissioners for Foreign Missions (ABCFM) and his party as far as the Green River rendezvous (see Parker's 1838 *Journal of an Exploring Tour* and Whitman's 1835 "Diary" in Hulbert and Hulburt 1936).

Parker deemed the Columbia ripe for missionaries, and in 1836 Whitman, his new bride Narcissa, Henry and Eliza Spalding, and William Gray set off overland for Oregon. After visiting Forts Nez Percés and Vancouver, Whitman and Spalding traveled to the interior, where they established mission stations at Waiilatpu and Lapwai (among the Cayuses and Nez Perces, respectively).

Waiilatpu was geographically close to Wascopam, and the Whitmans and Perkinses were friendly. They had similar histories prior to coming to Oregon. Both Marcus and Narcissa were native New Yorkers, with what Drury, their biographer, calls a "Presbygational" (Presbyterian-Congregational) background (Drury 1973: 1, 72). Neither had any formal religious training: Marcus was a medical doctor, Narcissa a teacher. Both were inspired to become missionaries to Oregon after hearing the Reverend Parker speak on the "Macedonian Call" on two separate occasions in November 1834. They were engaged before Marcus departed for the West in 1835 and married before they began their overland trek to Oregon in 1836. Henry Perkins made several visits to Waiilatpu, and the Wascopam and ABCFM missionaries sent a joint letter to the United States with Jason Lee in 1838.

The mission wives maintained a healthy correspondence. For the five years the Perkinses were at Wascopam, there are twenty-five extant letters from Narcissa, nine to Elvira Perkins and sixteen to Laura Brewer.

Elvira Perkins initiated the correspondence on July 4, 1838. The tie between her and Narcissa Whitman became quite strong after the drowning death of the Whitmans' daughter Alice, on June 23, 1839. Elvira had written a letter to Narcissa inquiring about Alice shortly before the accident, and Narcissa unloaded her grief to Elvira in a long letter dated June 25. Elvira in turn wrote a letter of condolence, and Henry watched over Narcissa in late July during one of Marcus's absences. Narcissa called Elvira's second letter a "cordial to my afflicted heart" and Henry's presence "like an angel's visit" (N. Whitman 1894:126). Thus it is not at all surprising that Narcissa should accept the Perkinses' invitation to stay for the winter of 1842–43 with them.

The major reason for Narcissa's stay was the absence of her husband, as Perkins says, in "Boston, on business for the Presbyterian Mission" (journal entry for Oct. 7, 1843, Archives of the Pacific Northwest Conference). The real reasons for Marcus Whitman's visit to the States have never been clear. Clifford Drury, who is the acknowledged expert on the topic, suggests that there were three interrelated purposes: to ensure the continued financial and moral support of the American Board of Commissioners for Foreign Missions for the establishments on the Columbia Plateau, to promote immigration to the Northwest, and to present the case of the Protestant missionaries against the "Catholic threat" to the leaders of the Presbyterian church (1973, 1:466–72). Apparently to those ends, Whitman visited Boston (the American Board headquarters), New York (where he talked with Horace Greeley and visited the Methodist Mission Society headquarters), and Washington, D.C. (where he is reputed to have had an audience with the secretaries of war and state and President Tyler) (1973, 2: chap. 18). It is probable that the Indian "excitement" of the spring of 1842 had also influenced his decision to make his famous trip (though one wonders why he left Narcissa alone and unprotected at Waiilatpu). On his return to Oregon he penned a "proposed bill" to Congress, which would have established a string of military posts from the Missouri along the Oregon Trail all the way to the Pacific Ocean (Drury, 2:395–401).

Marcus left Waiilatpu October 3. On the sixth an Indian attempted to break into the mission house, and by the eleventh Narcissa was at Fort Nez Percés.

Her stay at Wascopam commenced on October 29; shortly afterward the mill at Waiilatpu was burned. According to an undated letter of Elvira Perkins:

> Mrs. Whitman spent the winter with us. She has occupied the little room that was finished off last spring in the addition to our part of the house. . . . Her health is poor, and her nervous system much debilitated, and in her afflicted, lonely state, it is a great comfort for her to be with us. She has two half-breed children with her, which with mine make quite a family, though she visits days part of the time with Mrs. Lee and Mrs. Brewer. She is an active energetic business woman when in health, and calculated to exert influence wherever she moves. [E. Perkins, letter of early 1843, Canse Collection]

Narcissa's bad health consisted of gynecological problems, for which she would be treated by Dr. Forbes Barclay at Vancouver; failing eyesight, which forced her to wear eyeglasses that gave her headaches; and depression, brought on by her health and Marcus's absence. In her letter of February 7, 1843, she stated: "I have too many gloomy and depressing hours, and evil forebodings" (1893:176).

Despite those trials, Narcissa appears to have been well liked. Henry Brewer called her "a very agreeable friend & a good christian" (letter of Jan. 2, 1843, Canse Collection); Daniel Lee said she "endeared herself greatly to us" (D. Lee and Frost 1844:259). Narcissa also spoke well of her hosts: "I am spending a very happy winter here . . . the society and prayers of such a company of living and growing Christians is very refreshing to me" (N. Whitman 1893:172).

Henry Perkins's assessment of Narcissa, in a letter to her sister written two years after the Whitman Massacre (Oct. 19, 1849), is less complimentary than those of Brewer or Lee. He saw her as a "highly gifted, polished American lady," out of her "proper sphere," who loved the "company" of others but was "considered haughty" by the natives. Perkins was harder on Marcus Whitman, whom he found distant, toward both his wife and the Indians. Drury, who has printed Perkins's letter in full, disputes his evaluation of Mrs. Whitman, stating that Perkins knew her only in a time and place when she was both lonely and ill and not in her normal character (1973, 2:36, 392–94).

After her departure from Wascopam, Narcissa stayed for six weeks at Waiilatpu and then proceeded to the lower country, where she spent time at Vancouver and Willamette Falls and saw the Daniel Lees off to the States at Clatsop. Her return inland with Jason Lee is documented in Perkins's journal entry for October 7, 1843 (Appendix 1, Doc. 5). She remained at Wascopam until Marcus, back from the East, picked her up on the twenty-seventh.

The definitive study of the lives of the Whitmans is Clifford Drury's *Marcus and Narcissa Whitman and the Opening of Old Oregon* (1973). The most complete collection of Marcus's writings is Archer Hulbert and Dorothy Hulbert's three-volume *Marcus Whitman, Crusader* (1936, 1938, 1941). Narcissa's 1836 overland diary has been printed in Drury's *First White Women over the Rockies*, vol. 1; several of her letters appear in the 1891 and 1893 *Transactions . . . of the Oregon Pioneer Association.*

## Wright, Benjamin

Ben Wright, the one visitor of 1839 who had the greatest impact on Wascopam Mission, is also the one about whom the least is known. That historical lacuna is particularly regrettable, as Wright was an important—indeed catalytic—agent in the Great Revival of 1839–40.

William Gray says that Benjamin Wright came west with the independent Congregationalist missionary John Griffin, who had intended to start a mission among the Snake Indians. That mission never got started, Griffin proceeded to the Tualatin Valley, and Wright, with his friends David Dutton and Peter Lawson, ended up at Wascopam (1870:186). Perkins's "Wonderful Work of God. . . ." contains more primary information on Wright than any other source, but even it is vague on the man's background.

There is a bit more detail in the "Narration" of Robert Shortess, another member—along with Sydney Smith and Thomas Farnham—of the "Peoria Party" of 1839 immigrants. Shortess met Wright in March 1840.

> Ben Wright had, according to his own story, once been a Methodist itinerant in missions, but, weary of the profession, had gone to Texas and engaged in trade. Being threatened with indictment for selling liquor to negroes and Indians, he left in haste and . . . crossed the plains . . . to Oregon, in 1839. [1955:112]

Daniel Lee's manuscript letter of January 15, 1840 (Canse Collection), summarizes some of Wright's activities in the preceding week, when both men were evangelizing at Fort Vancouver. Daily (at least between the eleventh and thirteenth), while Lee preached to the "Clicitats," Wright gave evening sermons to the company's employees. The sermons apparently had some impact. Lee reported, "He preached with power. They [the Hudson's Bay Company's men] are beginning to be alarmed" (D. Lee, letter of Jan. 15, 1840, Canse Collection). On January 16 (according to Lee; Perkins's January 21 is probably incorrect) Wright departed for Willamette. Here again we may assume his catalytic influence was felt. He may well have been present at the fiery January 31 service that resulted in the reawakening of William Willson (see his February 12, 1840, letter to Perkins, Canse Collection).

After some time at Willamette (how long is unknown) Wright returned to Wascopam, where he and Dutton were met by Shortess in mid-March. According to the latter, "He and Dutton were now buying horses from the Indians to drive to Willamette for sale" (Shortess 1955:112). In early April all three men left Wascopam and traveled downstream. The party got into a fracas with Indians over horses across from Claticut, continued downstream on the south side, crossed at The Cascades and proceeded to Vancouver, ferried to Sauvie Island with Cassino (the well-known chief of the Vancouver-area Chinookans), traveled south to the Pudding River, and ended up at the ranch of Thomas Hubbard and Calvin Tibbets. Here they parted company, Shortess remaining while "Wright and Dutton went on . . . to the Methodist Mission" (Shortess 1955:114). Shortess later included Wright, Dutton, and Lawson on a list of six who had come to Oregon in 1839 but stayed less than a year (1955:116). Perkins's cryptic statement in his 1844 journal ("A Wright, we have long heard say is no more" [entry for Feb. 8, Archives of the Pacific Northwest Conference]) may be a reference to Wright's ultimate fate.

An interesting aside to the Wright episode, which may reveal something else about his earlier history, is his labeling of the Wascopam Methodists as "nothing but Congregationalists." Perkins took that to mean that he considered the missionaries "formalists." Methodists, Baptists, and Presbyterians were all camp-going peoples; Congregationalists, with a Puritan heritage, were not. Wright, by his own statement, was an ex-circuit rider who "had been in successive revivals, fourteen years." Yet he had traveled west, as noted above, with the Congregational minister John Griffin. That party had broken up, for unrecorded reasons. There is a good possibility that doctrinal differences contributed to the split.

Whatever Wright's true genesis, his effect on the missionary effort is obvious. He was apparently a very effective preacher who spoke in the "old fashioned Methodist style"; listeners were both "stirred" and "alarmed." He seems to have been the catalyst that sparked the Great Revival or "Wonderful Work of God" of 1839–40. And his behavior appears to have led directly to Henry Perkins's own "day of salvation": October 28, 1839.


# Indians


## Bear-Cap

"Bear-Cap," the slave owner who argued with Henry Perkins in 1843, is not otherwise mentioned in the missionary documents. But his name does reappear twelve years later, in the June 1855 Warm Springs treaty negotiations, where he was called "a prominent old man of the Wasco tribe." He spoke in favor of signing the treaty and against any Wascos removing to Yakama (Pitt 1915).

## Canacissa

Canacissa is mentioned several times in the Wascopam documents. He seems to have moved very quickly to establish ties with the missionaries. It is surprising to see him take so readily to the spade, as digging was an activity normally associated with women. On the first Sunday at Wascopam, it was Canacissa who translated the sermon from Jargon into Chinookan. Ten days later he accompanied the missionaries to The Dalles, where he showed them his fishing station.

Canacissa is not mentioned again until May 1843, when he provided eight horses for Elijah White's interior trip. As Gustavus Hines described it, the old man attempted to extort an extra blanket in payment and insisted upon accompanying the party upstream, but he was denied by White (1850:158). During the dysentery epidemic of 1844, Elvira Perkins reported: "Canacissa's son was taken dangerously ill. . . . Mr. P. attended upon him constantly till he got better and since we have had him almost as a boarder" (letter of Sept. 1, 1844, Canse Collection). A year later Laura Brewer reported that "Ticicash, Carnicissa's son" had died of dysentery, one of the few cases during 1845 (letter of Aug. 15, 1845, Canse Collection).

## Celest

See Seletsa

## Chinook, Billy

Billy Chinook was one of the three local Indians who joined Fremont's party in 1843. Of the other two, one was employed, in Fremont's words, "as a guide to the Tlamath lake . . . [he] had been there, and bore the marks of several wounds he had received from some of the Indians in the territory" (Jackson and Spence 1970:576). That is undoubtedly the Indian whose story was told in the entry for August 19, named (by Brewer) Skakaps (Mudge 1854:16). Fremont's names for the two guides were "White Crane" and "Stiletsi" (Seletsa?) (Jackson and Spence 1970:578).

Fremont describes the third Indian as follows:

> At the request of Mr. Perkins, a Chinook Indian, a lad of nineteen, who was extremely desirous to "see the whites," and make some acquaintance with our institutions, was received into the party, under my special charge, with the understanding that I would again return him to his friends. He had lived for some time in the household of Mr. Perkins, and

spoke a few words of the English Language. [Jackson and Spence 1970: 577]

Brewer (Mudge 1854:109-10) supplies some additional information. The boy was named "William M'Kendree" (after a prominent Methodist minister) and was an orphan who had resided at the mission since shortly after its establishment. He had experienced a "change of heart" at the Wascopam Revival of 1839-40.

Although winter was fast approaching, Fremont was determined to explore the high lake country of the Great Basin. Freezing weather prompted the two Indian guides to turn back at White River, only twenty-five miles south of Wascopam. William (by now known as William Perkins or William Chinook) held on but began to have second thoughts in the deep snow of the rugged area near Mono Lake (now on the California-Nevada border). Fremont reported:

> Our Chinook . . . believed our situation hopeless, covered his head with his blanket, and began to weep and lament. "I wanted to see the whites," said he; "I came away from my own people to see the whites, and I wouldn't care to die among them; but here"—and he looked around into the cold night and gloomy forest, and drawing his blanket over his head, began again to lament. [Jackson and Spence 1970:630]

Fremont's party eventually crossed the Sierras, spent some time at Sutter's Fort, and then returned east by way of the San Joaquin Valley, the Mohave Desert, and Utah. In the fall of 1844 Fremont took William to the East Coast. Here:

> Our Chinook Indian had his wish to see the whites fully gratified. He accompanied me to Washington, and after remaining several months at the Columbia college, was sent by the Indian department to Philadelphia where, among other things, he learned to read and write well, and speak the English language with some fluency. [Jackson and Spence 1970:725]

Scattered documents recount William's story after 1844. In May 1845, he was under a doctor's care in Philadelphia with "a severe attack of indisposition" and was "anxious about his return home" (letter of May 5, 1945, Jackson and Spence 1970:417). Fremont's third expedition started west in June, and William was with it. Brewer reports: "He returned with Colonel Fremont to California, was with him during the war in that region, and acquitted himself much to the satisfaction of his employer" (Mudge 1854:113). The war in question, of course, was the Bear Flag Revolt, in which Fremont played a large part. The last mention of William in the Fremont papers states that he "was discharged as a voyageur at Johnson's ranch, Upper California, 6/6/47"

(Jackson and Spence 1970:388n). Here, according to Brewer, "he married a Spanish woman." His whereabouts for the next four years, the unsettled period of the Cayuse wars, are unknown.

By 1851, however, William had returned to Wascopam and with a "large herd" of California cattle had a home on Mill Creek (Clark and Clark 1978: 156n). In November 1853 Billy Chinook wrote a letter to Joel Palmer, then superintendent of Indian affairs for Oregon territory, requesting help in protecting Indian land near The Dalles from White encroachment (O'Donnell 1991). The 1855 "Treaty with the tribes of Middle Oregon" lists him as one of the three principal chiefs of the "Dalles band of Wascoes." He was an Indian Scout during the 1866–67 Snake war (Clark and Clark 1978:320). And finally, in 1870, when William was in his midforties, he is mentioned again, in Myron Eells's *History of the Indian Missions on the Pacific Coast. . . .*:

> Billy Chinook, or rather W. C. Parker [*sic:* probably Perkins], who received instruction at the Dalles more than thirty-five years ago is an elder in the church, and always takes his Testament to the Agency, and has some one hear him read and expound the lesson to him. . . . In 1870, Billy Chinook and John Mission had not forgotten the instruction which they had received at the Dalles, and acknowledged the vows then taken, and were taking a leading part in the progress of their tribe. [1882:106, 61]

William Chinook died December 9, 1890. Lake Billy Chinook, a reservoir on the Deschutes River, preserves the name of that prominent graduate of Wascopam Mission (Clark and Clark 1978).

## Hanecunewitt

The wood chopper who was given a shirt by Perkins in early April 1838 is not again mentioned in the Mission records.

## Hedding, Elijah

Elijah Hedding (To–a yah–nu), a son of the Walla Walla chief Piupiumaks-maks, was admitted to the Willamette Mission school on August 13, 1836. With the possible exception of William Brooks, the Chinook boy who traveled east with Jason Lee, he was the most notable of the school's alumni.

Elijah was named after the bishop of the Methodist Episcopal Church (1780–1852) who had appointed the Lees to the Oregon Mission. Elijah arrived at the mission with a second Walla Walla, To–man–as–ulta, dubbed "Osman Baker" (Carey 1922:265). The mission record book entry reads: "This day two chiefs from Walla–walla came to the mission house with two boys whom they wish to leave to be educated, of course their request is not refused"

(Carey 1922:245). As the Mission Record Book notes (Santee 1933:165), the friendly Walla Walla chief encountered by the Lees in autumn 1834 was probably Piupiumaksmaks, Elijah's father.

In early 1839, following the Willamette Revival, there are two probable references to Elijah in the mission documents. Both indicate that he was taking his religious lessons seriously. The first, undated, is from Margaret Smith. Although the identification of that passage with Elijah is not definite (given the reference to Whitman), the Indian's version of the death and resurrection is instructive in itself.

> Conversed with a young Indian from Walla Walla, who can speak English tolerably well, having been for some time under the instruction of Dr. Whitman. He has, since his stay among us, manifested a disposition to absent himself from the lodges of his people and spending the time in our houses, seeking instruction in reading, etc. He has been singing me some of the hymns he has learned and telling me what he knows about the bible. He says that Jesus Christ came here, and wicked men made holes in his hands, and feet, and sides, and he died and was put in the ground—came up again and went to heaven—and that by-and-bye he will come here again, blow a trumpet and all the people will come to him—to the good he will say, "come, come"—but to the bad he will say, "go away." Also, if good people wish to speak to him he will turn his ear and listen, but if bad people speak to him he will stop his ears. Repeating the names of the apostles he said Judas was bad and put something around his neck and he died. He also spoke of the Holy spirit, and of angels, but I could not comprehend what he wished to convey concerning them. I was much gratified in witnessing this proof of the capacity of these Indians to learn. [Bailey 1986:145-46]

The second reference is from Perkins, via Cyrus Shepard:

> Elijah Hedding . . . came the other day to Br Shepard,—told him that his heart had "come a little bad," for in doing a sum, he was some puzzled, & had been impatient & spoken a bad word. After telling his story, he went to his chamber, & fell upon his knees, where he continued for an hour. An example worthy of imitation, truly. [H. Perkins, letter of Mar. 7, 1839, Western Americana Collection]

Susan Shepard spoke of that incident also. By her account, Elijah "got angry with his enumeration table, and called it a dog" (Mudge 1848:184).

By 1842, Elijah had returned home. He is first mentioned by Joseph Williams, in late April, among a camp of "about twenty" Indians at the mouth of the Umatilla:

I sung and prayed with them, and exhorted them to turn to the Lord and seek for religion. A young Indian by the name of Elijah, a son of one of the chiefs, who could talk some English, had obtained religion, and was my interpreter. He exhorted them some himself. [1921:70]

On July 13, at Wascopam, Henry Brewer noted, "Elijah and his company arrived from Willamette" (1986:75), bringing "a few head of cattle" with him (Mudge 1854:61). A week later "Elijah's cousin . . . stole a two-year-old heifer" (Mudge 1854:61).

In fall 1842 Elijah White made his ill-starred trip to the interior, which resulted in confusion and upset among the Indians. The Wascopam missionaries began to worry about Elijah Hedding. An undated letter (probably early 1843, Canse Collection) from Elvira Perkins states:

It is thought if Elijah does well, he will succeed his father, or take his place in three or four years. He is now with his people, and what influence they will exert upon him we do not know, but have some fears it will not be of the best kind, as he is connected with the principal Kayuse chiefs, who you know, are not very well disposed to the whites.

Narcissa Whitman, then resident at Wascopam, knew from firsthand experience what was going on among the Cayuses and the Walla Wallas and must have conveyed that information to her hosts. Elvira Perkins's letter names "Towente [Tawatoy?] . . . Elijah's uncle . . . one of the ringleaders . . . making preparations for fighting with the Americans." In early February Piupiumaksmaks was at Wascopam, questioning Jason Lee about White's laws. With him, apparently, was his son. Elijah stayed for a while, "to pursue still further his English education," as Brewer put it. On Sunday, February 12, Jason Lee, about to leave the mission after a two-week stay, states, "Elijah Hedding was with us and seemed anxious to return to the Lord, from whom he has been wandering for some time past" (letter of Mar. 27, 1843, Archives of the Pacific Northwest Conference). According to Brewer:

Soon after his arrival at the Dalles, a camp-meeting was held in the vicinity. Elijah attended during the day, and returned to the mission house at night, to perform the little domestic business of the evening. Returning one night with a fellow Indian, the Spirit of God met him, in great power, by the way. So deep was his conviction, that he returned to the camp ground, craving the prayers of God's people. Earnest and believing supplication was offered in his behalf. The conflict was not long Victory was soon announced in favor of the burdened heart. Elijah arose from his knees, exclaiming, with rapture, "I am rich,—I am rich!" [Mudge 1854: 61]

Following the camp meeting, Elijah was married in a Christian ceremony to the Wasco Lahart, another convert. The marriage did not survive Elijah's impending return to the interior, however, and because of "the hatred existing against her people," according to Brewer, his wife was driven back to Wascopam (Mudge 1854:61). In the May following, White made his second, corrective visit to the interior, and Perkins had his meeting with Tawatoy, Piupiumaksmaks, and Elijah at their camping site (see related biographical sketches).

After spring 1843 there is a gap of more than fifteen months in the record. By autumn 1844, however, Elijah, his father, Tawatoy, some Nez Perces, and perhaps even Spokan Garry, with a multiethnic task force of more than thirty-six men, were in the Sacramento Valley, in the vicinity of Sutter's Fort. The details of what happened next are controversial, but the upshot is that Elijah was shot to death by an American, probably about the same time that Henry Perkins was leaving Oregon on the *Peru*. The remainder of the California party was back home by January 1845, and the news spread rapidly. That incident cast a pall over Indian-White relations on the Plateau that has never been fully forgotten or forgiven.

There are a number of contemporary documents that discuss the murder. Those closest chronologically to the event, and thus more likely to be factual, include letters by McLoughlin (Mar. 5, 1845, in Douglas 1944:183); Elijah White (Apr. 4, 1845, in Allen 1850:243–46) (both McLoughlin's and White's accounts were from the Nez Perce Ellice); Henry Brewer (Apr. 29, 1845, Canse Collection), who got his information from Spokan Garry; and Sutter himself (letter of July 21, 1845, 1960:148– 49). Combining those accounts yields the following reconstruction:

The Indians went to California to obtain cattle in exchange for horses and furs. In the vicinity of the fort they captured some more horses and mules, probably wild or from free-running herds, but perhaps from horse thieves. Some of those animals, it turned out, were branded and belonged to settlers in the vicinity. At the fort, an American, Grove Cook, demanded a mule with his brand. Elijah, in response, brandished a gun, "with the intention to shoot the mule if he took it,—this enraged [Cook], as he thought Elijah intended to kill him," according to Brewer (Sutter has Elijah aiming the gun at Cook).

The Indians were then informed by the authorities (Sutter or the Spanish, or both) that such animals must be returned to their owners. They refused, maintaining that (in E. White's words):

in their country six nations were on terms of amity, and that in case any one of these six nations stole a horse, the tribe was responsible for the safe delivery of that animal to the rightful owner; but in the case the Blackfeet or other formidable enemy steal or capture, the property is supposed lost, without redemption; and as we have captured these horses at the hazard of our lives from your openly declared enemies, we think they ought in justice to be ours. [Allen 1850:244-45]

The Indians would only yield the animals if they were paid for them.

Negotiations apparently followed (here the accounts vary considerably), and during them, Grove Cook shot Elijah through the heart. White has Elijah dying while on his knees in prayer, McLoughlin has him falling at Sutter's feet, Sutter claims he was not present and calls Elijah "a great Rascal" who had murdered one of his own countrymen, and Spokan Garry (Brewer's informant) "blame[d] Elijah's uncle" [Tawatoy] for the incident. At any rate, the Indians fled (Garry said Piupiumaksmaks had already left), leaving their cattle behind, and were pursued by a party of Spaniards or Americans.

By May the effects of that incident were already being felt in the Northwest. Marcus Whitman reported:

The death of Elijah Heading . . . has given much trouble since . . . February. . . . Some have urged that as Elijah was educated and was a leader in religious worship and learning and so in revenge one of the same grade must be killed of the Americans & Mr. Spalding or myself were proposed as suitable victims. [M. Whitman, letter of May 20, 1845, in Hulbert and Hulbert 1941:143]

## Marnicoon

Marnicoon is mentioned only in Perkins's 1838 journal (Appendix 1, Doc. 1), as a guide between Vancouver and Wascopam.

## Papeus

The "old man" of Claticut village was encountered by Daniel Lee, Ben Wright, and Tumsowit in late December 1839, during the "Wonderful Work of God" (Appendix 1, Doc. 3). He is mentioned again in the missionary papers in 1845, on the occasion of his death. As described by Laura Brewer, it is a prime example of the woeful consequences of a continuing blood feud:

Papas and Huaps had for a long time some difficulty about a canoe, which the former had given the latter, on account of the death of a woman, but it happened she did not die, and Papas demanded the canoe again, but it was not returned, therefore his son took a horse and rifle from Huaps. This aroused his anger, and he took a rifle, and shot the young man, wounding him severely in the arm. Papas was absent, but when he came and beheld his son,—Huaps thinking he would revenge it on him, took

an axe, and cut him to pieces, so that he died on the spot. The son, seeing
this, called to some one to shoot Huaps, which was done. He died this
morning. It is thought the son will recover. This has created great
excitement among the Indians. [L. Brewer, letter of Aug. 15, 1845, Canse
Collection]

## Piupiumaksmaks

Along with the better-known *k̓amáyaqan,* Piupiumaksmaks (among many
spellings, Peopeomoxmox is most common; this transcription, from the
Sahaptin, is from Theodore Stern forthcoming) was one of the most influential
Sahaptin Indians during the 1840s and 1850s. Like *k̓amáyaqan,* he is best
known for his activities during the treaty and war period of the midfifties.
Important information on his earlier life is contained in 1840s missionary
papers.

Piupiumaksmaks appears to have been the hereditary chief of the Walla
Wallas. In the early decades of the nineteenth century that position was held
by Yellepit, met by both Lewis and Clark (1988:303) and David Thompson
(1962:350–51). Yellepit (reported to be thirty-five in 1805 and forty in 1811)
would have been the proper age to be Piupiumaksmaks's father, but no such
tie can be demonstrated. Piupiumaksmaks was definitely grooming one of *his*
sons, Elijah Hedding (a.k.a. Toayahnu) to succeed him (E. Perkins letter of
early 1843, Canse Collection).

Piupiumaksmaks was born sometime in the late eighteenth century
(Santee 1933:164). We may assume that he had become a principal chief of
the Walla Wallas by the 1830s, if not earlier. From the mid-1830s there are two
accounts of a "Walla Walla chief" that, on the basis of internal evidence,
probably refer to Piupiumaksmaks. The first is from Jason Lee's diary, August
29 1834. On their way west, the Lees encountered a camp of friendly Walla
Wallas and Cayuses. The Walla Walla chief showed Jason Lee a calendar with
Sundays marked—from Hudson's Bay Company people, he assumed:

> I then, in red ink, wrote my name and Daniel's, stating what we were,
> dated it and gave it to him and he seemed pleased with it. He soon made
> a sign for me to follow him, and he took me out and presented me an
> elegant horse. . . . We smoked with them, sang a hymn, and commended
> them to God in prayer. [1916:255–56]

In company with the "Kioos chief" (perhaps Tawatoy), the Walla Walla chief
guided the Lees for a few miles before parting ways. Jason Lee wondered at
his "kindness."

Santee (1933:165) notes that two years following that incident, Elijah
Hedding was admitted to the Willamette Mission school. He assumes that the

Lee-Piupiumaksmaks relationship began with the above friendly encounter.

The Perkins and Daniel Lee initial encounter with the Walla Walla chief, dated March 31, 1838, (the second week of their mission), is similar to that of Jason Lee. Again the Walla Walla and Cayuse chiefs appear in close association (Tawatoy on the twenty-second—see biographical sketch of Tuetasomittlecum), and again there is a present of a horse (D. Lee, "Notebook," entry for Apr. 5, 1838, Daniel Lee Collection). It is notable that in both of those instances the Walla Walla and Cayuse chiefs moved quickly to establish friendly ties with the missionaries.

Perkins visited Fort Nez Percés (Walla Wallas) in July 1839. At that time the Walla Walla chief was absent in the Great Plains hunting bison, and the missionary did not meet him. In a letter of August 4, 1839, Perkins refers to him as "Elijah's father" (Canse Collection). In January he called him "Peu peu muchmuks, which means Yellow bird"—the first known reference to the chief by name—and termed him "principal chief" of the Walla Wallas.

In 1841 members of the Wilkes Expedition met the chief at Fort Nez Percés:

> The chief of the Wallawallas, who is called Puipui-Marmox (Yellow Bird) and the Nez Perce [*sic:* actually Cayuse] chief Tousatui (or Young Chief) seemed intelligent and friendly, but the white residents consider them great rogues. They were going to the Shaste country to trade for blankets, together with trinkets and beads, in exchange for their horses and beaver-skins. [Wilkes 1844, 4:397]

Elijah returned to Walla Walla in summer 1842. That fall, the upper country was visited by Dr. Elijah White, newly appointed sub-Indian agent for the Oregon territory, in order to (as Henry Brewer put it) "instruct the different tribes in their intercourse with the Whites, give them law to some extent, etc." (letter of Jan. 2, 1843, Canse Collection) Details on the law code and how Piupiumaksmaks dealt with it are given in chapter 8.

In February 1843 Piupiumaksmaks was in the Willamette Valley (J. Lee, letter of Mar. 27, 1843, Archives of the Pacific Northwest Conference). It was probably at that time that he made contact with John Sutter, who in early 1844 established Sutter's Fort or New Helvetia on the Sacramento River. Brewer said:

> Captain Sutton [*sic*], of California, sent a message to . . . Pea-pea-mux-mux, inviting him to come, with all his good hunters, into the region of his fort, and kill elk and deer, and catch wild horses; and, bringing them into the fort, receive, in return, cattle so highly prized by the Indians. [Mudge 1854:61]

The Indians could not obtain cattle from normal sources and probably knew of Ewing Young's overland voyage to California to purchase a herd for the Willamette Valley (Josephy 1965:240). Mounted southern Plateau task groups had traveled to California before (Wilkes, above), so Sutter's proposition undoubtedly looked good. A party of more than thirty-six, including Piupiumaksmaks and Elijah, Tawatoy, some prominent Nez Perces, and Spokan Garry, arrived in California, probably sometime in August or September 1844. Here Elijah was murdered (the circumstances surrounding the incident are covered in his biographical sketch).

Events after that time fall outside the Perkins period and therefore will be only summarized here. It may be said that Piupiumaksmaks led a colorful life and continued to play an important role in Oregon affairs until his death in 1855.

The California party arrived home early in 1845. All were greatly incensed over Elijah's death, and there was talk of sending a large force to California to avenge him. Early in March Piupiumaksmaks visited Vancouver and consulted with McLoughlin, who warned him not to take action (Josephy 1965:241). More meetings between Ellice, McLoughlin, and White may have helped, but the Walla Walla chief was definitely not satisfied. Traveling upstream for five days with him after the McLoughlin meeting, John Minto reported that the chief's mood was one "of sullen disappointment" and that he "rarely spoke" (1901:249). In summer 1846 Piupiumaksmaks was back in California with a larger party, the presence of which precipitated an unfounded scare among the settlers. At Sutter's Fort the chief told one of them the reasons for his presence:

> I have come from the forests of Oregon with no hostile intentions . . . to hunt . . . to trade our horses for cattle . . . [and] to visit the grave of my son Elijah. . . . But I have not traveled thus far only to mourn. . . . I demand justice! The blood of my slaughtered son calls for vengeance! I have told you what brought me here; and when these objects have been accomplished, I shall be satisfied, and shall return peacefully to my country. [Revere in Heizer 1942:3]

Ominous indeed, but the Indians remained in California through mid-1847 without ill effect. Ten young men even participated (on the American side) in the Bear Flag Revolt (Heizer 1942:3).

Upon his return to Fort Nez Percés in late July 1847, the old chief posed for a painting by artist Paul Kane (plate 17). The California party unfortunately brought measles to Oregon, which rapidly developed into an epidemic. The Whitman Massacre followed on November 29 (Boyd 1994a). Piupiumaksmaks was not involved, but the desire to avenge Elijah has been mentioned as a causative factor. As early as 1845, visitors to Waiilatpu were informed that "because his son had been killed by an American in California, the Walawala Chief demanded the life of Dr. Whitman" (Johnson and Winter 1846:136; see also M. Whitman, letter of May 20, 1845, in Hulbert and Hulbert 1941:143).

Piupiumaksmaks played an important role in the Walla Walla Treaty of 1855, in which the peoples of the southern Plateau ceded most of their land. The treaty proceedings reveal a suspicious and eloquent man, very unlike his counterparts kamáyaqan of the Yakamas, who was morose and taciturn, and the Nez Perce Lawyer, the principal Indian proponent of the treaties. Excerpts from Piupiumaksmaks's principal speech, which was given June 2, following talks by the White principals, Isaac I. Stevens and Joel Palmer, are reproduced below:

> We have listened to all you have to say, and we desire you should listen when any Indian speaks. . . . I know the value of your speech from having experienced the same in California, having seen treaties there. We have not seen in a true light the object of your speeches, as if there was a post set between us. . . . Should I speak to you of things that have been long ago as you have done? The whites made me do what they pleased, they told me to do this and that, and I did it. . . . From what you have said I think you intend to win our country, or how is it to be? . . . you have spoken in a round about way. Speak straight, I have ears to hear you and here is my heart. Suppose you show me goods, shall I run up and take them? Goods and the Earth are not equal; goods are for using on the earth. I do not know where they have given land for goods. We require time to think. . . . Speak plain to us. I am a poor Indian, show me charity. If there was a chief among the Nez Perces or Cayuses, if they saw evil done they would put a stop to it. . . . Such chiefs I hope Gov. Stevens and Gen'l Palmer are. I should feel very much ashamed if the Americans should do anything wrong. . . . Think over what I have said. [I. Stevens 1985:55-57]

The intransigence of the Walla Walla and Cayuse chiefs paid off, at least in part. Five days later the commissioners proposed that a third reservation, besides those already planned for the Nez Perces and the Yakamas, be set apart for their people. That was the Umatilla Reservation.

Following the treaties, and due in large part to them, the Columbia Plateau disintegrated into war. Six months later, at the battle of Walla Walla, Piupiumaksmaks and six others came in under a white flag. They were held, there was a fracas, and all but one were shot. The incident has been variously blamed on either side. But the responsibility for what followed falls squarely on the Whites. The old chief's scalp and ears were taken by one of the volunteers and carried triumphantly to Portland.

*Seletsa (Celest)*

Seletsa (Celest, Seletsee, Celetec, Celitsa), who visited Perkins and Lee shortly after their arrival at The Dalles in late March 1838 (Appendix 1, Doc. 1), was a Tenino chief (Ruby and Brown 1972:148). He had apparently received some religious instruction at Waiilatpu, hence Perkins's reference to singing the Protestant hymn "Greenville." It is interesting that his people prayed "in their own tongue," however, as they spoke the Columbia River dialect of Sahaptin, whereas it was the Northeastern branch that was current at Waiilatpu. Perhaps Seletsa (as he was known in the late forties) was an innovator, who translated or modified the Holy Word for his own people. That supposition receives some support from a later occurrence.

In late July 1842 "Celetec" traveled to Willamette to trade horses for cattle (Brewer 1986:75). At Willamette he and his family stayed with Dr. William and Margaret Bailey, while the remainder of his party camped outdoors. Margaret reported: "He invited me in to join them in their evening devotions in which he took the lead. Speaking in Chenook [Jargon] I was able to understand him" (1986:198). "Seletsee's Prayer" follows. It is obviously ad lib and follows no set pattern. Seletsa gave thanks for a safe voyage and place to stay and "for such a good day as the Sabbath day, when we can leave all our other thoughts, and think only of Thee." He wished for a good day (Sunday) of worship, that the Holy Spirit would "wash the hearts" of his people who "have forgotten thee" and that God would give him and his wife "angel hearts" (Bailey 1986:198–99). There was more, but Mrs. Bailey cut his "narrative" short.

A year later, "Celitsa" was again in the Willamette Valley, trying to trade horses for cattle. That time there was some kind of misunderstanding (the source is not clear on the exact nature of the problem). Apparently Seletsa had arrived with a note from Daniel Lee explaining the reason for his trip. He traded one horse to Jason Lee for a plow but could not get rid of the others. The text of Jason Lee's letter suggests the horses were not of good quality. At any rate, Seletsa left in a huff: "He threw down your letter—said he did not care much about cows and would go home as he was" (Jason Lee, letter of Aug. 1, 1843, Archives of the Oregon-Idaho Conference).

The last mention of "Siletsi" in the mission documents is on July 24, 1844, when he delivered a letter from Oregon Mission superintendent George Gary to Perkins (H. Perkins, letter, Archives of the Pacific Northwest Conference). His name appears again in early 1848 during the Cayuse War, when he was taken to The Dalles to protect him from the renegade Cayuses, whom he had refused to join (Ruby and Brown 1972: 122; O'Donnell 1991:82–83).

The available information on Seletsa is interesting in a number of respects:

(1) it shows how Christian elements spread, even to peoples peripheral to missions, and were utilized and modified by influential men; (2) it underlines the importance of that rare commodity, cattle, that prompted Sahaptin peoples to make long-distance trips to Willamette, and later to California, using horses in trade; and (3) it again shows that bargaining with Indians was not easy and that leading men were haughty and easily offended.

## *Tucknawack (Pucknawuck)*

The "young chief at the village opposite the Lower Dalles," encountered by the missionaries in April 1838, is not otherwise noted in the missionary records.

## *Tuetasomittlecum*

Tuetasomittlecum is probably Tawatoy (transcription from Stern forthcoming; also called "Young Chief"; *mittlecum* is perhaps a garbling of the Chinook Jargon tillicum 'people' [Yvonne Hajda, personal communication, 1988-93]), a prominent Cayuse chief throughout the 1830s and 1840s. He was brother to Pahkatos Qohqoh (Five Crows) and uncle to Cayuse Halket, sent to Red River by the Hudson's Bay Company in 1830. Tawatoy and his brother were principal men of the Umatilla band of Cayuses (Ruby and Brown 1972:51).

Despite occasional difficulties, Tawatoy's ties with the Hudson's Bay Company, and in particular Pierre Pambrun, head of the post at Fort Nez Perces, appear to have been strong. Pambrun supposedly built Tawatoy a house at his Umatilla village (Josephy 1965:203) and was probably influential in his supposed elevation to high chief in 1835 (Allen 1850: 191). Tawatoy's position explains his regal bearing and elaborate costume. In November 1837 Tawatoy's son had been baptized by Father Blanchet at Walla Walla, and it is probable that Tawatoy identified himself as Catholic by the time of his initial meeting with Perkins.

Territorial Indian agent Elijah White met with Tawatoy during both his trips to the interior in 1842 and 1843. The second of those, in May 1843, was the occasion of another encounter between Henry Perkins and the Cayuse chief. Perkins was along as interpreter and had been assigned to bring the Young Chief, Five Crows, and the Yellow Bird in to parley, from their camp on the headwaters of the Umatilla. Perkins encountered a mix of recent religious converts. Five Crows had been converted by the (Presbyterian) Whitmans, Piupiumaksmaks's son Elijah was ten months from the (Methodist) Willamette Mission school, and Tawatoy was a practicing Catholic. Perkins stayed the first night with Piupiumaksmaks and his son, with whom he shared prayers.

The next morning, quite early, he called at Tauitau's lodge, and was informed, on entering, that they had not yet had their morning prayers. The chief caused a bell to be rung, at the sound of which all his band came together for devotion. Tauitau then said to Mr. Perkins, "We are Catholics, and our worship is different from yours." He then fell upon his knees, all the rest kneeling and facing him. The chief had a long string of beads on his neck, to which was attached a brass cross. After all were knelt, they devoutly crossed themselves, and commenced their prayers as follows: "We are poor, we are poor." repeating it ten times, and then closing with "Good Father, good Son, good Spirit," and then the chief would slip a bead on the string. This was continued until all the beads were removed from one part of the string to the other. When their devotions closed, Tauitau said, "This is the way in which the priest taught us to worship God." [G. Hines 1850:169-70]

In the ensuing meetings, the Cayuses accepted White's law code and elected a principal chief. Tawatoy won on the first ballot but withdrew because his religious views conflicted with the majority of the Cayuses. His brother, Pahkatos Qohqoh, was elected on the second ballot.

In 1844 Tawatoy traveled with Piupiumaksmaks, Spokan Garry, and others to California, where Elijah was murdered (see Hedding, Elijah). Shortly before the Whitman Massacre, in November 1847, the Young Chief offered his house at the Umatilla village to the Catholics. It ultimately became Sainte Anne Mission (Ruby and Brown 1972:106-8). Tawatoy was a moderating influence in the Cayuse War; he himself captured and held the renegade murderers of the Whitmans (Ruby and Brown: chaps. 7-9). He died in September 1853, at 54 years, in the buffalo country (Ruby and Brown:183).

## Tumeocool

The conversion experience of the Wascopam native Tumeocool is described by Perkins in the "Wonderful Work of God. . . ." (Appendix 1, Doc. 3) and by D. Lee and Frost (1844:185-86). Lee states that Tumeocool initially "stood aloof" because the first converts were "of a lower class." Note Tumeocool's prayer "behind a hill," as if he were searching for a guardian spirit. Tumeocool is mentioned in the missionary papers only one other time, as a guide to Waiilatpu Mission (Brewer 1986:69, entry for Aug. 11, 1841).

## Tumsowit

Tumsowit and Yacooeter were both pivotal individuals in the 1839-40 Wascopam Revival. As a shaman, Tumsowit already had prestige among the Indians. His adoption of the trappings of Christianity undoubtedly served as a model for others who had heretofore held back.

What is most interesting about Tumsowit's conversion (Appendix 1, Doc. 3) is that it was accomplished in a purely Indian fashion. It is of a type with the conversions of natives also recorded by Perkins during the 1838–39 Willamette Revival. In the eyes of the missionaries, Tumsowit was receiving salvation; from an Indian perspective he was obtaining new powers. The roads to those ends were similar enough in the two cultures that the old man might be seen as accomplishing both, simultaneously.

Prayers must have been seen by Tumsowit as the missionaries' power songs; if he learned them by rote, he would acquire the powers that they gave the missionaries. Tumsowit's time "alone among the rocks and hills on his knees" was the missionaries' equivalent of Christ's forty days and nights in the wilderness, which preceded revelation; to the old shaman and his Indian observers it was a standard power quest. Isolation from family, marathon "searching" to the point of exhaustion—both were perfectly understandable to the Indians. Although the final "salvation" (read vision experience) was not remarkable from either Christian or Indian perspective, the "change was immediately observable," and Tumsowit was accepted as a "new man" (that is, Christian, or more powerful shaman), apparently in both cultures. Tumsowit's conversion is reprinted in Mudge (1848:170–72). A summary version is in D. Lee and Frost (1844:183).

Tumsowit's behavior after his conversion follows a pattern that would be understandable to Max Weber: simultaneously, as he began to exhort and spread the word, he was filling the roles of apostle and Indian prophet. Tumsowit traveled with Lee and Wright downstream, stopping at all the villages on the way to Fort Vancouver and preaching in Chinookan. In late May he was with Perkins, visiting "from house to house" at Wascopam village (H. Perkins, letter of June 2, 1840, Canse Collection).

The only other definite mention of Tumsowit in the missionary documents is in a letter of August 15, 1845. Laura Brewer states that he was doctoring again, in that case Canacissa's son, sick with dysentery: "There is no doubt that he would have lived, if Tumsowit had left him alone. He worked on him till the evening he died, when at his earnest request, he was brought here, but it was too late, for he died during the night" (Canse Collection).

As late as the 1850s Tumsowit was still practicing "medicine" at The Dalles. George Gibbs's description of one of his curing sessions is reprinted in chapter 6.

## Wamcutta

Wamcutta ("Wamcutsul") is mentioned several times in missionary documents between 1838 and 1841, but not thereafter. The earliest accounts suggest an individual of considerable influence, perhaps a hereditary chief.

Perkins's initial citation of March 18 at The Cascades is followed by two descriptions, from the pens of both Perkins and Daniel Lee, on April 3, when Wamcutta arrived at Wascopam. Perkins's account appears in Appendix 1, Document 1; Lee's follows:

> The chief, whose name is *Wamcatta,* returned from a trip down the Columbia and in the evening he called to see us when we told him why we had come to reside in his country. The next day he held a council with his people, which Seems to have had a favorable result for . . . April 5th he came out with a large party and assisted us in preparing timber for a house. ["Notebook," Daniel Lee Collection]

The chiefly behavior includes holding "council with his people," serving as itermediary with the Whites, and a definite chiefly bearing ("Honor to whom honor is due"). The missionaries' "present" at The Cascades and tea at Wascopam was reciprocated by help in preparing timbers and the use of two horses. (Lee says they were presented by a visiting Walla Walla chief.)

Wamcutta is next mentioned (in D. Lee and Frost 1844:158, 161) as one of the guides for Daniel Lee's trip over the Cascade mountains to Willamette Falls. Unfortunately he did not carry through with that venture: Lee was supposed to meet him at the (huckle)berry grounds, but Wamcutta was absent on an elk hunt, and the missionary was forced to forge ahead without his help. That account and the earliest indicate that Wamcutta had ties to the west of the mountains, at both Fort Vancouver and Willamette Falls (not an unusual situation for prominent men of the area).

Within a year, relations with the missionaries had soured. According to Perkins: "A report spread that Wamcutsul and his people were going to tie me today and whip me, because I would not sell them an axe for six dozen salmon. Wamcutsul insisted that he had threatened no such thing. God only knows" (H. Perkins, letter of Dec. 24, 1839, Canse Collection). The phrase Wamcutsul "and his people" suggests possible factionalism among the locals. By that time other Indians (for example, Yacooetar) were beginning to establish close ties with the missionaries. Wamcutta is mentioned only one more time, in 1841, by Henry Brewer: "Bought Wamcuttas claim on a small piece of land west of the spring. We pay 1 blanket, 1 pair pants, 1 vest, 1 common shirt" (1986:69, entry for July 31, 1841).

## Yacooetar

Yacooetar (frequently "Equator" or "Boston") was probably the single most influential man in Wascopam village, and his name recurs often in letters from 1839 to his death in 1847.

The earliest mention is in the autumn of 1839, by Thomas Farnham, who noted, "Boston, although of mean origin has, on account of his superior energy and inteliigence, become the war chief of the Dalles" (1843:87). That passage is notable on two counts: first, the Columbia Plateau and the Plains Indians had war chiefs, but they were not typical of Northwest Coast societies, of which the Upper Chinooks are sometimes considered a part. Second, Yacooetar had obtained that position because of his own innate qualities, not because of any inherited (kin) status. It is interesting that two individuals of high acquired status—Yacooetar and Tumsowit—according to Perkins, erstwhile competitors, resided in the same house. Postmarital residence patterns in the area were flexible, with relatives in the male line usually residing together. The Sahaptin Teninos frequently had joint family residences occupied by two brothers and their families. If Tumsowit and Yacooetar were indeed blood kin, Perkins offers no other evidence of it. It is possible, though not likely, that they were in-laws, with wives who were blood relatives, residing in a matricentric household. Perhaps Tumsowit's former status as a slave had something to do with that unusual residence pattern.

Yacooetar's first recorded interaction with a Euroamerican outsider, befitting a war chief, was aggressive. Farnham (1843:87-88) describes a confrontation on October 14, 1839, that resulted from the theft of a rifle and all the metal parts of a saddle. Supposedly—in that obviously overblown account—Farnham confronted the thieves and was surrounded by thirty-eight to forty Indians, eight to ten of them armed. Yacooetar was in their midst, facing him with a dueling pistol. They stood eye to eye for "an hour" until, with Daniel Lee interpreting, the goods were returned.

The early establishment of close ties between the Methodist missionaries and two important Indian leaders, Tumsowit and Yacooetar, was mutually beneficial. The two Indians increased their status and influence throughout the extent of Upper Chinookan territory by their association with the "powerful" newcomers, and the missionaries, through the medium of two respected native leaders and interpreters, found it much easier to spread their religious messages. Indians were more likely to listen closely to sermons or exhortations delivered by important men from their own culture speaking in their own tongue than they were to outsiders who communicated only in Chinook Jargon. Although the Wascopam Revival was initiated and carried out by three Whites—Perkins, Lee, and Wright—it would never have been as effective as it was without the help of the Indian associates Tumsowit and Yacooetar.

The story of Yacooetar's conversion also appears in the "Wonderful Work of God. . . ." (Appendix 1, Doc. 3), in Mudge (1848:173-74), and (abbreviated) in D. Lee and Frost (1844:184-86). Brewer's sketch of "Equator" (Mudge 1854:37-39) reiterates much of Perkins's description of the man and adds details on his family. Brewer states that

when first known at the mission station, he had two wives, after the
practice of most of the chiefs. The missionaries tried to show him the
wickedness of polygamy, and he finally acknowledged it, and put away
one of them, but supported her as before. [Mudge 1854:38]

Perkins's short diatribe on polygamy, not present in the published version of
the "Wonderful Work of God," was added from the 1952 typescript (see
Appendix 1, Doc. 3, and chap. 5). As with gambling, there is no evidence that
the Wascopam missionaries made any concerted effort to halt that "evil,"
though they spoke of it in sermons and paid lip service in writings intended for
consumption by East Coast audiences. Other factions of the Methodist
mission, of course, placed the elimination of "sins" such as gambling and
polygamy at the top of their list of priorities, much above the "religious
experience" or "salvation." Solidly entrenched in Indian culture, polygamy
would have been exceedingly difficult to eradicate, especially at the onset of
a missionary endeavor. That disagreement on priorities was a major source of
contention among the Oregon Mission family and a chronic problem for
Perkins.

Brewer's statement on the disposition of Yacooetar's first wife is
ambiguous: he "put her away" but continued to "support" her. What probably
happened was that living arrangements changed, and the polygamous
household was terminated. Brewer's statement suggests that the marriage itself
was not dissolved, however, as he "supported her as before." In other words,
Yacooetar made a cosmetic (and diplomatically astute) move that improved
his status with the Christian newcomers while maintaining his standing in the
Indian community.

Yacooetar's resident wife apparently attended Laura Brewer's classes
regularly. Brewer states she was "ambitious to learn the domestic habits of her
female Christian friends, who took much pains to instruct her . . . and won the
affections of her teachers" (Mudge 1854:38). As the resident wife of a leading
man, she was certainly a role model for the other women of Kaclasko. That
wife and Yacooetar's resident children all appear to have been converted.
Talispam, Yacooetar's eldest daughter, "was taken into the mission family"
and "gave good evidence that she was born again" but died shortly after from
tuberculosis.

Yacooetar is next mentioned in a letter of Sept. 1, 1844 (Elvira Perkins to
the absent Laura Brewer, Canse Collection), when his family "moved up"
(apparently from Kaclasko village to the mission grounds) because he was
afraid of catching the prevailing dysentery. The Perkinses treated his youngest
child, and Yacooetar responded by performing favors. "You know what a
faithful friend he is," reported Elvira. A few days later (Sept. 7) Laura Brewer

wrote, "Equator says tell Mr. B[rewer, absent at Willamette] halo wappato conawa tilicum sick, closeaiak chanev" (Canse Collection). (The message, translated from Chinook Jargon, means "no potatoes, all Indians sick, better be quick with the canoe[s]" [Henry Zenk, personal communication, 1993]). In the next few years Yacooetar showed continuing signs of civilization. By spring 1845 he had acquired a cow "from the emigrants by taking care of their horse last winter" (H. Brewer, letter of Apr. 29, 1845, Canse Collection). In April 1847 he had "commenced . . . to cultivate a small piece of ground" (H. Brewer, letter of Apr. 26, 1847, Canse Collection).

The year 1847, however, was destined to be a year of troubles, terminating in Yacooetar's death. On January 18, Alvan Waller recorded a visit by "Equator" on behalf of his "brother-in-law Hallicula" concerning compensation for goods lost in a fire that occurred while Waller was giving a sermon; on the twenty-fifth Yacooetar transmitted a "bitter complaint about the cold weather" that had caused many horses to die. Rumors were circulating that it was a result of Hudson's Bay Company "medicine" against the Americans. In both of those cases Yacooetar was serving as spokesman for various factions of aggrieved Indians; neither appears to have been the result of his own peculiar problems or initiative. Not all the Kaclasko people respected Yacooetar's influence, however; Waller stated: "One of the first and best disposed men of the clan about us has asked me why I allowed Equator to talk so much? that his talk was nothing but sound . . . and advised me to pay no attention" (letter of Feb. 3, 1847, Canse Collection).

On August 22 an incident occurred that led to Yacooetar's death. It is reported in four sources, all from the Brewer papers: Henry Brewer's letters of October 6, 1847, and December 7, 1848, Laura Brewer's letter of October 7, 1847 (all in Canse Collection), and Mudge (1854:38–39). The following reconstruction combines passages from those accounts.

Ten men, Immigrants . . . allowed certain lewd vicious Indian women to come to their camp. . . . Early next morning the women left & stole . . . two sacks containing clothing a pistol etc. . . .

Most of the Indians were off on the berry ground, except perhaps 15 men . . . when [some of these] Indians visited their camp the next morning they [the immigrants] . . . took 3 horses and a rifle from the chief's [Yacooetar] son. This enraged the Indians they gathered around our house 12 or 15 in number & commenced their war yell. . . . Br Waller advised the chief to keep quiet & he would get back the horses but he nor his people would not.

The Indians gathered around the Americans . . . an Indian . . . fired without doing injury . . . the old chief came up to one of the whites and seized a mule . . . and at the same time raised his hatchet. . . . Then

Shepherd shot the chief . . . through the heart . . . mortally. Then two Indians shot Shepherd . . . he died in a few minutes. . . . It is an awful sight to see two men shooting each other. . . . Another American was shot through his arm & another in his leg . . . Markomer's brother . . . was shot through his leg. . . .

The wounded chief walked a few rods, and laid down near our house, and in about 20 minutes died. . . . Equator said to Br. Waller before he died, "What a fool I am. I might have lived had I followed your advice.". . . The dead body of one of my country men was in view, stript by the savages and exposed to their continued insults, not one of our people daring to go near him for some hours. . . .

As their chief was dead they wished the blood of a chief among the whites. Br. Waller was afraid of his life as they considered him more of a chief than myself [H. Brewer]. . . . The Indians demanded 4 horses of the Americans . . . fled to Willamette after leaving a horse & two blankets for the Indians for peace.

Br Roberts [Reverend William Roberts, successor to George Gary] & Br Waller promised them 4 cows . . . this satisfied them. . . . Br Roberts started the same evening for Willamette, and on the next sabbath morning, arrived agin with Gov. Abernethy by whom the affair was amicably settled by the exchange of property, according to Indian custom. . . .

We left Wascopam on the 7th of September for the lower country. Br. Hinman and family and Perrin Whitman, the Dr.'s nephew, were left in charge of the Dalles station.

The timing of the above incident is crucial. It preceded the Whitman Massacre and the ensuing Cayuse War by three months and was certainly a contributing factor to the general disruption among the natives that led to both events. It will be recalled that another Indian leader, Elijah Hedding, son of the Walla Walla chief Piupiumaksmaks, had been murdered by Americans almost three years earlier (see the biographical sketch of Hedding). Both of those deaths—Elijah and Yacooetar—required, by Indian custom, the sacrifice of an equally high-placed White. Note also that the severe winter of 1847 was attributed by the natives to white "medicine." Similar explanations, consistent with native beliefs on disease causation, were given for the measles epidemic that preceded the Whitman Massacre. It is obvious that the factors that led to the massacre were not limited to those natives (Cayuses and Walla Wallas) in the vicinity of Waiilatpu alone. The Indians of The Dalles had similar experiences.

# Notes

## Preface

1. All of those documents are now kept in the office of the director of the University of Puget Sound Collins Memorial Library and have been copied on microfilm.

## Introduction

1. Excluding The Cascades. David French (personal communication, 1989–93) suggests that there is a natural boundary in the thinly occupied area of the Columbia Gorge between The Cascades and the White Salmon and Hood River areas. The orientation of The Cascades people's social ties, subsistence round, and culture was to the west and the Portland Basin; the orientation of the White Salmon River, Hood River, and other upstream Chinookans was to the east, or the Plateau.

## Chapter 1

1. Until that structure was built, Sunday services were held in the open "among the oaks and under a pine" (D. Lee, "Ten Years in Oregon," partial draft, Archives of the Oregon-Idaho Conference). Pulpit Rock, according to recent tradition the meeting site, is nowhere mentioned in the mission documents.

## Chapter 2

1. Linguists disagree on whether Kathlamet merits the status of a separate language or whether it should be considered a divergent dialect of Upper Chinookan.

2. As with Yehhuh and *wáiaxix*, those two words are variants of a single name. Wah- and Clah– (*tla*) are feminine singular and collective neuter markers (David French, personal communication, 1989–93). Lewis and Clark's "Clahclellah" is probably the ethnographers' *wimałgikšat*, at Bonneville, and "Wahclellah" is *nimišxáya*, a mile below Beacon Rock (D. French forthcoming).

3. David French (forthcoming) notes that the deep water of that stretch of the Columbia made Indian fishing difficult.

4. I have used the name standardized in the historical literature by Washington Irving (1836: chap. 10) and Biddle (1926). As noted in the text, Wishram is the *Sahaptin* name for

349

the site; Chinookans have always called it *nixlúidix. Spearfish* was the name of the historic community that occupied the site of *nixlúidix* until 1957; the contemporary town of Wishram is ten miles upstream at the former Sahaptin village of sk'in.

5. The estimates' "Eneshur," "Wahhowpum," and "Pishquitpah."

## Chapter 3

1. There are several alternate and colloquial names for the four salmon species: chinook = king, coho = silver or silversides, sockeye = blueback or red, chum = dog, pink = humpback (Netboy 1980:39-41)

2. The large number of stations recorded from the mid-twentieth century were not all traditional (according to Columbia Sahaptin elder James Selam [Eugene Hunn, personal communication, 1982-93]). Technological changes, particularly the addition of cables with moving box cars, allowed Indians to reach and lay claim to sites previously inaccessible (David French, personal communication, 1989-93).

3. That list of known sites is certainly incomplete. Huckleberry grounds fluctuated widely in productivity from year to year: old fields became overgrown with vegetation, and new fields were added when fire cleared the land of competing vegetation at the elevation favored by *V. membranaceum.*

4. The "mullet" mentioned by Lewis and Clark were various species of the genus *Catostomus,* which ran in small streams in early spring (Hunn 1990:155).

5. After dating that letter February 3, Waller proceeded to write later entries until he sent it off.

6. The latter two are both bison products: a parfleche is a rawhide bag; an apishamore is a hide saddle blanket.

## Chapter 4

1. The Hudson's Bay Company's Peter Skene Ogden.

2. Catholic priest Honoré Mesplier.

3. "Casineau" (usually Cassino) was chief of the Vancouver-area Indians; his home village originally appears to have been at Kalama. See Spencer (1933).

4. Probably Bache, founder of the 1829 trading post at Wascopam (see chap. 1).

5. In Columbia Sahaptin those two words translate as follows: *šapa–wanp–ɫa–ma*: *šapa* = a causative prefix, *wanp* = to sing (as a power song), *ɫa* = agentive suffix, *ma* = plural suffix. *taymu–ɫa–ma*: *taymu* = news; *ɫa* = agentive suffix, *ma* = plural suffix (Eugene Hunn, personal communication, 1982-93).

6. That distinction is relative. A few wealthy Sahaptins did hold slaves, and slaves were present in large numbers among the westernmost bands of Klickitats.

## Chapter 5

1. Pam-a wa-nicht pam-a ti-kuat-at, the name of the ceremony, translates as follows: *pama* = for the purpose of; *wani* = to name" *t* = verbal nominalizer; *pama* = for the purpose of; *tkʷata* = to eat; *t* = verbal nominalizer. Perkins's translation as the "Feast of the Naming" is perfectly appropriate (Eugene Hunn, personal communication, 1982-93)

2. A taboo on the name of a dead person was general throughout aboriginal Oregon. It was strongly developed among the lower Chinooks, who dropped the name of the deceased from the vocabulary and also "changed . . . the names of all the chief mourners" (Ray 1938:74). A notable example of the latter custom was the renowned chief Concomly, who, after the 1824 death of a favored son, became known as Madsu (Thunder):

> The old man had conferred his name & authority on one of his deceased sons, on his death the name forever ceased to be used among his country men as being unlucky & calling to remembrance a lamented chief; hence it is esteemed cruel & unfeeling ever to pronounce it; & when they speak of the deceased chief they say the old man's favorite son, or some such expression. [Scouler 1905:168]

3. Perkins's parenthetical assertion that that list represents all things in the order that they were created is interesting and raises several questions. There is an order in the first quotation that could be interpreted as representing the biblical order of creation in the seven days of Genesis. If so, that was an addition to the ritual that may have entered under missionary influence or—conceivably—even earlier. The second quotation shifts the sequence around and may represent a breakdown of an original Christian order. But then again, neither sequence is clearly Christian, and they may both represent an aboriginal system. Curtis's resume of the rite has the speaker referring to "roads of five kinds" over which the "reborn" person will travel (1911a:179). There is no evidence of Christian influence anywhere else in the ritual.

4. Social ranking is not a part of contemporary Warm Springs ceremonies. Instead, "the order is for close kin and/or those who helped a great deal to be 'gifted' first" (Yvonne Hajda, personal communication, 1988-93).

5. Perkins's "pam-a si-akt pam-a ti-kuat-at" is identical to his phrase for *Feast of the Naming,* with the exception of the root *si-akt,* which has not been identified. The identifiable portion of the phrase translates as "Feast for the purpose of . . ."; *si-akt,* therefore, following Perkins, should mean "boring," and the name of the ceremony should be "Feast of the Boring."

6. Hunn notes: "In Columbia Sahaptin . . . co-wife terms vary depending on whether the co-wives are coresident (from the same village, thus probably classificatory 'sisters') or not; in the first case they call one another X'*aks,* literally 'a woman's sister or female friend;' otherwise they call one another X'*awi,* literally 'rival, enemy'" (Eugene Hunn, personal communication, 1982-93).

7. The usual practice in that area is for the head to be oriented to the *west* (see Kuykendall 1889:94; Spier and Sapir 1930:271; Ray 1942:217), though several northern

Plateau peoples oriented the corpse to the east (Ray 1942:217). Farnham is probably incorrect on that point.


## Chapter 6

1. *i-t'alap'as* was the term used by Chinookans below The Cascades; *i-sk'u'l-a* by those between The Cascades and The Dalles (David French, personal communication, 1989-93); Columbia Sahaptins called Coyote *spílya* (Rigsby 1965:202-3).

2. Among contemporary Warm Springs Indians, revealing one's spirit quest experience leads to "the loss of power" (David French, personal communication, 1989-93).

3. Farnham's account is securely dated to 1839. Lee's is undated, but fits in the bracket 1839-42. It is possible that it also dates from 1839 and records the same performance witnessed and described by Farnham.

4. Two phrases used by Perkins in Appendix 1, Document 5, are based on skep. As analyzed by Eugene Hunn, "skep-i pau-a-cha" (p. 000) means "perhaps 'They were skep.'", 'They had skep.', or 'They were skep-like.' *pa-* is third person singular intransitive verb prefix, *wa-* is the verb stem 'to be', and *-cha* is the past tense suffix . . . *i* is an adjectivizing suffix indicating possession of a quality . . . 'skep-in pu-kui-a' = skep plus 'subject marker' plus '*pa-ku-ya*(?)' 'they [the spirits] did [something]'? *ku-* is the verb stem 'to do' and *-ya* is the past tense; *pu-* is perhaps properly *pa-*." Hunn makes the interesting observation that skep is the root of the Sahaptin word for wild rose bush, *šk'apášway*. The "rose is a powerful charm to protect one from ghosts" (Eugene Hunn, personal communication, Feb. 2, 1988).


## Chapter 7

1. The Waiilatpu herd, by contrast, numbered twenty in mid-1840, and the first steer was slaughtered in mid-1841 (Drury 1973, 1:256).

2. The earliest recorded instance of native cultivation of potatoes was by the Haidas of the Queen Charlotte Islands, by 1829 (Green 1915:51fn). The Haidas had an especially strong impetus to grow the plant: starchy foods are especially rare in the north, and demand was great. Haidas traded their surplus for other goods with Tsimshians and Tlingits in a potato fair during the annual eulachon run at the mouth of the Nass River.


## Chapter 8

1. This letter, received on the twentieth, has also not survived.

Chapter 9

1. Itself a variation on the "disease in a bottle" threat first attributed to Astorian Duncan McDougall in 1811 (Irving 1836:117-18).

2. Despite Bishop Rosati's claim that the Iroquois introduced the "seeds of Catholicity" (in Blanchet 1932:94-95), it may have been a different, adumbrated form of Christianity that they brought. Nathaniel Wyeth, who spent the first half of 1833 among the Flathead Indians, told Wilbur Fiske and Jason Lee in a December 1833 briefing before Lee's departure to Oregon that "the religion of these tribes is Deism" (Hulbert 1935:118). Deism was popular among eighteenth-century rationalists such as Thomas Jefferson and Benjamin Franklin and held that although God was responsible for the Creation, he had no working involvement in the present world. "God as watchmaker" is a common metaphor.

3. The phrase "my heart is good" appears constantly in later translations from Sahaptian languages, especially treaty negotiations. Yvonne Hajda (personal communication, 1988-93) notes that "The idea that the heart was the organ of thought was widespread. In Kalapuya, for instance 'How is your heart?' means 'What do you think?'"

4. The word appears to have spread from Colvile to Puget Sound. Heron was at Fort Nisqually in 1833, where, with the recently arrived William Tolmie, he attempted (in both Chinook Jargon and through an interpreter) to impart the basics of Christianity to the local Puget Sound Salish (Tolmie 1963:221-22, 249;Huggins 1833-39). Writing in May 1840 from Whidbey Island, the Reverend Norbert Blanchet stated:

> Ten years ago the natives heard tell for the first time of a great Master of heaven and of a time when they would come to serve Him.... This knowledge caused them to sanctify Sunday, after their fashion, by games and dances to the point of exhaustion. [Blanchet in Landerholm 1956:68]

Chapter 10

1. For the postcontact camp see Samarin (1986); an argument for precontact origins appears in Hymes (1980). Hajda, Zenk, and Boyd (1988) provide the most up-to-date treatment of the origins of Chinook Jargon.

2. Brewer records that the Halls passed through Wascopam on their way to Lapwai (1986:60).

3. According to Eugene Hunn: "*winš* = man, *áyat* = woman, *miyánaš* = child, *ínaw* = young man, *wapsíni* = unmarried woman, *k'úsi* = horse, *músmuscin* = cow, *huqhúq* = pig, *lulúk'aš* = milk, breast, *tápaš* = pine, *cuníps* = oak, *núsux̣* = salmon, *ayłalu* = wheat, native grass sp., *iłays* = type of root bread. 'Stinostino' (potatoes) is unfamiliar" (Eugene Hunn, personal communication, 1982-93).

4. The native terms in this letter are all Chinookan, indicating that the missionaries were instructing in both languages, not just one. David French (personal communication,

1989-93) translates (literally) "Etokte mika Mr. Brewer" as "good you Mr. Brewer." The words in lines 15–18 of the quotation he calls "bad Chinookan" or "jargonized" Chinookan. It is true that there are no r sounds in Chinookan. If the r's in *Brewer* were hard to pronounce, those in *Herbert* would have been more so. No wonder Brewer did not name any children after his nephew.

5. See Durkheim's *Elementary Forms of the Religious Life* (1915), Weber's *Protestant Ethic and the Spirit of Capitalism* (1930), Wallace's *Culture and Personality* (1970), and V. Turner's *Ritual Process* (1969).

6. The text reads "Kaclasko," but from internal evidence it is obvious that Wishram is the settlement described.

7. Whether through the medium of Henry Perkins or another missionary, the myth of the Gadarene was incorporated into at least one other Pacific Northwest Indian mythology, that of the Klamaths and Modocs. In the 1880s anthropologist Albert Gatschet recorded a free translation of "The Story of the Hog" from half-breed J. C. D. Riddle, born in 1862:

> The Klamath Lakes (and) Modocs believe a wicked spirit in the hog, in the coyote also to reside. That time, when hogs all into the sea running perished, one only black hog escaped, that time into hogs a wicked spirit entered. Not therefore the Indians black hogs kill.

Gatschet says in a footnote, "This hog story is evidently the result of the consolidation of aboriginal superstitions with the evangelist's relation of the Gergesene swine throwing themselves into the Lake of Galilee from the headlands of Gadara" (1890:127–28).

## Appendix 1
## Document 2

1. The reference is to the "Wonderful Work of God among the Indians of the Oregon Territory," which originally appeared in the *Christian Advocate and Journal* 15, no. 9 (October 14, 1840):1. The document is printed in its entirety as Document 3 of Appendix 1.

2. The distance to Willamette is 150 miles; the distance to Vancouver is 100.

3. In the "Autobiography," two "natives."

4. Perkins's unpublished account of the Willamette Revival is held in the Daniel Lee Collection, Mss. 1211, Manuscripts Department, Regional Research Library, Oregon Historical Society, Portland.

## Document 3

1. The 1952 journal typescript reads:

> There were but three of us at the station who understood English—Mr. Wright, myself and wife.... Mr Wright ... felt he must begin preaching.... So earnest was his desire for an immediate resumption of duty, that we arranged that he

should preach in our kitchen, stipulating that we should take turns and have preaching every evening. To this I assented, and our meetings began. Mr. Wright was so terribly in earnest that we were both very much stirred. He stated that he had been in successive revivals, fourteen years, and he launched out in the old fashioned Methodist style, preaching to me and my wife as if we were both on the road to Hell! Our only season was about an hour at twilight, but the Lord blessed us greatly. We spoke only English, but the Lord spoke so to our hearts that we became very earnest declaimers.

2. The 1952 version reads "heaven on earth."

## Document 5

1. Dr. Charles Pittman (variously Pitman) was corresponding secretary of the Methodist Episcopal Church at the time that journal was written. He was apparently not related to Anna Maria Pittman Lee, Jason Lee's first wife.

2. In the *Christian Advocate and Journal.*

3. Bells persist today as important ritual items in such native religions as the *Wáašat* and Indian Shaker Church (Schuster 1975:384, 415). The standard explanation of their introduction ascribes them to Catholic missionaries (Barnett 1957:293), but it is quite possible that Methodist influence was also important. A second example of the use of bells by Methodists (in that case Henry Brewer at Wishram) follows: "I took a hand bell & went from house to house & invited them to meet on nature's green carpet."

4.Presumably Perkins refers here to big sagebrush *(Artemisia tridentata)* (Eugene Hunn, personal communication, 1982-93).

5. Probably the leaves of wild iris *(Iris missouriensis),* sometimes woven into mats by Plateau peoples.

6. Ananias and Sapphira (Acts 5:1-11): A parable on the sins of greediness and lying. After the crucifixion the followers of Christ, at the behest of the Apostles, sold their worldly goods and redistributed the proceeds, "every man according to his needs." Ananias and his wife Sapphira contributed only part of their profit, pretending it was the entire amount. When Peter discovered that deception, he accused Ananias and his wife of being influenced by Satan, and both were struck dead by the wrath of God.

7. Fleas.

8. Literally, "much (matter) in small (compass)" (Latin).

9. Not identified.

10. Slavery was an emotional issue among Methodists of the time. Perkins, coming from Maine, was naturally a member of the antislavery faction. Feelings were so strong that in 1844, shortly after that journal was penned, the Methodist Episcopal Church split into two independent regional bodies: the Northern abolitionist and the Southern proslavery (Johnson 1955: chap. 17).

11. "This is a fact & the reason they assign, is "They are poor, & exiled from their

country, & people, & it would make them feel bas to be called *slaves,* so we call them brothers & sisters." (Perkins)

12. "This is his name whose speech I have put down above." (Perkins)

13. Bison apparently inhabited the Columbia Plateau until shortly before the historic period (Kingston 1932). After the introduction of the horse, most eastern Plateau groups were able to travel to the plains to hunt bison, and some Nez Perces and Flatheads did so annually (Anastasio 1972:130-32). Although there are reports of Upper Chinookans accompanying those parties, and although Indians from The Dalles were known at the Green River rendezvous, that robe was likely a trade item, probably from Nez Perces.

14. That is a semisubterranean storage lodge *(wulči* in Umatilla Sahaptin), which doubled as a place of seclusion for menstruating women (Theodore Stern, personal communication, 1982).

15. "They obtain the poison of these animals & put upon their arrows which immediately entering into the circulation makes the death of their victim sure when once pierced by them." (Perkins)

16. Bishop John Emory (1789-1835) served in Maryland and Pennsylvania. He was best known as an editor, especially of the American edition of the works of John Wesley and the *Methodist Magazine.* He also wrote several articles defending Methodist doctrine and helped found Wesleyan University (Harmon 1974:773-74). Several other individuals, indicative of Perkins's reading at the time, are named in the passage (deleted here) that follows in the complete journal. Adam Clarke (1760-1832), one of the founders of British Methodism, wrote eight volumes of commentaries between 1810 and 1826. John Wesley (1707-88), an Episcopal priest whose teaching was strongly influenced by the Moravians, is recognized as the father of Methodism. John Newton (1725-1807) was influential in the British evangelical revival of the early eighteenth century that preceded the rise of Methodism. David Brainerd (1718-47) was a Presbyterian missionary to the Delaware and Seneca Indians; John Summerfield (1798-1825) was a noted American Methodist preacher of the early 1820s. Martin is unidentified.

17. Perkins's "skesh" 'shadow of death' is a different concept from "skep." The former appears to be the soul of a dead person, akin to our concept of ghost, while the latter was the guardian spirit of a dead person. In the Indian mind, one possessed both a soul and a guardian spirit, and both were released after death. The two concepts are not always clearly separated in the ethnographies (and may not always have been so by Indians). Both were associated with illness. "Soul-loss," which was treated by a trip to the land of the dead to recover the lost soul, was believed to cause physical ailments. Possession by the guardian spirit of a deceased person, however, apparently resulted in psychotic aberrations. "Spirit sickness," the uneasy state one experienced prior to the catharsis of performing spirit songs and dances at winter ceremonies, is more closely akin to the latter state. Like "skep," words akin to "skesh" occur in the Sahaptin (?) and Salishan languages. Quinault has *spes* as 'soul' (Olson 1936:154); Sanpoil-Nespelem has *ske'is* for dream and *sku'susqa* for ghost (Ray 1933:180, 167).

18. A coyote.

19. The Gadarene. See chapter 10.

20. Dr. Otto Jahn (1813-67) was a prominent German philologist, art critic, and archaeologist.

21. "Juggler" and "jugglery" were nineteenth-century terms that referred to native curers and their activities. The words also have a connotation of skill in sleight of hand.

22. John Howard (1726-90), known as "the philanthropist," was a leading figure in prison reform and institutional hygiene in eighteenth-century Britain. He was instrumental in the passage of the 1774 Prison Reform Act, which improved prison sanitation and provided for medical care in jails, and published the results of a prison survey in the 1777 report *The State of Prisons in England and Wales.* In the 1780s he became interested in hospital hygiene and, in two tours, investigated the lazarettos (leprosaria) and military hospitals of Europe. He was constantly exposed to disease and died of typhus ("prison fever") in 1790. Jeremy Bentham eulogized him thus: "He died a martyr, after living the life of an apostle" (Encyclopedia Britannica, 1875 ed.).

23. Calomel (mercurous chloride), a white powder, was used as a cathartic. The danger of mercury poisoning was not recognized at the time.

24. The "blister" refers to a mustard plaster. Powdered mustard paste was used as a "counterirritant," which produced a rush of blood wherever it was applied, supposedly depressing the pain at its original source.

25. Philip Doddridge (1702-51) was a "celebrated nonconformist" minister at Northampton (1729-51). According to the 1875 *Encyclopaedia Britannica* (7:1320):

> His sermons were mostly practical in character. . . . He endeavoured to write on the common general principles of Christianity, and not in the narrow spirit of any particular party. There is a remarkable delicacy and caution evinced in the works of Dr. Doddridge whenever the subject approaches the disputed points of theology. The general expressions of the sacred writers are then employed, and the reader is allowed to draw his own conclusions, unbiased by the prejudices of human authorities.

The *Family Expositor* is listed as one of his four major works.

26. Clarke's *Commentaries* were mentioned earlier (note 13). Along with the *44 Sermons* and *24 Articles,* John Wesley's *Explanatory Notes on the New Testament* (1755) is said to comprise "the doctrinal standards of American Methodism" (Bucke 1964:225). George Campbell (1719-96) was a Presbyterian theologian and professor at Marichal College in Aberdeen. The 1875 *Encyclopaedia Britannica* (4:754) describes him as

> the acutest and most cultivated theologian and scholar . . . that the Church of Scotland has produced. . . . In 1778 his last and in some respects his greatest work appeared, *A New Translation of the Gospels.* The translation is a good one, but it is the critical and explanatory notes which accompany it that give the book its high value.

27. Perkins nowhere identifies his Walla Walla interpreter(s). Brewer (in Mudge 1854:55–56) names two: John and his friend Luxillu. John (perhaps the "John Mission" of reservation days) was called "an apt interpreter," but Luxillu "was an excellent interpreter. He seemed to catch, as the missionaries never knew any other Indian to do, the *spirit* of the language communicated to him." Luxillu is the most frequently mentioned Walla Walla in the Perkins and Brewer papers. He lived into the twentieth century and is pictured in a well-known photograph atop Pulpit Rock on the occasion of the seventieth-anniversary celebration of the founding of the mission, March 22, 1908.

28. A number of Indians were employed at various times in the mission household. One of the earliest was William M'Kendree (or Billy Chinook: see Appendix 3). The female servant Tilustina is mentioned frequently in entries from 1842 and 1843. The orphaned daughter of Kis–kis, the Indian killed by the Klamaths, she eventually married an American and moved to the Willamette Valley. Appearing in late 1844 was the redeemed slave Ransom (see chapter 5). Two other names that are mentioned more than once in Brewer's papers are Penessar and Howalt.

29. One of the strongest statements about the Second Coming in the Bible. See chapter 10.

30. Luke 2:25–38. Simeon and Anna (Phanuel's daughter) were both prophets who predicted that the infant Jesus was the "Lord's Christ . . . thy salvation . . . A light to lighten the Gentiles, and the glory of thy people Israel."

31. A note on the left margin reads *"Omit this page."*

32. Not identified.


## Appendix 3


1. Loewenberg 1973:72 provides information on the source of Victor's appellation "a dessicated Dominie Sampson." It came ultimately from the notoriously mean-spirited and narrow-minded Anglican preacher Herbert Beaver, who served at Fort Vancouver between 1836 and 1838. Beaver could neither understand nor abide most Indian customs, the local tolerance for non-Anglican religions, nor the employees' common-law marriages. Following a few choice adjectives applied by Beaver to Chief Factor McLoughlin's common-law wife in a report to London, the good doctor, in a fit of rage, hit him with his cane. Beaver shortly afterward left for London in a huff (Jessett 1959: intro.). Beaver quite likely disapproved of McLoughlin's good relations with the Methodists.

2. The latter assessment should be taken with a grain of salt. Simpson was notoriously biased against all "breeds" (Lavender 1968:259)

# References

Abbot, Henry L.
1857    Report . . . upon Explorations for a Railroad Route, from the Sacramento Valley to the Columbia River. *In* Reports of Exploration and Surveys . . . from the Mississippi River to the Pacific Ocean . . ., vol. 6. 33rd Cong., 2d sess., Senate Exec. Doc. 78, serial 763.

Aberle, David
1959    The Prophet Dance and Reactions to White Contact. Southwestern Journal of Anthropology 15:74-83.

Adams, Barbara
1958    The Cascade Indians: Ethnographic Notes and an Analysis of Early Relations with Whites. B.A. thesis, Reed College, Portland, Oreg.

Allen, A. J.
1850    Ten Years in Oregon: Travels and Adventures of Doctor E. White and Lady. Ithaca: Press of Andrus, Gauntlett, and Co.

Alvord, Benjamin
1884    The Doctor-Killing Oregons. Harper's New Monthly Magazine, January: 364-66.

Amoss, Pamela
1984    A Little More than Kin, and Less than Kind: The Ambiguous Northwest Coast Dog. *In* The Tsimshian and Their Neighbors of the North Pacific Coast, edited by Jay Miller and Carol Eastman, 292-305. Seattle: University of Washington Press.

1987    The Fish God Gave Us: The First Salmon Ceremony Revived. Arctic Anthropology 24(1):56-66.

1990    The Indian Shaker Church. *In* Handbook of North American Indians, edited by William C. Sturtevant. Vol. 7, Northwest Coast, edited by Wayne Suttles, 633-39. Washington, D.C.: Smithsonian Institution.

Anastasio, Angelo
1972    The Southern Plateau: An Ecological Analysis of Intergroup Relations. Northwest Anthropological Research Notes 6:109-229. Moscow, Idaho.

Applegate, Jesse
1851    [Letter of June 2 to Anson Dart (from Yonkalla)]. Records of the Oregon Superintendency of Indian Affairs, 1848-73, no. 2, roll 12, Letters Received, September 30, 1848-December 25, 1852, RG 75. National Archives. Washington, D.C.

1914    Recollections of My Boyhood. Roseburg, Oreg.: Press of Review Publishing Co.

Axtell, James
1979    The Ethnohistory of Early America: A Review Essay. William and Mary Quarterly 35:110-44.

Bagley, Clarence
1932    Early Catholic Missions in Old Oregon. Seattle: Lowman and Hanford.

Bailey, Margaret Jewett (Smith)
1986     The Grains, or Passages in the Life of Ruth Rover. Corvallis: Oregon State
         University Press.
Ballou, Howard
1922     History of the Oregon Mission Press. Oregon Historical Quarterly 23:95–110.
Bancroft, Hubert (with Frances Fuller Victor)
1886     History of Oregon, 1834–1848. The Works of Hubert Howe Bancroft, vol. 29,
         History of the Pacific States. San Francisco: History Co.
Barclay, Wade
1950     History of Methodist Missions. Part 1, Early American Methodism, 1769–
         1844. Vol. 2, To Reform the Nation. New York: Board of Missions and
         Church Extension of the Methodist Church.
Barker, Burt, ed.
1948     Letters of Dr. John McLoughlin, 1829–32. Portland, Oreg.: Binfords and
         Mort.
Barnett, Homer
1938     The Nature of the Potlatch. American Anthropologist 40:349–57.
1957     Indian Shakers: A Messianic Cult of the Pacific Northwest. Carbondale:
         Southern Illinois University Press.
Beavert, Virginia
1974     The Way It Was: "Anaku Iwacha": Yakima Indian Legends. Consortium of
         Johnson O'Malley Committees of Region IV: State of Washington.
Beckham, Stephen
1984     "This Place Is Romantic and Wild:" An Historical Overview of the Cascades
         Area, Fort Cascades, and the Cascades Townsite, Washington Territory.
         Heritage Research Associates Report no. 27. U.S. Army Corps of Engineers,
         Portland District. Portland, Oreg.
Benedict, Ruth
1923     The Concept of the Guardian Spirit in North America. American
         Anthropological Association Memoir 29. Menasha, Wis.
Biddle, Henry
1926     Wishram. Oregon Historical Quarterly 27:113–30.
Billington, Ray
1968     Oregon Epic: A Letter That Jarred America. Pacific Historian (Summer):30–
         37.
Bishop, Charles
1967     Journal and Letters of Capt. Charles Bishop on the Northwest Coast of North
         America, 1794–1799, edited by Michael Roe. Cambridge: Hakluyt Society.
Black, Samuel
1829     Nez Percés Report. Hudson's Bay Company Archives ms. B.146/e/2.
         Winnipeg.
Blanchet, Francis Norbert
1932     Historical Sketches of the Catholic Church in Oregon, 1838–1878. In Early
         Catholic Missions in Oregon. Vol. 1, edited by Clarence Bagley, 9–149.
         Seattle: Lowman and Hanford.
Boas, Franz
1894     Chinook Texts. Bureau of American Ethnology Bulletin no. 20. Washington,
         D.C.

1901      Kathlamet Texts. Bureau of American Ethnology Bulletin no. 26. Washington, D.C.

Bolduc, Jean Baptiste
1979      Journal, Cowlitz, February 15, 1844. *In* Mission of the Columbia, translated by Edward Kowrach, 103-21. Fairfield, Wash.: Ye Galleon Press.

Bolon, Gustavus
1854      Annual Indian Report for 1854, Central District, to Isaac I. Stevens, September 3. Records of the Washington Superintendency of Indian Affairs, 1853-74, no. 5, roll 20, Letters from employees assigned to the Central or Middle district, February 24, 1854-July 13, 1874, RG 75. National Archives. Washington, D.C.

Boxberger, Daniel
1984      The Introduction of Horses to the Southern Puget Sound Salish. *In* Western Washington Indian Socio-Economics: Papers in Honor of Angelo Anastasio, edited by Herbert Taylor and Garland Grabert, 103-19. Bellingham: Western Washington State University.

Boyd, Robert
1984      'Doctor Killings' on the Southern Coast: An Index of Systemic Stress Associated with Epidemic Mortality and Rapid Culture Change. Manuscript in Boyd's possession.

1985      The Introduction of Infectious Diseases among the Indians of the Pacific Northwest, 1774-1874. Ph.D. diss., University of Washington.

1990      Demographic History, 1774-1874. *In* Handbook of North American Indians, edited by William C. Sturtevant. Vol. 7, Northwest Coast, edited by Wayne Suttles, 135-48. Washington, D.C.: Smithsonian Institution.

1994a     The 1847-1848 Pacific Northwest Measles Epidemic. Oregon Historical Quarterly 95:6-47.

1994b     Smallpox in the Pacific Northwest: The First Epidemics. BC Studies 101:5-40.

Boyd, Robert, and Yvonne Hajda
1987      Seasonal Population Movement along the Lower Columbia River: The Social and Ecological Context. American Ethnologist 14:309-26.

Brackenridge, Williaam
1931      Our First Horticulturist: The Brackenridge Journal, part 4. Edited by O. B. Sperlin. Washington Historical Quarterly 22:129-45.

Brewer, Henry
1928      Log of the Lausanne. Oregon Historical Quarterly 29-30:53-62, 111-19, 189-208, 288-309, 347-62.

1986      The Journal of Henry Bridgman Brewer, September 3, 1839 to February 13, 1843. . . . Edited by Richard Seiber. Fairfield, Wash.: Ye Galleon Press.

Brosnan, Cornelius
1932      Jason Lee: Prophet of the New Oregon. New York: Macmillan.

1933      The Oregon Memorial of 1838. Oregon Historical Quarterly 34:68-77.

Brunot, Felix
1871      Minutes of a Council Held with Simcoe Indians, at Their Reservation, Washington Territory. *In* Report of the Commissioner of Indian Affairs. 42nd Cong., 2d sess., House Exec. Doc. 1, serial 1505, 547-51.

Bucke, Emory
1964    The History of American Methodism. New York: Abingdon Press.
Burnett, Peter
1880    Recollections and Opinions of an Old Pioneer. New York: D. Appleton.
Caldwell, Warren
1956    The Archaeology of Wakemap Mound: A Stratified Site near the Dalles on the Columbia River. Ph.D. diss., University of Washington.
Canse Collection
Mss.    Papers of Henry B. Brewer and Henry K. W. Perkins Papers. Washington State Historical Society. Tacoma.
Canse, John
1930    Pilgrim and Pioneer: Dawn in the Northwest. New York: Abingdon Press.
Carey, Charles
1932    Lee, Waller and McLoughlin. Oregon Historical Quarterly 33:187–213.
Carey, Charles, ed.
1922    The Mission Record Book of the Methodist Episcopal Church, Willamette Station. . . . Oregon Historical Quarterly 23:230–66.
Carter, Thomas
1937    Photographs of Columbia River Fishing Places Located above Bonneville Dam. Yakima Agency Records, RG 75. National Archives, Seattle Branch.
Chance, David
1973    Influences of the Hudson's Bay Company on the Native Cultures of the Colvile District. Northwest Anthropological Research Notes Memoir no. 2. Moscow, Idaho.
Clark, Keith, and Donna Clark
1978    William McKay's Journal, 1866–67: Indian Scouts. Part 1. Oregon Historical Quarterly 79:121–71, 269–333.
Clarke, Samuel
1905    Pioneer Days of Oregon History. Portland, Oreg.: J. K. Gill.
Coale, George
1958    Notes on the Guardian Spirit Concept among the Nez Perce. National Archives of Ethnography 48:135–48.
Codere, Helen
1950    Fighting with Property: A Study of Kwakiutl Potlatching and Warfare, 1792–1930. American Ethnological Society Monograph 18. New York.
Collins, June
1974    Valley of the Spirits: The Upper Skagit Indians of Western Washington. American Ethnological Society Monograph 56. Seattle: University of Washington Press.
Colvocoresses, George
1852    Four Years in a Government Exploring Expedition. New York: Cornish, Lamport.
Corps of Engineers
1955    Summary Report on the Indian Fishery at Celilo Falls and Vicinity, Columbia River, 1947–1954. Portland, Oreg.
Cressman, Luther
1948    Lower Columbia Indian Weapons. Oregon Historical Quarterly 49:297–98.

Cross, Osborne
1850    A Report, in the Form of a Journal . . . of the March of the Regiment of
        Mounted Riflemen to Oregon, from May 10 to October 5, 1849 . . . *In* Report
        of the Secretary of War. 31st Cong., 2d sess., Senate Exec. Doc. 1, pt. 2, serial
        587, 126-244.
Curtin, Jeremiah
1909    Wasco Tales and Myths. *In* Wishram Texts, edited by Edward Sapir, 237-314.
        Publications of the American Ethnological Society, vol. 2. Leiden: E. J. Brill.
Curtis, Edward
1911a   The Chinookan Tribes. *In* The North American Indian, vol. 8, 85-154, 172-
        83. Norwood, Mass.: Plimpton Press. Reprint, New York: Johnson Reprint,
        1970.
1911b   The Yakima and The Klickitat. *In* The North American Indian, vol. 7, 3-42.
        Norwood, Mass.: Plimpton Press. Reprint, New York: Johnson Reprint, 1970.
Demers, Modeste
1871    Chinook Dictionary, Catechism, Prayers and Hymns. Montreal.
DeSmet, Pierre
1905    Life, Letters and Travels of Father Pierre-Jean DeSmet, S.J., 1801-1873 . . .
        Edited by Hiram M. Chittenden and Alfred T. Richardson. 4 vols. New York:
        Francis P. Harper.
Desmond, Gerald
1952    Gambling among the Yakima. Catholic University of America Anthropo-
        logical Series 14. Washington, D.C.: Catholic University of America Press.
Dickeman, Mildred
1975    Demographic Consequences of Infanticide in Man. Annual Review of
        Ecology and Systematics 6:107-37.
Dixon, Roland
1907    The Shasta. Bulletin of the American Museum of Natural History 17(5):
        381-498.
Dobbs, Caroline
1932    Men of Champoeg. Portland, Oreg.: Metropolitan Press.
Donald, Leland
1983    Was Nuu-chah-nulth-aht (Nootka) Society Based on Slave Labor? *In* The
        Development of Political Organization in Native America, edited by Morton
        Fried, 108-19. Proceedings of the American Ethnological Society for 1979.
        Philadelphia.
Douglas, David
1953    Journal of Travels in North America 1823-1827. New York: Antiquarian
        Press.
Douglas, James
1944    Letter of March 5, 1845. *In* The Letters of John McLoughlin from Fort Van-
        couver to the Governor and Committee: Third Series, 1844-46, edited by E.
        E. Rich, 177-88. The Publications of the Champlain Society, vol. 7. Toronto:
        Champlain Society.
Douglas, Mary, ed.
1970    Witchcraft Confessions and Accusations. London: Tavistock.

Drucker, Philip
1940    Kwakiutl Dancing Societies. University of California Anthropological Records 2(6):201-30. Berkeley.
1950    Northwest Coast: Culture Element Distributions XXVI. University of California Anthropological Records 9(3):157-294. Berkeley.
1951    The Northern and Central Nootkan Tribes. Bureau of American Ethnology Bulletin no. 144. Washington, D.C.
1955    Sources of Northwest Coast Culture. In New Interpretations of Aboriginal American Culture History, 59-81. Washington, D.C.: Anthropological Society of Washington.
1965    Cultures of the North Pacific Coast. San Francisco: Chandler.
1983    Ecology and Political Organization on the Northwest Coast of America. In The Development of Political Organization in Native America, edited by Morton Fried, 86-96. Proceedings of the American Ethnological Society for 1979. Philadelphia.

Drury, Clifford
1958    The Diaries and Letters of Henry H. Spalding and Asa Bowen Smith Relating to the Nez Perce Mission, 1838-1842. Glendale, Calif.: Arthur H. Clark.
1973    Marcus and Narcissa Whitman and the Opening of Old Oregon. 2 vols. Glendale, Calif.: Arthur H. Clark.

DuBois, Cora
1938    The Feather Cult of the Middle Columbia. General Series in Anthropology, no. 7. Menasha, Wis.

Duff, Wilson
1956    Prehistoric Stone Sculpture of the Fraser Valley and Gulf of Georgia. Anthropology in British Columbia 5:15-151.
1975    Images: Stone: B.C. Seattle: University of Washington Press.

Duncan, Janice
1972    Minority without a Champion: Kanakas on the Pacific Coast. Portland: Oregon Historical Society.

Dunn, John
1845    The Oregon Territory and the British North American Fur Trade. Philadelphia: G. B. Zieber.

Durkheim, Émile
1915    The Elementary Forms of the Religious Life: A Study in Religious Sociology. London: Allen.

Eells, Myron
1882    History of the Indian Missions on the Pacific Coast, Oregon, Washington and Idaho. New York: American Sunday School Union.
1887    Decrease of Population among the Indians of Puget Sound. American Antiquarian and Oriental Journal 9:271-76.
1985    The Indians of Puget Sound: The Notebooks of Myron Eells, edited by George Castile. Seattle: University of Washington Press.

Eld, Henry
1841    Journal, Statistics etc. in Oregon and California. Western Americana Collection, WA ms. 161. Beinecke Library. Yale University.

Elmendorf, William
1971   Coast Salish Status Ranking and Intergroup Ties. Southwestern Journal of Anthropology 27:353–80.

Emmons, George
1841   Journal Kept While Attached to the Exploring Expedition... No. 3. Western Americana Collection, WA ms. 166. Beinecke Library. Yale University.

Encyclopaedia Britannica
1875   Encyclopaedia Britannica: A Dictionary of Arts, Sciences, and General Literature. 9th ed. Edinburgh: A. C. Black.

Ermatinger, Francis
1980   Fur Trade Letters of Francis Ermatinger, edited by Lois McDonald. Glendale, Calif.: Arthur H. Clark.

Ewers, John
1955   The Horse in Blackfoot Culture; with Comparative Material from Other Western Tribes. Bureau of American Ethnology Bulletin no. 159. Washington, D.C.

Farnham, Thomas
1843   Travels in the Great Western Prairies, the Anahuac and Rocky Mountains, and in the Oregon Territory. New York: Greeley and McElrath.

Ferguson, R. Brian
1984   A Reexamination of the Causes of Northwest Coast Warfare. In Warfare, Culture and Environment, edited by R. Brian Ferguson, 267–328. Orlando: Academic Press.

Filloon, Roy
1952   Huckleberry Pilgrimage. Pacific Discovery 5:4–13.

French, David
1958   Cultural Matrices of Chinookan Non-Casual Language. International Journal of American Linguistics 24:258–63.
1961   Wasco-Wishram. In Perspectives in American Indian Culture Change, edited by Edward Spicer, 337–430. Chicago: University of Chicago Press.
1998   Wasco, Wishram, Cascades. In Handbook of North American Indians, edited by William C. Sturtevant. Vol. 12, Plateau, edited by Deward Walker. Washington, D.C.: Smithsonian Institution.

French, Kathrine
1955   Culture Segments and Variation in Contemporary Social Ceremonialism on the Warm Springs Reservation, Oregon. Ph.D. diss., Columbia University.
1963   Ceremonial Segmentation. In Sixth International Congress of Anthropological and Ethnological Sciences, 1960. Tome 2, vol. 1, 101–4. Paris: Musée de l'Homme.

French, Kathrine, and Yvonne Hajda
1985   The Changing Structure of Warm Springs Alliances. Paper read at the 84th annual meeting of the American Anthropological Association, Washington, D.C., December 5.

Frisch, Jack
1978   Iroquois in the West. In Handbook of North American Indians, edited by William C. Sturtevant. Vol. 15, Northeast, edited by Bruce Trigger, 544–46. Washington, D.C.: Smithsonian Institution.

Frost, Joseph
1934    Journal of John [sic] H. Frost, 1840–43. Edited by Nellie Pipes. Oregon
        Historical Quarterly 35:50–73, 139–67, 235–62, 348–75.
Fulton, Leonard
1968    Spawning Areas and Abundance of Chinook Salmon in the Columbia River
        Past and Present. Fish and Wildlife Service Special Scientific Report—
        Fisheries, no. 571. Washington, D.C.
1970    Spawning Areas and Abundance of Steelhead Trout, and Coho, Sockeye, and
        Chum Salmon in the Columbia River Basin—Past and Present. National
        Marine Fisheries Special Scientific Report—Fisheries, no. 618. Washington,
        D.C.
Gairdner, Meredith
1841    Notes on the Geography of the Columbia River. Journal of the Royal Geo-
        graphic Society 11:250–57.
Garth, Thomas
1965    The Plateau Whipping Complex and Its Relationship to Plateau Southwest
        Contacts. Ethnohistory 12:141–70.
Gary, George
1923    Diary of Rev. George Gary. Edited by Charles Carey. Oregon Historical
        Quarterly 24:68–105, 152–85, 269–333, 386–433.
Gatschet, Albert
1890    The Klamath Indians of Southwestern Oregon. Contributions to North
        American Ethnology no. 2. 2 vols. Washington, D.C.
Geo-Recon International
1983    Cultural Resource Overview and Survey of Select Parcels in The Dalles
        Reservoir, Oregon and Washington. U.S. Army Corps of Engineers, Portland
        District. Portland, Oreg.
Geyer, Carl Augustus
1846    Notes on the Vegetation and General Character of the Missouri and Oregon
        Territories, Made during a Botanical Journey, . . . during the Years 1843 and
        1844. Hooker's London Journal of Botany 5:22–41, 198–208, 285–310, 509–
        24.
Gibbs, George
1854    Report of Mr. George Gibbs to Captain Mc'Clellan, on the Indian Tribes of
        the Territory of Washington. In Reports of Exploration and Surveys . . . from
        the Mississippi River to the Pacific Ocean . . ., vol. 1. 33rd Cong., 2d sess.,
        House Exec. Doc. 91, serial 736, 402-49.
1863    Dictionary of the Chinook Jargon, or Trade Language of Oregon. Shea's
        Library of American Linguistics, vol. 12. New York: Cramoisy Press.
1956    Account of Indian Mythology in Oregon and Washington Territory. Edited
        by Ella Clark. Oregon Historical Quarterly 57:125–67.
Gill, John
1891    Gill's Dictionary of the Chinook Jargon, 13th ed. Portland, Oreg.: J. K. Gill.
Glazebrook, G. P.
1938    The Hargreave Correspondence, 1821–1843. Toronto: Champlain Society.
Gordon, George
1889    Report upon the Subject of the Fishing Privileges etc. . . . Bureau of Indian
        Affairs, Portland Area Office. Portland, Oreg. Typescript.

Gray, William
 1870    A History of Oregon, 1792–1849. Portland, Oreg.: Harris and Holman.
Green, Jonathan
 1915    Journal of a Tour on the Northwest Coast of America in the Year 1829. New York: Charles F. Heartman.
Griswold, Gillett
 1970    Aboriginal Patterns of Trade between the Columbia Basin and the Northern Plains. Archaeology in Montana 11(2–3).
Grubbs, Francis H.
 1908    Early History . . . History of Pulpit Rock. The Dalles Daily Chronicle, April 30.
Gunther, Erna
 1926    Analysis of the First Salmon Ceremony. American Anthropologist 28:605–17.
 1928    A Further Analysis of the First Salmon Ceremony. University of Washington Publications in Anthropology 2(5):129–73. Seattle.
 1950    The Western Movement of Some Plains Traits. American Anthropologist 52: 174–80.
Habersham, Robert A.
 1874a   The Columbia River through the Cascade Range. Map made under the Direction of Major N. Michler, U.S. Engineer. Oregon Historical Society. Portland.
 1874b   Survey of the Columbia River from The Dalles to Celilo. Map made under the Direction of Major N. Michler, U.S. Engineer. Oregon Historical Society. Portland.
Haeberlin, Herman, and Erna Gunther
 1930    The Indians of Puget Sound. University of Washington Publications in Anthropology 4(1). Seattle.
Haines, Francis
 1937    The Nez Perce Delegation to St. Louis in 1831. Pacific Historical Review 6: 71–78.
 1938    The Northward Spread of Horses among the Plains Indians. American Anthropologist 40:429–37.
 1960    Nez Perce Horses: How They Changed the Indian Way of Life. Idaho Yesterdays 4:8–11.
Hajda, Yvonne
 1984    Regional Social Organization in the Greater Lower Columbia, 1792–1838. Ph.D. diss., University of Washington.
 1987    Exchange Spheres on the Greater Lower Columbia. Paper read at the 86th annual meeting of the American Anthropological Association, Chicago, November 22.
Hajda, Yvonne, Henry Zenk, and Robert Boyd
 1988    The Early Historiography of Chinook Jargon. Paper read at the 87th annual meeting of the American Anthropological Association, Phoenix, November 17.
Hale, Horatio
 1846    Ethnography and Philology. Philadelphia: C. Sherman.
 1890    An International Idiom: A Manual of the Oregon Trade Language or "Chinook Jargon." London: Whittaker.

Harmon, Nolan, ed.
1974      The Encyclopedia of World Methodism. Nashville: United Methodist Publishing House.
Harper, J. Russell, ed.
1971      Paul Kane's Frontier. Austin: University of Texas Press.
Heizer, Robert
1942      Walla Walla Indian Expeditions to the Sacramento Valley, 1844–1847. Quarterly of the California Historical Society 21:1-7.
Henry, Alexander
1992      The Journal of Alexander Henry the Younger, 1799–1814. Vol. 2, The . . . Columbia. . . ., 609–749. Edited by Barry Gough. Toronto: Champlain Society.
Heron, Charles
1830-31   Fort Colvile Journal, April 12, 1830–April 13, 1831. Hudson's Bay Company Archives. B.45/a/1. Winnipeg.
Hillgen, Marcella
1938      The Wascopam Mission. Oregon Historical Quarterly 39:221-34.
Hilty, Ivy, et al.
1972      Nutritive Values of Native Foods of Warm Springs Indians. Oregon State University Circular 809. Corvallis.
Hines, Donald, ed.
1992      Ghost Voices: Yakima Indian Myths, Legends, Humor and Hunting Stories. Collected by Lucullus McWhorter. Issaquah, Wash.: Great Eagle Publishing.
Hines, Gustavus
1850      A Voyage Round the World: With a History of the Oregon Mission. . . . Buffalo: G. H. Derby.
1868      Oregon and Its Institutions. New York: Carlton and Porter.
Hines, Harvey
1899      Missionary History of the Pacific Northwest, Containing the Wonderful Story of Jason Lee, with Sketches of Many of His Co-Laborers. Portland, Oreg.: Published by the author.
Hudson's Bay Company
1838      Census of Indian Population at Fort Vancouver: Klikitat Tribe, Cathlacanasese Tribe, Cath–lal–thlalah Tribe. Hudson's Bay Company Archives, ms. B.223/z/1, fols. 26–28. Winnipeg.
Huggins, Edward
1833-39   Fort Nisqually Journal. Suzzallo Library. University of Washington, Seattle.
Hulbert, Archer, ed.
1935      The Oregon Crusade. Vol. 5 of Overland to the Pacific. Denver: Denver Public Library.
Hulbert, Archer, and Dorothy Hulbert, eds.
1936      Marcus Whitman, Crusader: Part One, 1802 to 1839. Vol. 6 of Overland to the Pacific. Denver: Denver Public Library.
1938      Marcus Whitman, Crusader: Part Two, 1839 to 1843. Vol. 7 of Overland to the Pacific. Denver: Denver Public Library.
1941      Marcus Whitman, Crusader: Part Three, 1843–47. Vol. 8 of Overland to the Pacific. Denver: Denver Public Library.

Hunn, Eugene
1980    Sahaptin Fish Classification. Northwest Anthropological Research Notes
        14:1–19. Moscow, Idaho.
1981    On the Relative Contribution of Men and Women to Subsistence among
        Hunter-Gatherers of the Columbia Plateau: A Comparison with *Ethnographic
        Atlas* Summaries. Journal of Ethnobiology 1:124–34.
1990    Nch'i Wana, "The Big River": Mid-Columbia River Indians and Their Land.
        Seattle: University of Washington Press.
Hunn, Eugene, and David French
1981    Lomatium: A Key Resource for Columbia Plateau Native Subsistence. North-
        west Science 55:87–94.
Hunn, Eugene, George Murdock, and David French
1998    Western Columbia River Sahaptins, *In* Handbook of North American In-
        dians, edited by William C. Sturtevant. Vol. 12, Plateau, edited by Deward
        Walker. Washington, D.C.: Smithsonian Institution.
Hymes, Dell
1980    Commentary. *In* Theoretical Orientations in Creole Studies, edited by Albert
        Valdman and Arnold Highfield, 389–423. San Francisco: Academic Press.
1981    "In vain I tried to tell you": Essays in Native American Ethnopoetics. Phila-
        delphia: University of Pennsylvania Press.
Irving, Washington
1836    Astoria, or Anecdotes of an Enterprise beyond the Rocky Mountains. Phila-
        delphia: Carey, Lea, and Blanchard. Reprint, edited by Edgeley Todd,
        Norman: University of Oklahoma, 1964 (page citations are to the reprint
        edition).
1837    The Adventures of Captain Bonneville U.S.A. in the Rocky Mountains and
        the Far West. Philadelphia: Carey, Lea and Blanchard. Reprint, edited by
        Edgeley Todd, Norman: University of Oklahoma, 1961 (page citations are to
        the reprint edition).
Jackson, Donald, and Mary Lee Spence, eds.
1970    The Expeditions of John Charles Fremont. Vol. 1, Travels from 1838 to 1844.
        Urbana: University of Illinois Press.
Jacobs, Melville
1934    Northwest Sahaptin Texts, Part I (in English). Columbia University Contri-
        butions to Anthropology 19. New York.
1945    Kalapuya Texts. University of Washington Publications in Anthropology 11.
        Seattle.
1958    Clackamas Chinook Texts. Vol. 1. Indiana University Research Center in
        Anthropology, Folklore and Linguistics, Publication 11. Bloomington.
1959    The Content and Style of an Oral Literature. Viking Fund Publications in
        Anthropology no. 26. New York.
1960    The People Are Coming Soon: Analyses of Clackamas Chinook Myths and
        Texts. Seattle: University of Washington Press.
Jessett, Thomas
1960    Chief Spokan Garry, 1811–1892: Christian, Statesman, and Friend of the
        White Man. Minneapolis: T. S. Denison.
Jessett, Thomas, ed.
1959    Reports and Letters of Herbert Beaver. Portland, Oreg.: Champoeg Press.

Johnson, Allen, and Dumas Malone, eds.
1931      Dictionary of American Biography. 20 vols. New York: Charles Scribner's
          Sons.
Johnson, Charles
1955      The Frontier Camp Meeting: Religion's Harvest Time. Dallas: Southern
          Methodist University Press.
Johnson, Overton, and William Winter
1846      Route across the Rocky Mountains, with a Description of Oregon and Cali-
          fornia . . . Lafayette, Ind.: J. B. Semans. Reprint, Princeton, N.J.: Princeton
          University Press, 1932 (page citations are to the reprint edition).
Jorgensen, Joseph
1980      Western Indians: Comparative Environments, Languages, and Cultures of 172
          Western North American Indian Tribes. San Francisco: W. H. Freeman.
Josephy, Alvin
1965      The Nez Perce Indians and the Opening of the Northwest. New Haven: Yale
          University Press.
Joyce, Sally Ann
1939      Affidavit, June 9. Yakima Agency Records, RG 75. National Archives.
          Seattle.
Judson, Lewis
1971      Reflections on the Jason Lee Mission and the Opening of Civilization in the
          Oregon Country. Salem: Wynkoop-Blair Printing Service.
Kane, Paul
1859      Wanderings of an Artist among the Indians of North America. London:
          Longman, Brown, Green, Longmans, and Roberts.
Kardas, Susan
1971      The People Bought This and the Clatsop Became Rich. A View of Nineteenth
          Century Fur Trade Relationships on the Lower Columbia between Chinookan
          Speakers, Whites, and Kanakas. Ph.D. diss. Bryn Mawr College.
Kingston, Ceylon Samuel
1932      Buffalo in the Pacific Northwest. Washington Historical Quarterly 23:163-72.
Kip, Lawrence
1897      The Indian Council at Walla Walla, May and June, 1855. Sources of the
          History of Oregon 1(2). Eugene, Oreg.: University Press.
Kroeber, Alfred L.
1923      American Culture and the Northwest Coast. American Anthropologist 25:1-
          20.
1939      Cultural and Natural Areas of Native North America. University of California
          Publications in American Archaeology and Ethnology 38. Berkeley.
1941      Salt, Dogs, Tobacco. University of California Anthropological Records 6(1).
          Berkeley.
Kuykendall, George
n.d.      Dreams, Trances, Going to Heaven and Coming Back. George Kuykendall
          Papers. Manuscripts Collection. Holland Library. Washington State Univer-
          sity, Pullman.
1887      Death of the Wisham Chief's Daughter. George Kuykendall Papers. Manu-
          scripts Collection. Holland Library. Washington State University, Pullman.

1889       A Graphic Account of the Religions or Mythology of the Indians of the Pacific
           Northwest, Including a History of Their Superstitions, Marriage Customs,
           Moral Ideas and Domestic Relations, and Their Conception of a Future State,
           and the Re-habiliment of the Dead. *In* History of the Pacific Northwest:
           Oregon and Washington. . . ., compiled by Elwood Evans et al. Vol. 2, 60-95.
           Portland, Oreg.: North Pacific History Co.

Landerholm, Carl
1956       Notices and Voyages of the Famed Quebec Mission to the Pacific
           Northwest . . . Portland: Oregon Historical Society.

Lavender, David
1968       Thomas McKay. *In* The Mountain Men and the Fur Trade of the Far West,
           edited by LeRoy Hafen. Vol. 6, 259-77. Glendale, Calif.: Arthur H. Clark.

Layton, Thomas
1981       Traders and Raiders: Aspects of Trans-Basin and California-Plateau Com-
           merce, 1800-1830. Journal of California and Great Basin Anthropology 3:
           127-37.

Lee, Daniel
Mss.       Manuscripts, collection 1211. Manuscripts Department, Oregon Historical
           Society.

Lee, Daniel, and Joseph Frost
1844       Ten Years in Oregon. New York: Published for the authors by J. Collard.

Lee, Jason
1835       Flathead Indians [communication of Oct. 29, 1834]. Christian Advocate and
           Journal, October 30.

1841       Journal of Jason Lee, Mission House, Willamette, March 15, 1841. Christian
           Advocate and Journal, August 25.

1916       Diary. Oregon Historical Quarterly 17:116-46, 240-66, 397-430.

Leslie, David
1838       Letters from Oregon. The Oregonian and Indians' Advocate 1(2)(November):
           58-59.

Leslie, David
Mss.       Manuscripts, collection 1216. Oregon Historical Society. Portland.

Lévi-Strauss, Claude
1981       The Naked Man [*L'Homme nu*]. New York: Harper and Row.

Lewis, Meriwether, and William Clark
1983       Atlas of the Lewis and Clark Expedition. Vol. 1 of The Journals of the Lewis
           and Clark Expedition, edited by Gary Moulton. Lincoln: University of
           Nebraska Press.

1988       July 28-November 1, 1805. Vol. 5 of The Journals of the Lewis and Clark
           Expedition, edited by Gary Moulton. Lincoln: University of Nebraska Press.

1990       November 2, 1805-March 22, 1806. Vol. 6 of The Journals of the Lewis and
           Clark Expedition, edited by Gary Moulton. Lincoln: University of Nebraska
           Press.

1991       March 23-June 9, 1806. Vol. 7 of The Journals of the Lewis and Clark
           Expedition, edited by Gary Moulton. Lincoln: University of Nebraska Press.

Lockley, Fred
1923       Impressions and Observations of the Journal Man [David Carter]. Portland
           Oregon Journal, July 11:8.

Loewenberg, Robert
  1972       Elijah White vs. Jason Lee: A Tale of Hard Times. Journal of the West 11:636–
             62.
  1973       'Not . . . by feeble means': Daniel Lee's Plan to Save Oregon. Oregon Histor-
             ical Quarterly 74:71–78.
  1976a      Equality on the Oregon Frontier: Jason Lee and the Methodist Mission, 1834–
             43. Seattle: University of Washington Press.
  1976b      The Missionary Idea in Oregon: Illustration from the Life and Times of
             Methodist Henry Perkins. In The Western Shore: Oregon Country Essays
             Honoring the American Revolution, edited by Thomas Vaughan, 151–80.
             Portland: Oregon Historical Society.
McArthur, Lewis
  1974       Oregon Geographic Names. Portland: Oregon Historical Society.
McClellan, George
  1853       Journal, May 20–December 10, 1853. Mf A228. Suzzallo Library, University
             of Washington. Seattle.
McGillivray, Simon, Jr., and William Kittson
  1831–32 Fort Nez Percés Journal. Ms. B.146/a. Hudson's Bay Company Archives.
             Winnipeg.
McKay, William
  1869       The Early History of the Dalles. The Dalles Weekly Mountaineer, May 28:1.
Mackenzie, Alexander
  1970       The Journals and Letters of Sir Alexander Mackenzie. Edited by W. Kaye
             Lamb. Cambridge: Cambridge University Press.
McKeown, Martha
  1959       Come to Our Salmon Feast. Portland, Oreg.: Binfords and Mort.
McKinlay, Archibald
  1911       The Gun Powder Story. Oregon Historical Quarterly 12:369–74.
McLoughlin, John
  1830       [Letter of March 19]. John Work Collection, ms. 319. Oregon Historical
             Society. Portland.
  1840       [Letters of August 19 and 21 and September 2]. Ms. B.223/b/27, fols. 32–34.
             Hudson's Bay Company Archives. Winnipeg.
  1941       The Letters of John McLoughlin from Fort Vancouver to the Governor and
             Committee: First Series, 1825–38. Edited by E. E. Rich. Vol. 4. Toronto: Pub-
             lications of the Champlain Society.
  1943       The Letters of John McLoughlin from Fort Vancouver to the Governor and
             Committee: Second Series, 1839–44. Edited by E. E. Rich. Vol. 6. Toronto:
             Publications of the Champlain Society.
McWhorter, Lucullus
  Mss.       Manuscript collection. Holland Library, Washington State University.
             Pullman.
Marshall, Alan
  1977       Nez Perce Social Groups: An Ecological Interpretation. Ph.D. diss., Washing-
             ton State University.
Marwick, Max
  1964       Witchcraft and Sorcery. Harmondsworth, England: Penguin.

Meinig, Donald
1968    The Great Columbia Plain: A Historical Geography, 1805-1910. Seattle: University of Washington Press.
Merk, Frederick
1931    Fur Trade and Empire: George Simpson's Journal. Cambridge: Harvard University Press.
Miller, Alfred Jacob
1968    The West of Alfred Jacob Miller. Norman: University of Oklahoma Press.
Miller, Christopher
1985    Prophetic Worlds: Indians and Whites on the Columbia Plateau. New Brunswick, N.J.: Rutgers University Press.
Minor, Rick, Kathryn Toepel, and Stephen Beckham
1986    An Overview of Investigations at 45SA11: Archaeology in the Columbia River Gorge. Heritage Research Associates Report no. 39. U.S. Army Corps of Engineers, Portland District. Portland, Oreg.
Minto, John
1901    Reminiscences. Oregon Historical Quarterly 2:245-54.
Mooney, James
1896    The Ghost-Dance Religion and the Sioux Outbreak of 1890. Bureau of American Ethnology Annual Report no. 14, 640-1136. Washington, D.C.
Morison, Samuel
1927    New England and the Opening of the Columbia River Salmon Trade, 1830. Oregon Historical Quarterly 28:111-32.
Mudge, Zachariah, ed.
1848    The Missionary Teacher: A Memoir of Cyrus Shepard. New York: Lane and Tippett, for the Sunday-school Union of the Methodist Episcopal Church.
1854    Sketches of Mission Life among the Indians of Oregon. New York: Carlton and Porter. Reprint, Fairfield, Wash.: Ye Galleon Press, 1983 (page citations are to the reprint edition).
Murdock, George
1958    Tenino Sorcery. Miscellanea Paul Rivet 1, 299-315. Mexico City.
1965    Tenino Shamanism. Ethnology 4:165-71. Reprinted in Culture and Society, by George Murdock, 251-61. Pittsburgh: University of Pittsburgh Press, 1965 (page citations are to the reprint edition).
1980    The Tenino Indians. Ethnology 19:129-50.
Nesmith, James
1906    Diary of the Emigration of 1843. Oregon Historical Quarterly 7:329-59.
Netboy, Anthony
1980    The Columbia River Salmon and Steelhead Trout: Their Fight for Survival. Seattle: University of Washington Press.
Nevins, Allen
1964    John Charles Fremont.The Dictionary of American Biography, vol. 7. New York: Charles Scribner's Sons.
Newell, Robert
1867    Early History of Oregon. Portland Oregon [Daily] Herald. March 3:3(2-3).
Nicandri, David
1986    Northwest Chiefs: Gustave Sohon's View of the 1855 Stevens Treaty Councils. Tacoma: Washington Historical Society.

1987      John Mix Stanley: Paintings and Sketches of the Oregon Country and Its Inhabitants. Oregon Historical Quarterly 88:149-73.

Norton, Helen, Robert Boyd, and Eugene Hunn
1983      The Klickitat Trail of South Central Washington: A Reconstruction of Seasonally-Used Resource Sites. *In* Prehistoric Places on the Southern Northwest Coast, edited by Robert Greengo, 121-52. Thomas Burke Memorial Washington State Museum Research Report no. 4. Seattle.

Oberg, Kalervo
1934      Crime and Punishment in Tlingit Society. American Anthropologist 36:145-56.

O'Donnell, Terence
1991      An Arrow in the Earth: General Joel Palmer and the Indians of Oregon. Portland: Oregon Historical Society Press.

Ogden, Peter
1961      Peter Skene Ogden's Snake Country Journal, 1826-27. Edited by K. G. Davies. The Hudson's Bay Record Society, vol. 23. London.

Olson, Ronald
1936      The Quinault Indians. University of Washington Publications in Anthropology 6(1). Seattle.

Oregonian (Portland)
1893      An Oregon Pioneer, Dr. Wm. C. M'Kay, of Pendleton. January 3:2(1-2).

Pambrun, Andrew
1978      Sixty Years on the Frontier in the Pacific Northwest. Fairfield, Wash.: Ye Galleon Press.

Pandosy, Marie Charles
1862      Grammar and Dictionary of the Yakima Language. Translated by George Gibbs and J. G. Shea. Shea's Library of American Linguistics, 6. Reprint, New York: AMS Press, 1970 (page citations are to the reprint edition).

Parker, Samuel
1838      Journal of an Exploring Tour beyond the Rocky Mountains, under the direction of the A.B.C.F.M., Performed in the Years 1835, '36, and '37. . . . Ithaca, N.Y.: Published by the author.
1936      Report of a tour west of the Rocky Mountains in 1835-7. *In* Marcus Whitman, Crusader, edited by Archer Hulbert and Dorothy Hulbert. Vol. 6, Overland to the Pacific, 90-135. Denver: Denver Public Library.

Peterson, Marilyn
1978      Prehistoric Mobile Stone Sculpture of the Lower Columbia River Valley. Master's thesis, Portland State University.

Phebus, George
1978      The Smithsonian Institution 1934 Bonneville Reservoir Salvage Archaeology Project. Northwest Anthropological Research Notes 12:113-51. Moscow, Idaho.

Pipes, Nellie
1936      The Protestant Ladder. Oregon Historical Quarterly 37:237-40.

Pitt, Charles
1915      Palmer Treaty, 1855. Dorrington Papers, RG 75. National Archives. San Bruno (photocopy at Seattle branch).

Pulpit Rock
   1925      Pulpit Rock, Site of Early Missionary Efforts, to Have Spectacular Service.
             (Newspaper clipping dated April 12, 1925). Lulu Crandall Collection. The
             Dalles Public Library. The Dalles, Oregon.
Quimby, George
   1972      Hawaiians in the Fur Trade of North-West America, 1785-1820. Journal of
             Pacific History 7:92-103.
   1985      Japanese Wrecks, Iron Tools, and Prehistoric Indians of the Northwest Coast.
             Arctic Anthropology 22(2):7-15.
Ramsey, Jarold
   1977      Coyote Was Going There: Indian Literature of the Oregon Country. Seattle:
             University of Washington Press.
   1983      The Bible in Western Indian Mythology. In Reading the Fire: Essays in the
             Traditional Indian Literatures of the Far West, by Jarold Ramsey, 166-80.
             Lincoln: University of Nebraska Press.
Ray, Verne
   1933      The Sanpoil and Nespelem: Salishan Peoples of Northeastern Washington.
             University of Washington Publications in Anthropology 5. Seattle.
   1936      Native Villages and Groupings of the Columbia Basin. Pacific Northwest
             Quarterly 27:99-152.
   1938      Lower Chinook Ethnographic Notes. University of Washington Publications
             in Anthropology 7(2). Seattle.
   1939      Cultural Relations in the Plateau of Northwestern America. Los Angeles:
             Southwestern Museum.
   1942      Plateau: Culture Element Distributions XXII. University of California
             Anthropological Records 8(2). Berkeley.
Ray, Verne, George Murdock, Beatrice Blyth, Omer Stewart, Jack Harris, E. Adamson
   Hoebel, and D. B. Shimkin
   1938      Tribal Distribution in Eastern Oregon and Adjacent Regions. American
             Anthropologist 40:384-415.
Rice, Harvey
   1984      Native American Dwellings and Attendant Structures of the Southern Plateau.
             Ph.D. diss., Washington State University.
Rickard, T. A.
   1939      The Use of Iron and Copper by the Indians of British Columbia. British
             Columbia Historical Quarterly 3:25-50.
Rigsby, Bruce
   1965      Linguistic Relations in the Southern Plateau. Ph.D. diss., University of
             Oregon.
Rockwell, Cleveland
   1888      Columbia River, Sheet No. 6: Fales Landing to Portland. U.S. Coast and Geo-
             detic Survey. Multnomah County Library. Portland, Oreg.
Ross, Alexander
   1849      Adventures of the First Settlers on the Oregon or Columbia River. London:
             Smith, Elder and Co.
   1854      The Fur Hunters of the Far West. Reprint, edited by Kenneth Spalding,
             Norman: University of Oklahoma Press, 1956 (page citations are to the reprint
             edition).

Rousseau, Jacques
    1965        Caravane vers l'Oregon. *In* Cahier des Dix, no. 30. Montréal: Les Éditions des
                Dix.
Ruby, Robert, and John Brown
    1972        The Cayuse Indians: Imperial Tribesmen of Old Oregon. Norman: University
                of Oklahoma Press.
    1989        Dreamer-Prophets of the Columbia Plateau: Smohalla and Skolaskin. Nor-
                man: University of Oklahoma Press.
Saleeby, Becky, and Richard Pettigrew
    1983        Seasonality of Occupation of Ethnohistorically-Documented Villages on the
                Lower Columbia River. *In* Prehistoric Places on the Southern Northwest
                Coast, edited by Robert Greengo, 169–93. Thomas Burke Memorial Washing-
                ton State Museum Research Report no. 4. Seattle.
Samarin, William
    1986        Chinook Jargon and Pidgin Historiography. Canadian Journal of Anthro-
                pology 5:23–34.
Santee, Joseph
    1933        Pio–Pio–Mox–Mox. Oregon Historical Quarterly 34:164–76.
Sapir, Edward
    1910        Wasco. *In* Handbook of American Indians North of Mexico, edited by Frede-
                rick Webb Hodge, 917–18. Bureau of American Ethnology Bulletin no. 30,
                vol. 2. Washington, D.C.
    1990        Wishram Texts and Ethnography. *In* The Collected Works of Edward Sapir.
                Vol. 7, edited by William Bright. New York: Mouton de Gruyter.
Sapir, Edward, ed.
    1909        Wishram Texts. Publications of the American Ethnological Society, vol. 2.
                Leiden: Late E. J. Brill.
Schaeffer, Claude
    1965        The Kutenai Female Berdache: Courier, Guide, Prophetess, and Warrior.
                Ethnohistory 12:193–236.
Schafer, Joseph, ed.
    1934        A Day with the Cow Column in 1843 and Recollections of My Boyhood.
                Chicago: Caxton Club.
Schoenberg, Wilfred
    1962        A Chronicle of the Catholic History of the Pacific Northwest, 1743–1960.
                Spokane: Gonzaga Preparatory School.
    1987        A History of the Catholic Church in the Pacific Northwest, 1743–1983. Wash-
                ington, D.C.: Pastoral Press.
Schoning, Robert W., T. R. Merrell, and D. R. Johnson
    1951        The Indian Dip Net Fishery at Celilo Falls on the Columbia River. Oregon Fish
                Commission Contribution no. 17. Portland, Oreg.
Schuster, Helen
    1975        Yakima Indian Traditionalism: A Study in Continuity and Change. Ph.D. diss.,
                University of Washington.
Schwede, Madge
    1970        The Relationship of Aboriginal Nez Perce Settlement Patterns to Physical
                Environment and to Generalized Distribution of Food Resources. Northwest
                Anthropological Research Notes 4:129–36. Moscow, Idaho.

Scouler, John
    1905    Dr. John Scouler's Journal of a Voyage to Northwest America. Oregon Historical Quarterly 6:54-75, 159-205, 276-87.

Service, Elman
    1979    The Hunters. Englewood Cliffs, N.J.: Prentice-Hall.

Seufert Brothers Company
    1916    United States of America vs. Seufert Brothers Company. In the District Court of the United States for the District of Oregon. Plaintiff's testimony. Multnomah County Library. Portland, Oreg.

Shortess, Robert
    1955    Narration. In To the Rockies and Oregon, 1839-1843, edited by LeRoy Hafen and Ann Hafen, 94-120. Vol. 3 of The Far West and the Rockies Historical Series. Glendale, Calif.: Arthur H. Clark.

Simpson, George
    1830    [Letter of August 20]. Ms. D.4/97. Hudson's Bay Company Archives. Winnipeg.
    1847    Narrative of a Journey Round the World during the Years 1841 and 1842. London: H. Colburn.
    1975    The "Character Book" of George Simpson, 1832. In Hudson's Bay Miscellany, 1670-1870, edited by Glyndwr Williams, 151-236. Publications of the Hudson's Bay Record Society, vol. 30. Winnipeg.

Slacum, William
    1837    Memorial of William A. Slacum, Dec.18, 1837. 25th Cong., 2nd sess., Senate Exec. Doc. 24, vol. 1, serial 314.

Smith, Sidney
    1955    Sidney Smith Diary. In To the Rockies and Oregon, 1839-1842, edited by LeRoy Hafen and Ann Hafen, 67-93. Vol. 3 of The Far West and the Rockies Historical Series. Glendale, Calif.: Arthur H. Clark.

Smith, Silas
    1899    Mr. Smith's Address. September 18 newspaper clipping (source unidentified). Scrapbook 35:30-31. Oregon Historical Society. Portland.

Spalding, Eliza
    1838    [Letter of April 21]. Manuscripts Collection. Holland Library. Washington State University, Pullman.

Spalding, Henry
    1837    Letter of February 16. Missionary Herald (December):33.
    1839    Introduction of the Gospel to Northwest America. Oregon and Indian's Advocate 1(10):300-301.
    1840    Letter of October 2, 1839. Missionary Herald, vol. 36 (June):230.
    1842    [Letter of February 18]. Manuscript collection. Holland Library, Washington State University. Pullman.
    1846    [Letter of February 12]. Manuscript collection. Holland Library, Washington State University. Pullman.

Spencer, Omar
    1933    Chief Cassino. Oregon Historical Quarterly 34:19-30.

Spier, Leslie
   1930      The Klamath and Western Culture. *In* Klamath Ethnography, 224–325. University of California Publications in American Archaeology and Ethnology 30. Berkeley.
   1935      The Prophet Dance of the Northwest and Its Derivatives: The Source of the Ghost Dance. General Series in Anthropology 1. Menasha, Wis.: George Banta.
Spier, Leslie, and Edward Sapir
   1930      Wishram Ethnography. University of Washington Publications in Anthropology 3(3). Seattle.
Splawn, Andrew
   1917      Ka–Mi–Akin, the Last Hero of the Yakimas. Portland, Oreg.: Kilham Stationery and Printing.
Sprague, Roderick
   1967      Aboriginal Burial Practices in the Plateau Region of North America. Ph.D. diss., University of Arizona.
Sproat, Gilbert
   1868      Scenes and Studies of Savage Life. London: Smith, Elder.
Stern, Theodore
   1956      The Klamath Indians and the Treaty of 1864. Oregon Historical Quarterly 57: 229–73.
   1993      Chiefs and Chief Traders: Indian Relations at Fort Nez Percés, 1818–1855. Corvallis: Oregon State University Press.
   1998      Cayuse, Umatilla, Walla Walla. *In* Handbook of North American Indians, edited by William C. Sturtevant. Vol. 12, Plateau, edited by Deward Walker. Washington, D.C.: Smithsonian Institution.
Stevens, Hazard
   1900      The Life of Isaac Ingalls Stevens. New York: Houghton Mifflin.
Stevens, Isaac Ingalls
   1859      Narrative and Final Report of Explorations for a Route for a Pacific Railroad near the Forty-seventh and Forty-ninth Parallels of North Latitude, from St. Paul to Puget Sound. *In* Reports of Exploration and Surveys . . . from the Mississippi River to the Pacific Ocean, vol. 12, pt. 1. 35th Cong., 2d sess., Senate Exec. Doc. 46, serial 992.
   1985      A True Copy of the Record of the Official Proceedings at the Council in the Walla Walla Valley, 1855. Edited by Darrell Scott. Fairfield, Wash.: Ye Galleon Press.
Steward, Julian
   1927      A New Type of Carving from the Columbia Valley. American Anthropologist 29:255–61.
   1955      Theory and Application in a Social Science. Ethnohistory 2:292–302.
Stewart, Hilary
   1973      Indian Artifacts of the Northwest Coast. Seattle: University of Washington Press.
Strickland, William
   1850      History of the Missions of the Methodist Episcopal Church. Cincinnati: L. Swormstedt and J. H. Power.

Strong, Emory
1959    Stone Age on the Columbia River. Portland, Oreg.: Binfords and Mort.
1961    Prehistoric Sculpture from the Columbia River. Archaeology 14:131-37.
Strong, W. Duncan, W. Egbert Schenck, and Julian Steward
1930    Archaeology of the Dalles-Deschutes Region. University of California Publications in American Archaeology and Ethnology 29(1). Berkeley.
Stuart, Robert
1935    Robert Stuart's Narratives. *In* The Discovery of the Oregon Trail, edited by Phillip Rollins, 2-263. New York: Charles Scribner's Sons.
Sturtevant, William
1968    Anthropology, History, and Ethnography. *In* Introduction to Cultural Anthropology, edited by James Clifton, 451-75. Palo Alto: Houghton Mifflin.
Sutter, John (Johann)
n.d.    Sutter's Overland Journey. Typescript by Allan Lane from Personal Reminiscences, by John Sutter. Bancroft Library, University of California. Berkeley. Also available in the Biography File, Regional Research Library, Oregon Historical Society. Portland.
1960    Letter of July 21, 1845. *In* James Clyman Frontiersman, edited by Charles Camp, 148-49. Portland, Oreg.: Champoeg Press.
Suttles, Wayne
1951    The Early Diffusion of the Potato among the Coast Salish. Southwestern Journal of Anthropology 7:272-88. Reprinted *in* Coast Salish Essays, edited by Ralph Maud, 137-51. Seattle: University of Washington Press; Vancouver: Talonbooks, 1987 (page citations are to the original edition).
1957    The Plateau Prophet Dance among the Coast Salish. Southwestern Journal of Anthropology 13:352-93. Reprinted *in* Coast Salish Essays, edited by Ralph Maud, 152-98. Seattle: University of Washington Press; Vancouver: Talonbooks, 1987 (page citations are to the original edition).
1960a   Affinal Ties, Subsistence, and Prestige among the Coast Salish. American Anthropologist 62:296-305. Reprinted *in* Coast Salish Essays, edited by Ralph Maud, 15-25. Seattle: University of Washington Press; Vancouver: Talonbooks, 1987 (page citations are to the original edition).
1960b   Variation in Habitation and Culture on the Northwest Coast. *In* Transactions of the 34th International Congress of Americanists, 522-37. Vienna: Verlag Ferdinand Berger. Reprinted *in* Coast Salish Essays, edited by Ralph Maud, 26-44. Seattle: University of Washington Press; Vancouver: Talonbooks, 1987 (page citations are to the original edition).
1987    Loans from the South. *In* Four Anthropological-Linguistic Notes and Queries, 5-6. Manuscript in Suttles's possession.
1990a   Central Coast Salish Subsistence. Northwest Anthropological Research Notes 24:147-52. Moscow, Idaho.
1990b   Introduction. *In* Handbook of North American Indians, edited by William C. Sturtevant. Vol. 7, Northwest Coast, edited by Wayne Suttles, 1-16. Washington, D.C.: Smithsonian Institution.
Suttles, Wayne, and Aldona Jonaitis
1990    History of Research in Ethnology. *In* Handbook of North American Indians, edited by William C. Sturtevant. Vol. 7, Northwest Coast, edited by Wayne Suttles, 73-87. Washington, D.C.: Smithsonian Institution.

Swindell, Edward
    1942    Report on Source, Nature and Extent of the Fishing, Hunting and Miscellan-
            eous Related Rights of Certain Indian Tribes in Washington and Oregon. . . .
            U.S. Dept. of Interior. Office of Indian Affairs. Los Angeles.
Sylvester, Avery
    1933    Voyage of the Pallas and Chenamus, 1843-45. Oregon Historical Quarterly
            34:259-72, 359-71.
Tappan, William
    1854    Annual Report, Southern Indian District, Washington Territory. In Washing-
            ton Superintendency of Indian Affairs, 1853-74, no. 5, roll 17, Letters from
            employees assigned to the Columbia River or Southern district, and the
            Yakima Agency, May 1, 1854-July 20, 1861, RG 75. National Archives.
            Washington, D.C.
Taylor, Herbert, and Wilson Duff
    1956    A Post-Contact Southward Movement of the Kwakiutl. Research Studies of
            the State College of Washington 24:56-66. Pullman.
Teit, James
    1928    The Middle Columbia Salish. University of Washington Publications in
            Anthropology 2. Seattle.
Tetlow, Roger
    1969    There Were Black Pioneers Too. Portland Oregonian, October 5, Northwest
            Magazine:4-5, 16.
Thompson, David
    1962    David Thompson's Narrative, 1784-1812. Edited by Richard Glover.
            Toronto: Champlain Society.
Thompson, Laurence
    1973    The Northwest. In Current Trends in Linguistics, vol. 10, Linguistics in North
            America, edited by Thomas Sebeok, 979-1045. The Hague: Mouton.
Tolmie, William
    1963    The Journals of William Fraser Tolmie: Physician and Fur Trader. Vancouver:
            Mitchell Press.
Townsend, John
    1839    Narrative of a Journey across the Rocky Mountains to the Columbia River. . . .
            Philadelphia: H. Perkins. Reprint, Lincoln: University of Nebraska Press,
            1978 (page citations are to the reprint edition).
Turner, Nancy
    1978    Food Plants of British Columbia Indians, Part II: Interior Peoples. British
            Columbia Provincial Museum Handbook no. 36. Victoria.
    1983    Camas (Camassia spp.) and Riceroot (Fritillaria spp.): Two Lilaceous 'Root'
            Foods of the Northwest Coast Indians. Ecology of Food and Nutrition 13:199-
            219.
Turner, Victor
    1969    The Ritual Process: Structure and Anti-Structure. Chicago: Aldine.
United Methodist Church
    Mss.    Archives of the Oregon-Idaho Conference of the United Methodist Church.
            Willamette University. Salem, Oreg.
    Mss.    Archives of the Pacific Northwest Conference of the United Methodist
            Church. University of Puget Sound, Tacoma.

Victor, Frances Fuller
1870    The River of the West. Hartford, Conn.: Columbia Book Co.
Voegelin, Erminie
1942    Northeast California: Culture Element Distributions 20. University of California Anthropological Records 7(2):47–252. Berkeley.
Voorhis, Ernest
1930    Historic Forts and Trading Posts of the French Regime and of the English Fur Trading Companies. Department of the Interior (Canada). Natural Resources Intelligence Branch. Ottawa.
Walker, Deward
1967    Mutual Cross-Utilization of Economic Resources in the Plateau: An Example from Aboriginal Nez Perce Fishing Practices. Washington State University Laboratory of Anthropology Report of Investigation no. 41. Pullman.
1968    Conflict and Schism in Nez Perce Acculturation: A Study of Religion and Politics. Pullman: Washington State University Press.
1969    New Light on the Prophet Dance Controversy. Ethnohistory 16:245–55.
Walker, Deward, ed.
1998    Plateau. Vol. 12 of Handbook of North American Indians, edited by William C. Sturtevant. Washington, D.C.: Smithsonian Institution.
Wallace, Anthony
1970    Culture and Personality. New York: Random House.
Waller, Alvan
1843    Letter from Oregon, August 19, 1842. Christian Advocate and Journal, November 8.
Mss.    Manuscripts, collection 1210. Oregon Historical Society. Portland.
Warre, Henry
1976    Overland to Oregon in 1845: Impressions of a Journey across North America. Edited by Madeleine Major-Fregeau. Public Archives of Canada. Ottawa.
Weber, Max
1930    The Protestant Ethic and the Spirit of Capitalism, translated by Talcott Parsons. London: George Allen and Unwin.
Whitehead, Margaret
1981    Christianity, a Matter of Choice. Pacific Northwest Quarterly 72:98–105.
Whiting, Beatrice
1950    Paiute Sorcery. Viking Fund Publications in Anthropology no. 15. New York.
Whitman, Narcissa
1893    Letters Written by Mrs. Whitman from Oregon to Her Relatives in New York. Transactions of the 19th Annual Reunion of the Oregon Pioneer Association for 1891, 79–179. Portland, Oreg.
1894    Mrs. Whitman's Letters. Transactions of the 21st Annual Reunion of the Oregon Pioneer Association for 1893, 53–219. Portland, Oreg.
1963    Diary. In First White Women over the Rockies, edited by Clifford Drury. Vol. 1, 25–170. Glendale, Calif.: Arthur H. Clark.
Wilkes, Charles
1844    Narrative of the United States Exploring Expedition. Vols. 4 and 5. Philadelphia: C. Sherman.

Williams, Joseph
   1921     Narrative of a Tour from Indiana to the Oregon Territory, 1841–2. New York: Cadmus Book Shop.

Wingert, Paul
   1949     American Indian Sculpture: A Study of the Northwest Coast. New York: J. J. Augustin.

Wolf, Eric
   1982     Europe and the People without History. Berkeley: University of California Press.

Wood, W. Raymond
   1980     Plains Trade in Prehistoric and Protohistoric Intertribal Relations. *In* Anthropology in the Great Plains, edited by W. Raymond Wood and Margot Liberty, 98–109. Lincoln: University of Nebraska Press.

Work, John
   1824     Journal. Manuscript, collection 319. Oregon Historical Society. Portland.

Worsley, Peter
   1957     The Trumpet Shall Sound. London: MacGibbon and Kee.

Wyeth, Nathaniel
   1899     The Correspondence and Journals of Captain Nathaniel J. Wyeth. Edited by F. G. Young. Sources of the History of Oregon 1(3–6). Eugene, Oreg.: University Press.

# Index

In *Studies in the Anthropology of North American Indians*

*The Comanches: A History,*
*1706–1875*
By Thomas W. Kavanagh

*Koasati Dictionary*
By Geoffrey D. Kimball with the
assistance of Bel Abbey, Martha
John, and Ruth Poncho

*Koasati Grammar*
By Geoffrey D. Kimball with the
assistance of Bel Abbey, Nora
Abbey, Martha John, Ed John, and
Ruth Poncho

*The Salish Language Family:*
*Reconstructing Syntax*
By Paul D. Kroeber

*The Medicine Men: Oglala Sioux*
*Ceremony and Healing*
By Thomas H. Lewis

*A Dictionary of Creek / Muskogee*
By Jack B. Martin and Margaret
McKane Mauldin

*Wolverine Myths and Visions:*
*Dene Traditions from Northern*
*Alberta*
Edited by Patrick Moore and
Angela Wheelock

*Ceremonies of the Pawnee*
By James R. Murie
Edited by Douglas R. Parks

*Archaeology and Ethnohistory*
*of the Omaha Indians: The Big*
*Village Site*
By John M. O'Shea and John
Ludwickson

*Traditional Narratives of the*
*Arikara Indians* (4 vols.)
By Douglas R. Parks

*They Treated Us Just Like In-*
*dians: The Worlds of Bennett*
*County, South Dakota*
By Paula L. Wagoner

*A Grammar of Kiowa*
By Laurel J. Watkins with the
assistance of Parker McKenzie

*Native Languages and Language*
*Families of North America*
(folded study map and wall display map)
Compiled by Ives Goddard